I0824118

The Art of OZ

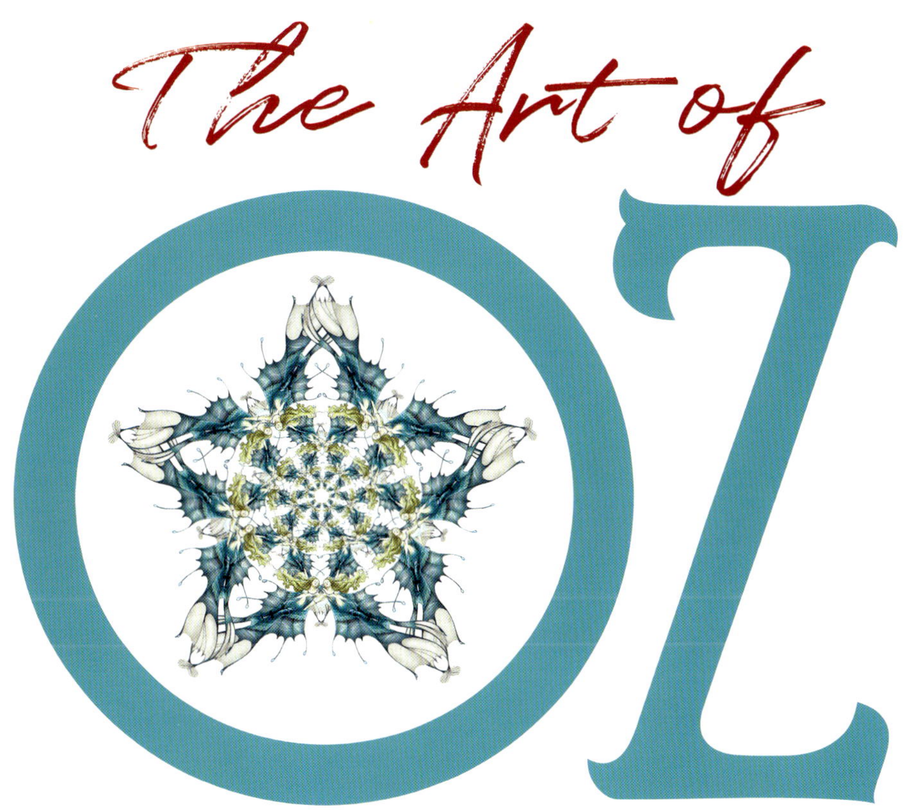

The Art of OZ

Witches, Wizards & Wonders Beyond the Yellow Brick Road

By GABRIEL GALE
Text by JOHN FRICKE

Afterword by MICHAEL PATRICK HEARN

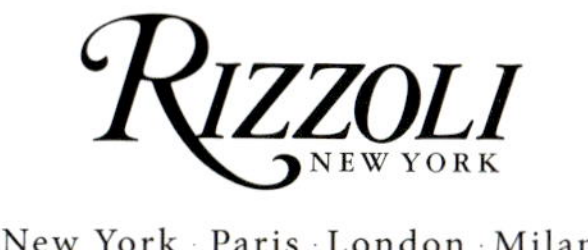

New York · Paris · London · Milan

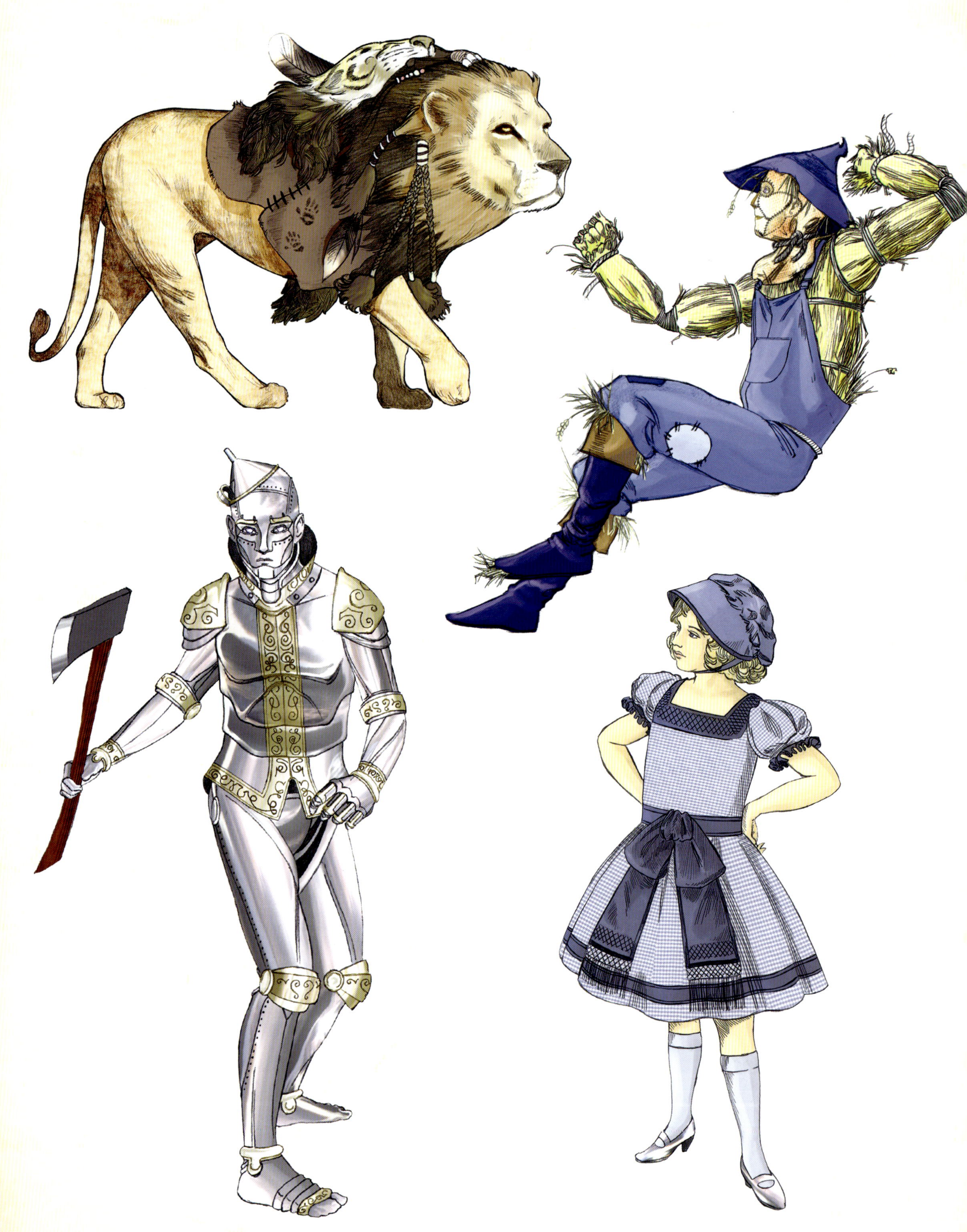

Contents

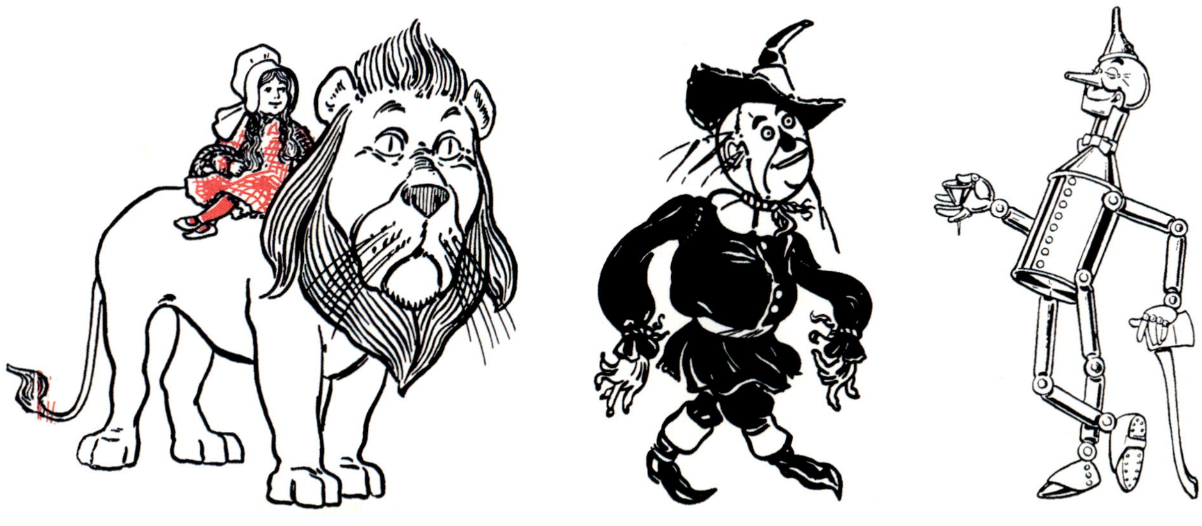

A Message from Gabriel Gale

ARTIST & *AGES OF OZ* HISTORIAN

Happy greetings to all of you—from the Marvelous Land of Oz.

For many years, it's been my privilege to visit and travel throughout this very special kingdom. Oz, of course, was first discovered by its "Royal Historian" L. Frank Baum. His books introduced me—and millions more—to the characters and amazing creatures who live there, to the Deadly Desert that surrounds and protects them, and to all the mysterious countries inside and outside the Ozian boundaries.

Because of Mr. Baum, I also grew up to become a writer and an explorer—and someone who tries to serve as a constant defender of the Good. Those who rule Oz eventually became aware of my genuine dedication; that is why I was invited to go there. If you know anything about Oz, you can imagine my excitement and delight at such an offer.

These trips have given me the opportunity to get to know much previously unrecorded Oz history, which I now share in Oz books of my own. Best of all, however, I have been accepted as a good friend by some of the extraordinary celebrities whose names I'm sure you will recognize: Dorothy Gale and her dog, Toto (both originally of Kansas); the Scarecrow, Tin Woodman, and Cowardly Lion (Dorothy's close companions on her first trip down the Yellow Brick Road); and two more who were—in their own ways—of great help to all of them: the Wizard of Oz and Glinda the Good Witch.

As we got to know one another, they learned that I am also an artist, and they gladly gave me the chance to draw new pictures of them *and* many, many more of the Ozites. The fact that they—and Her Highness, Princess Ozma of Oz—came to trust me and like my portraits has now resulted in Royal Permission to bring my artwork to you.

Additionally, we decided that it was most natural and correct to also include some of Mr. Baum's own descriptive and inspirational words from the original Oz books, along with a selection of their illustrations. He and his associates began all of this, and Dorothy, the Scarecrow, their friends, and I are overjoyed to continue, in this manner, the chronicles of the greatest American fantasyland.

One final admission: All of us have a special hope in creating *The Art of Oz*. We would like it to serve as your own present-day passport to the wonders and endless magic of that enchanted realm.

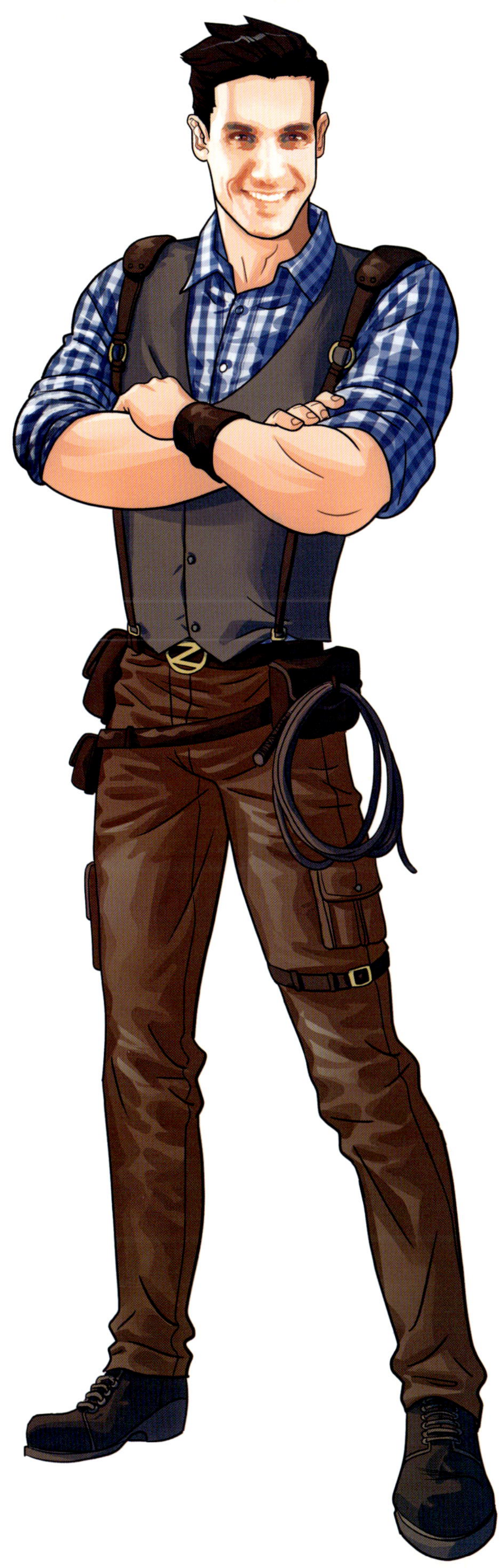

Welcoming You to Oz!

BY PROFESSOR H. M. WOGGLE-BUG, T. E.

How happy I am to meet you on your pictorial visit to our enchanted kingdom!

First of all, I want to assure you that everything I tell you about Oz and its people is The Truth. This means that I may now honestly introduce myself: I am the famous, the acclaimed, and the immeasurably intelligent Professor H. M. Woggle-Bug, T. E.

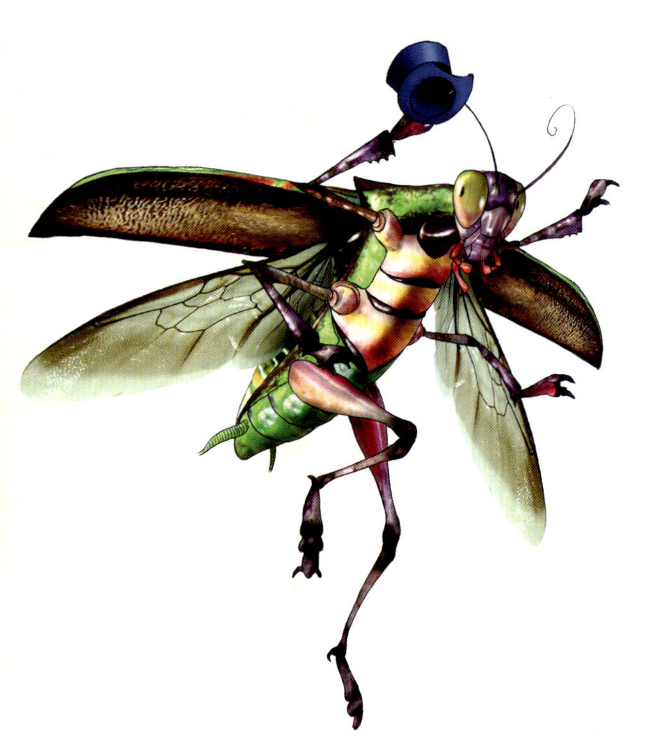

Once, I was a tiny insect—it's true!—living between the bricks on a fireplace hearth in an Oz schoolroom. For years, I carefully listened to Professor Nowitall; in the process, I became Thoroughly Educated (T. E.). Then, one day, he unexpectedly discovered me and decided to use his enlarging glass to project me onto a screen in a Highly Magnified (H. M.) state. In this manner, his students also could see me. The sight of such a Very Big Bug, however, startled them, and in the subsequent confusion, I stepped off the screen and—at full size—made my escape! Soon thereafter, I became friends with the Scarecrow, Tin Woodman, Jack Pumpkinhead, and others you will meet in these pages. I am also special counsel to our Princess Ozma and, under her gracious rule, I have become Dean of our Royal College.

There is much to tell you about us and our country. Most of you know L. Frank Baum's story, *The Wonderful Wizard of Oz*, and the famous motion picture that was made from it—all about Dorothy's first visit here. On the next page, pictures by W. W. Denslow from Mr. Baum's book will remind you of some of her adventures.

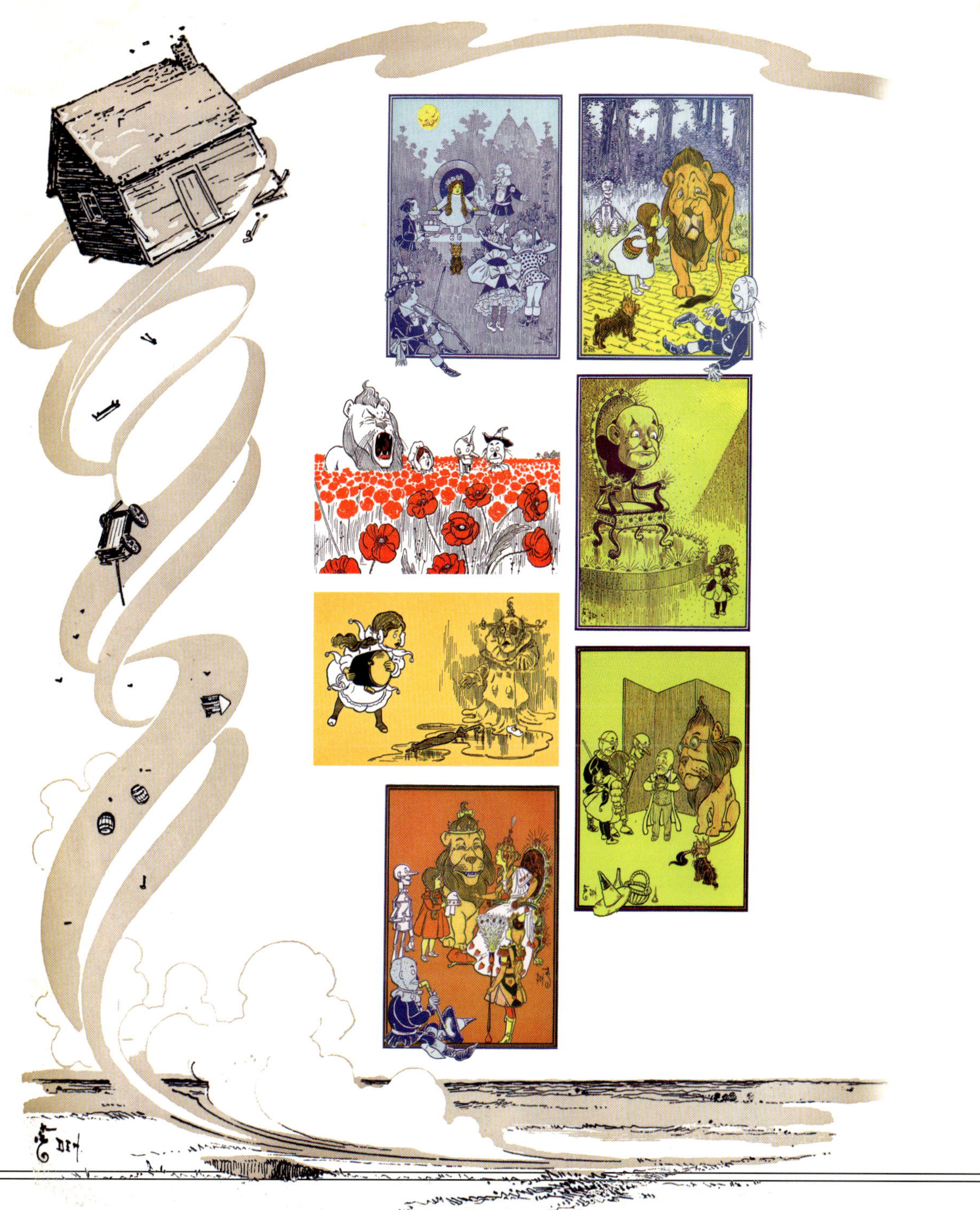

In The Wonderful Wizard of Oz *book and movie, Dorothy and her dog, Toto, are carried by tornado from Kansas to Oz in the family farmhouse (left). The Munchkins welcome her (top left) and direct her to the Emerald City, so that she might ask the Wizard of Oz to send her home. Along the way, she befriends the Scarecrow, Tin Woodman, and Cowardly Lion (top right), all of whom have requests of the Wizard as well. The Deadly Poppy Field proves to be a dangerous detour (second row, left), but the travelers finally meet the Great Oz (second row, right). When he tells them that he won't fulfill their wishes until they destroy the Wicked Witch of the West, Dorothy is lucky to do just that with a bucket of water (third row, left). Back at the Emerald City, however, she and her friends discover that the Wizard is a humbug (third row, right). Fortunately, he knows enough magic to give brains, a heart, and courage to the Scarecrow, Tin Woodman, and Lion, but he leaves Oz in his balloon before Dorothy can join him. Glinda the Good Witch is the one who finally explains the magic of Dorothy's silver shoes to the little girl (near left), and she and Toto at last return to Kansas.*

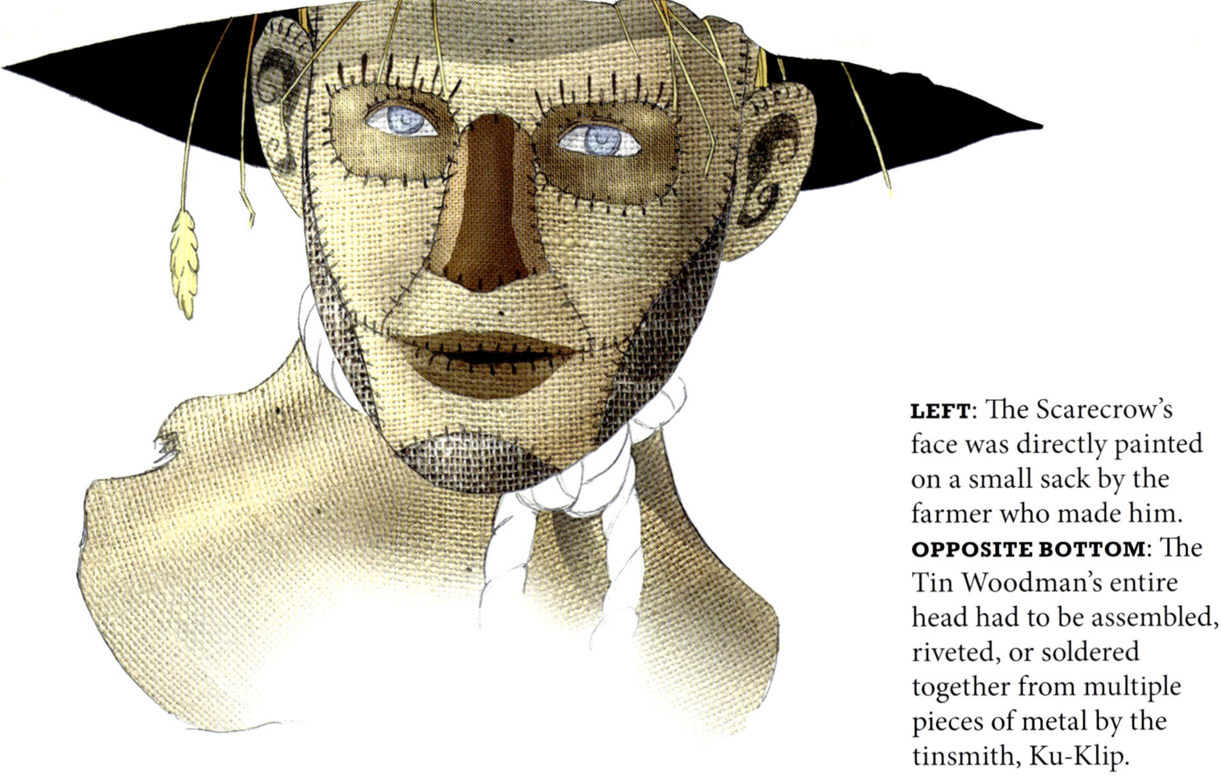

LEFT: The Scarecrow's face was directly painted on a small sack by the farmer who made him. **OPPOSITE BOTTOM**: The Tin Woodman's entire head had to be assembled, riveted, or soldered together from multiple pieces of metal by the tinsmith, Ku-Klip.

It's true that the moviemakers changed some of Mr. Baum's story. They decided the silver shoes should be ruby slippers, as that color would look brighter on the screen. The Good Witch of the North—who first welcomes Dorothy in the film—is actually a different Oz witch than Glinda, who is our Good Witch of the South. The film also omitted much history. Did you know that the Tin Woodman was once a real man and woodchopper? The Wicked Witch of the East was angry with him, because he planned to marry a Munchkin maiden who was her slave. To prevent the marriage, the Witch enchanted his ax so that it chopped off his arms, legs, and head—and cut his body in half! Of course, no one ever dies in Oz. (No one ever ages, either; as the song says, it's a "merry old land!") So, the clever Woodman went to a tinsmith, who made him new body parts of metal. Soon he was all tin, which was unfortunate because he got caught in a rainstorm and rusted solid; that's how Dorothy found him!

But there just wasn't time for all of this in the movie; that's one reason *The Wonderful Wizard of Oz* book is such fun: there's so much more story. Despite the alterations, however, the film is wonderful entertainment. We here in Oz have only one serious objection: the fact that those in charge of the motion picture thought that Dorothy's trip to Oz should be represented as a dream.

Well! I am here to tell you right now that Oz is a really, truly, "live" place! If this is not an honorable and accurate statement, how could Mr. Baum write so much about us in his other books? Here is the proof: You may remember that, when the Wizard left, he assigned the Scarecrow to rule Oz; it was later discovered that our Rightful Ruler was really Princess Ozma, hidden away by a magic spell.

Ozma took the throne as soon as the spell could be broken, and shortly afterward, Dorothy returned to Oz for more excitement of her own. (As you will read in these pages, the Wizard came back, too.) Mr. Baum reported all these things—and so much more—in his fourteen Oz books. He also discovered fantastic creatures and recorded thrilling events from the countries outside ours; these are known as his "Borderlands of Oz" stories. You are certain to find many Ozzy escapades referenced herein that will be new to you, and all of them are true to our world!

Mr. Baum eventually retired as our "Royal Historian"—and from the Great Outside World as well—and several other worthy authors were then enlisted to share Oz news with eager readers. Of course, many people who love Oz have composed their own stories about our land, and there are probably more of them now being written than ever before. This makes perfect sense: astounding, joyous, scary, thrilling things continue to happen here every day! Additionally, there are always more Oz movies, animated cartoons, stage plays, and musicals. Oz is here!—Oz is there with you!—Oz is everywhere that good triumphs over evil!

Meanwhile, you will find your favorites and countless more remarkable residents of Oz in these pages. The new Ozian art of Gabriel Gale paints them in memorable detail, whether beauteous, curious, monstrous, funny, or glorious; additionally, his delightful, detailed work is accompanied in several places by the original Oz pictures of the amusing Mr. Denslow and the incomparable John R. Neill.

On to your journey! As you turn these pages, you will be guided by seven Ozians, whose international importance precedes even mine, and I think you will recognize all of them. Never fear, though; I return to you later in the book to discuss the maps of Oz. And—once more in truth!—I'll also help explain things elsewhere. You'll see that many of Mr. Gale's drawings are accompanied by writings from Mr. Baum's Oz books; after all, no one knows us better than he! But there are some pictures that have thoroughly instructive captions instead; I have written those!

Eminently yours,

Professor H. M. Woggle-Bug, T. E.

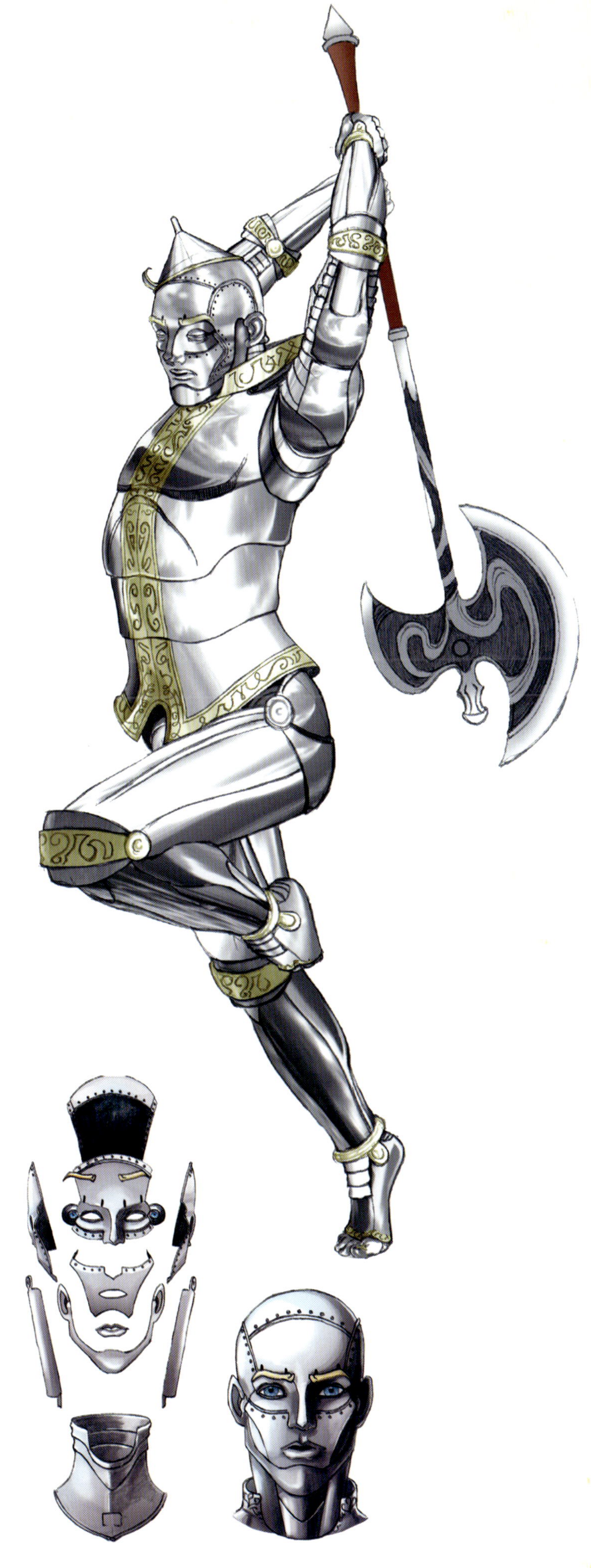

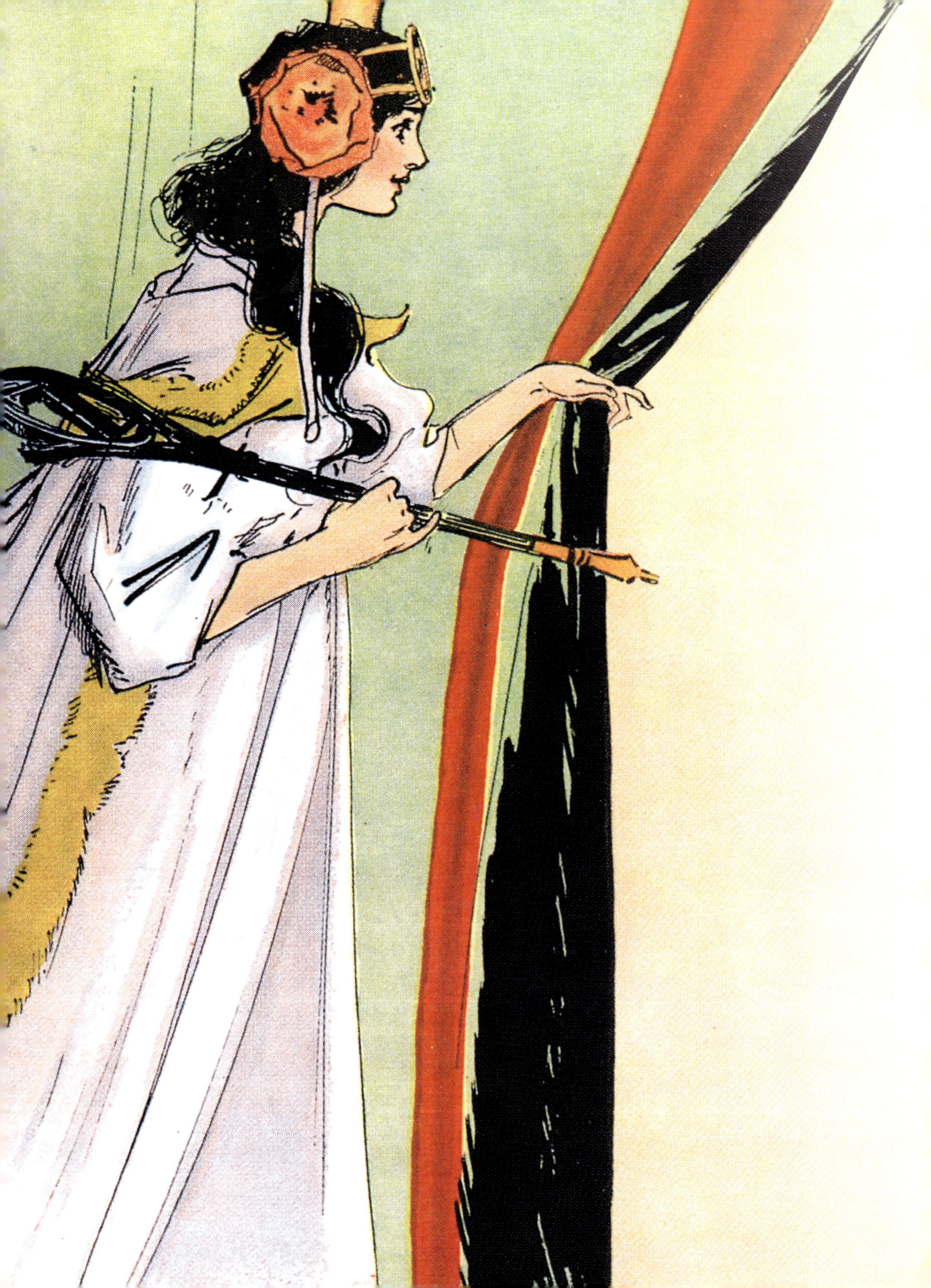

Royal Proclamation Extraordinary

from Princess Ozma of Oz

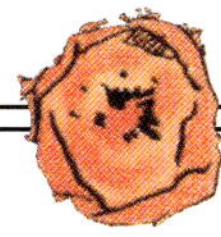

TO: MR. GABRIEL GALE
BY IMPERIAL APPOINTMENT,
HISTORIAN TO THE LAND OF OZ

Sir:

In your Illustrious and Illustrative Honor, this decree hereby and happily sanctions the sharing of your bright new pictorial entertainment with the Many Friends of Oz in the Great Outside World.

We, one and all, celebrate the publication of your Oz artwork, including portraits of some of our outstanding citizens; images of our historical figures; vivid considerations of our unique creations and creatures; and distinctive examinations of the topography of our universe.

In this manner, all children—and all those who used to be children—may view your fresh and present-day drawings of the best-loved characters who reside in Oz. Readers will also be introduced to those who dwell nearby, underneath, and in the depths of the oceans around and about our Marvelous Land.

I have additionally authorized eight of our most popular inhabitants to contribute the text that accompanies your drawings and paintings. I feel certain that people of all ages will delight in the personal comments of Dorothy Gale of Kansas, the Scarecrow, Tin Woodman, Cowardly Lion, Glinda the Good Witch, Toto the dog, Professor H. M. Woggle-Bug, T. E., and the wonderful Wizard himself. Of course, some booklovers will be familiar with our history; many others, however, may know only a small percentage of the countless adventures that have occurred here in Oz. That is why these eight celebrities have been selected to guide everyone through your pages, for there could be no better or more informed company than such treasured, close friends of the children.

Finally, I wholeheartedly endorse your commitment—and that of the Oz personalities—to herein honor the work of the man who first discovered Oz and introduced us to the world: legendary author and explorer L. Frank Baum. We all recognize Mr. Baum as Our Most Noble and Notable Champion, as it was his imagination and storytelling gift that launched the famous series of Oz books. To complete this past and present overview, I am further pleased that you have included a number of the extraordinary original pictures drawn by the first two Oz artists, W. W. Denslow and John R. Neill. It is gratifying that they, too, receive their due, as their incomparable interpretations of our populace and vistas are timeless indeed.

I thus warmly welcome this opportunity to commend Gabriel Gale, and I encourage everyone, on either side of the rainbow, to enjoy this chance to discover Oz!

Given under my Hand and Seal at the Royal Palace in the Emerald City of Oz in the One Hundred and Eighteenth Year, Second Division, of My Reign,

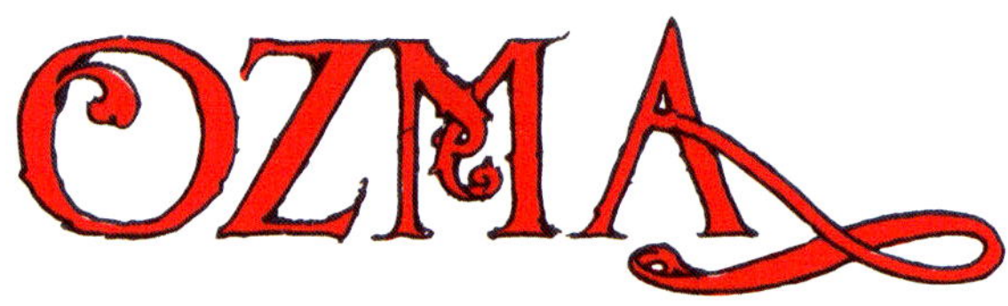

SUPREME RULER
OF THE LAND OF OZ

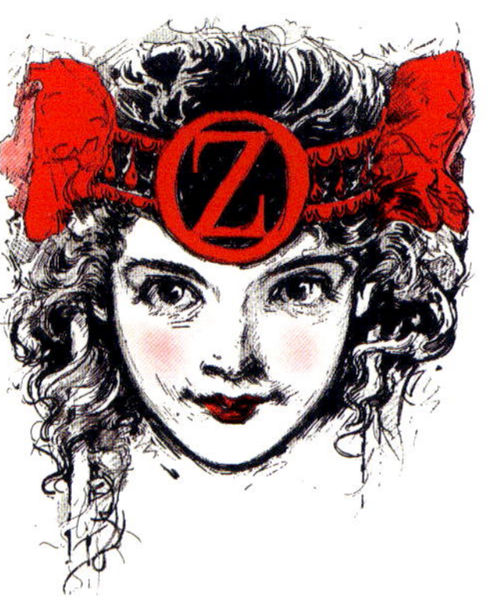

PAGE 13: Art by John R. Neill, *The Magic of Oz*
ABOVE: Art by Neill, *The Emerald City of Oz*
OPPOSITE: Art by Neill, *The Lost Princess of Oz*

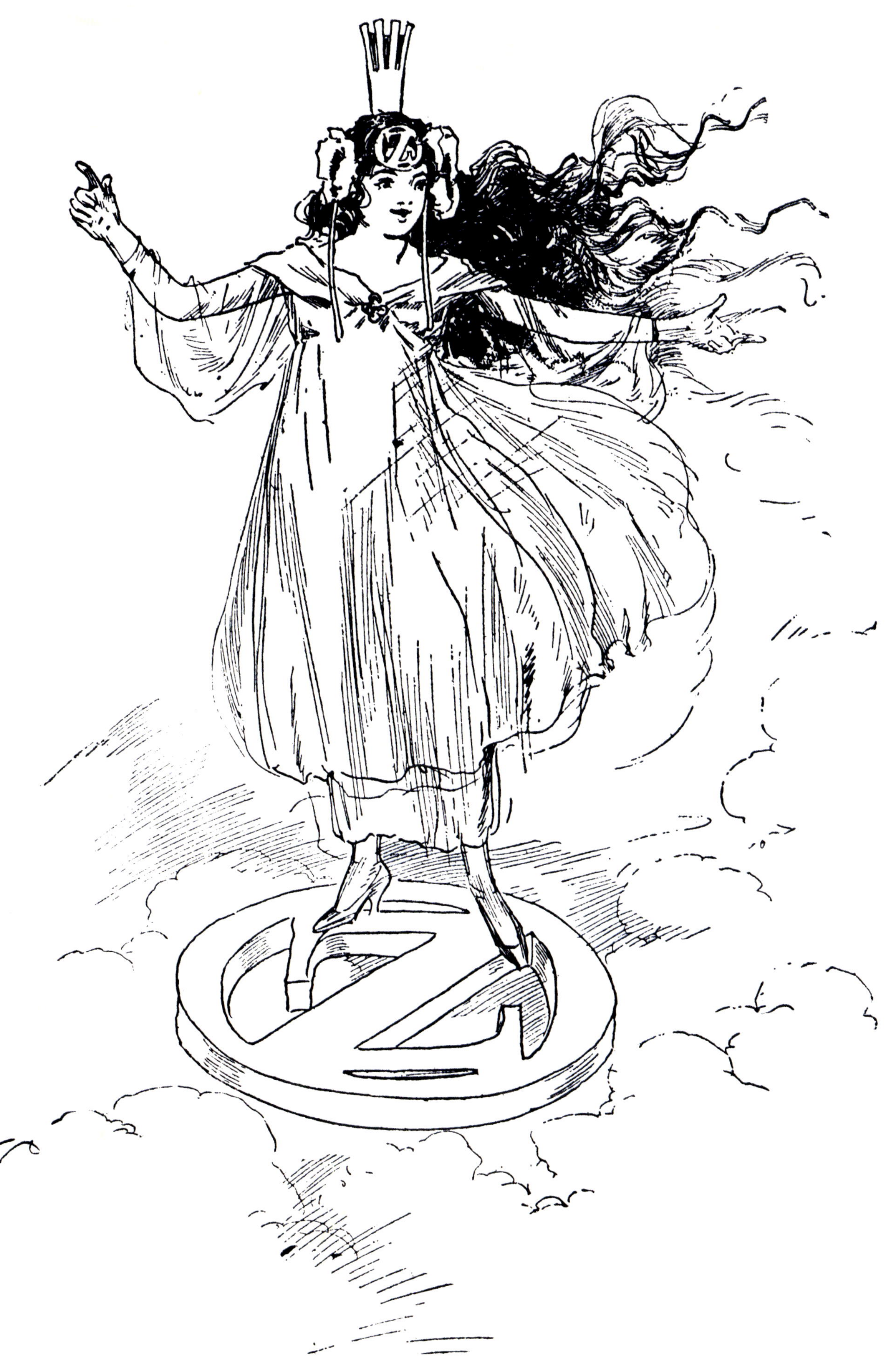

The Witches & Their Armies

INTRODUCED BY DOROTHY

My first visit to Oz was very exciting, and most of it was beautiful. Of course, it was frightening, too, but everything worked out all right, because Toto and I finally got home to Kansas! Meanwhile, we met the Scarecrow, Tin Woodman, and Cowardly Lion, and our adventures together were told by Mr. Baum in *The Wonderful Wizard of Oz*. I never expected, though, that I would return here again and again, finally coming to Oz to stay forever—with Toto, too! Naturally, we also sent for Aunt Em and Uncle Henry, and as nice as Kansas is, there just couldn't be a happier place for us than the Emerald City.

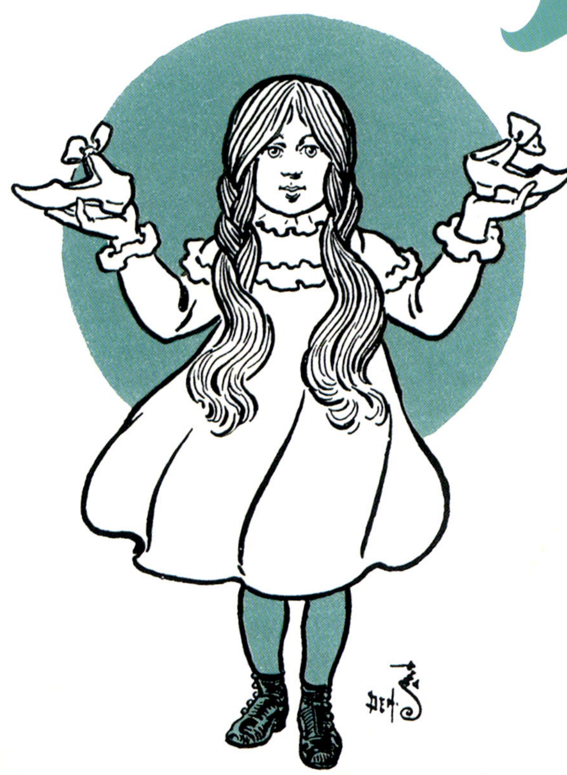

I have to admit I didn't realize that my earliest trip would be so important to the history of Oz—from the very moment I "landed" in the blue Munchkin Country. That's where the tornado

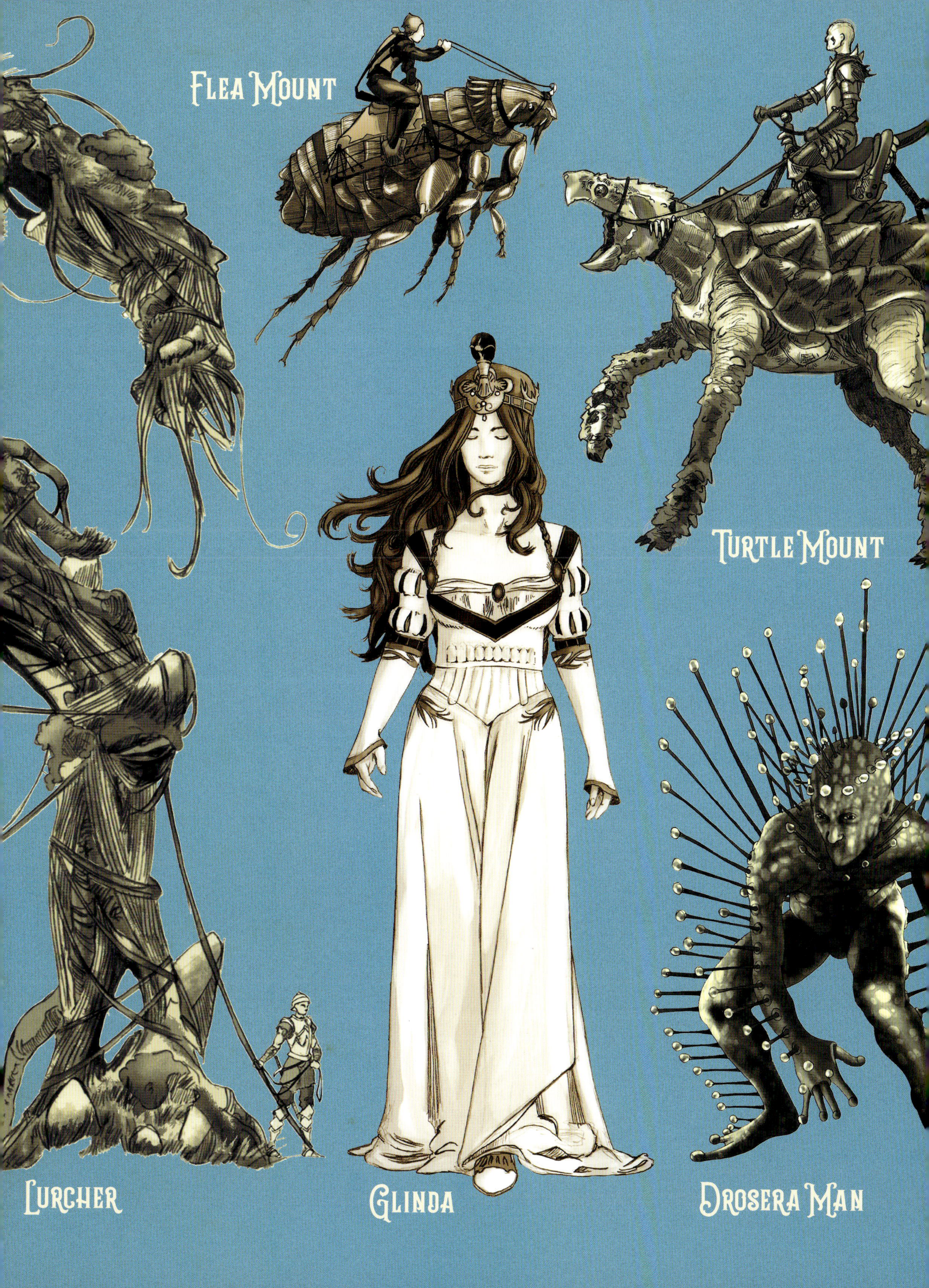
Flea Mount
Turtle Mount
Lurcher
Glinda
Drosera Man

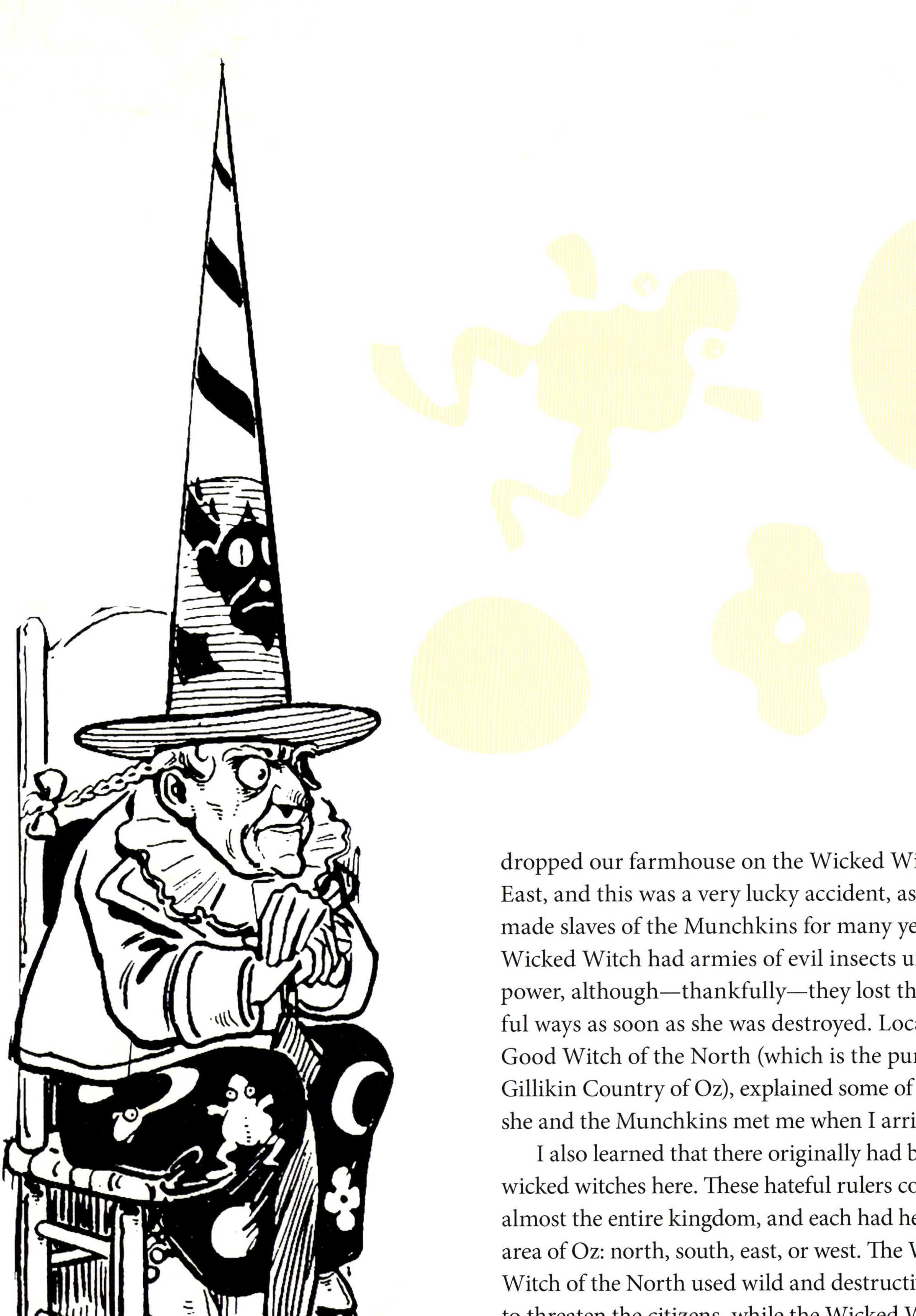

dropped our farmhouse on the Wicked Witch of the East, and this was a very lucky accident, as she had made slaves of the Munchkins for many years. This Wicked Witch had armies of evil insects under her power, although—thankfully—they lost their dreadful ways as soon as she was destroyed. Locasta, the Good Witch of the North (which is the purple Gillikin Country of Oz), explained some of this when she and the Munchkins met me when I arrived.

I also learned that there originally had been four wicked witches here. These hateful rulers controlled almost the entire kingdom, and each had her own area of Oz: north, south, east, or west. The Wicked Witch of the North used wild and destructive animals to threaten the citizens, while the Wicked Witch of the South (in the red Quadling Country) raised magic plants to trap or crush those she wanted to destroy. After many battles—and the use of *good* magic—Locasta and Glinda the Good were able to defeat the wretched witches of the north and south. Their frightening pets and plants remained in Oz, but you'll be glad to know that most of them are no longer mean and scary, just sometimes mischievous or menacing.

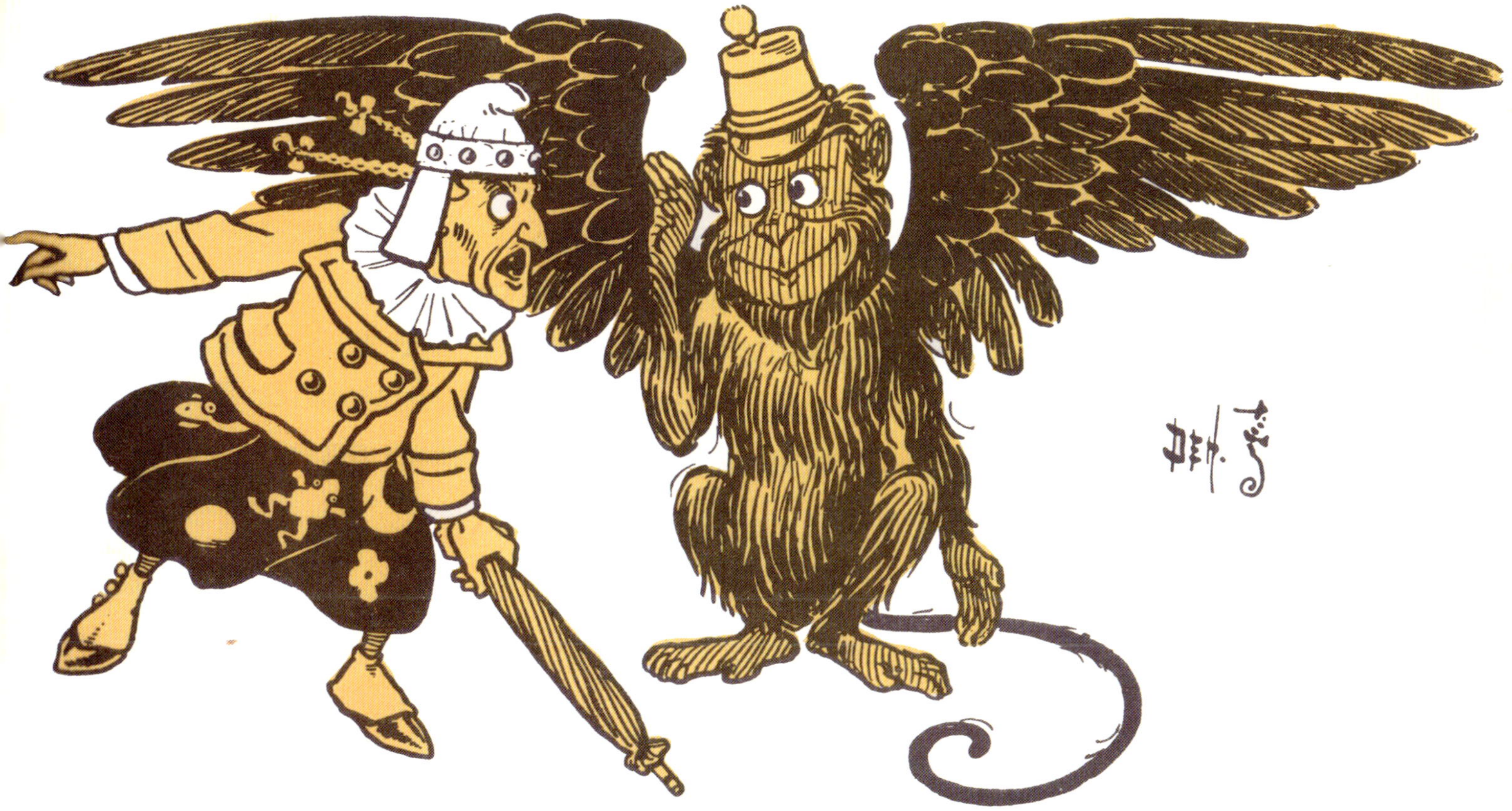

My next unexpected contribution to the saga of Oz happened when Toto and I—along with our friends—were sent to the yellow Winkie Country by the Wizard of Oz. He promised that he'd grant our requests if we killed the Wicked Witch of the West. Fortunately, we didn't meet her armies of horrible snakes and lizards, but she did send the Winged Monkeys to capture Toto and me, and she made me her slave. I was so scared that I did everything she asked, until the day she stole one of my magic shoes. In anger, I fought back with the only "weapon" I had: a bucket of water. I didn't know that she was so old and dried up that she would completely melt away, so this was the second history-changing coincidence in which I was involved. The Oz people have been lovely to me ever since!

PAGE 16: Dorothy
OPPOSITE: The Wicked Witch of the West
ABOVE: With the King of the Winged Monkeys
BELOW: Toto isn't pleased with either of them.
All art by W. W. Denslow, *The Wonderful Wizard of Oz*

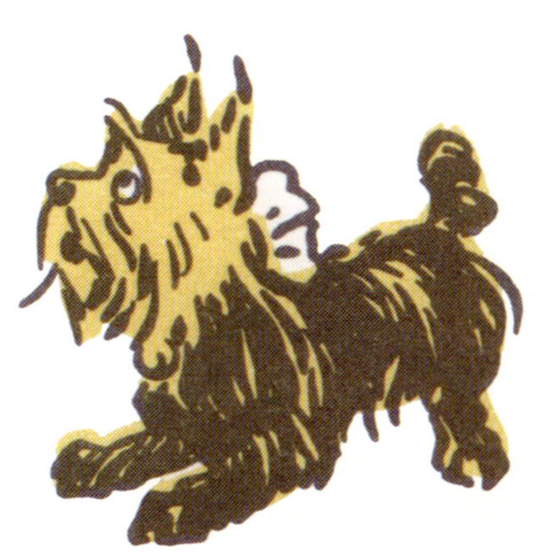

BELOW: Dorothy and the Wicked Witch of the West by Denslow, *The Wonderful Wizard of Oz*
OPPOSITE: Glinda the Good by Neill, *The Marvelous Land of Oz*

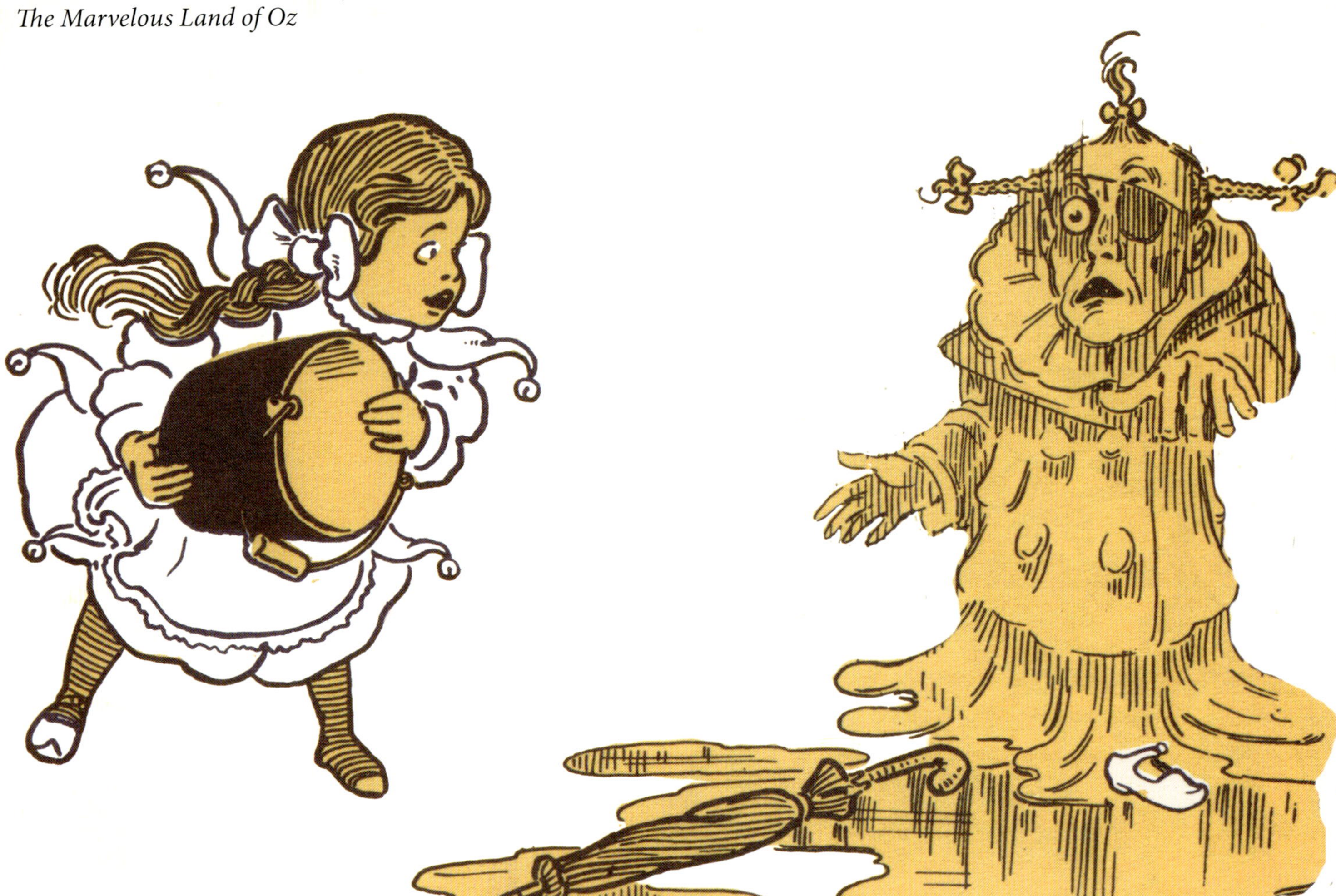

You will see pictures of Locasta—and the bad witches and their monster armies—in these pages. You'll also meet beauteous Glinda the Good, Witch of the South, whose remarkable sorcery has brought joy, protection, and glory to Oz. She's the one who revealed to me the power of the magic shoes of the Witch of the East. They had been given to me by Locasta, but it was Glinda who taught me to use them to travel to Kansas. Since then, she and Princess Ozma have shared in the work of making Oz the most wonderful kingdom anywhere.

There's one more army I should mention. "General" Jinjur was a bold Munchkin maiden, who decided that women should: 1) take over ruling the Land of Oz; 2) steal all the jewels from the Emerald City to make rings, bracelets, and necklaces; and 3) force men to do all the housework, laundry, cooking, and babysitting! Soon after I returned to Kansas, Jinjur's all-girl forces invaded the palace of Oz and took away the throne from the Scarecrow, who was then the king. Glinda came to the rescue, however, and sent Jinjur home. The girl realized that she knew how to run a farm but didn't know to manage a whole country.

Now, any new wicked witches or armies must be in hiding, for Princess Ozma is our rightful ruler, and her "law" is very simple: "Our Land of Oz is a Land of Love."

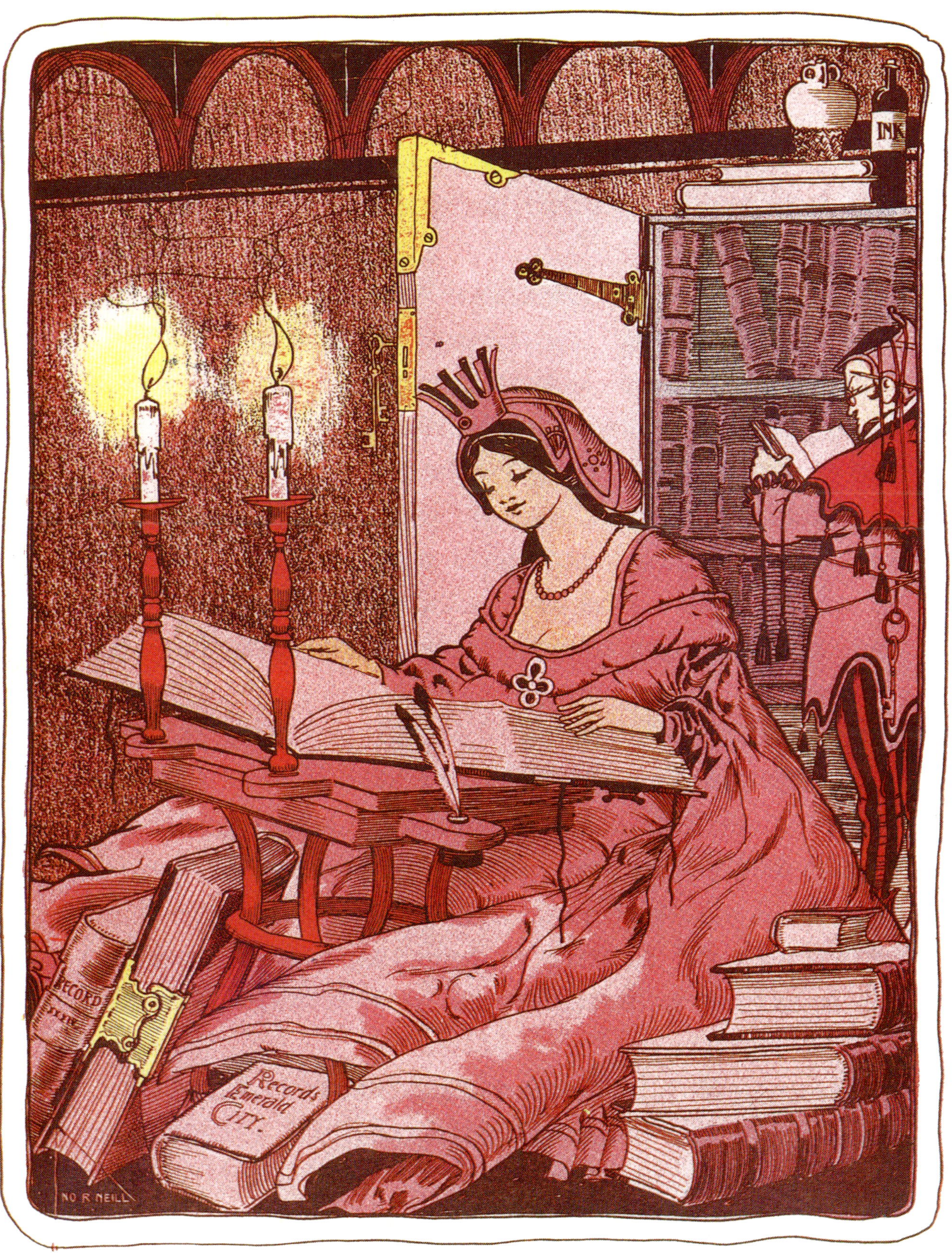
INK
Records
Emerald
City

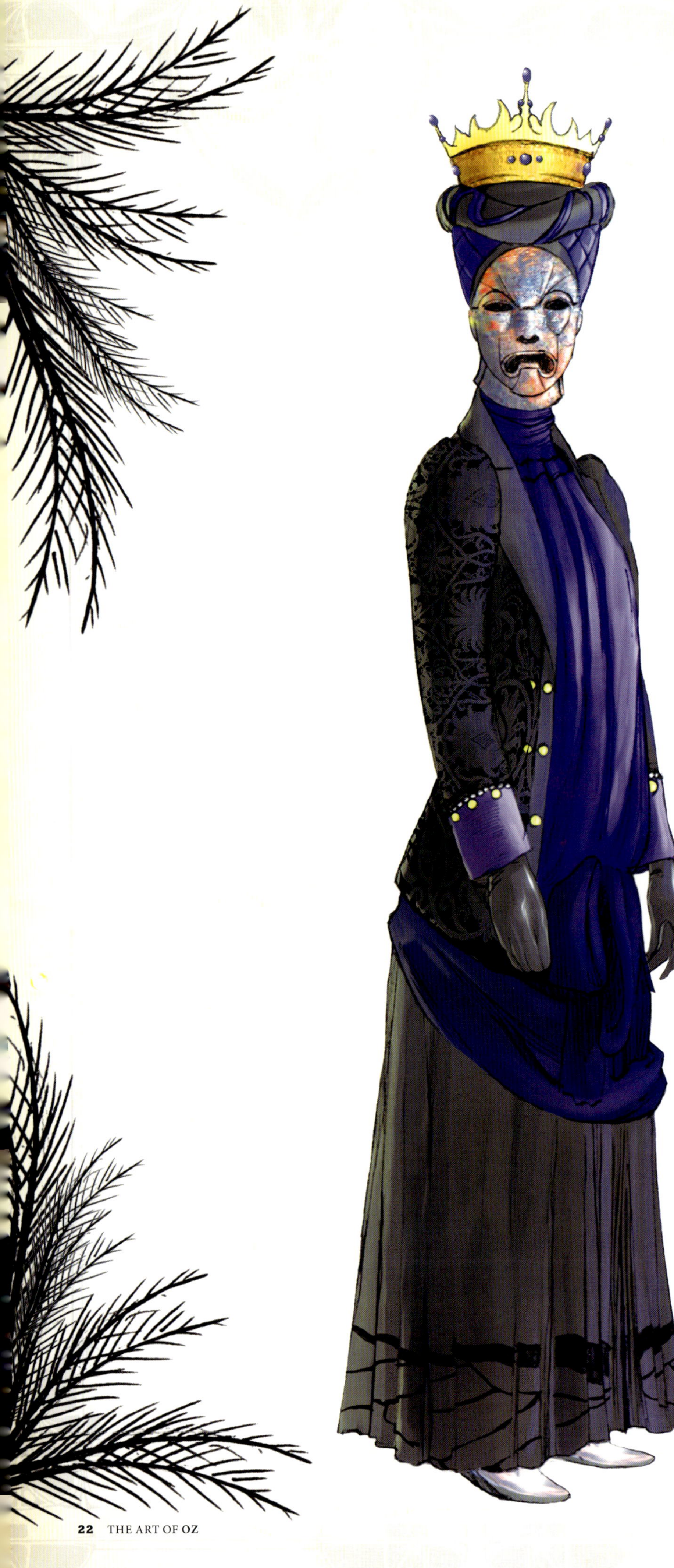

Ava Munch

The Wicked Witch of the East

Gabriel Gale's *Ages of Oz* is the saga of the wildly wicked magic workers who ruled our country during its earliest days. Ava Munch was the given name of the Wicked Witch of the East. She commanded an army "platoon of bulging-eyed creepy-crawlies: oversize wisp wasps, mosquitos, and fruit flies, beetles and tumble-bumbles with iridescent wings."

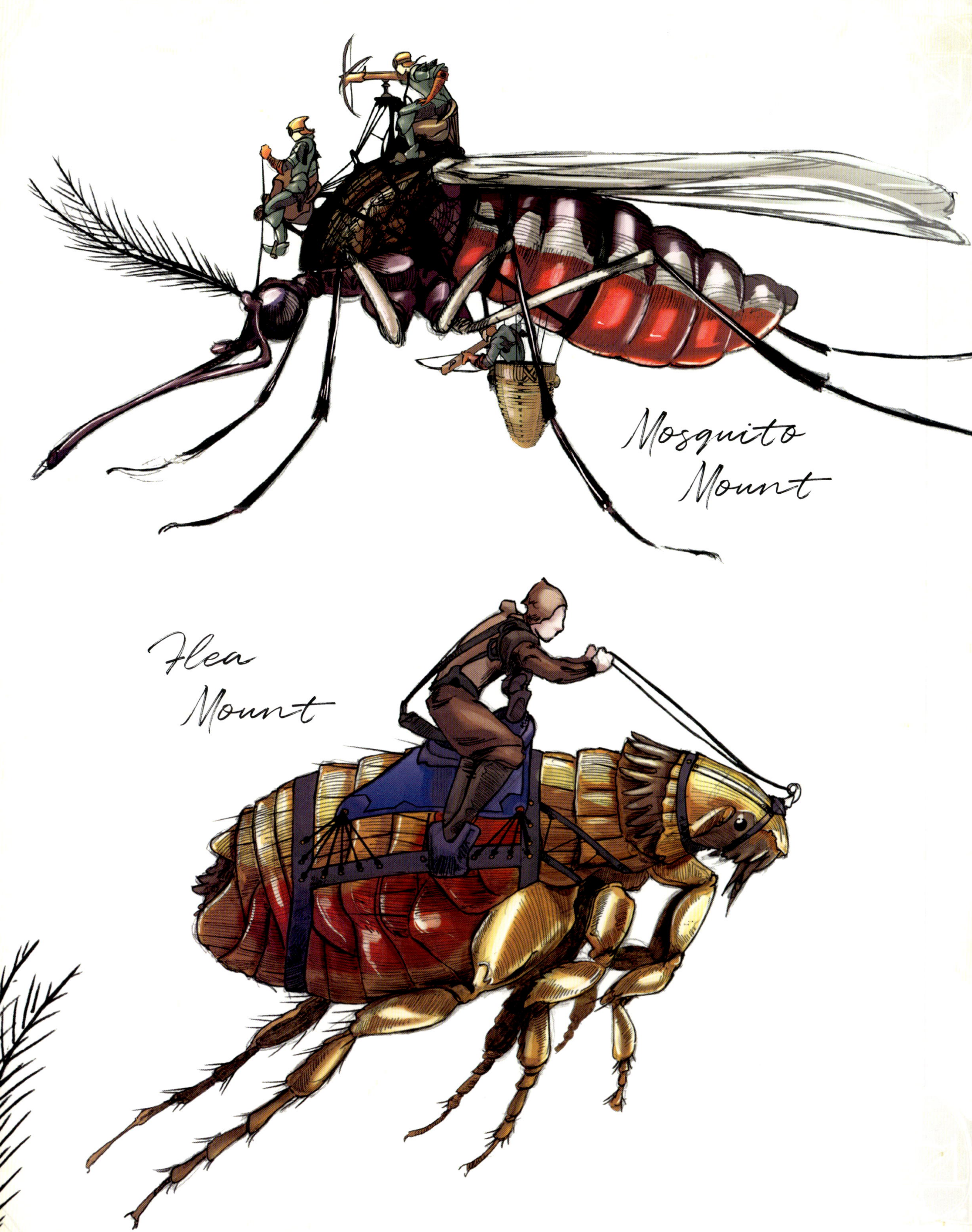
Mosquito
Mount
Flea
Mount

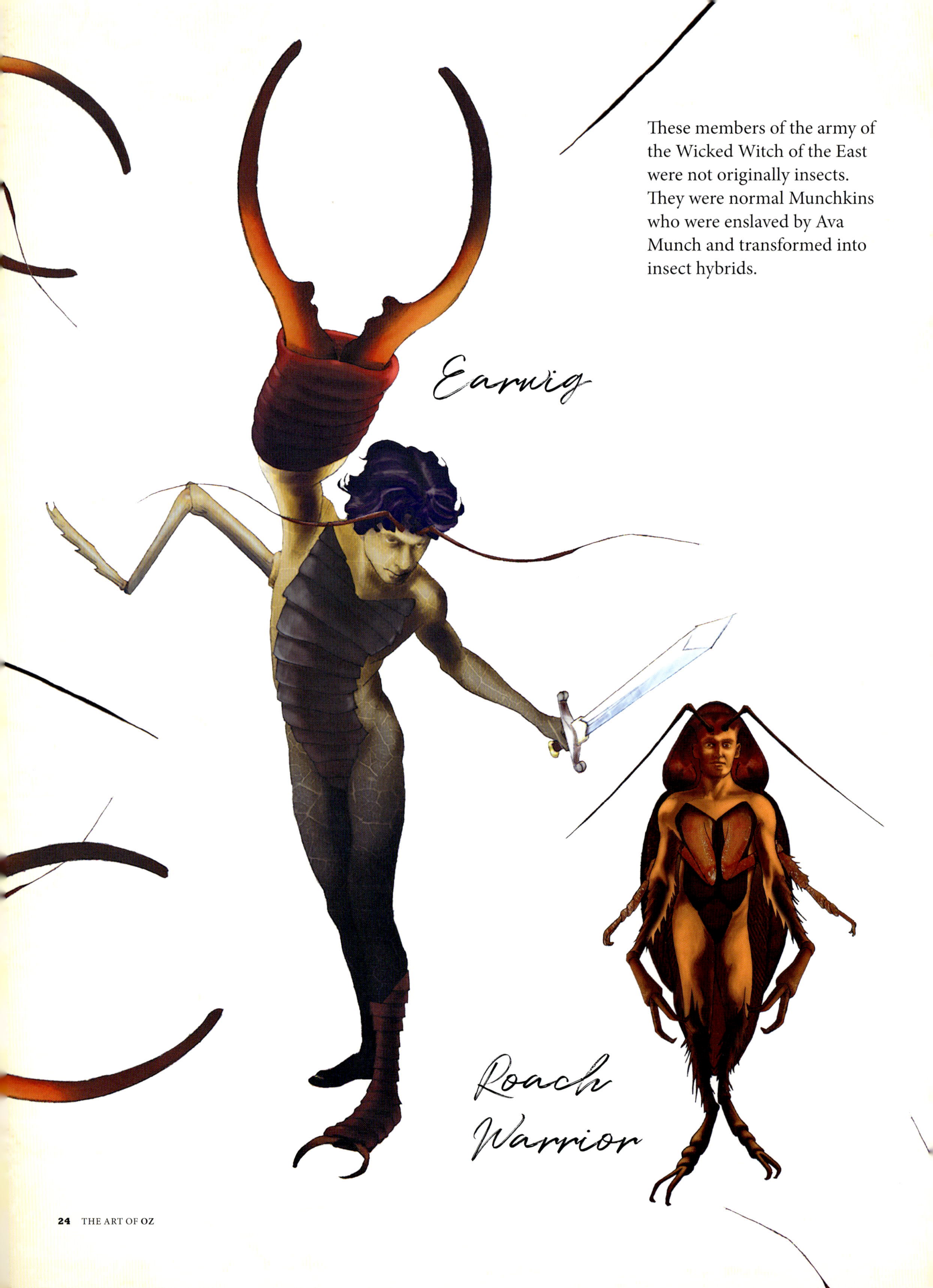

These members of the army of the Wicked Witch of the East were not originally insects. They were normal Munchkins who were enslaved by Ava Munch and transformed into insect hybrids.

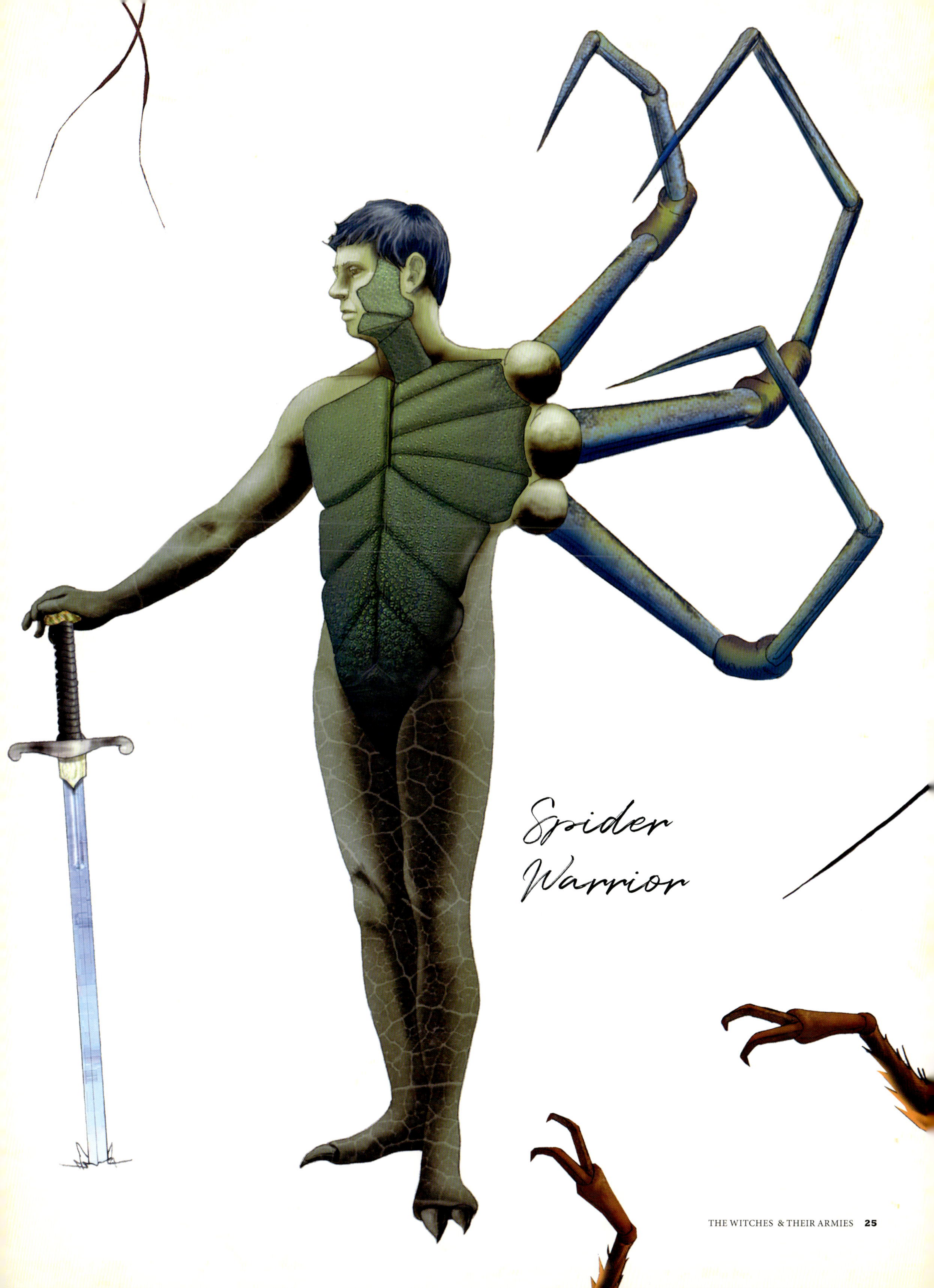
Spider
Warrior

Roach Chariot

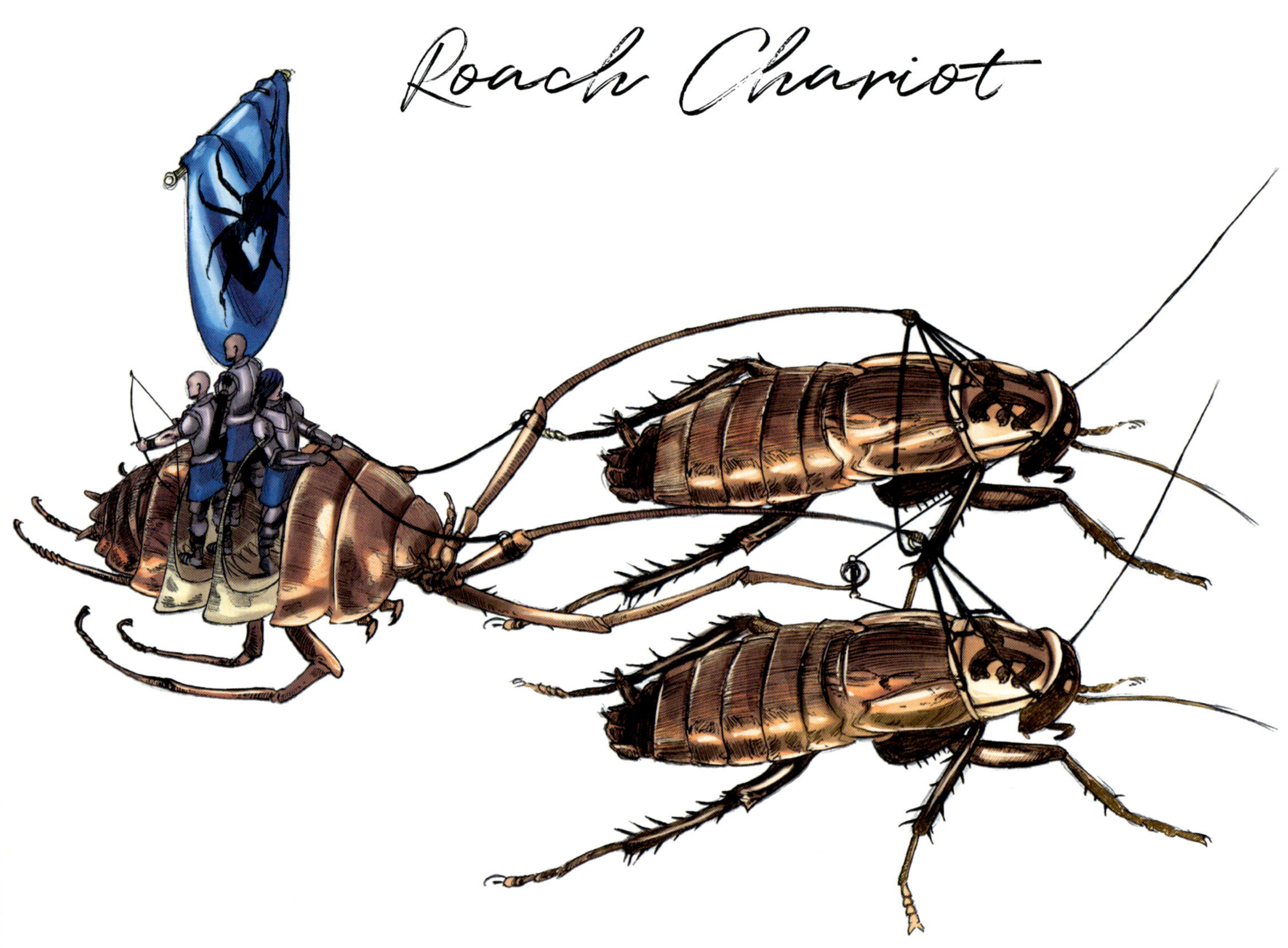

Whether enchanted Munchkins or oversize insects, they all had to do the evil bidding of Ava Munch.

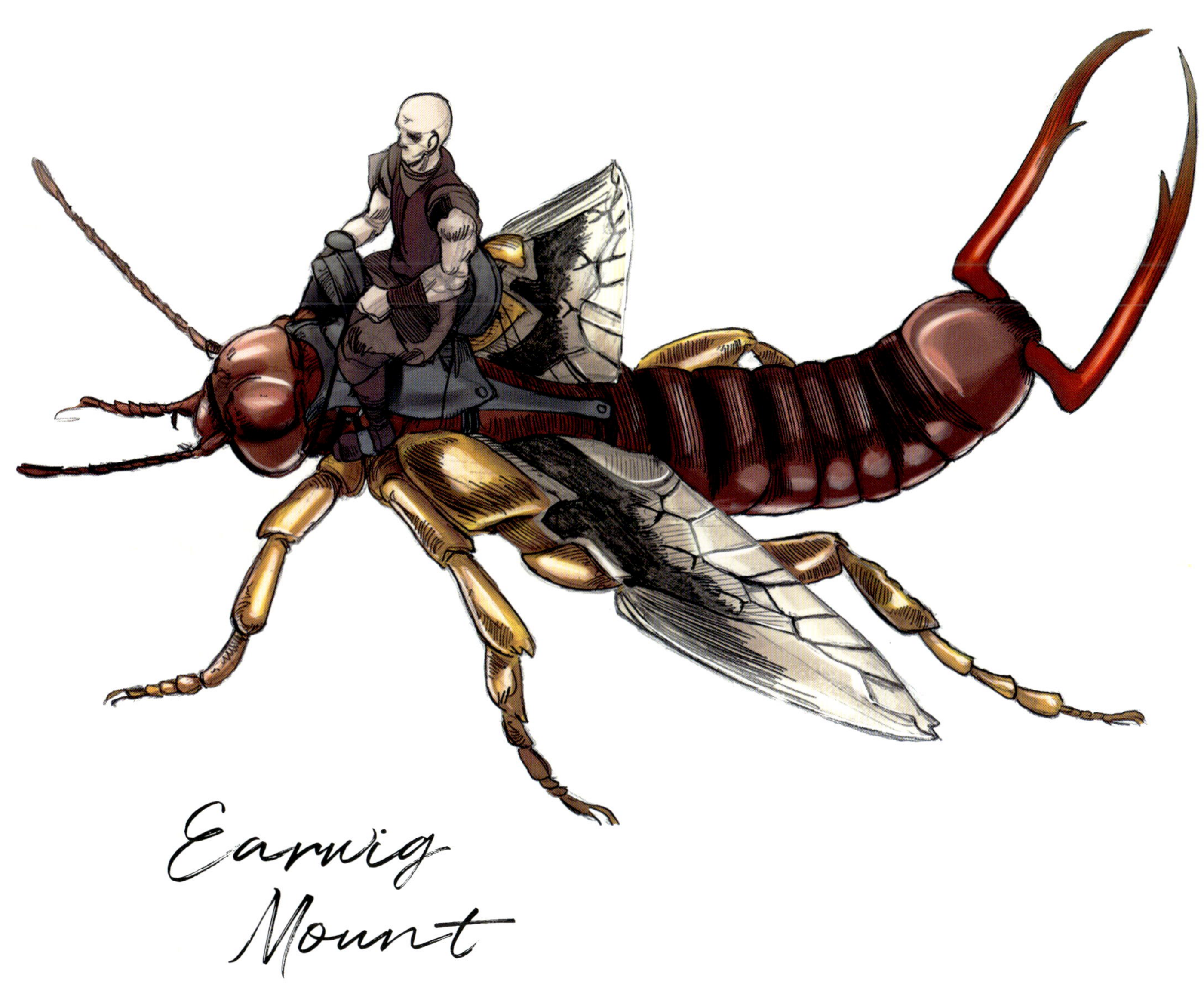
Earwig
Mount

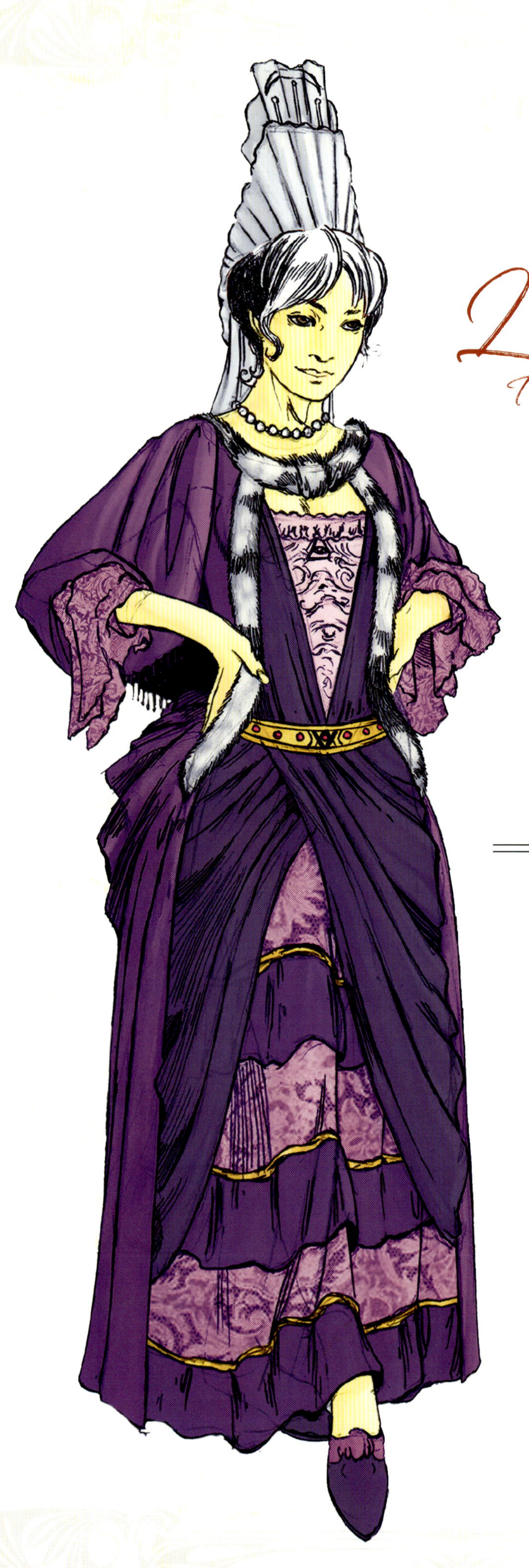

Locasta
The Good Witch of the North

The little woman wore a white gown that hung in plaits from her shoulders; over it were sprinkled little stars that glistened in the sun like diamonds. The woman was doubtless much older than the Munchkins; her face was covered with wrinkles, her hair was nearly white, and she walked rather stiffly.

—THE WONDERFUL WIZARD OF OZ

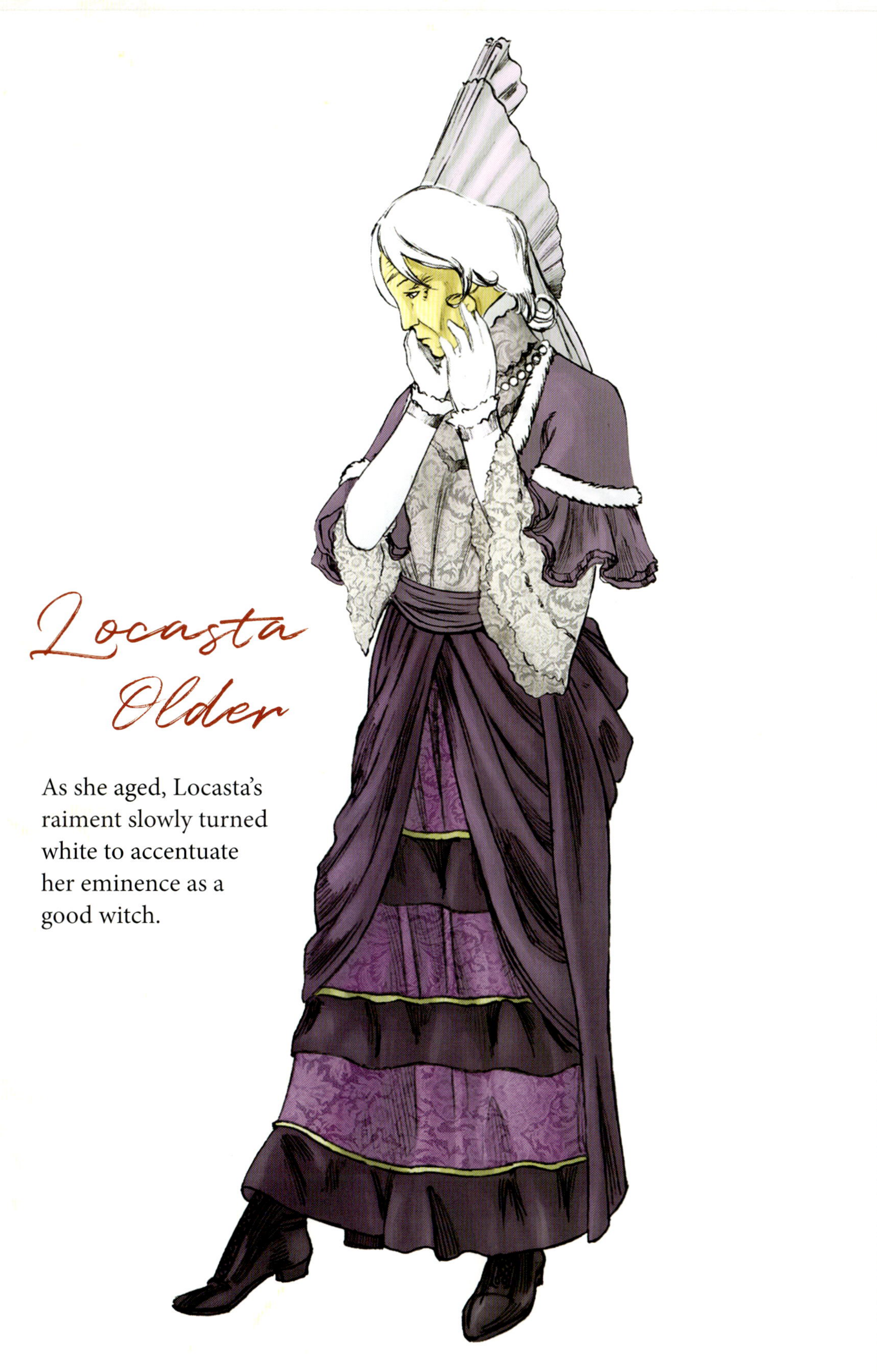

Locasta Older

As she aged, Locasta's raiment slowly turned white to accentuate her eminence as a good witch.

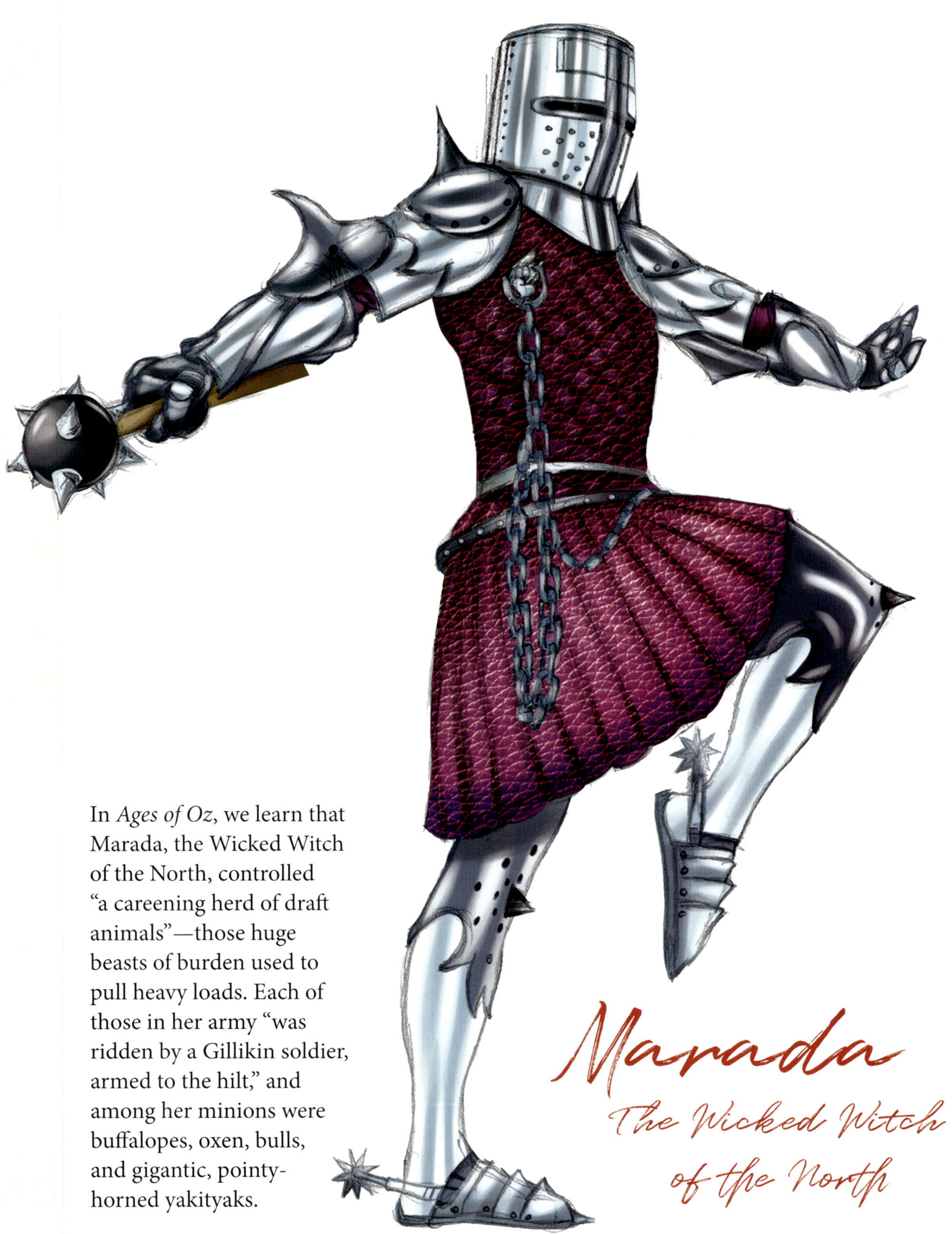

In *Ages of Oz*, we learn that Marada, the Wicked Witch of the North, controlled "a careening herd of draft animals"—those huge beasts of burden used to pull heavy loads. Each of those in her army "was ridden by a Gillikin soldier, armed to the hilt," and among her minions were buffalopes, oxen, bulls, and gigantic, pointy-horned yakityaks.

Marada

The Wicked Witch of the North

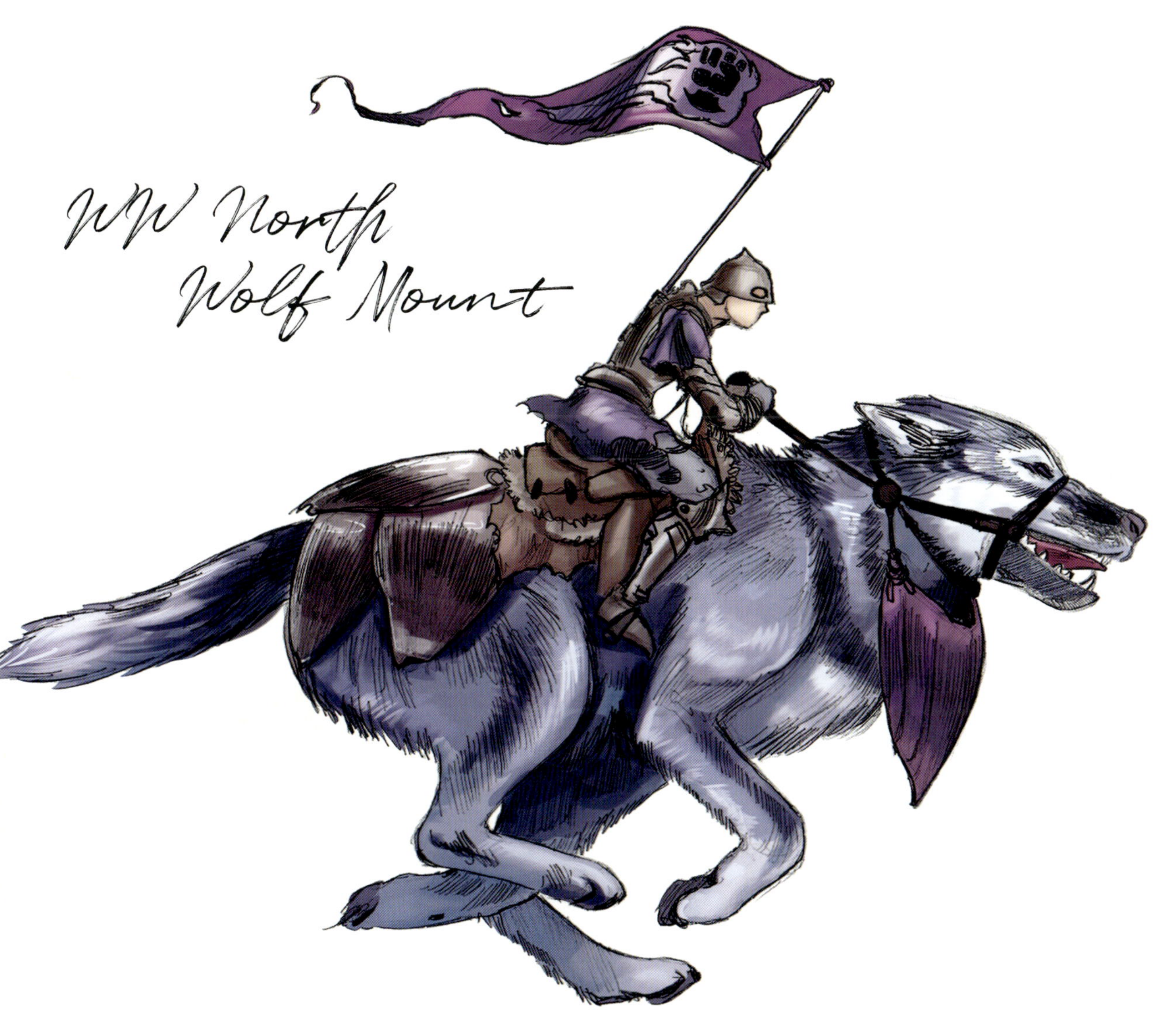
WW North
Wolf Mount

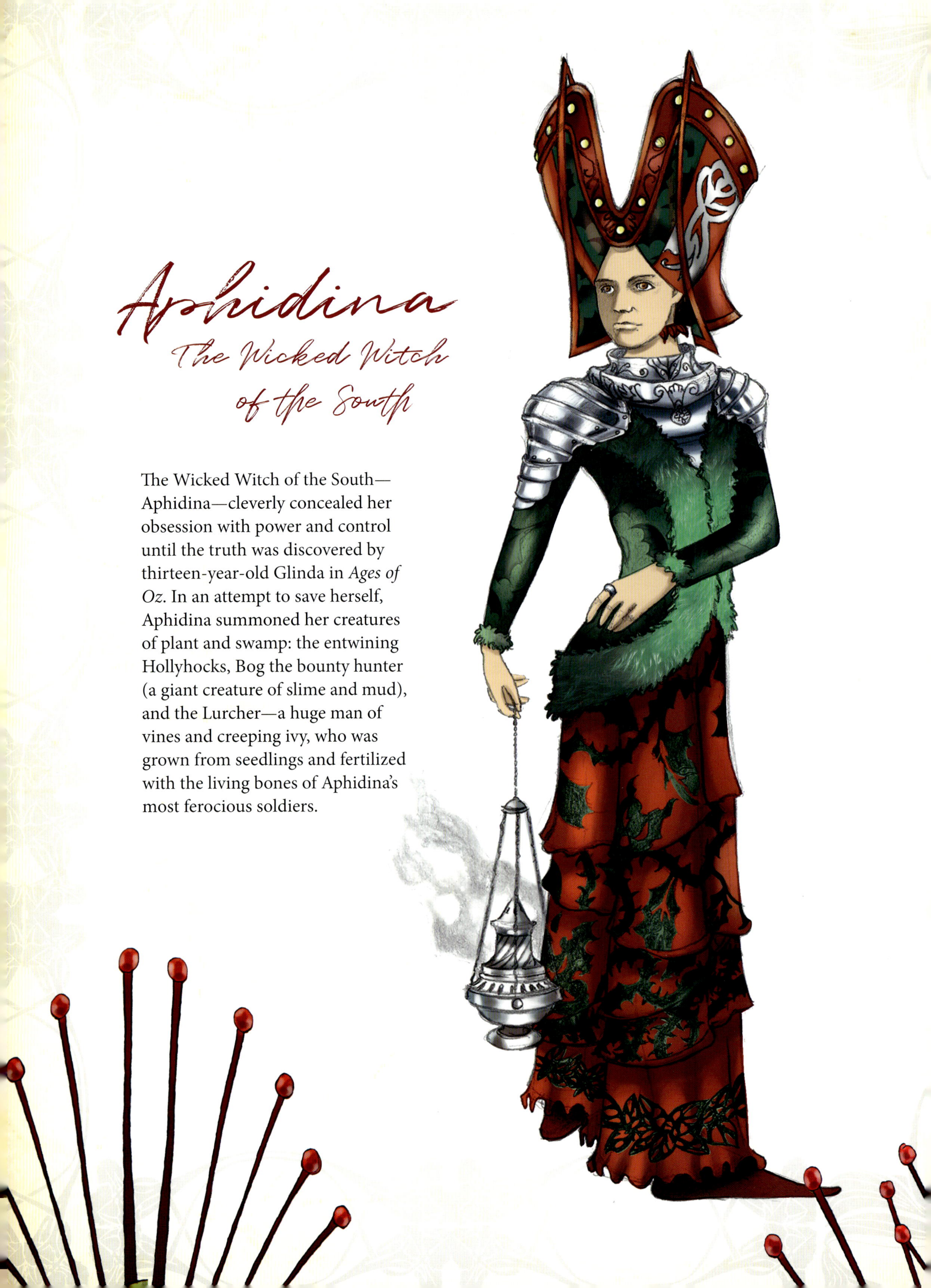

Aphidina

The Wicked Witch of the South

The Wicked Witch of the South—Aphidina—cleverly concealed her obsession with power and control until the truth was discovered by thirteen-year-old Glinda in *Ages of Oz*. In an attempt to save herself, Aphidina summoned her creatures of plant and swamp: the entwining Hollyhocks, Bog the bounty hunter (a giant creature of slime and mud), and the Lurcher—a huge man of vines and creeping ivy, who was grown from seedlings and fertilized with the living bones of Aphidina's most ferocious soldiers.

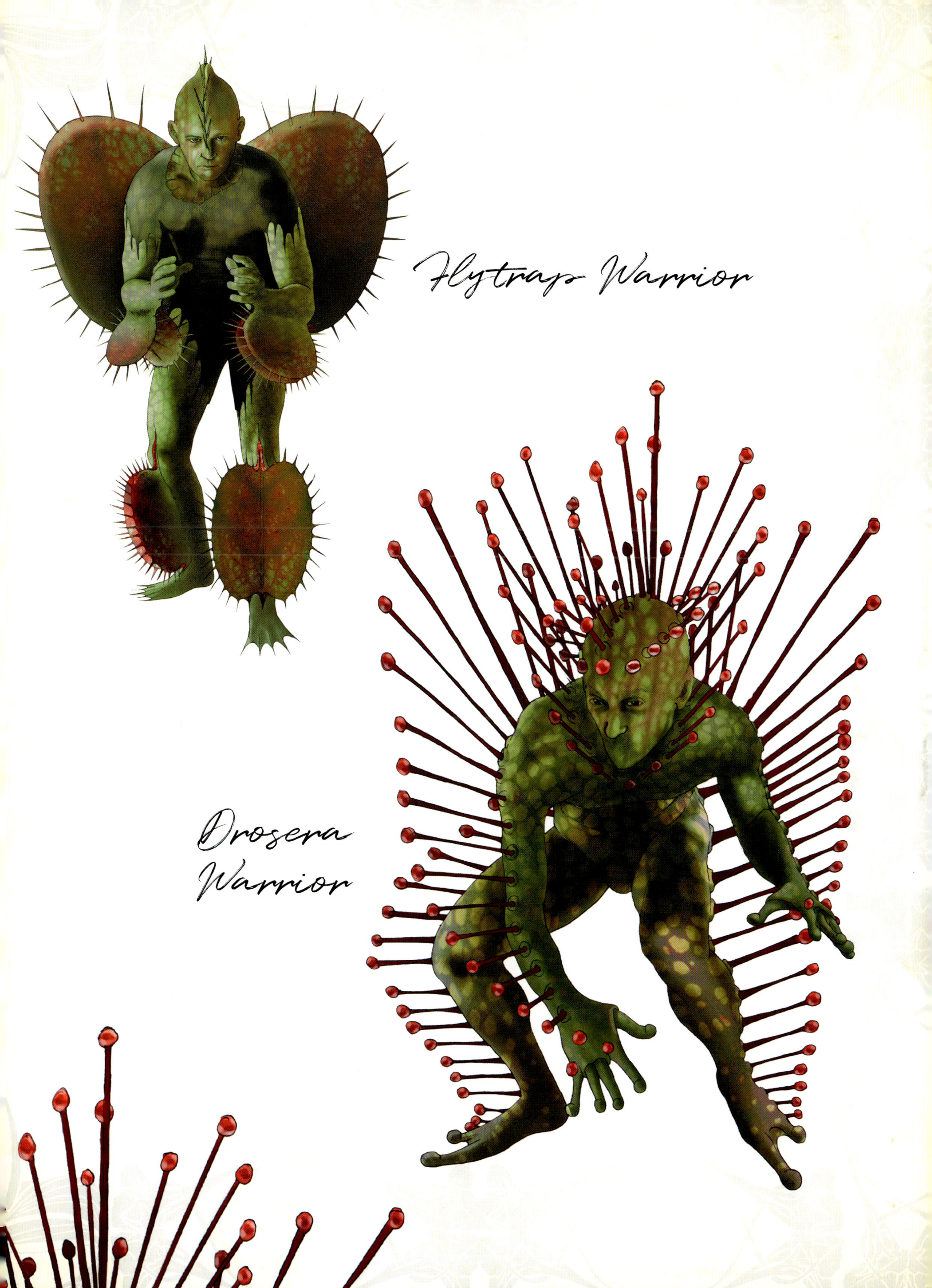
Flytraps Warrior
Drosera
Warrior

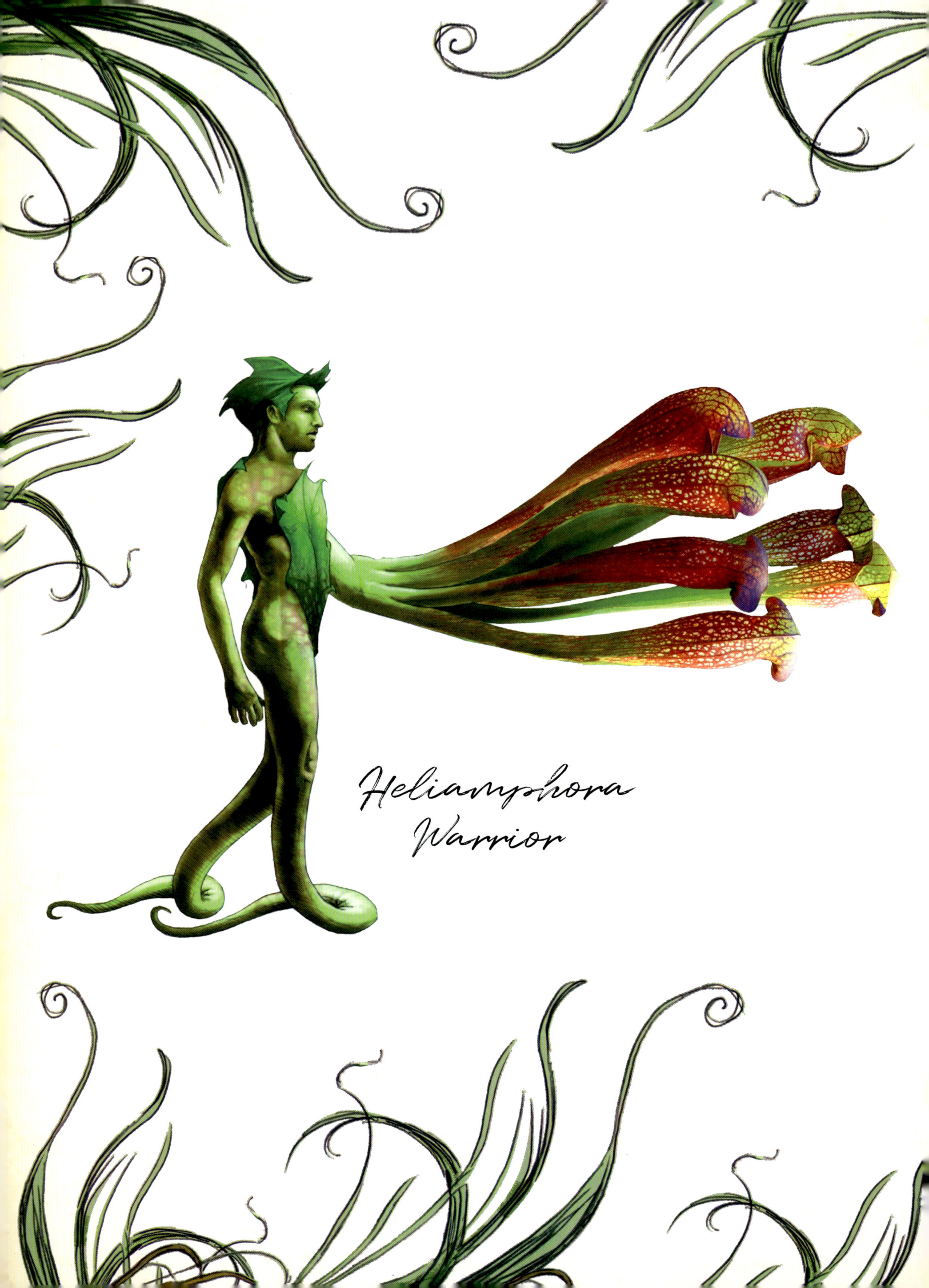
Heliamphora
Warrior

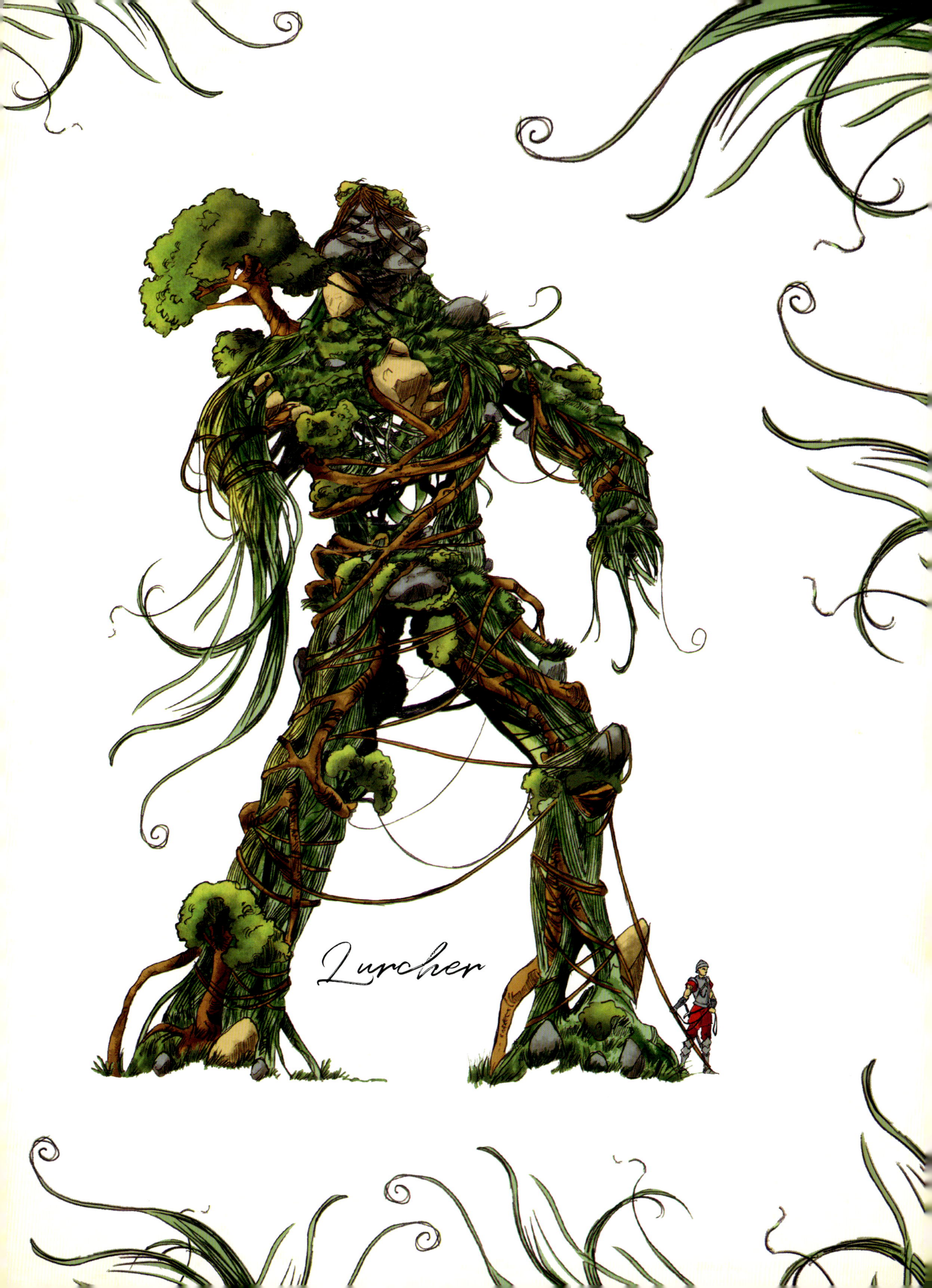
Lurcher

Daspina
The Wicked Witch Of the West

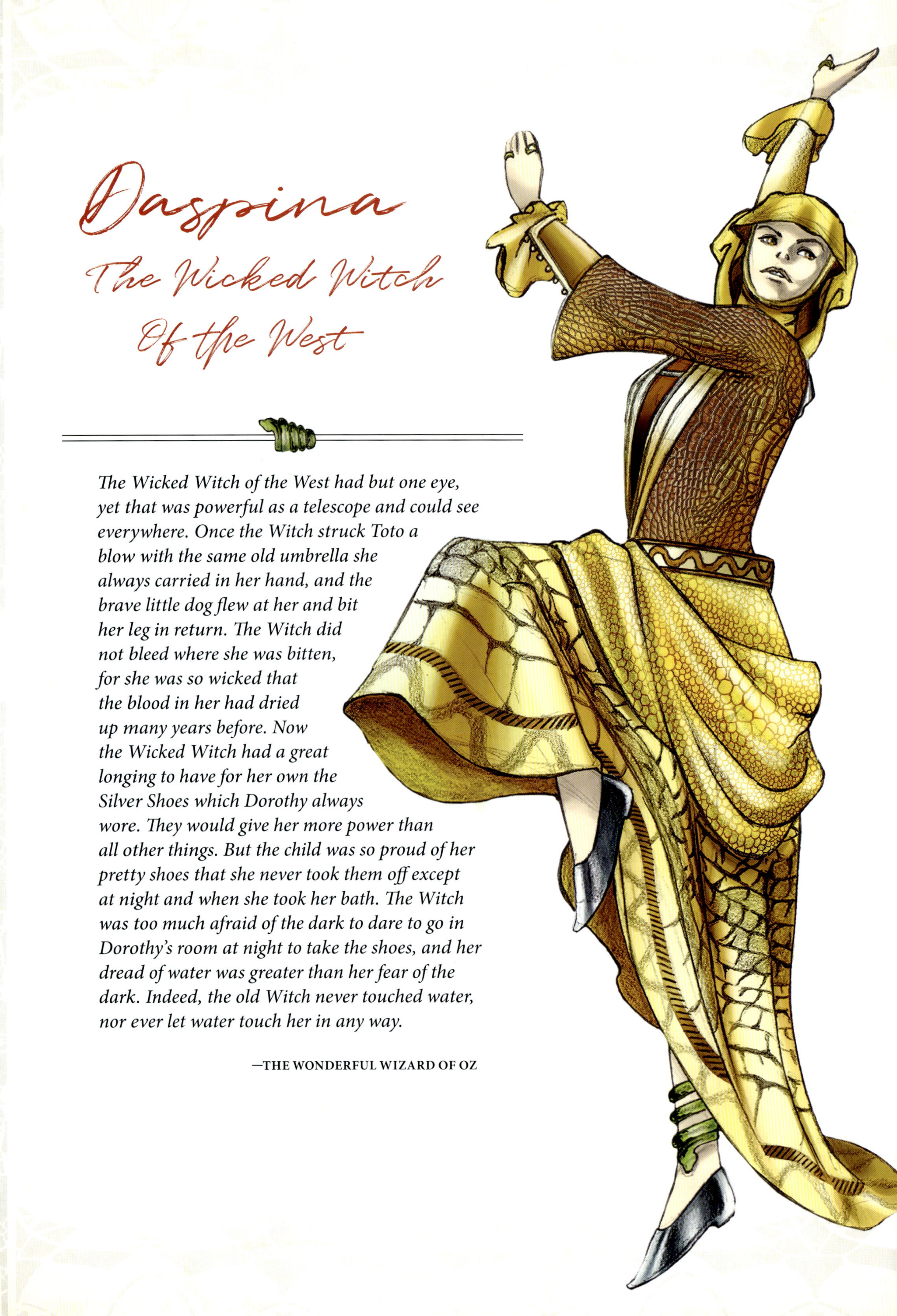

The Wicked Witch of the West had but one eye, yet that was powerful as a telescope and could see everywhere. Once the Witch struck Toto a blow with the same old umbrella she always carried in her hand, and the brave little dog flew at her and bit her leg in return. The Witch did not bleed where she was bitten, for she was so wicked that the blood in her had dried up many years before. Now the Wicked Witch had a great longing to have for her own the Silver Shoes which Dorothy always wore. They would give her more power than all other things. But the child was so proud of her pretty shoes that she never took them off except at night and when she took her bath. The Witch was too much afraid of the dark to dare to go in Dorothy's room at night to take the shoes, and her dread of water was greater than her fear of the dark. Indeed, the old Witch never touched water, nor ever let water touch her in any way.

—THE WONDERFUL WIZARD OF OZ

Lizard Warrior

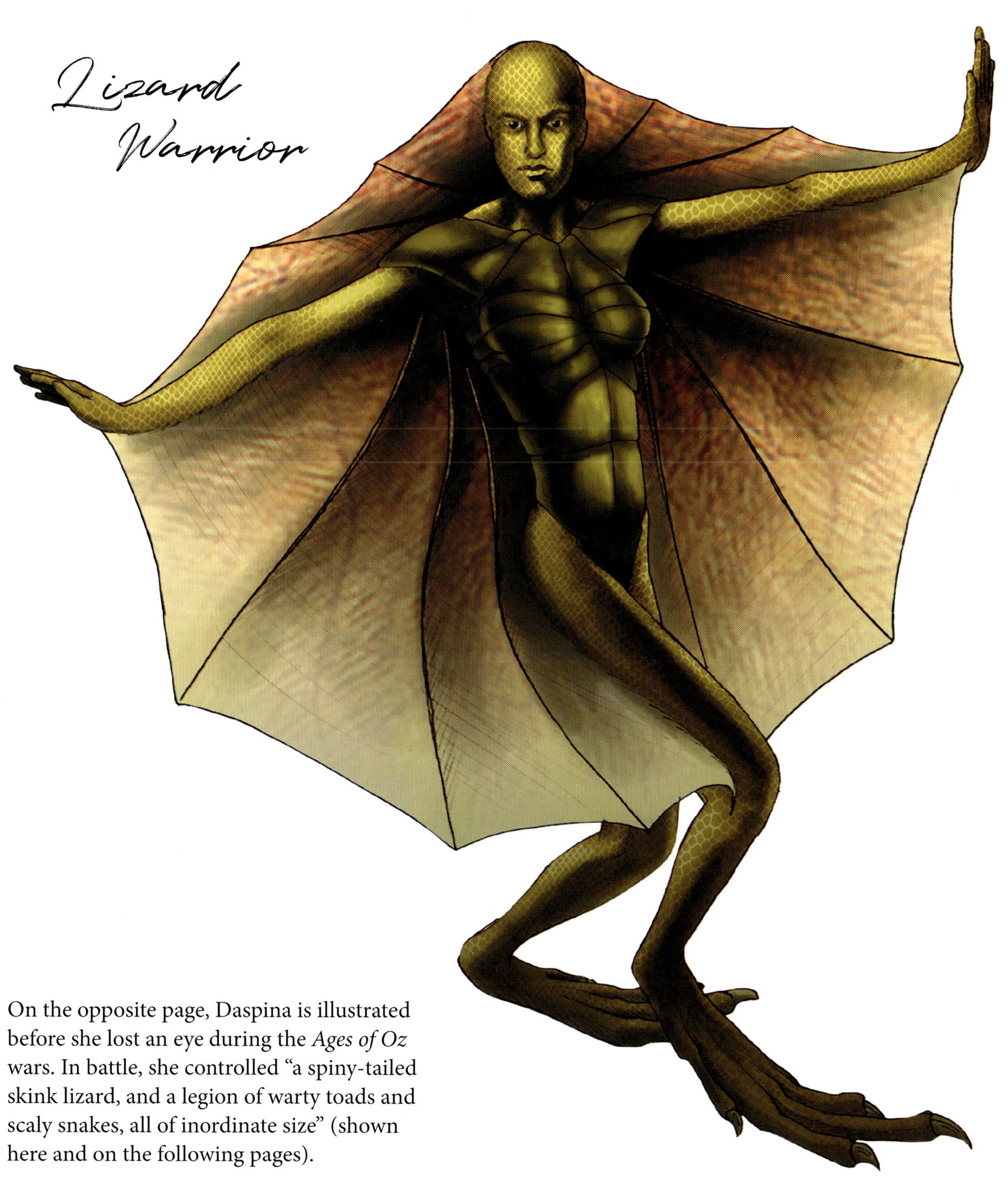

On the opposite page, Daspina is illustrated before she lost an eye during the *Ages of Oz* wars. In battle, she controlled "a spiny-tailed skink lizard, and a legion of warty toads and scaly snakes, all of inordinate size" (shown here and on the following pages).

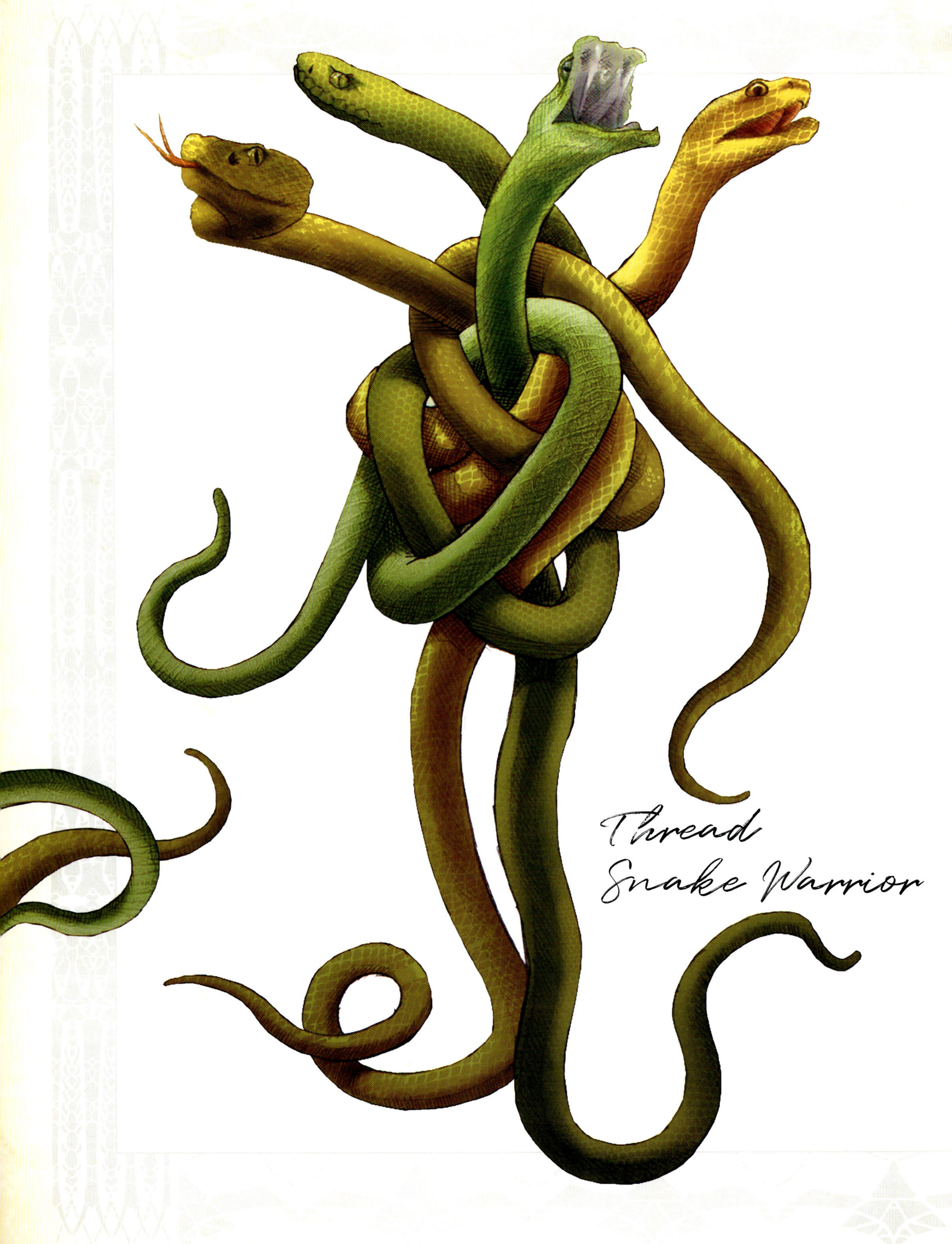

Thread
Snake Warrior

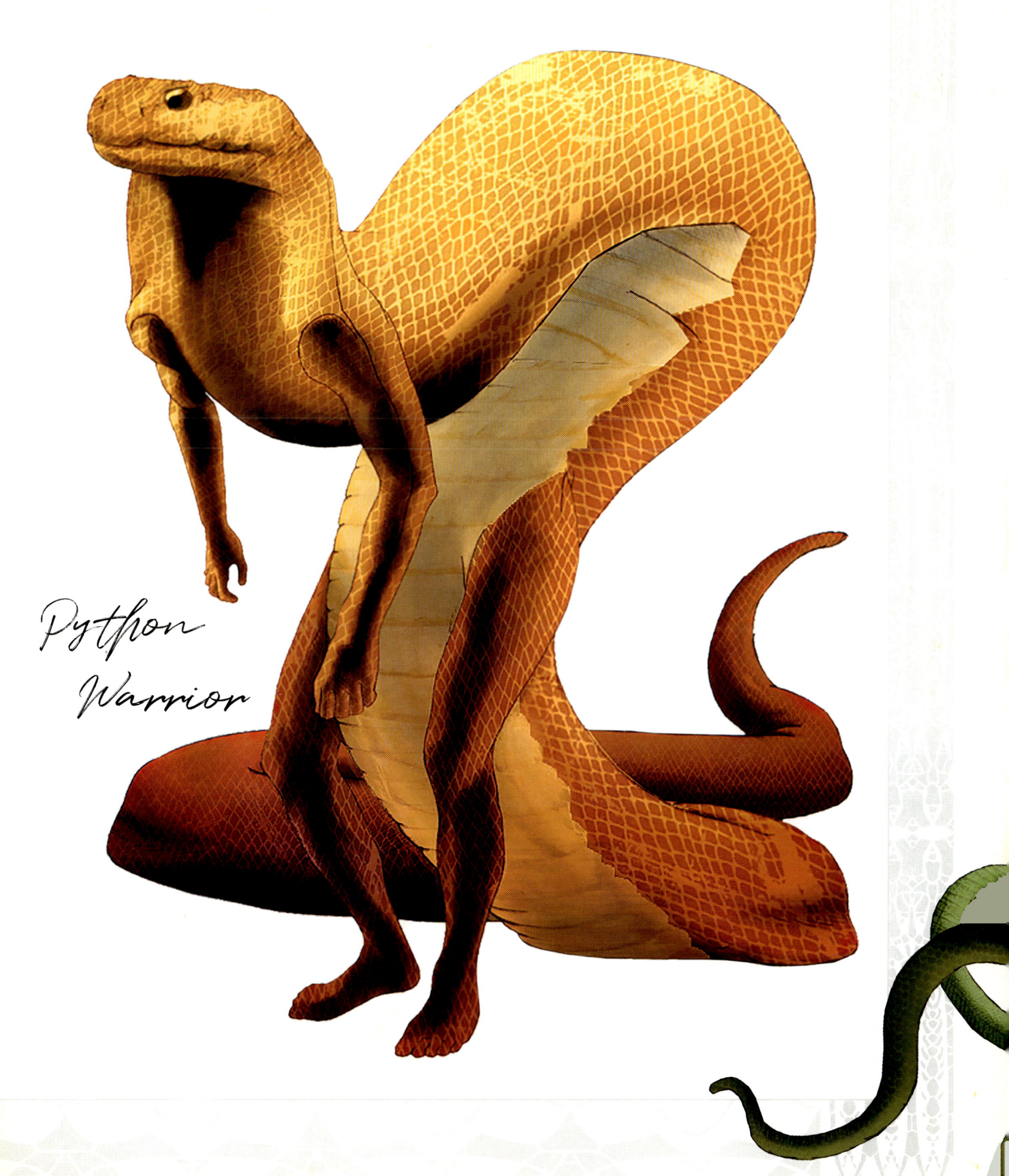
Python
Warrior

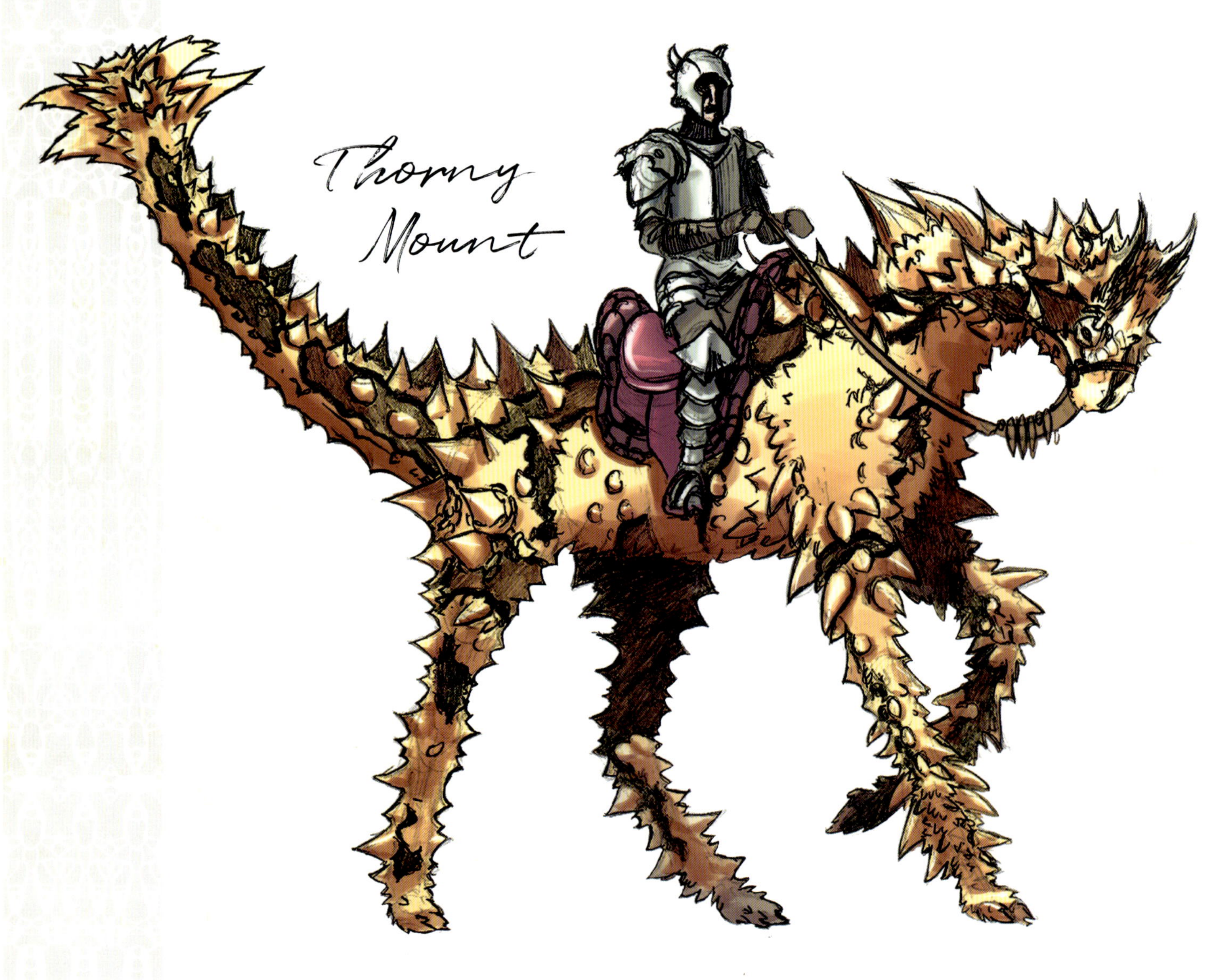
Thorny
Mount

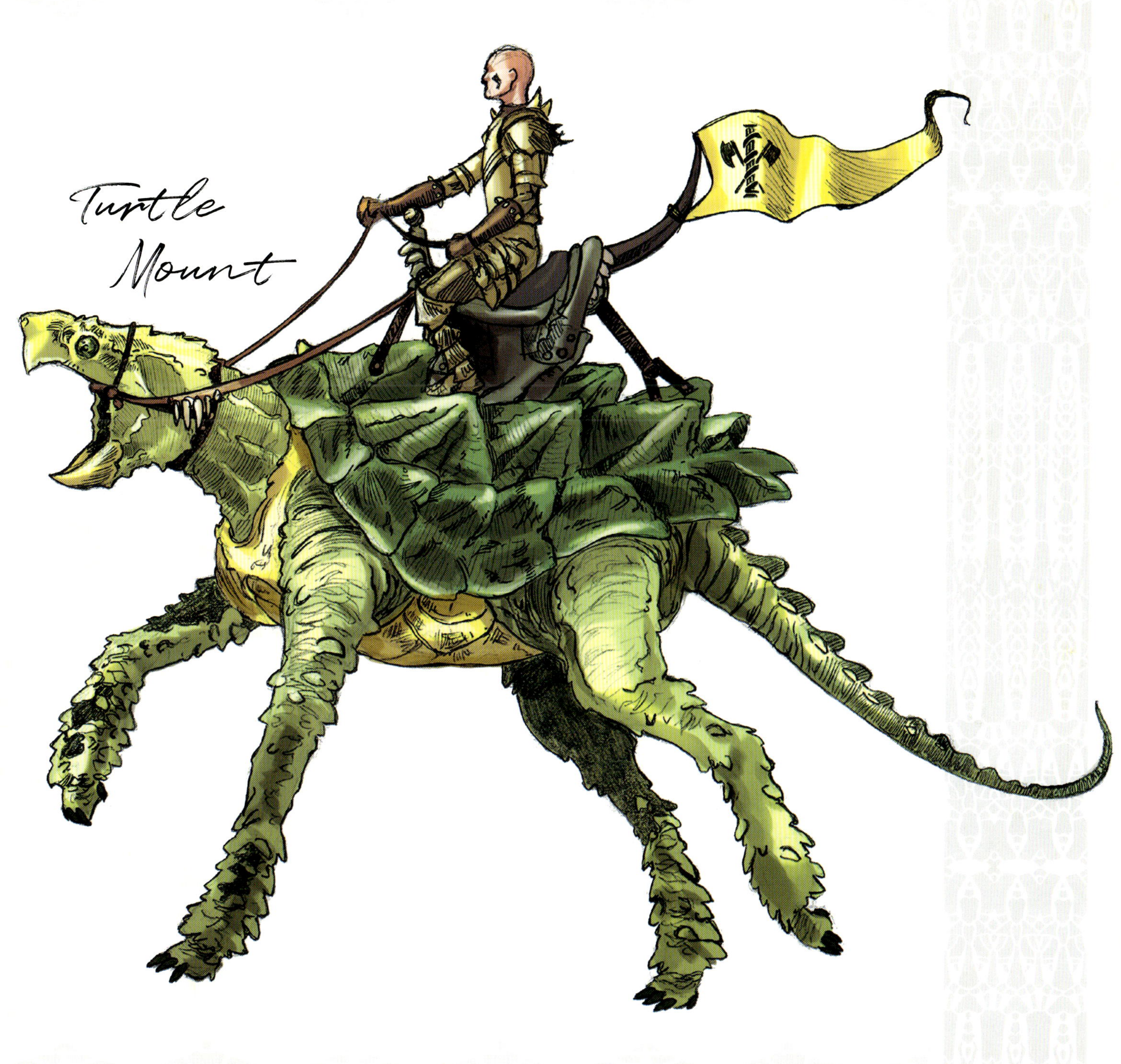
Turtle
Mount

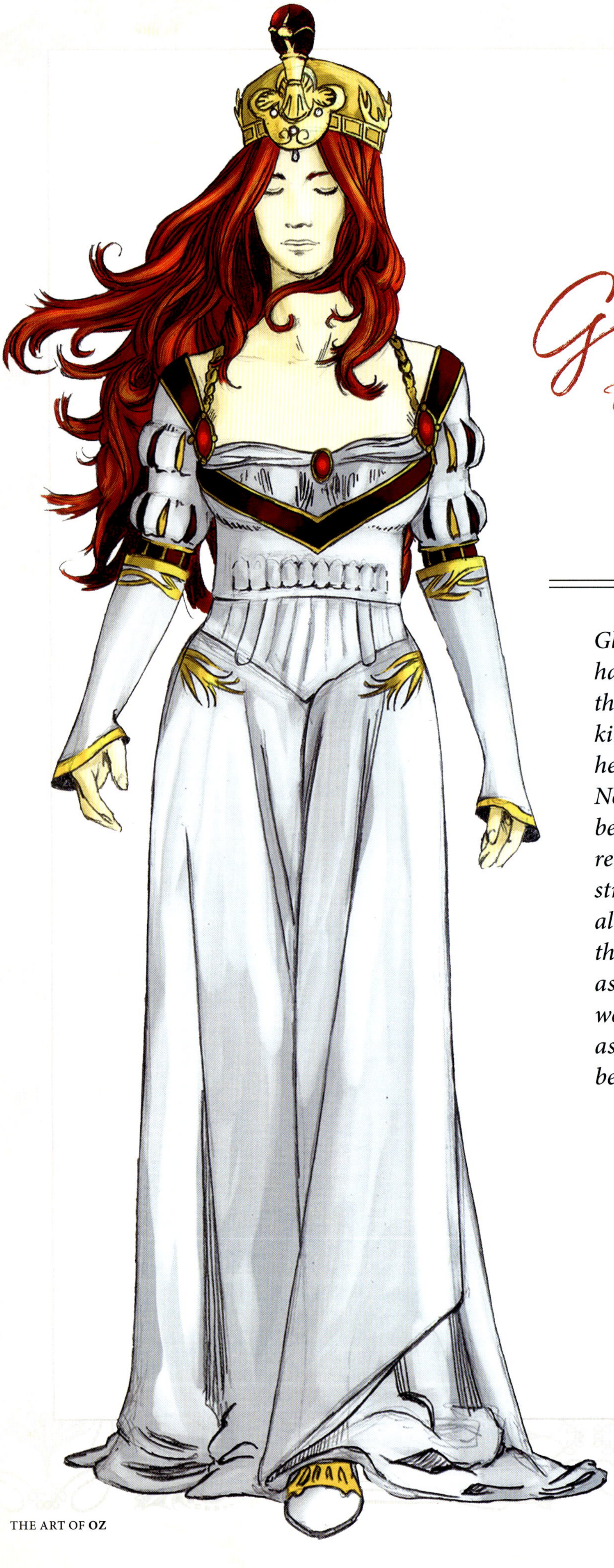

Glinda
The Good Witch of the South

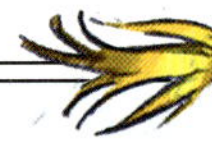

Glinda is the Royal Sorceress of Oz. She has wonderful magical powers and uses them only to benefit the subjects of Ozma's kingdom. Glinda is always kindly and helpful and willing to listen to their troubles. No one knows her age, but all can see how beautiful and stately she is. Her hair is like red gold and finer than the finest silken strands. Her eyes are blue as the sky and always frank and smiling. Her cheeks are the envy of peach-blows, and her mouth is as enticing as a rose bud. Glinda is tall and wears splendid gowns that trail behind her as she walks. She wears no jewels, for her beauty would shame them.

—THE SCARECROW OF OZ

Glinda's Mounts

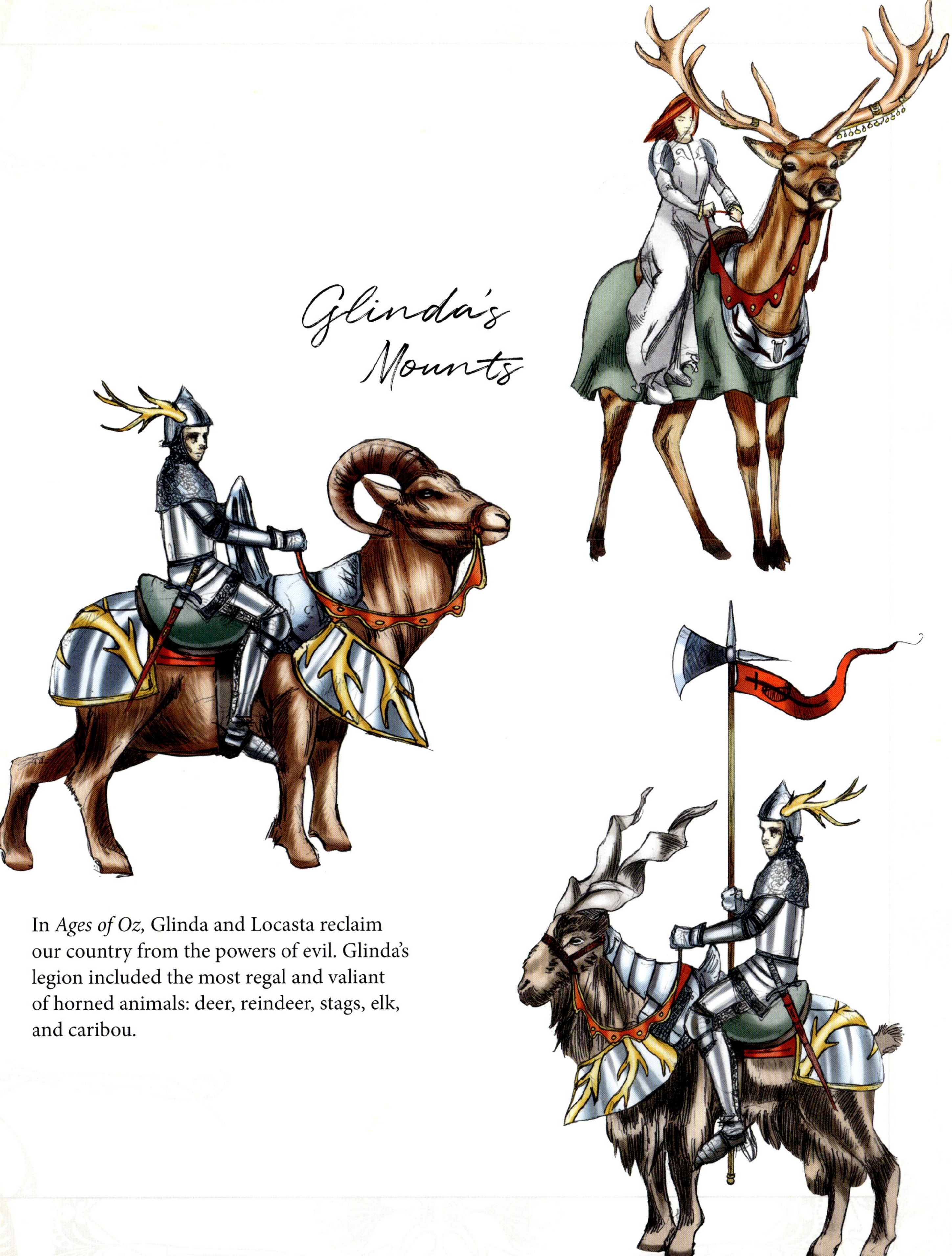

In *Ages of Oz,* Glinda and Locasta reclaim our country from the powers of evil. Glinda's legion included the most regal and valiant of horned animals: deer, reindeer, stags, elk, and caribou.

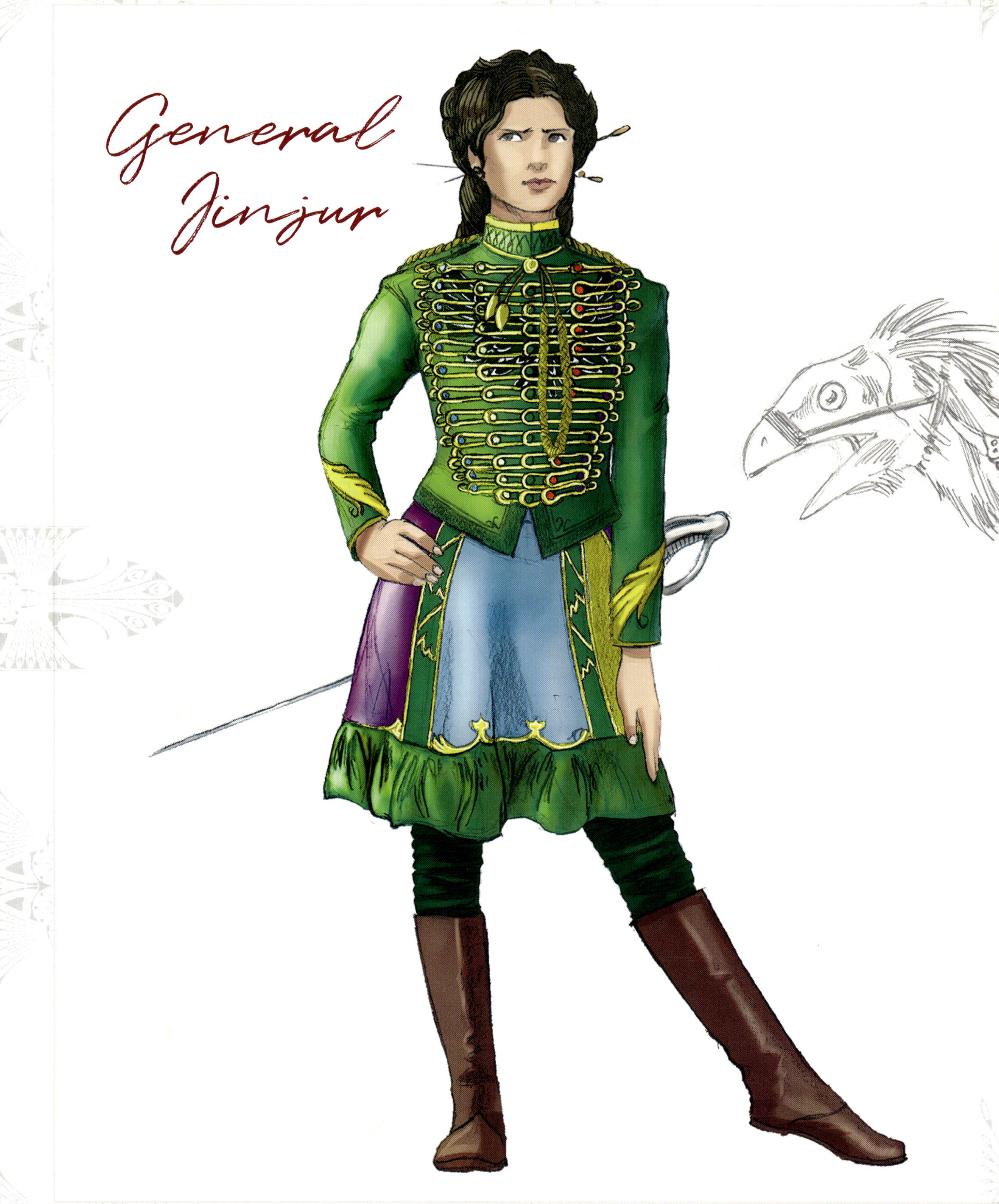
General Jinjur

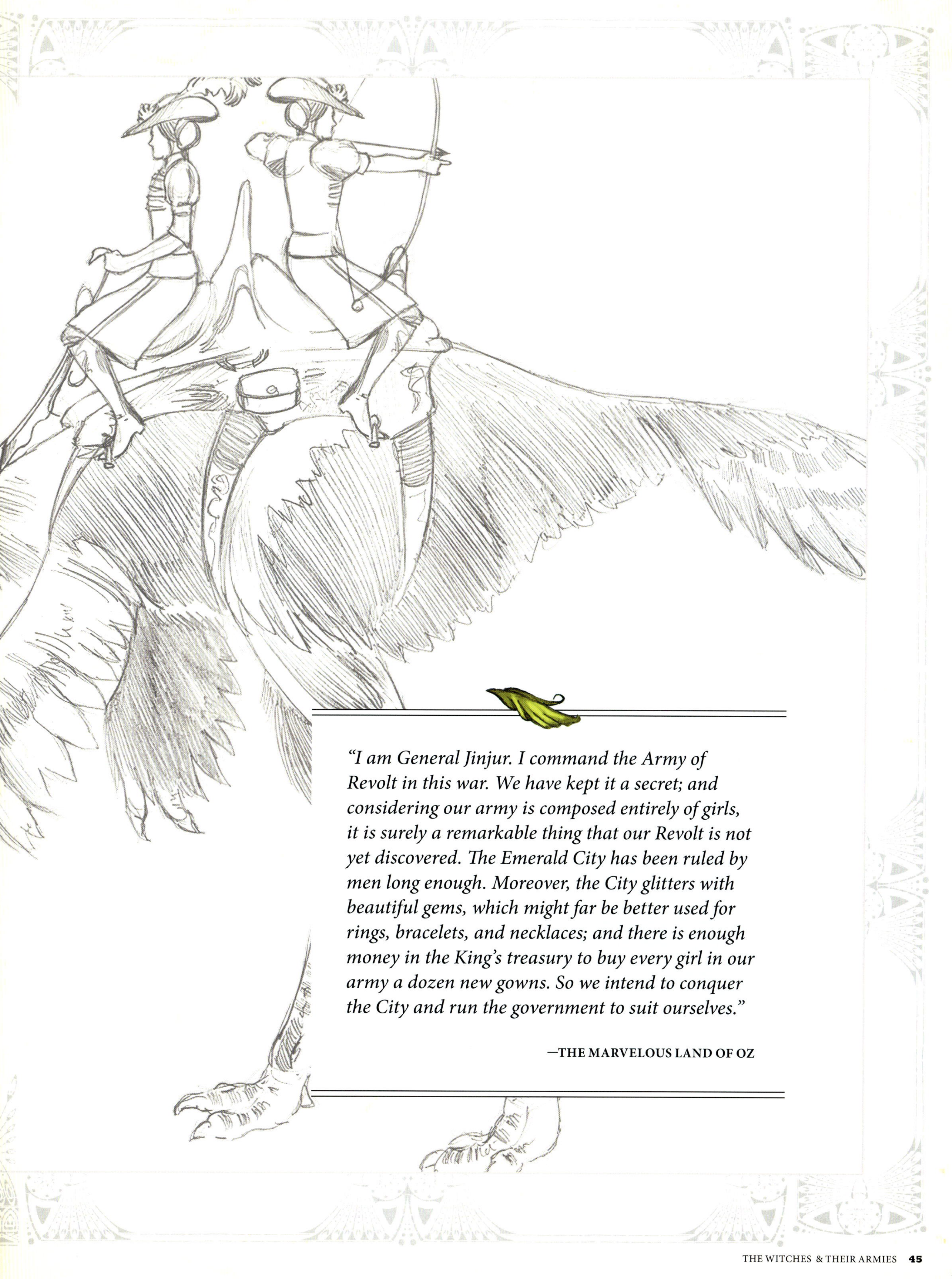

"I am General Jinjur. I command the Army of Revolt in this war. We have kept it a secret; and considering our army is composed entirely of girls, it is surely a remarkable thing that our Revolt is not yet discovered. The Emerald City has been ruled by men long enough. Moreover, the City glitters with beautiful gems, which might far be better used for rings, bracelets, and necklaces; and there is enough money in the King's treasury to buy every girl in our army a dozen new gowns. So we intend to conquer the City and run the government to suit ourselves."

—THE MARVELOUS LAND OF OZ

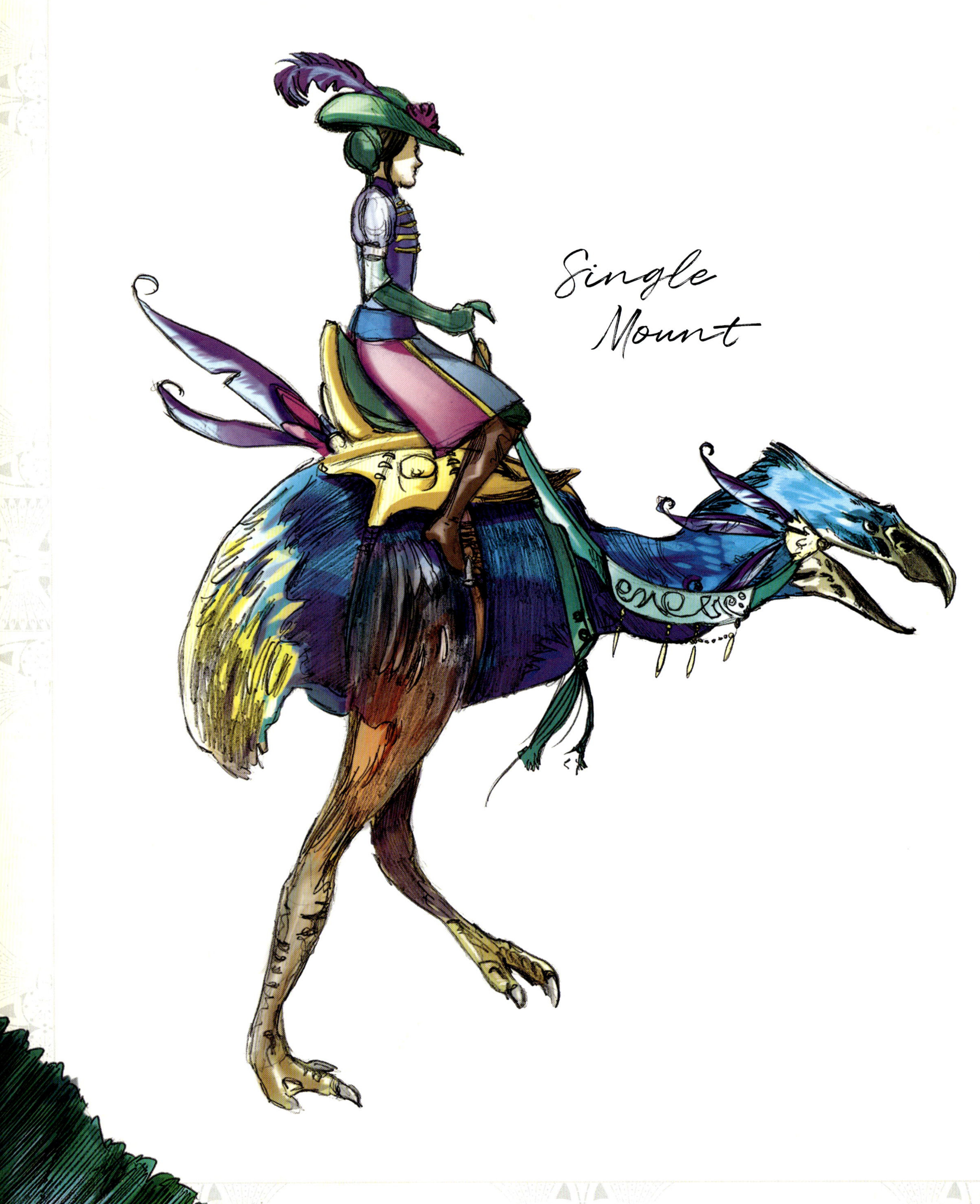
Single
Mount

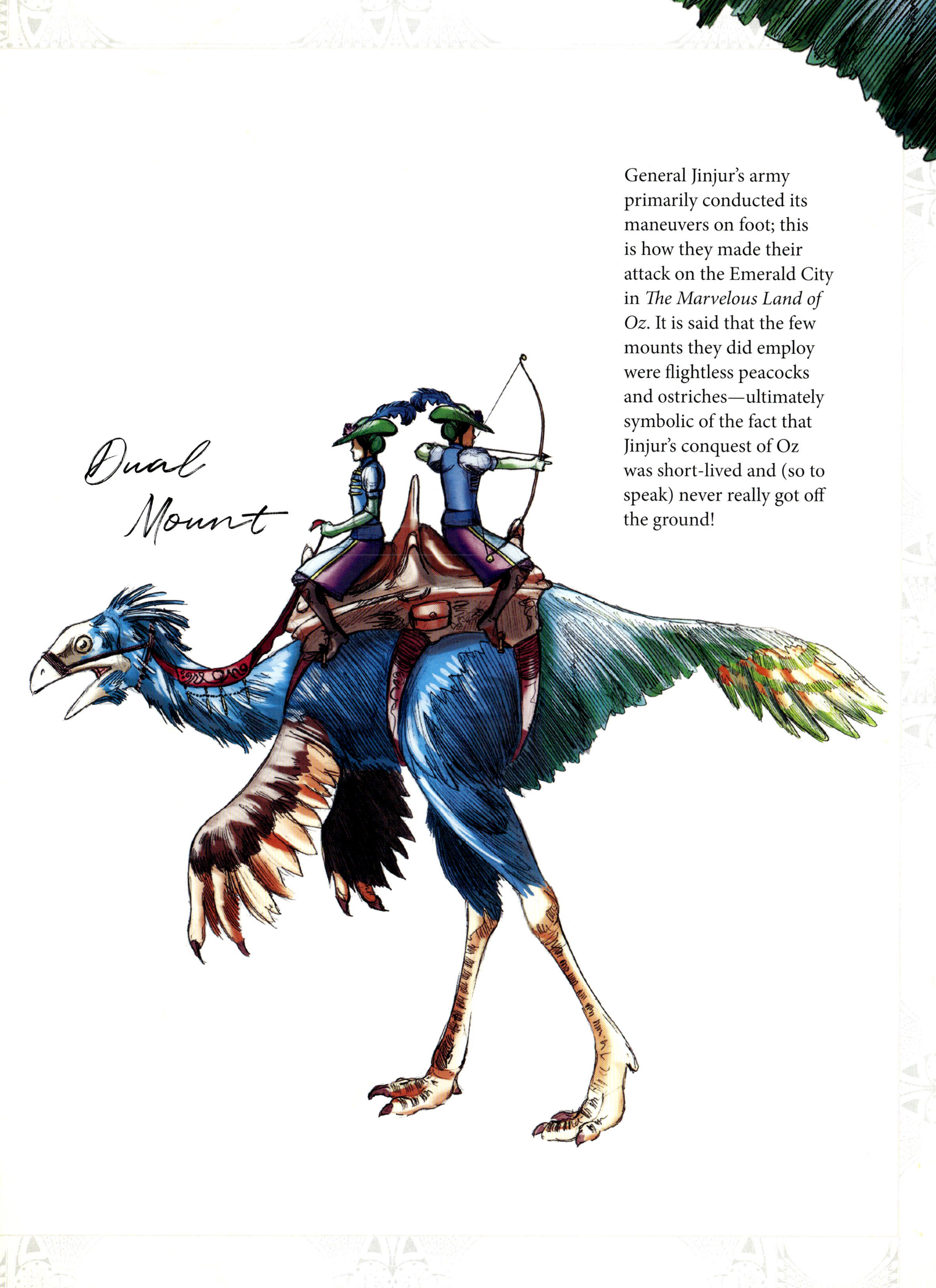

Dual Mount

General Jinjur's army primarily conducted its maneuvers on foot; this is how they made their attack on the Emerald City in *The Marvelous Land of Oz*. It is said that the few mounts they did employ were flightless peacocks and ostriches—ultimately symbolic of the fact that Jinjur's conquest of Oz was short-lived and (so to speak) never really got off the ground!

The Beasts

INTRODUCED BY THE COWARDLY LION

First of all, I'm pleased to say that the courage I received from the Wizard continues to keep me brave—because if it didn't, I just couldn't tell you about the most beastly beasts and monsters in history! As they come from Oz, or its surrounding countries, many are actually fine, helpful creatures. Others, however, have been ferocious in their attempts to destroy innocent Ozians, and I think we should—courageously—discuss them *first*.

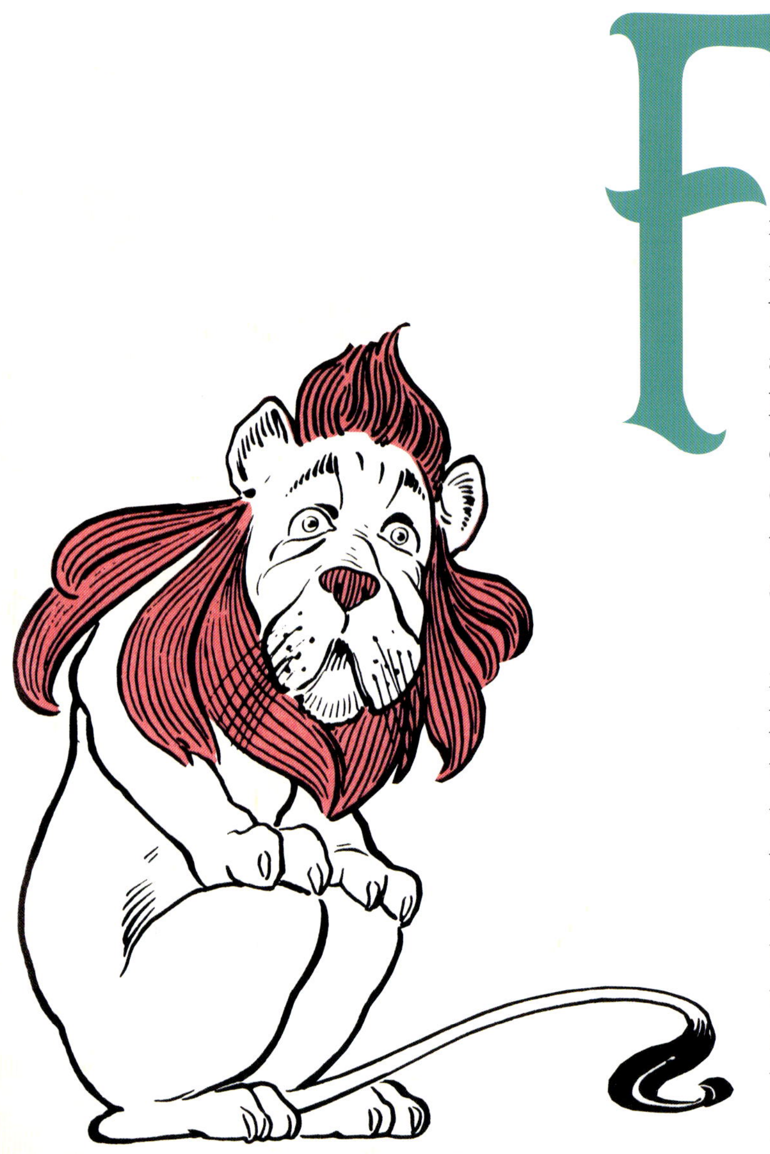

Among our terrifying animals are the Kalidahs: mammoth brutes with bodies like bears and heads like tigers. When Dorothy, Toto, the Scarecrow, the Tin Woodman, and I first made our way to the Emerald City, we passed through a forest where some Kalidahs lived. Two of them attacked us, but as panicked as I was, I roared very loudly to scare them . . . for a moment. This gave us time to escape across a tree-bridge spanning a deep ravine; when the Kalidahs followed us, the Tin Woodman chopped off the edge of the tree that rested on our side of the gulf. The bridge crashed

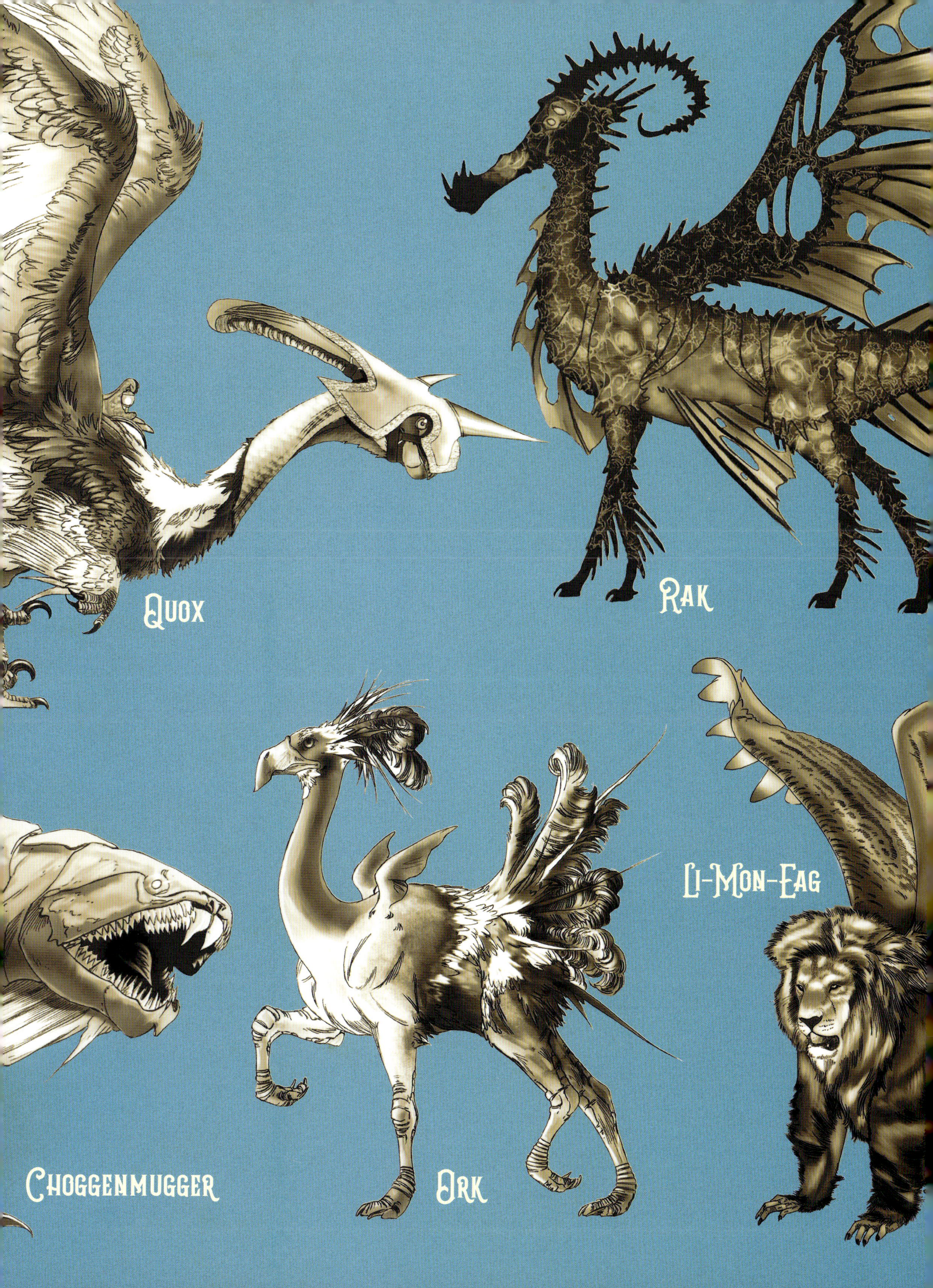

Quox
Rak
Li-Mon-Eag
Choggenmugger
Ork

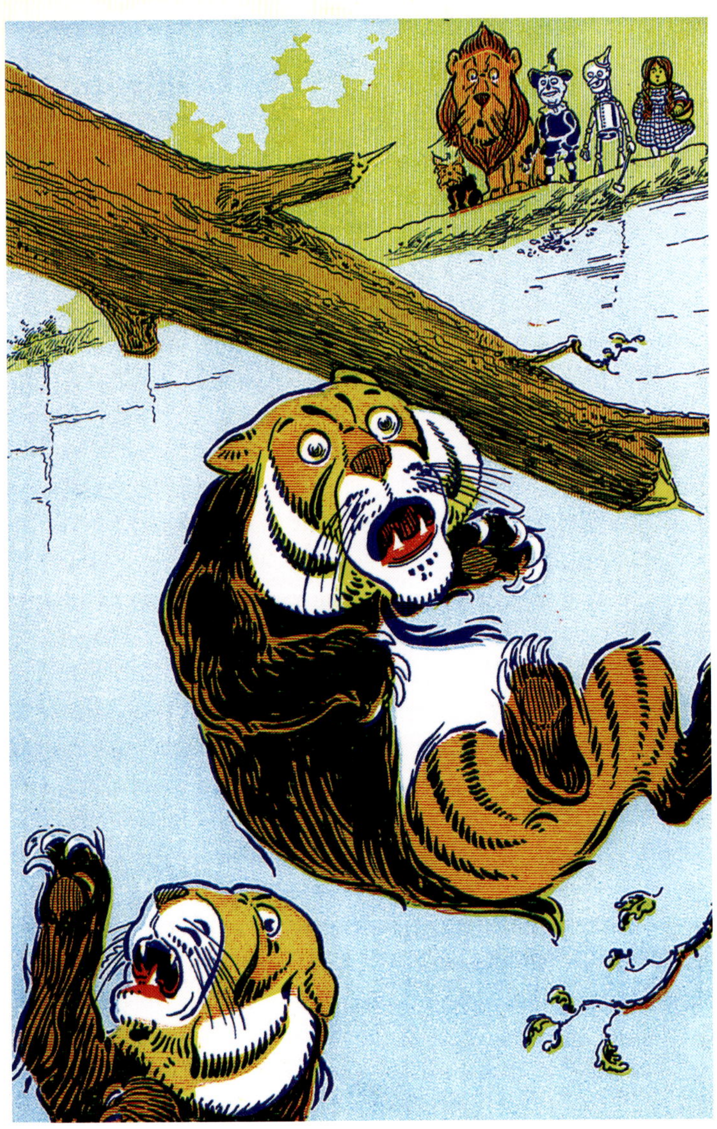

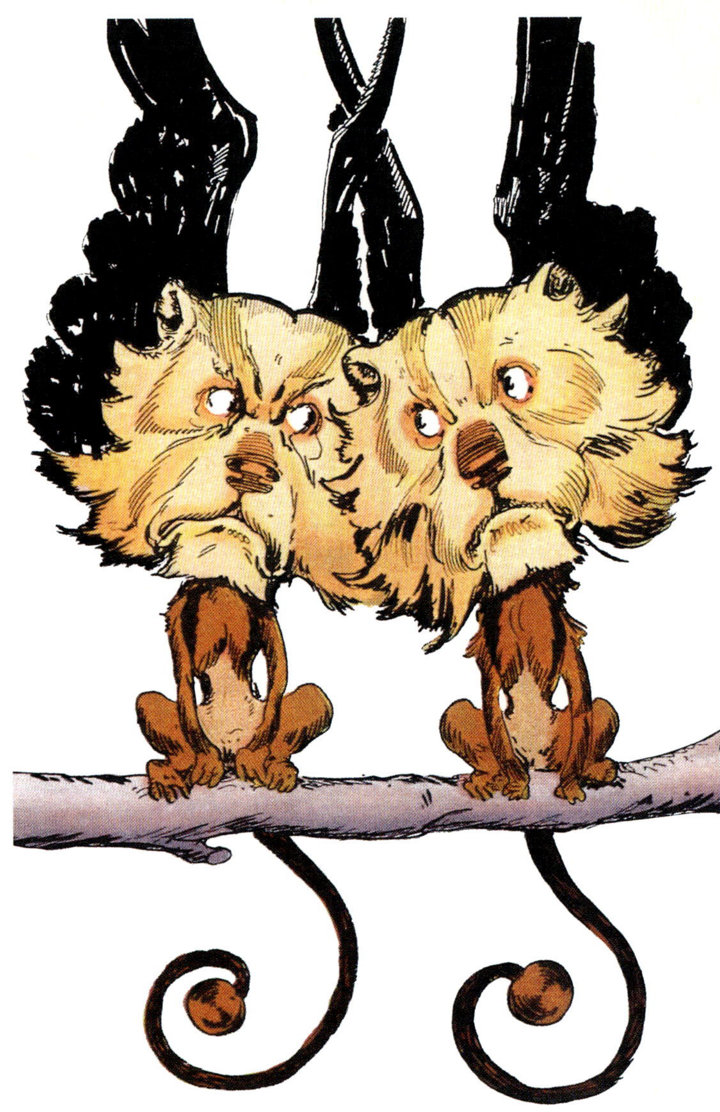

to the bottom of the chasm, taking the Kalidahs with it.

Another fiend was Choggenmugger—an enormous, long-tailed monstrosity, who snacked on full-grown dragons, giant crocodiles, and unfortunate residents of the Isle of Regos. He might still be terrorizing the natives (and any visitors, including me!), if it hadn't been for two magic pearls that were accidentally acquired by Nikobob, a stalwart charcoal-burner. Nikobob didn't know it, but the pearls gave him strength beyond measure and protected him from all danger. So, in Mr. Baum's own words: when the huge snake attacked Nikobob, he easily "chopped Choggenmugger into many small pieces."

The Li-Mon-Eags—a devious combination of lion, monkey, eagle, and wild ass—were actually supernatural disguises for the wicked Nome King and Kiki Aru, a disagreeable Munchkin boy. Kiki's knowledge of the magic word "Pyrzqxgl" almost started a war in the Forest of Gugu, because he used it to transform four monkeys into gigantic soldier men, and Gugu, the leopard king, into a fat woman! (It took our Wizard to change them back.) Another ever-hungry villain is the Rak, who breathed out smoke that smelled like salt and pepper. Some unlucky people thought that such heavy clouds were just a dense fog, which let the Rak sneak up on them. Even now, when we get a foggy day, I tremble until I'm positive I can't detect the aroma of spices in the air.

In his "Borderlands of Oz" book, *The Sea Fairies*, Mr. Baum wrote about an underwater beast, the Yell-Maker, who was best known

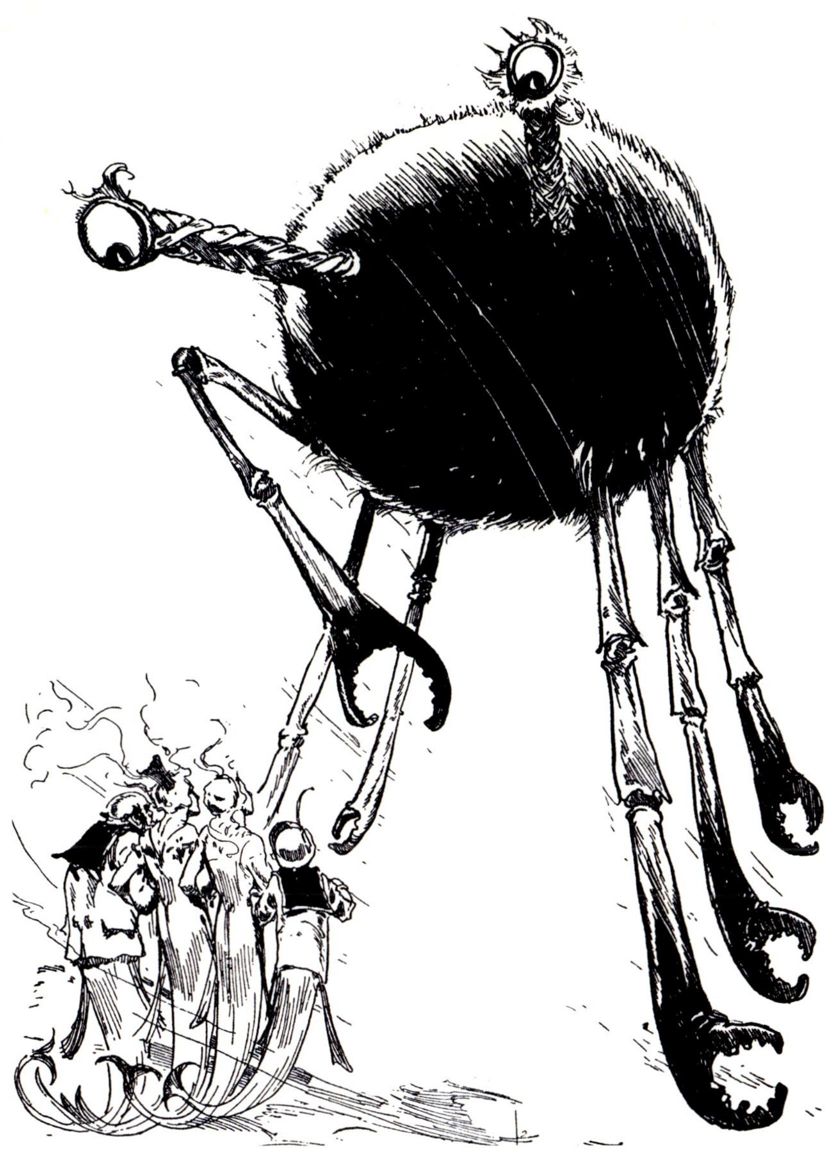

for inflicting terrible torture with his giant claws. Fortunately, he was withered away to a pulpy mass by the self-defense magic of the Queen of the Mermaids. Yet some other undersea monsters offer great friendship to those living in or visiting their realms. The finest of these is merry King Anko, the world's oldest and largest sea serpent.

Two of the oddest-looking Ozzy creatures are also among the jolliest: the flying Ork—who, with his countrymen, once rescued the Scarecrow from flaming, utter destruction—and Quox, the young dragon. Quox was considered young, as he was only 3,056 years old when he saved Tik-Tok, the Shaggy Man, the Rainbow's Daughter, and others from the Nome King.

Believe it or not, even the scary Winged Monkeys turned out to be excellent companions. They were only wicked when *controlled by* someone wicked. So,

PAGE 48: The Cowardly Lion by Denslow, *The Wonderful Wizard of Oz*
OPPOSITE LEFT: The Kalidahs by Denslow, *The Wonderful Wizard of Oz*
OPPOSITE RIGHT: The Li-Mon-Eags by Neill, *The Magic of Oz*
ABOVE: The Yell-Maker confronts (from left) Cap'n Bill, mermaids Queen Aquareine and Princess Clia, and Trot. Art by Neill, *The Sea Fairies.*

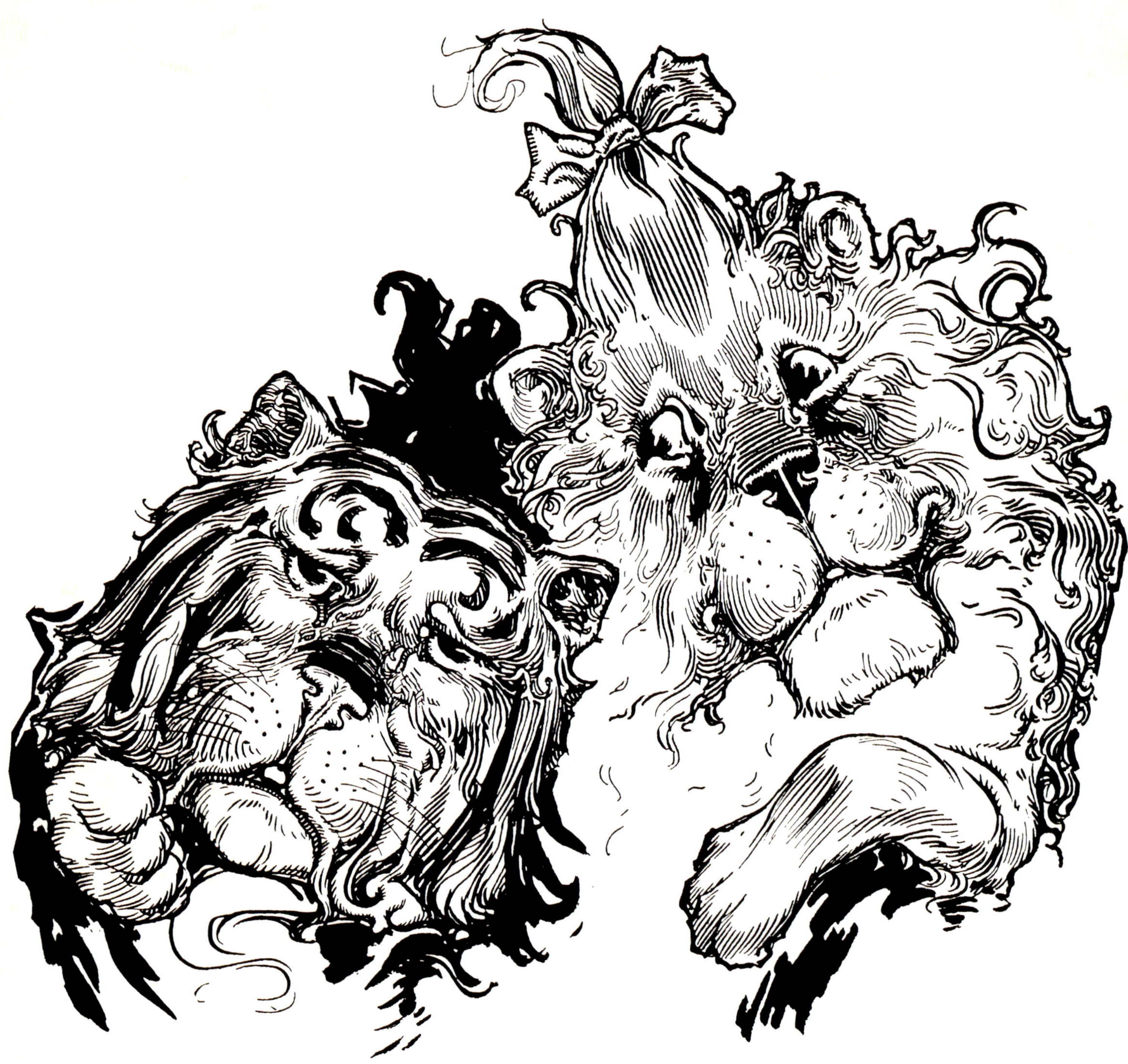

after the Wicked Witch of the West was melted, the Monkeys generously carried Dorothy and the rest of us back to see the Wizard. Later on, they served Glinda the Good, and flew the Tin Woodman to rule the Winkies, the Scarecrow to rule the Emerald City, and me to a nearby woodland, where I was proclaimed King of the Forest!

As you know, this was my dream come true. Eventually, though, I missed my friends and returned to the Emerald City with my companion, the Hungry Tiger. We've been proud bodyguards to Princess Ozma ever since. It's a responsibility that requires Courage, and—just between us—I confess that many things still worry me. Yet I realized long ago that fear is something I have in common with other beasts and humans and everyone. Now when I'm frightened, I remember what I learned from the gift given to me by the Wizard: Courage is always there, deep inside all of us. We just have to believe in it—and call upon it.

ABOVE: The Hungry Tiger and Cowardly Lion by Neill, *The Patchwork Girl of Oz*
OPPOSITE: Eggs are fatal to nomes, so Quox conquers the King. Art by Neill, *Tik-Tok of Oz*.

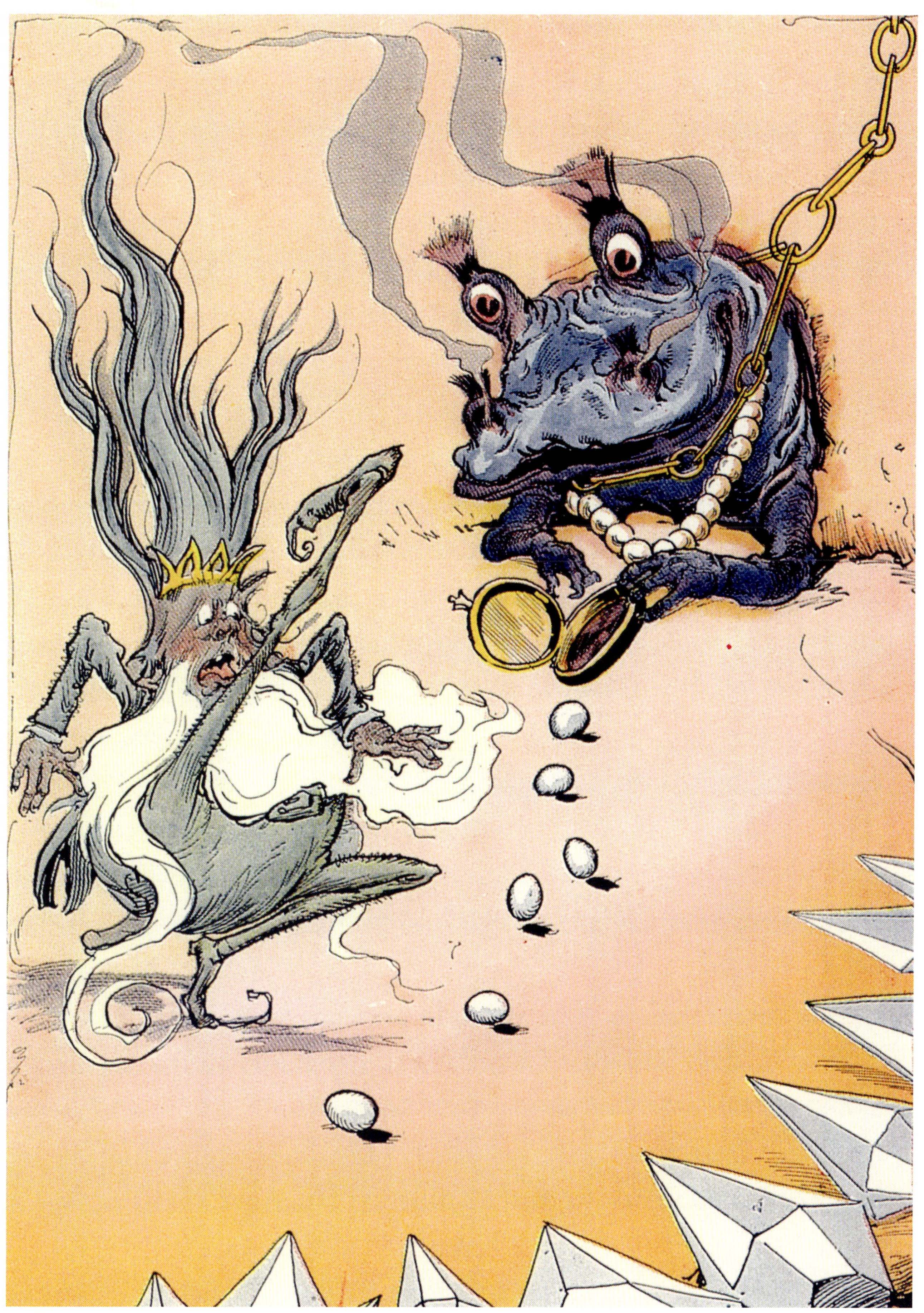

The Kalidahs

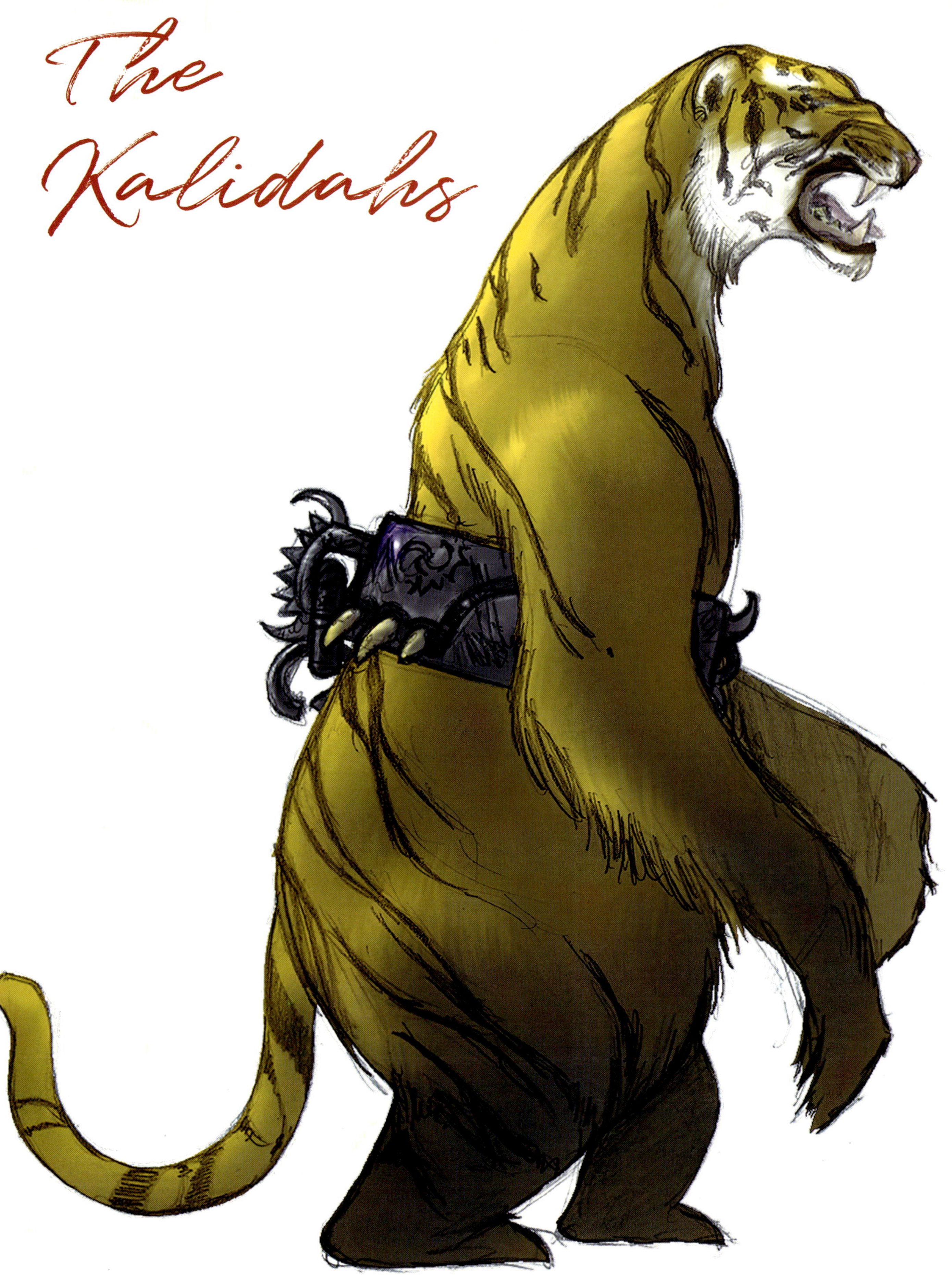

Kalidahs appear in two of Mr. Baum's books, *The Wonderful Wizard of Oz* and *The Magic of Oz*. In the second of these, one of the gigantic beasts threatens Trot—a young girl from California—who moved to Oz with her sailor companion, old Cap'n Bill. In Trot's defense, Cap'n Bill managed to pin the Kalidah to the ground by pounding a stake through its middle. This doesn't hurt the beast in any way (this is Oz, after all), but it does leave a see-through opening in his body. When the Kalidah later makes his escape, he scampers away and says to himself: "Our own Kalidah King has certain magic powers of his own. Perhaps he knows how to fill up these two holes in my body." (You can bet that he did.)

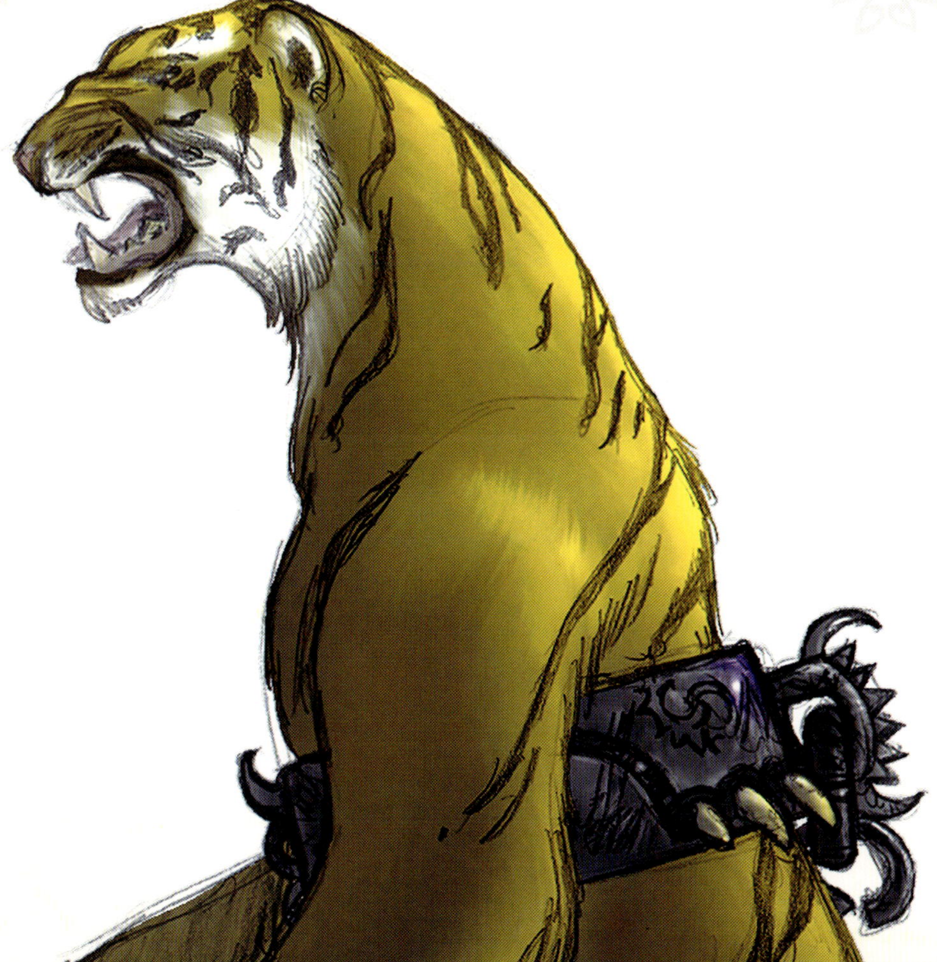

Fighting Kalidahs

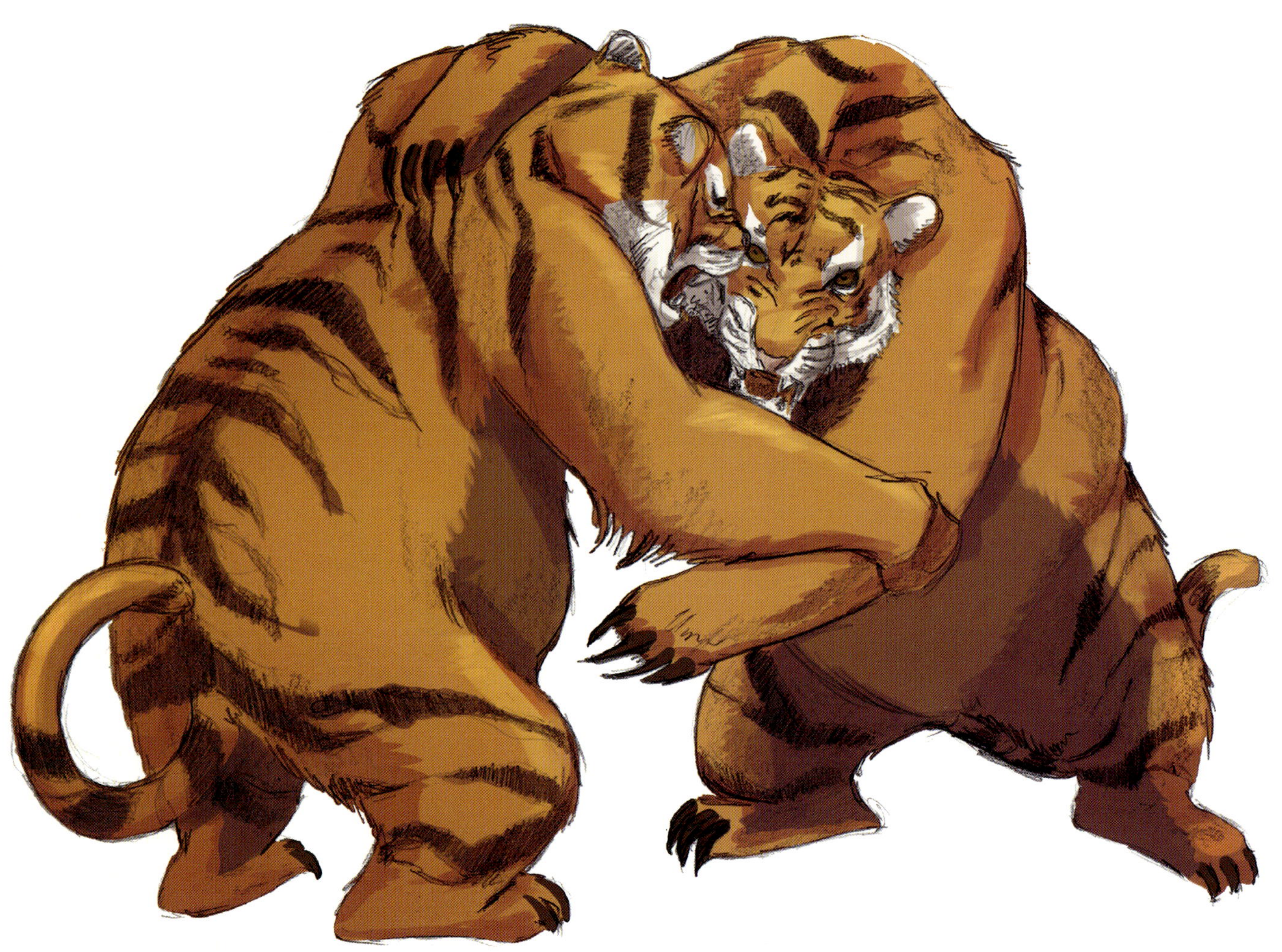

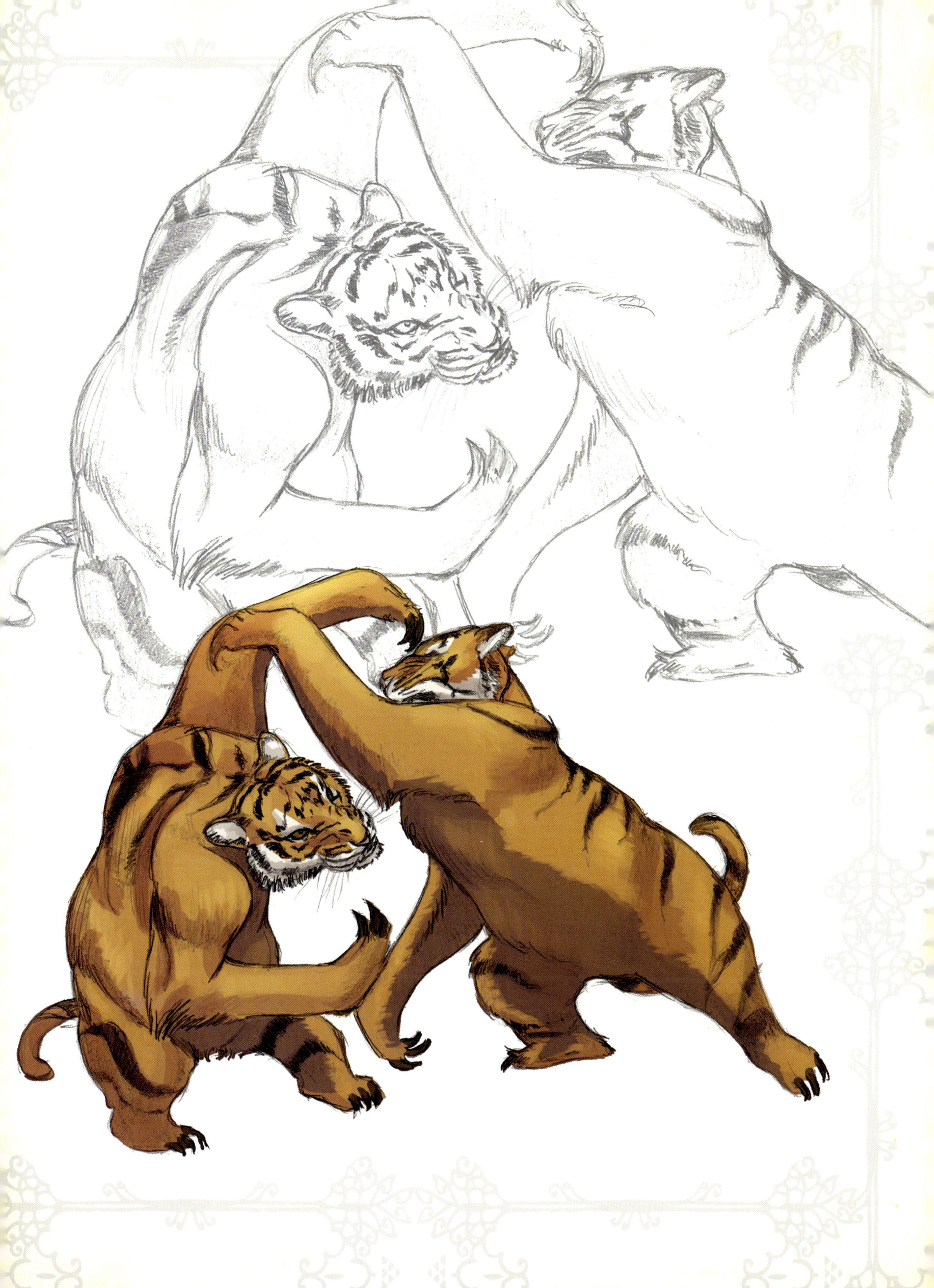

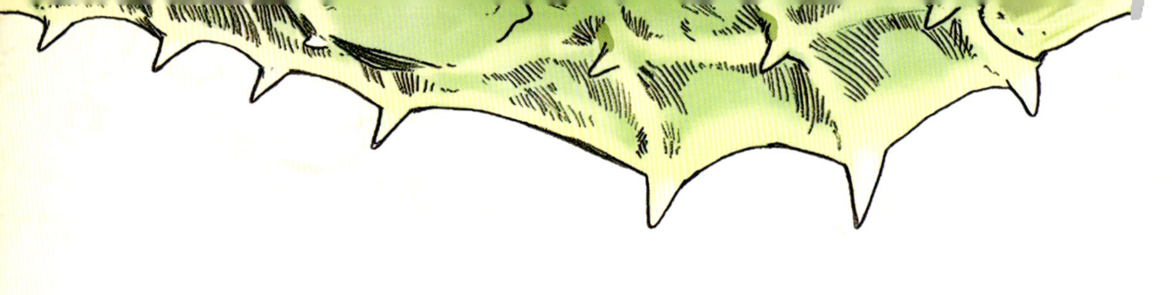

Choggenmugger

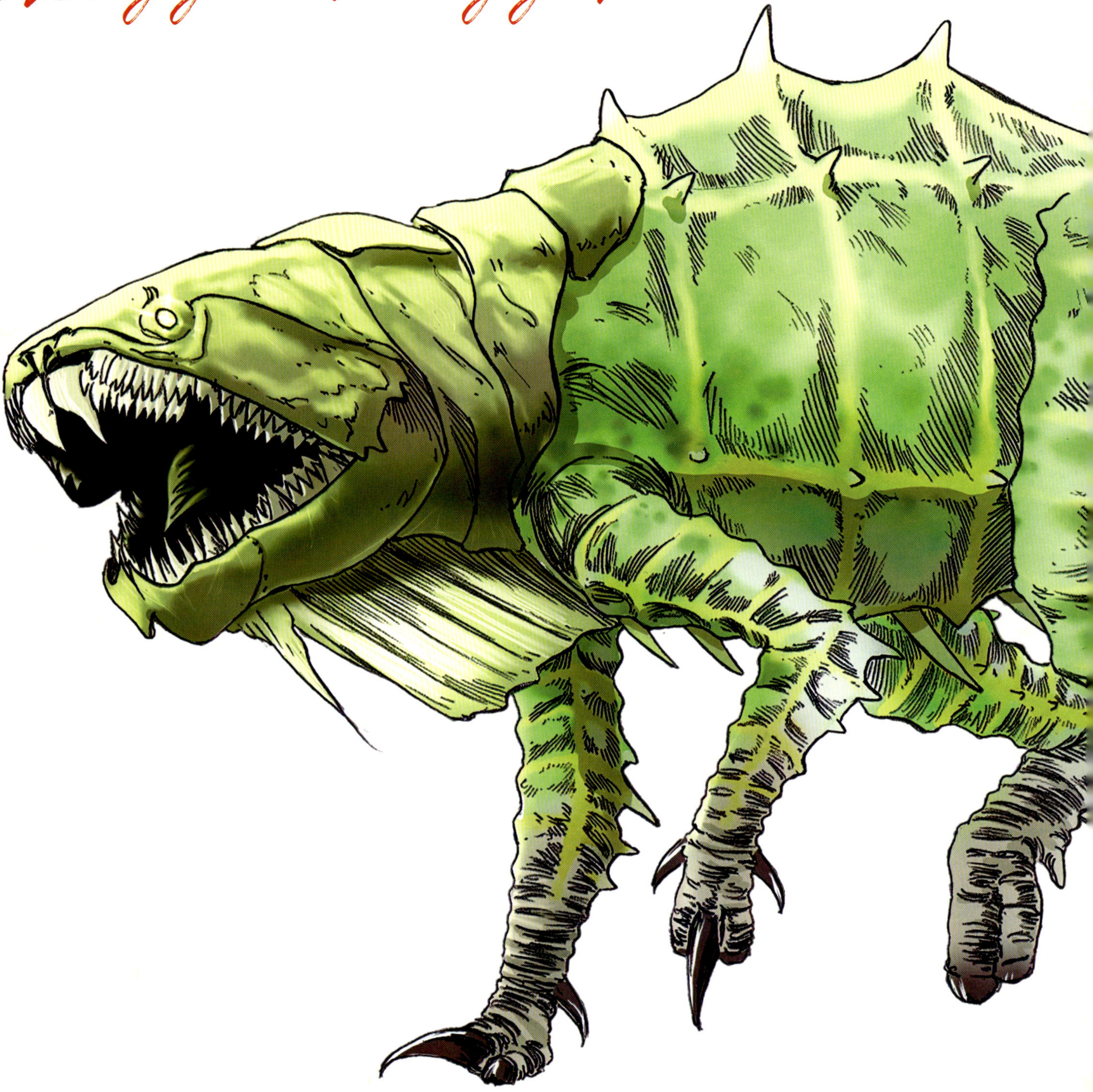

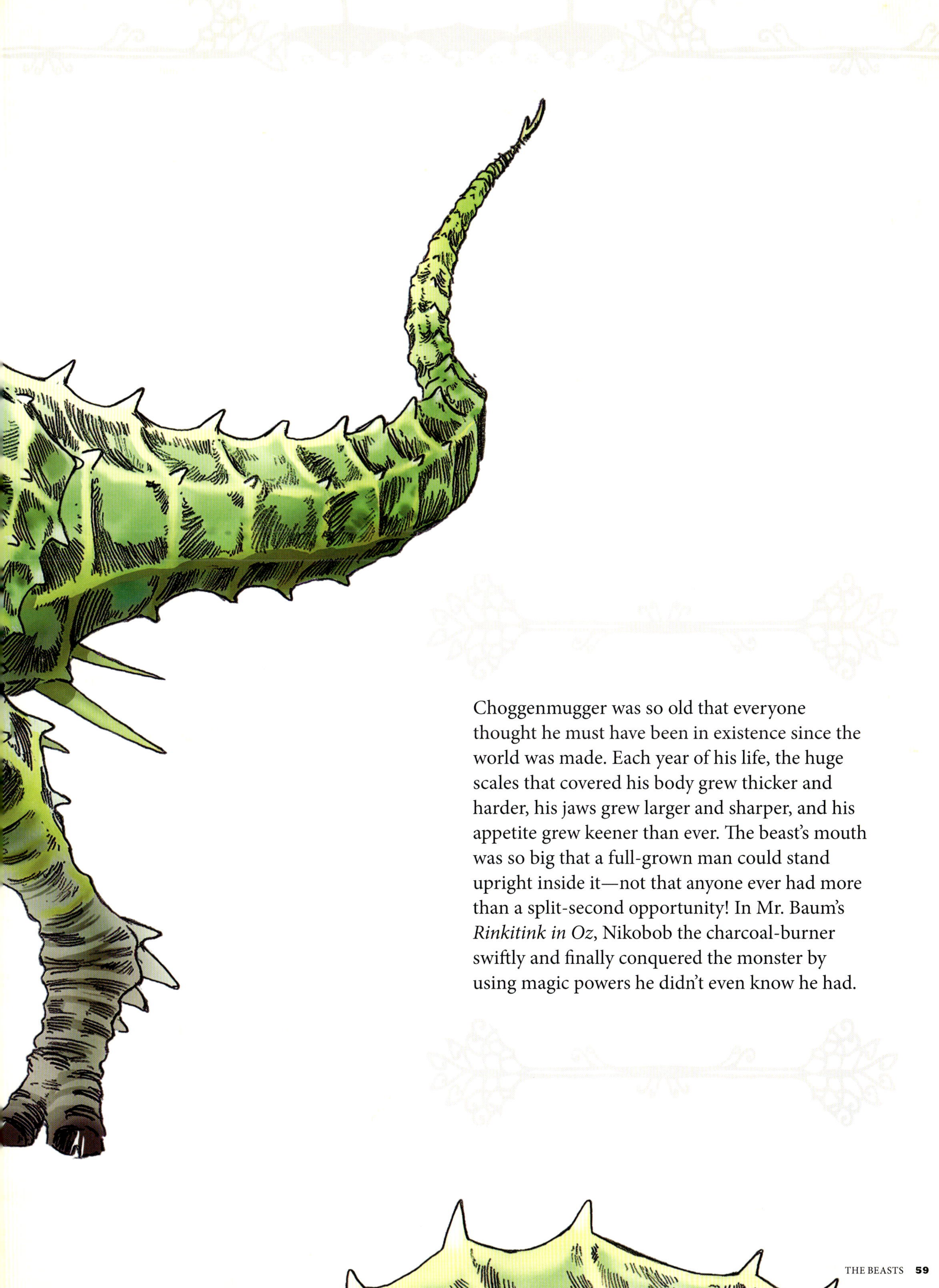

Choggenmugger was so old that everyone thought he must have been in existence since the world was made. Each year of his life, the huge scales that covered his body grew thicker and harder, his jaws grew larger and sharper, and his appetite grew keener than ever. The beast's mouth was so big that a full-grown man could stand upright inside it—not that anyone ever had more than a split-second opportunity! In Mr. Baum's *Rinkitink in Oz*, Nikobob the charcoal-burner swiftly and finally conquered the monster by using magic powers he didn't even know he had.

Li-Mon-Eags

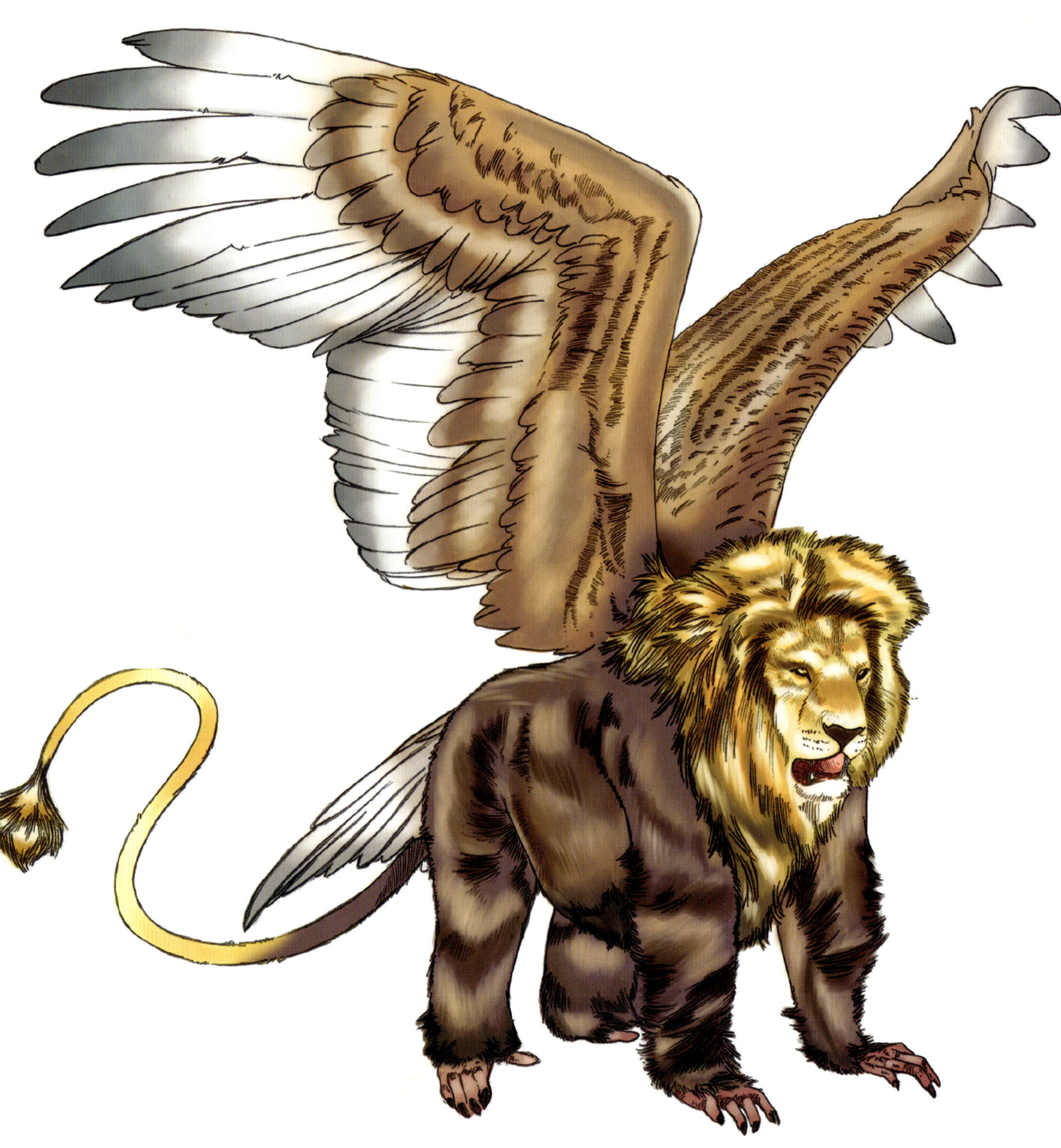

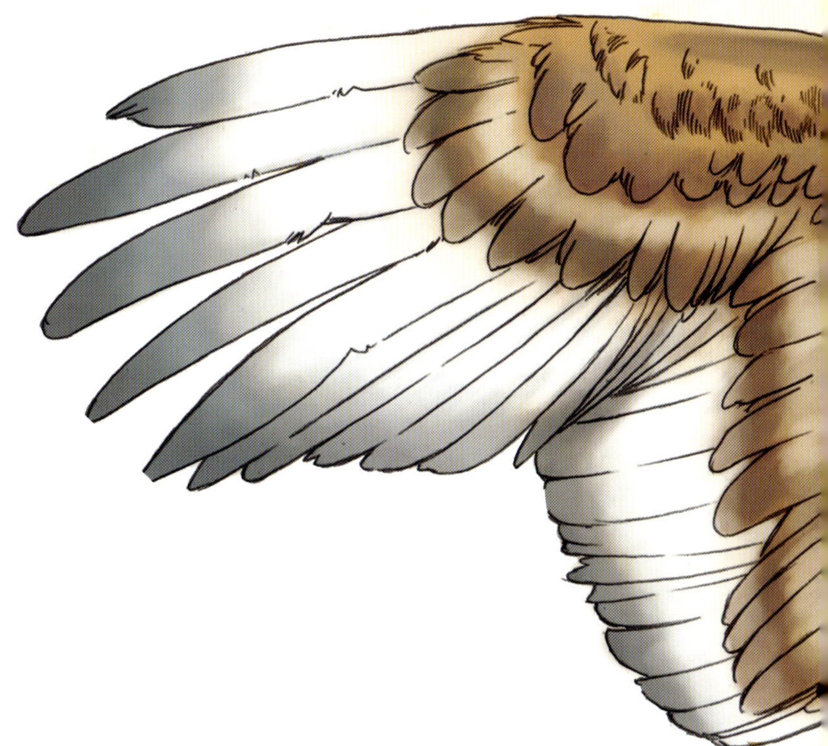

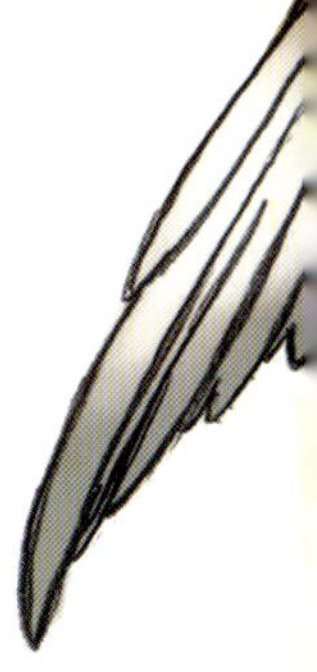

Kiki Aru, the magician Munchkin boy, used the following phrase when transforming himself and his evil companion into Li-Mon-Eags: “I want Ruggedo, the Nome, and myself to have the heads of lions, the bodies of monkeys, the wings of eagles, and the tails of wild asses, with knobs of gold on the end of them instead of bunches of hair—*Pyrzqxgl*!” He pronounced that final (and extraordinary) magic word in the proper manner, and at once their forms changed to those he’d described.

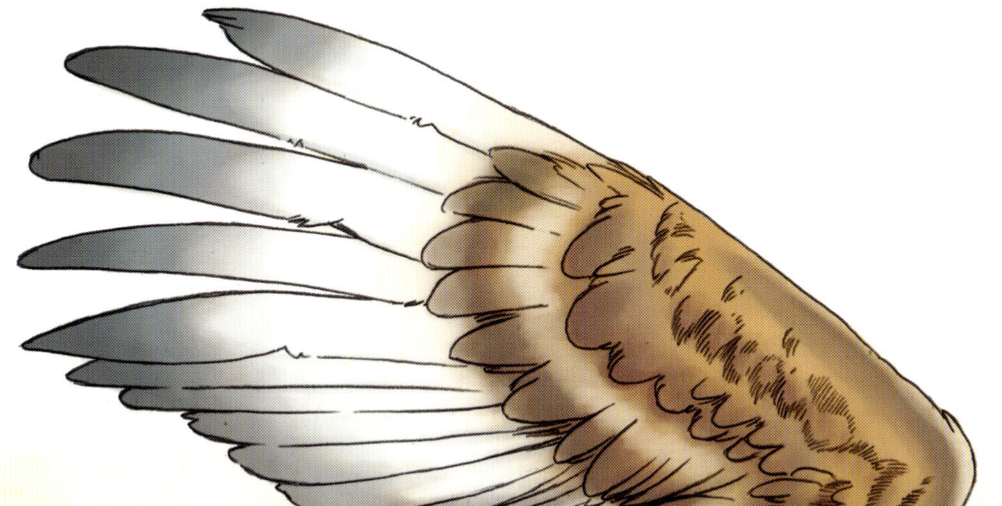

The Rak

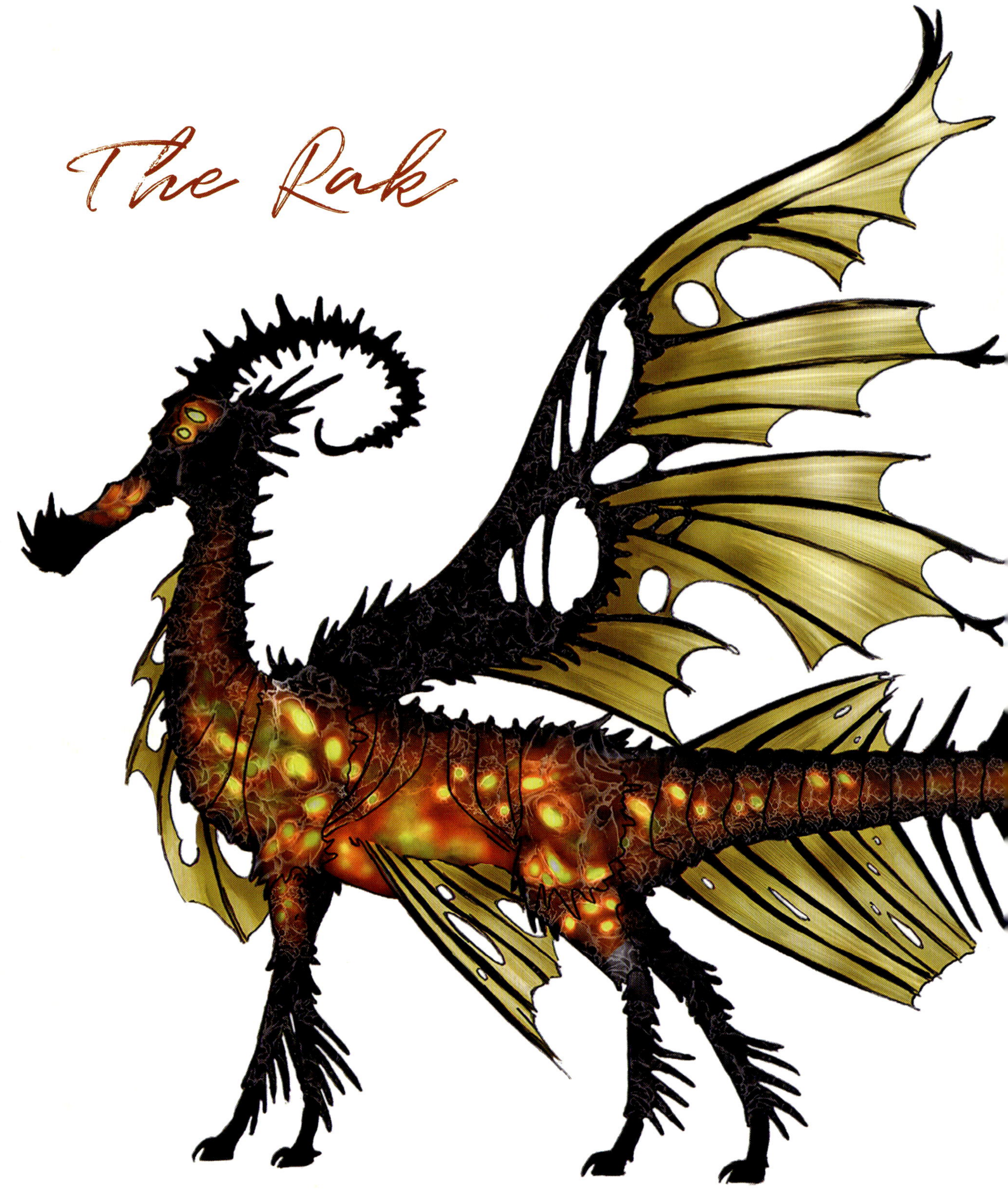

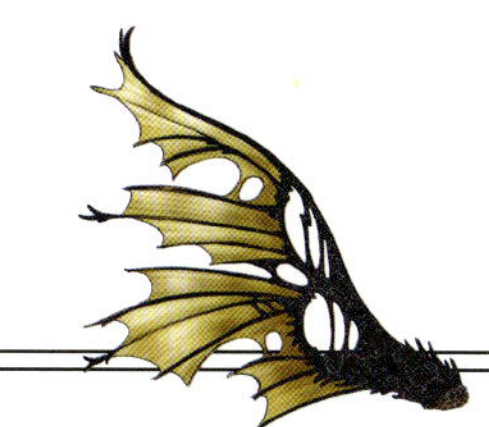

The Rak can fly in the air and run like a deer and swim like a fish. Inside its body is a glowing furnace of fire, and the Rak breathes in air and breathes out smoke, which darkens the sky for miles around, wherever it goes. It is bigger than a hundred men and feeds on any living thing.

—TIK-TOK OF OZ

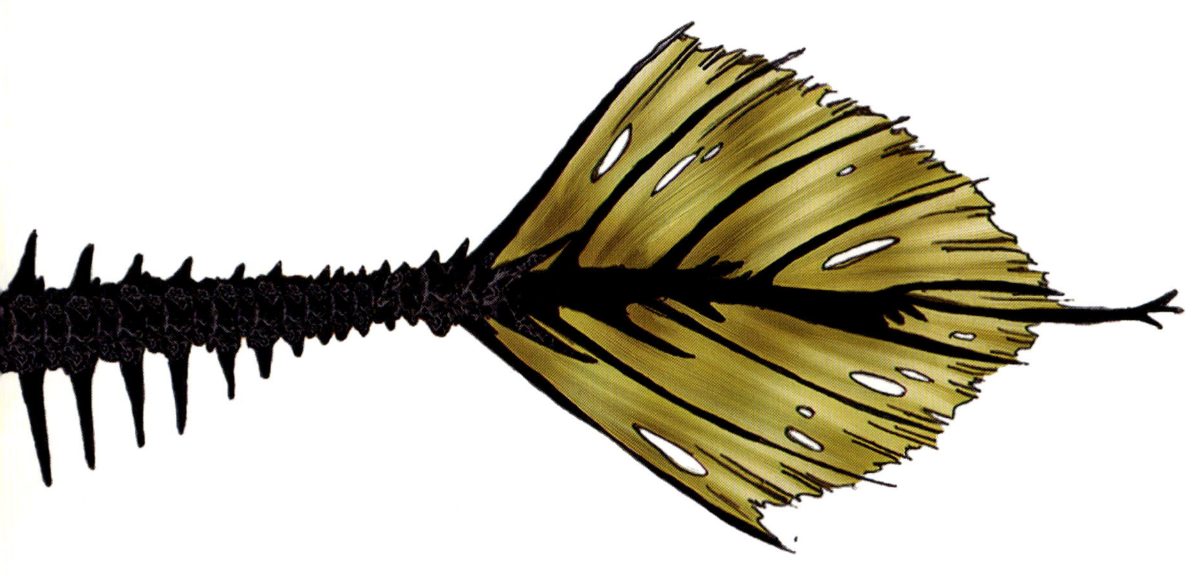

The Yell-Maker

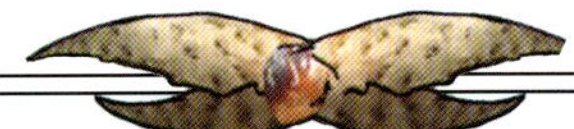

A dreadful sea creature swam into the hall. It had a body much like that of a crab, only more round and of a jet-black color. Its eyes were bright yellow balls set on the ends of two horns that stuck out of its head. They were cruel-looking eyes, too, and seemed able to see every person in the room at the same time. The legs of the Yell-Maker, however, were the most curious part of the creature. There were six of them, slender and black as coal, and each extended twelve to fifteen feet from its body. At the end of these thin legs were immense claws shaped like those of a lobster, and they were real "nippers" of the most dangerous sort.

—THE SEA FAIRIES [A "BORDERLANDS OF OZ" STORY]

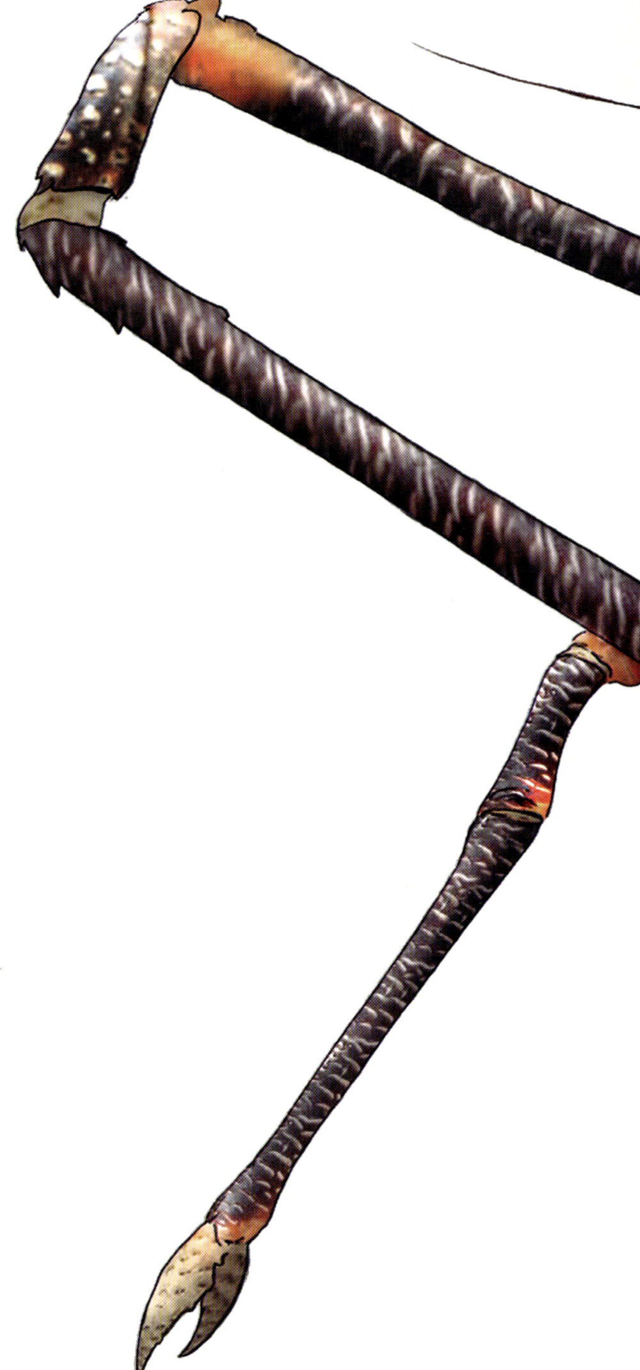

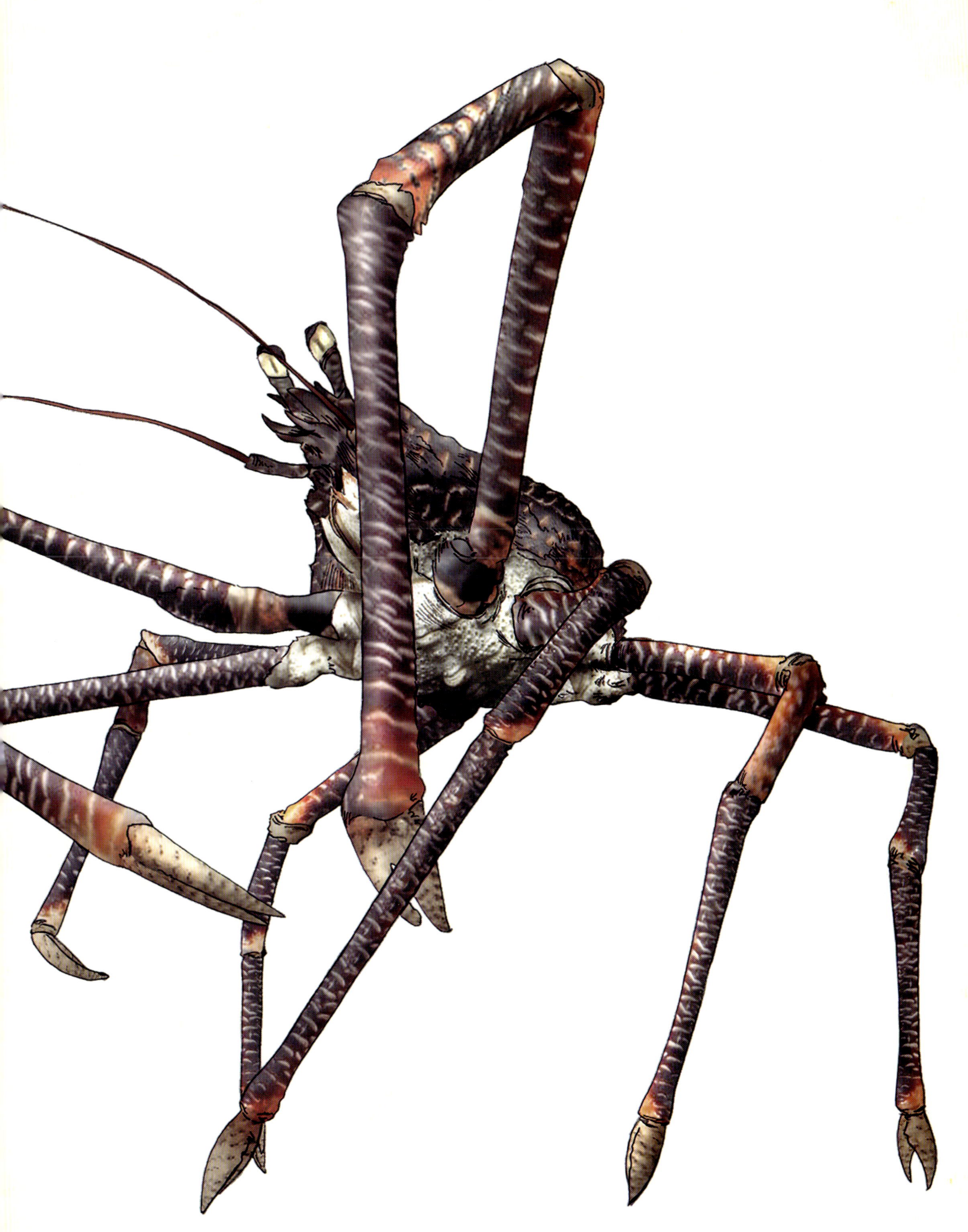

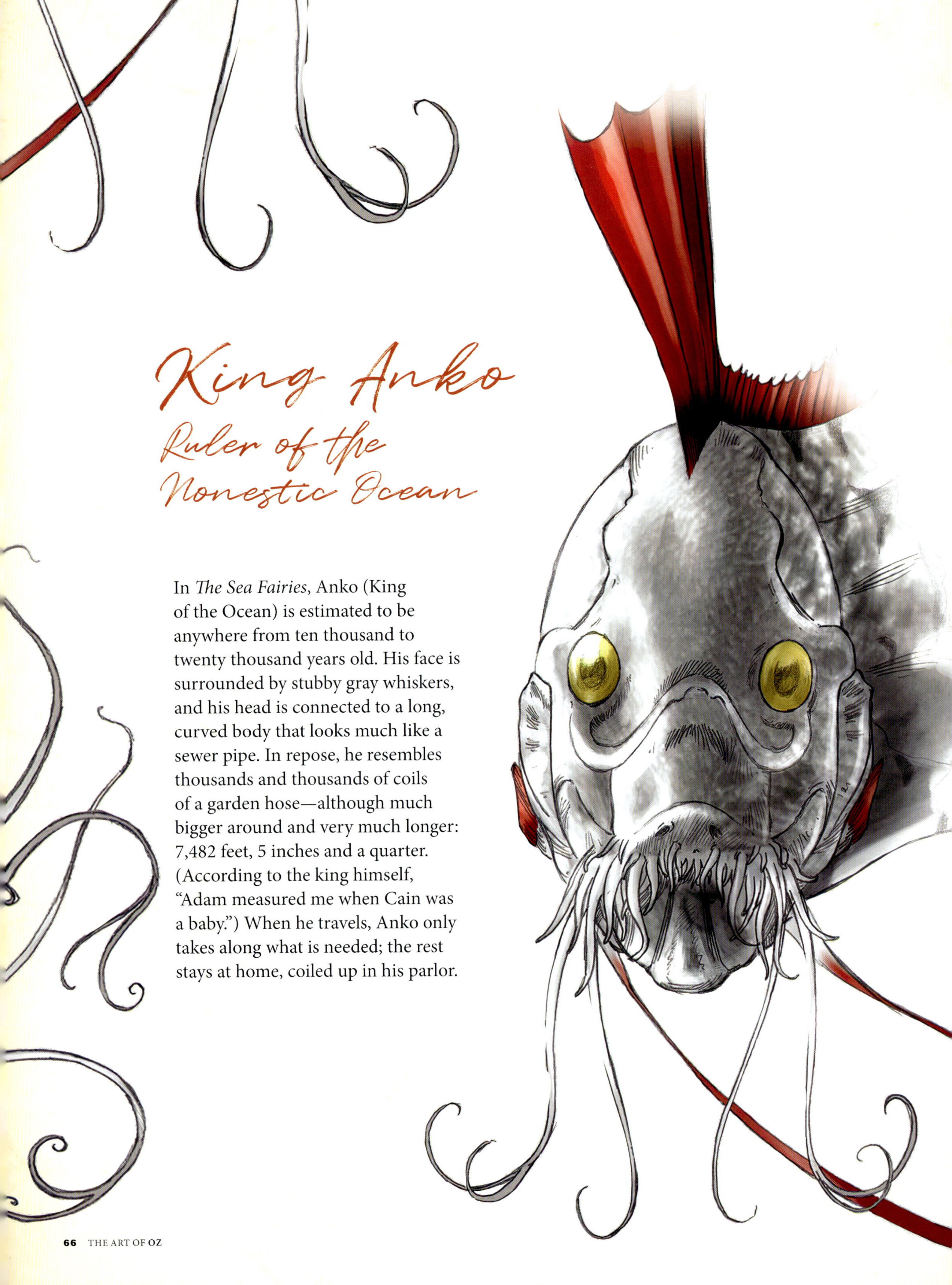

King Anko
Ruler of the Nonestic Ocean

In *The Sea Fairies*, Anko (King of the Ocean) is estimated to be anywhere from ten thousand to twenty thousand years old. His face is surrounded by stubby gray whiskers, and his head is connected to a long, curved body that looks much like a sewer pipe. In repose, he resembles thousands and thousands of coils of a garden hose—although much bigger around and very much longer: 7,482 feet, 5 inches and a quarter. (According to the king himself, "Adam measured me when Cain was a baby.") When he travels, Anko only takes along what is needed; the rest stays at home, coiled up in his parlor.

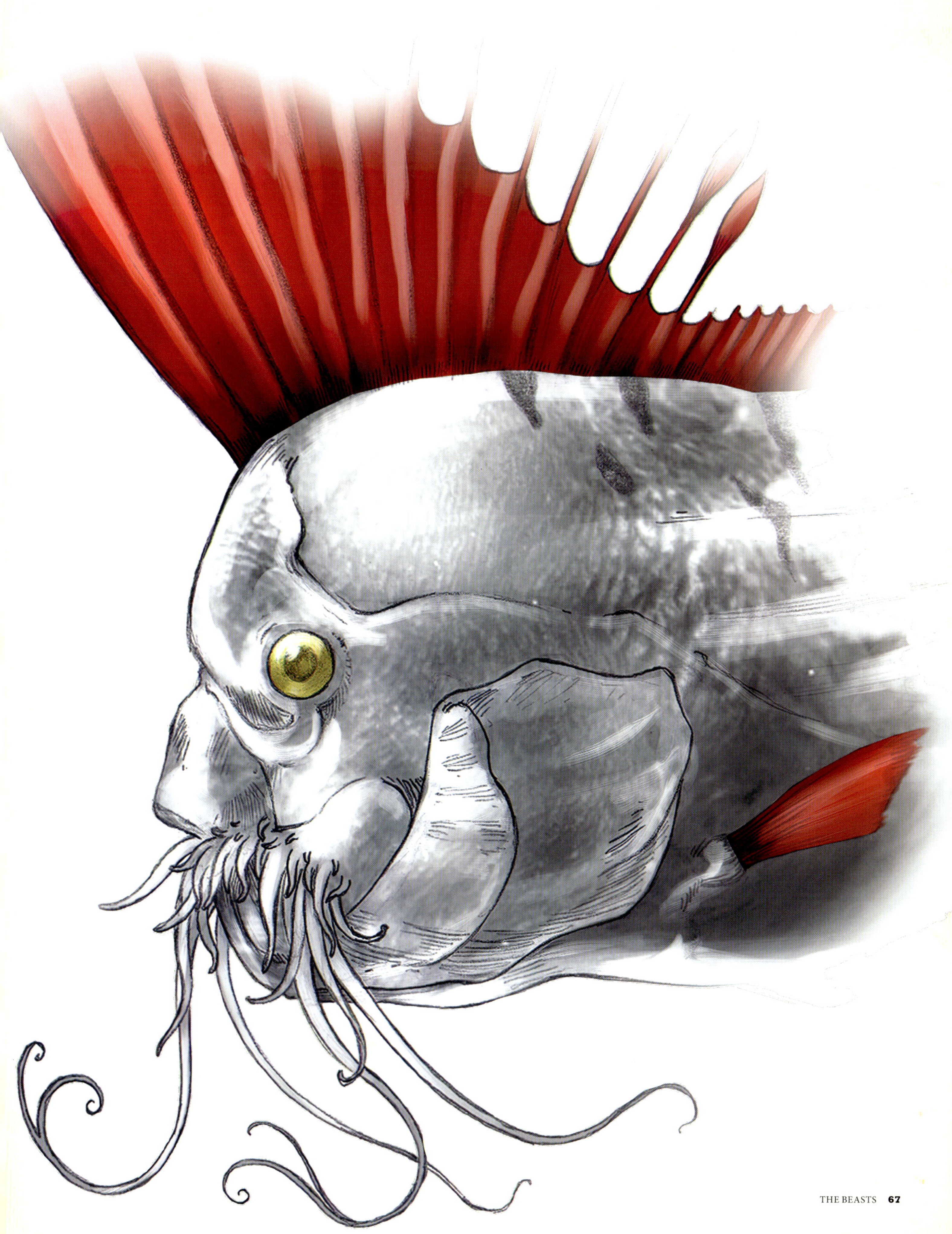

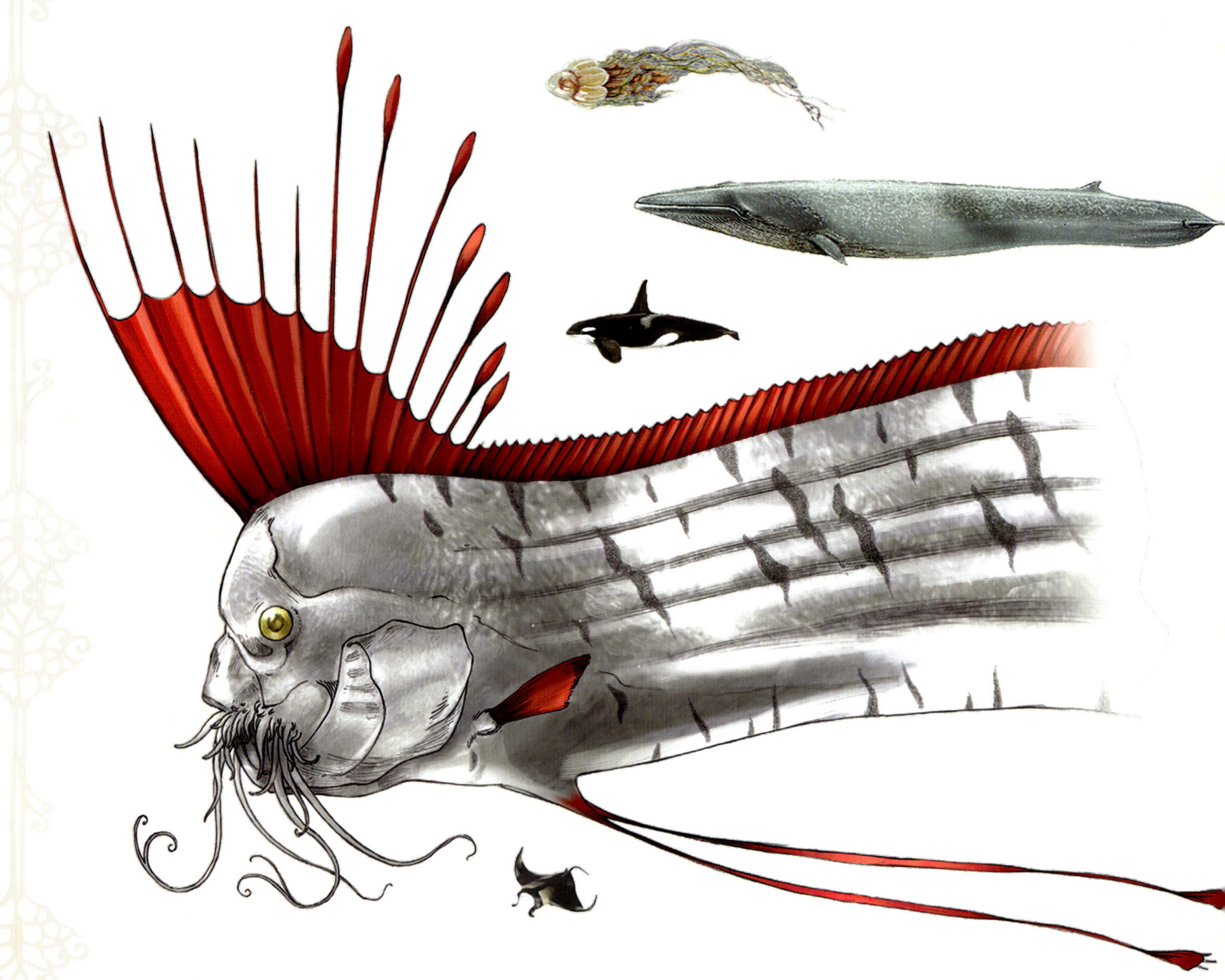

To give a sense of the extreme size of the King of the Ocean, Anko is here compared to (this page, from the top) a giant jellyfish, a blue whale, the orca (or killer whale), a manta ray, (opposite page, from the top) a giant squid, a sperm whale, a white shark, and a humpback whale.

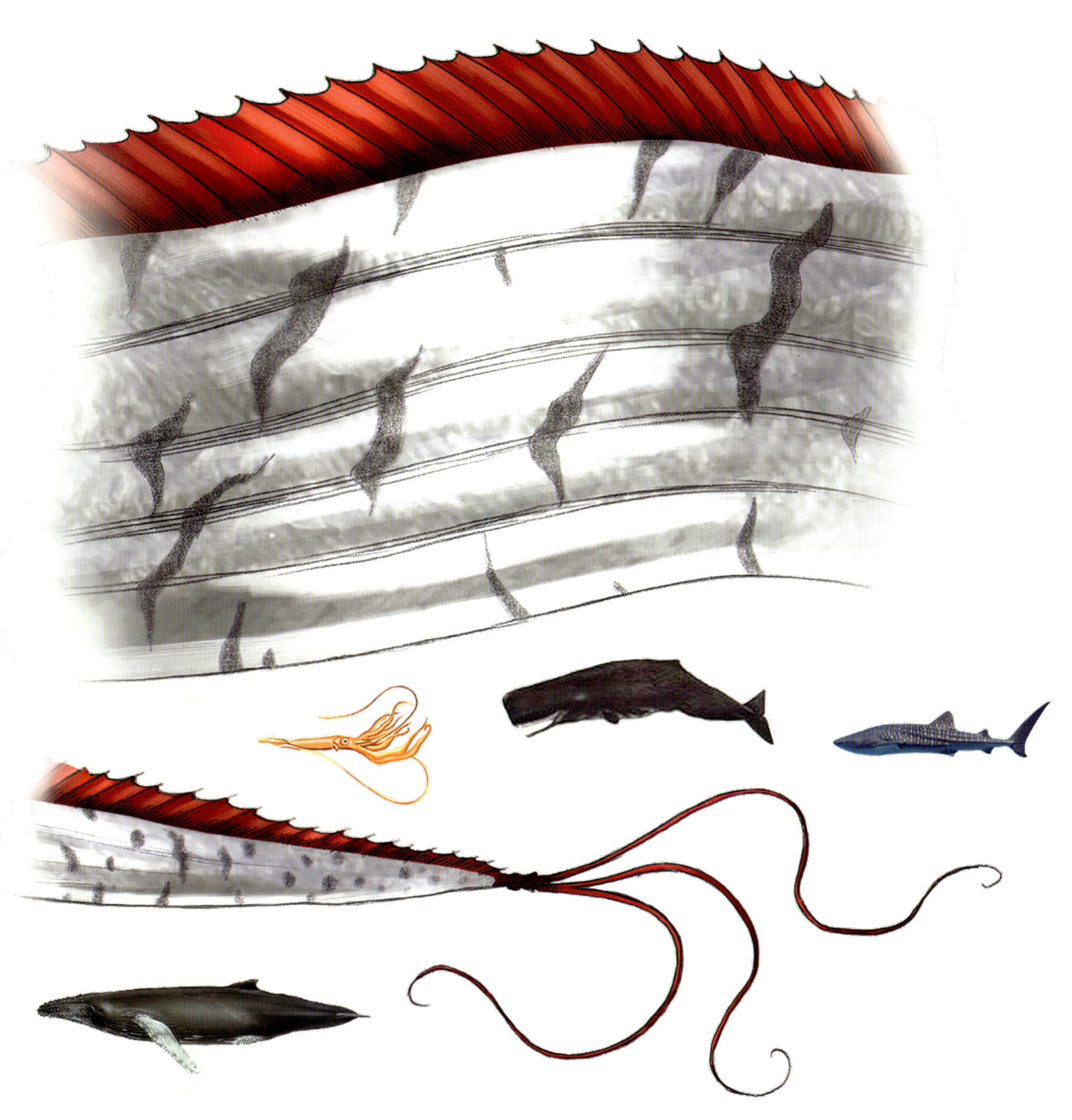

The Ork

The Ork wasn't a fish, nor was it a beast. It had wings, shaped like an inverted chopping bowl and covered with tough skin instead of feathers. It had four legs, and its head was shaped a good deal like a poll parrot, with a beak that curved downward in front and upward at the edges, and was half bill and half mouth. But to call it a bird was out of the question, because it had no feathers whatsoever, except a crest of wavy plumes of a scarlet color on the very top of its head. Perhaps the most curious thing about the creature was its tail. This queer arrangement of skin, bones, and muscle was shaped like the propellers used on boats and airships, having fan-like surfaces and being pivoted to its body.

—THE SCARECROW OF OZ

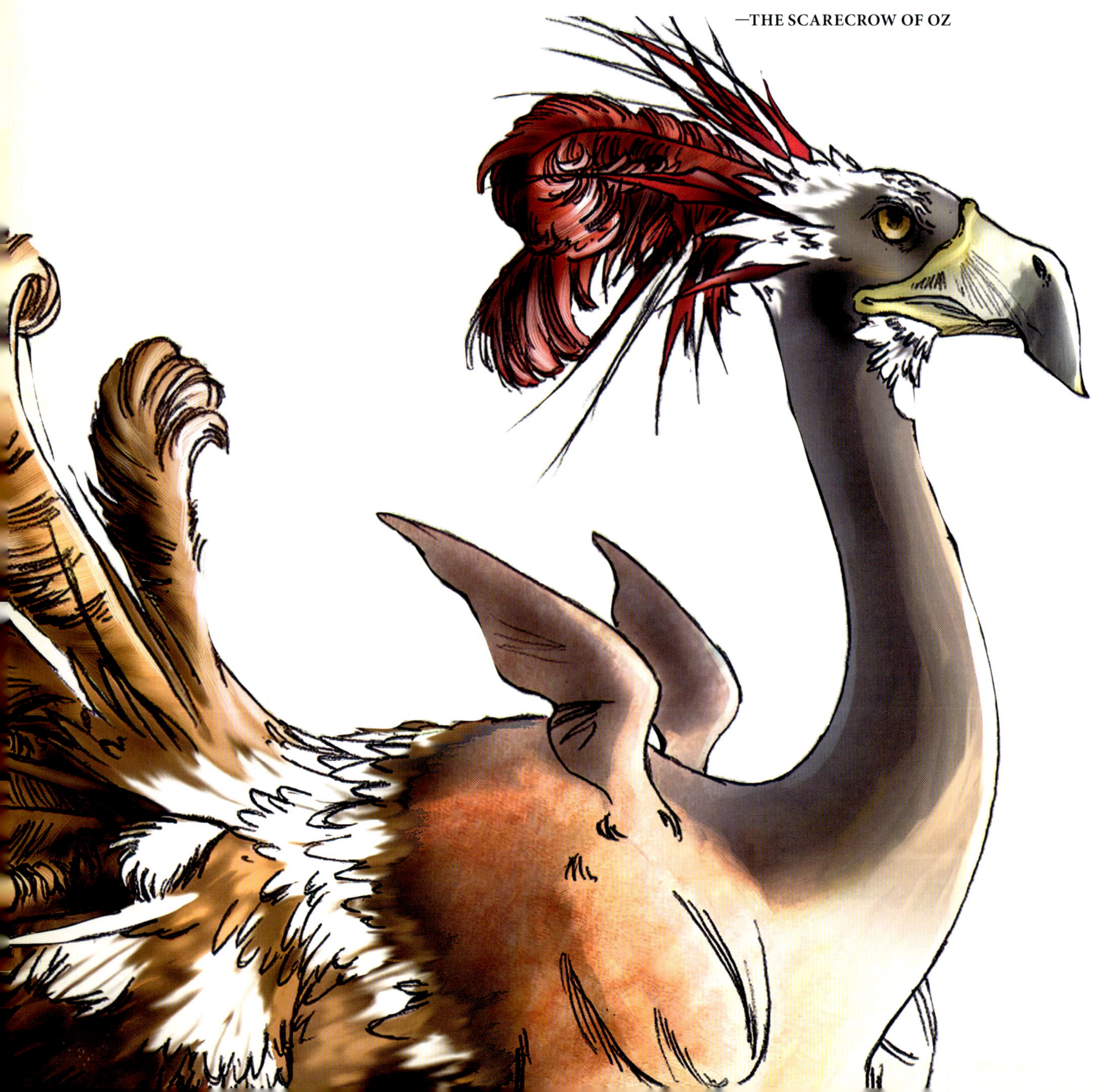

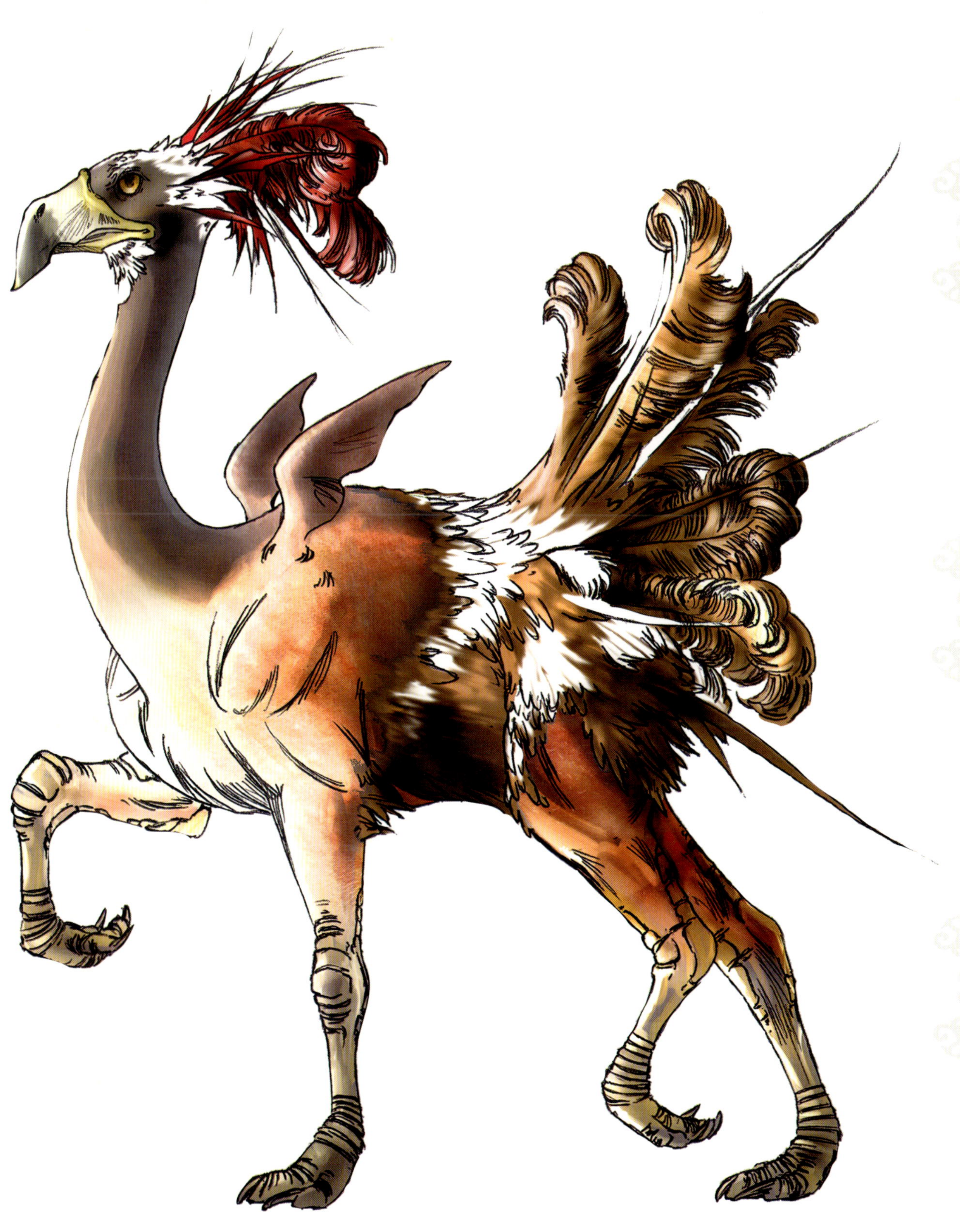

Featherless Quox

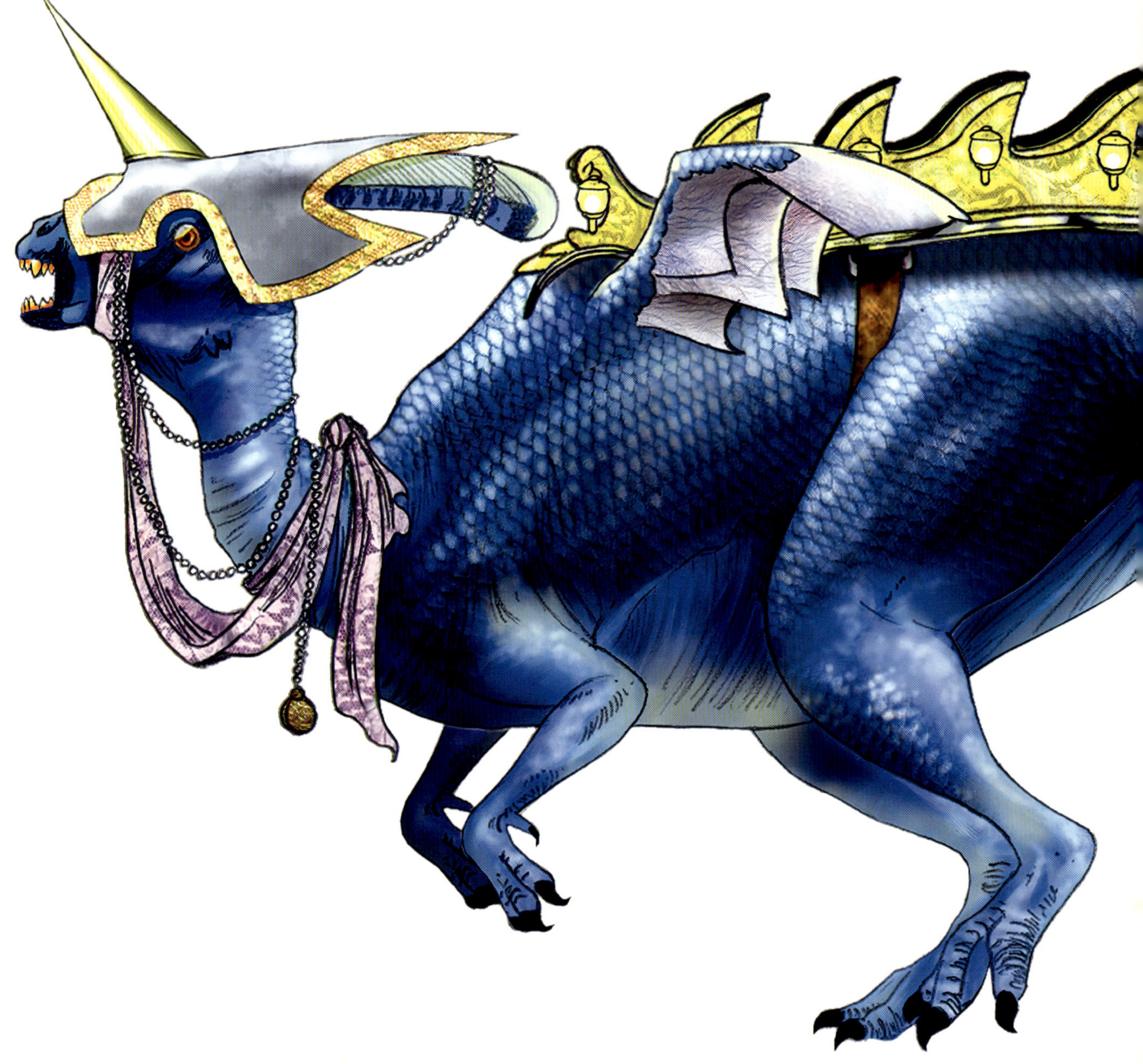

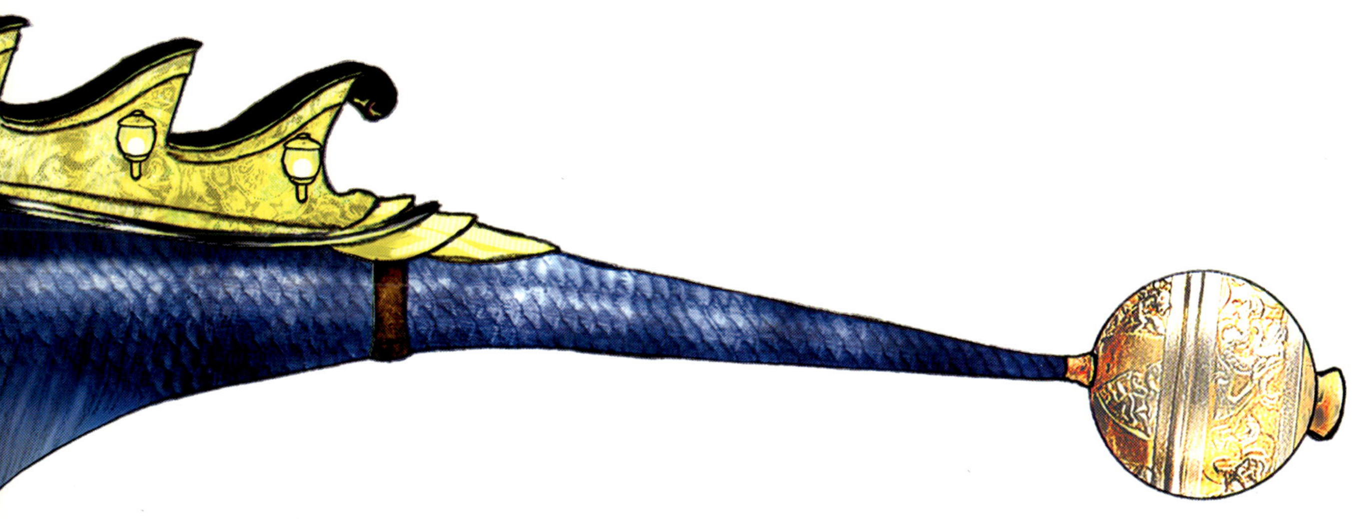

In *Tik-Tok of Oz,* the Nome King rids himself of twenty-three confrontational visitors—and Hank the Mule—by dropping them into a Hollow Tube in the ground that goes clear through to the other side of the world. The Great JinJin of the kingdom there determines the travelers' innocence and commandeers young dragon Quox to transport them back to the Nome Kingdom and depose the evil King Ruggedo from his throne. (Quox is given this beast-of-burden duty because of a cavalier but disrespectful comment he made to his most ancient ancestor, the Original Dragon.)

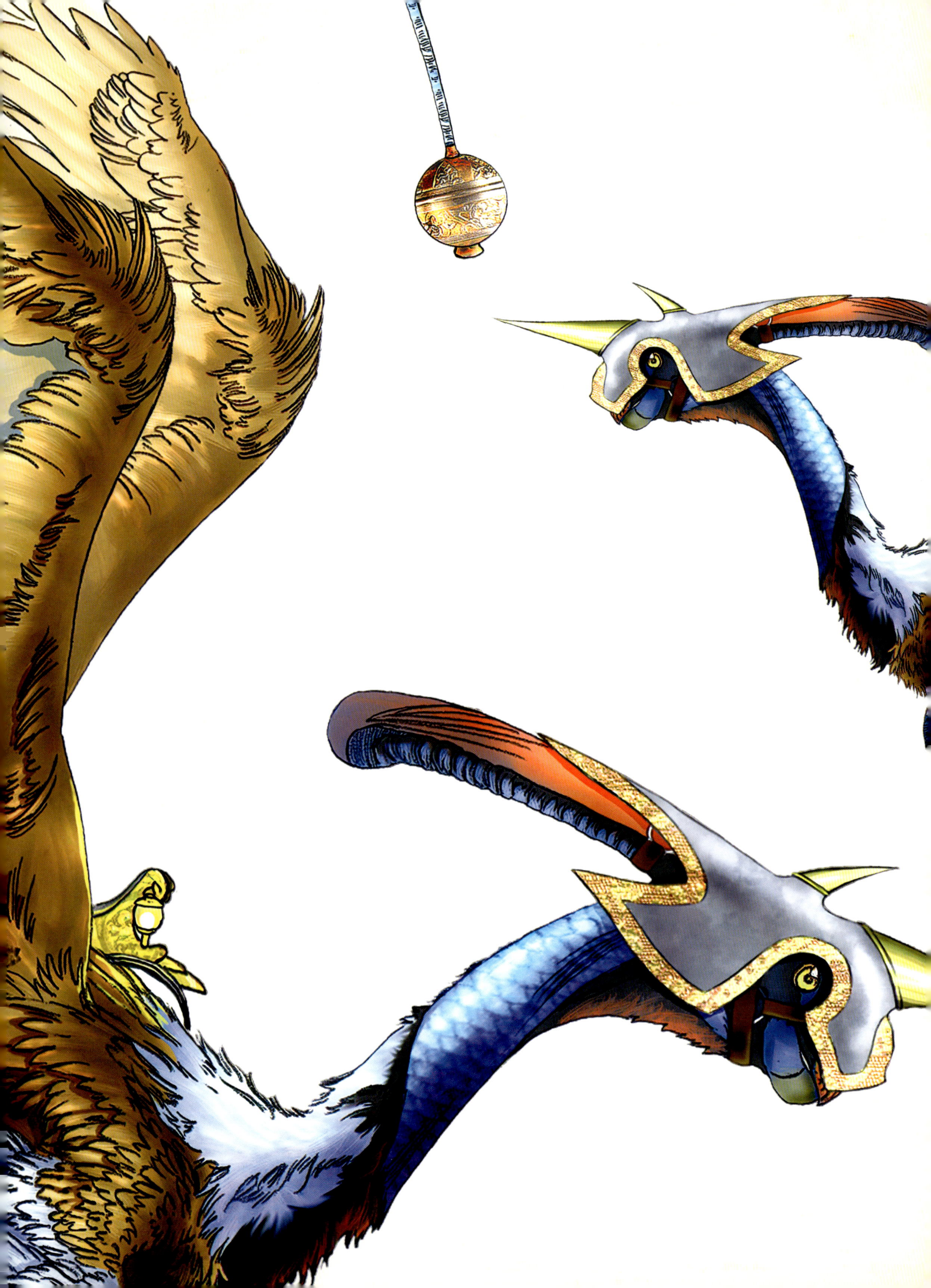

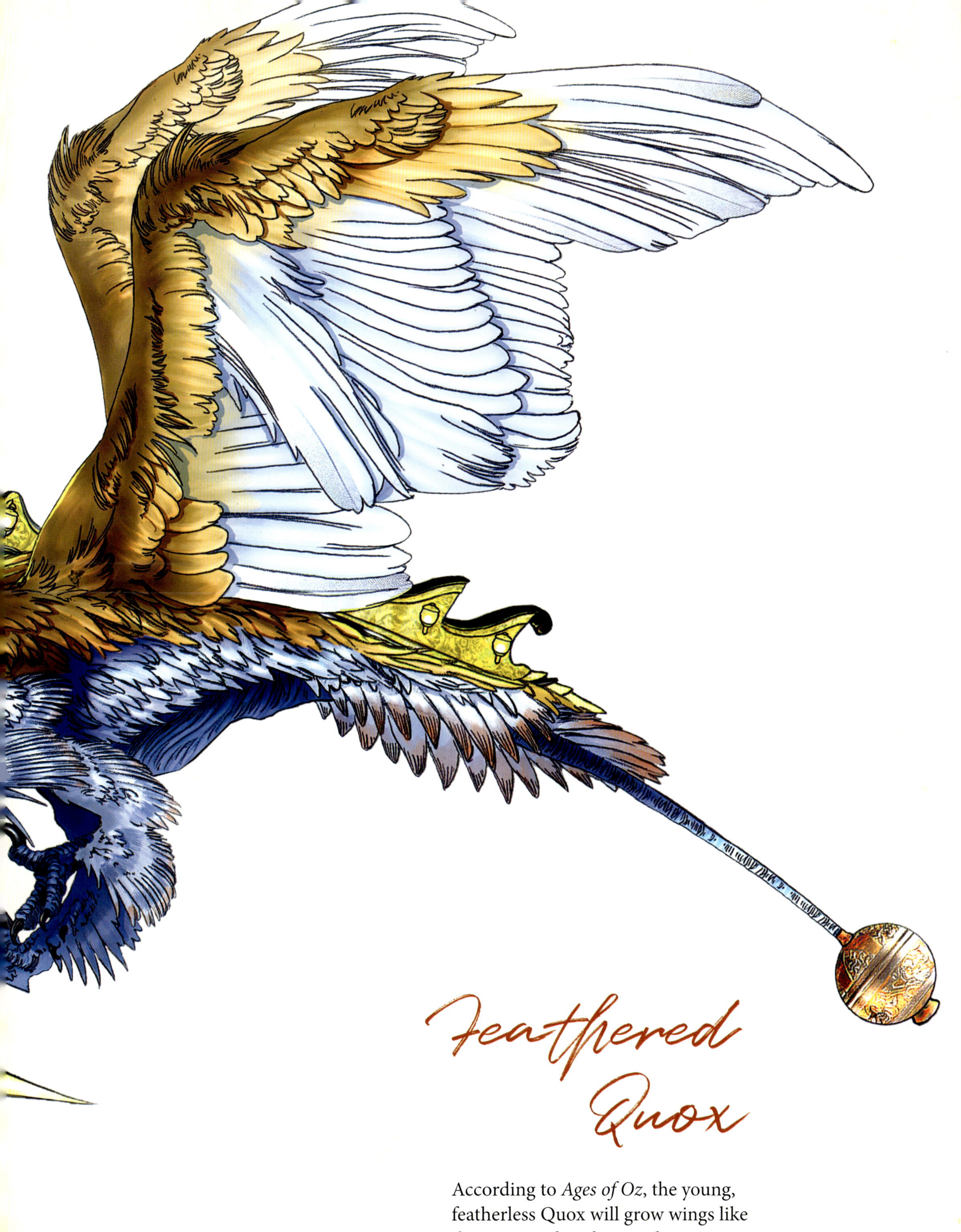

Feathered Quox

According to *Ages of Oz*, the young, featherless Quox will grow wings like these in another thousand years.

Winged Monkey

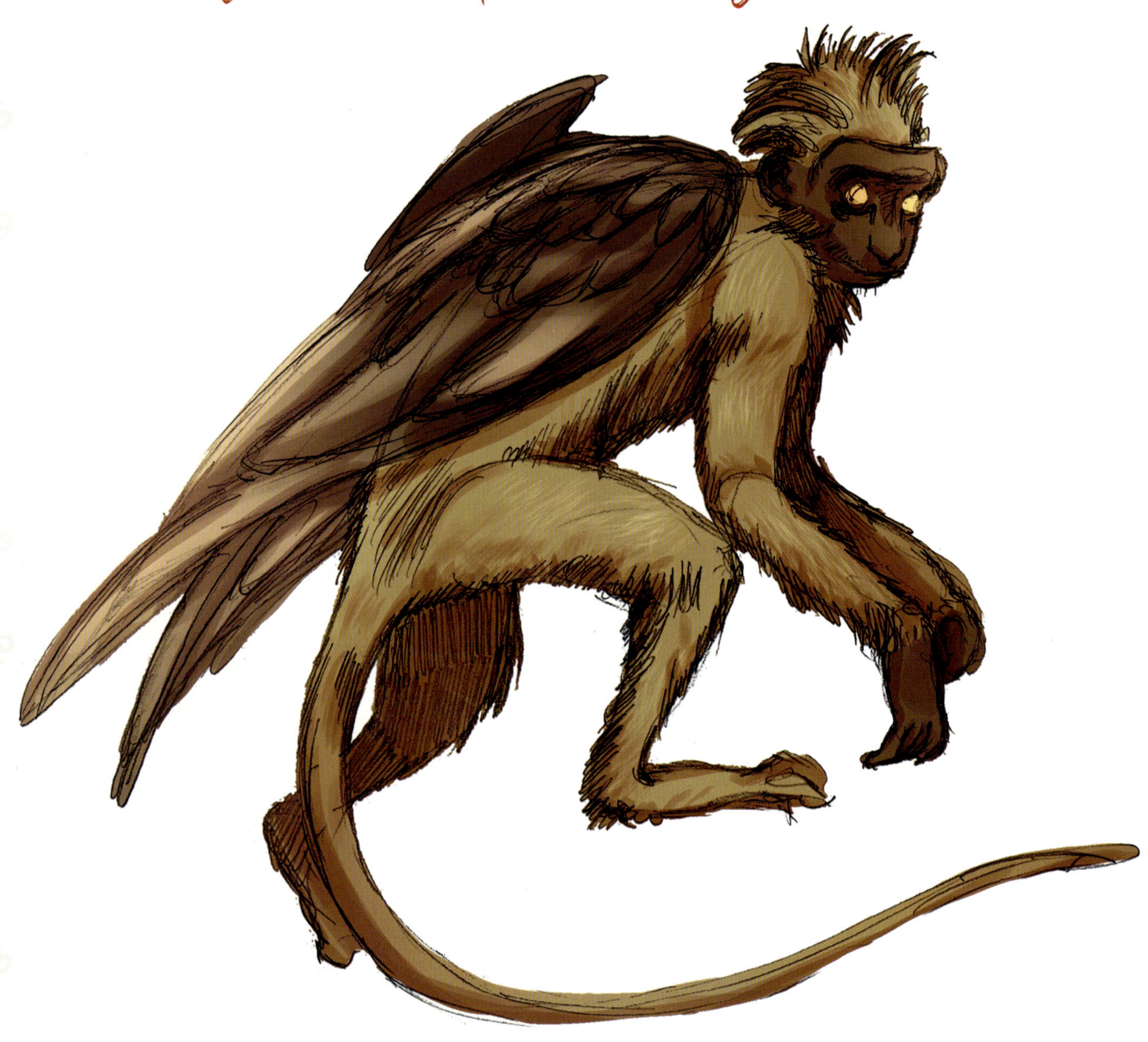

Winged Monkey Regiment

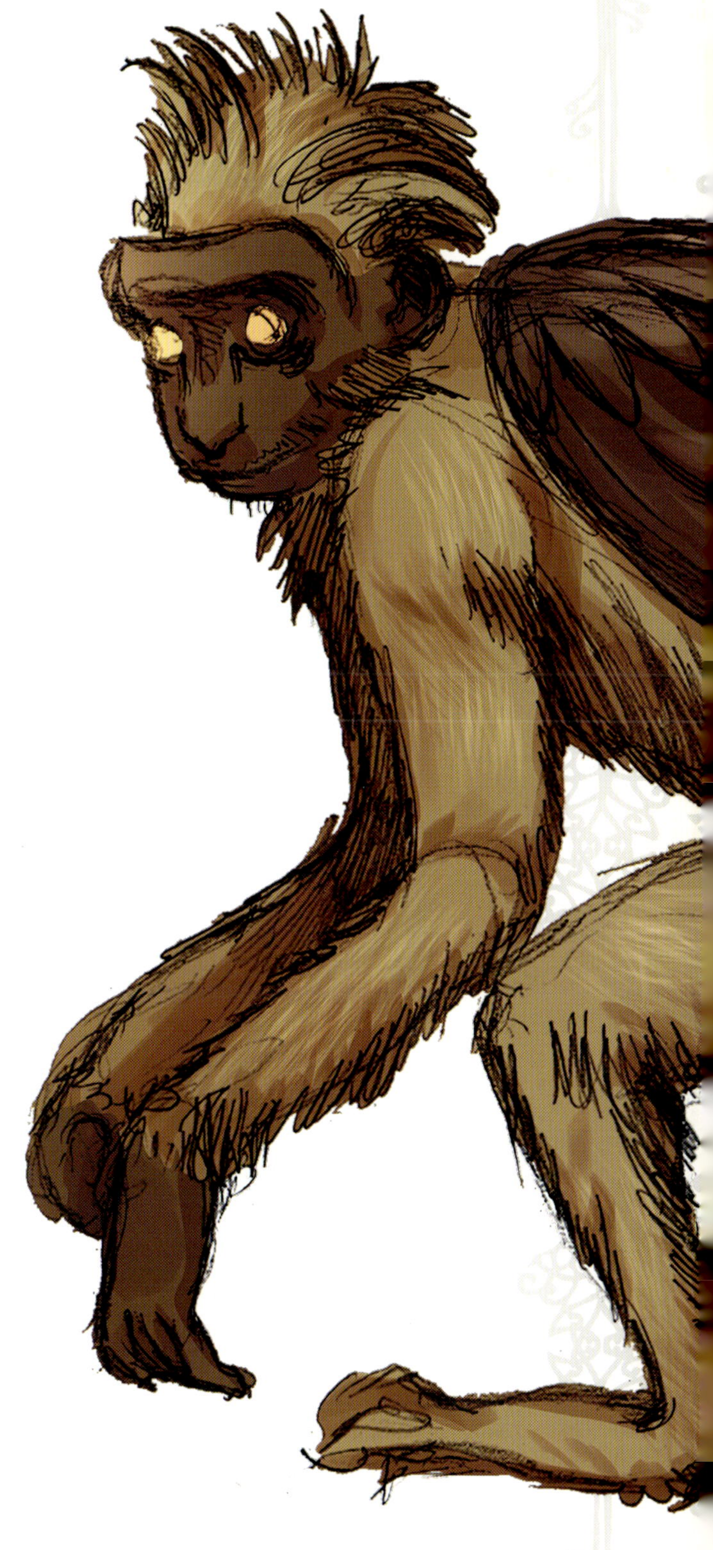

The complicated history of the Winged Monkeys is told in *The Wonderful Wizard of Oz*: how, after a relatively harmless prank, they were compelled by the sorceress Gaylette to obey three commands of the owner of a valuable Golden Cap. The Monkeys remained happy and free until that Cap fell into the hands of the Wicked Witch of the West. She ordered them to help her conquer the Winkie Country and drive the Wizard of Oz from her land. Her third demand was that the Monkeys destroy the Tin Woodman and Scarecrow and capture and bring to her the Cowardly Lion, Dorothy, and Toto. Soon thereafter, the Witch was melted by the little Kansas girl, and Dorothy herself acquired the Golden Cap. She and Glinda each used it three times (for good purposes), after which the Good Sorceress set the Monkeys free. They are no longer slaves of the Golden Cap.

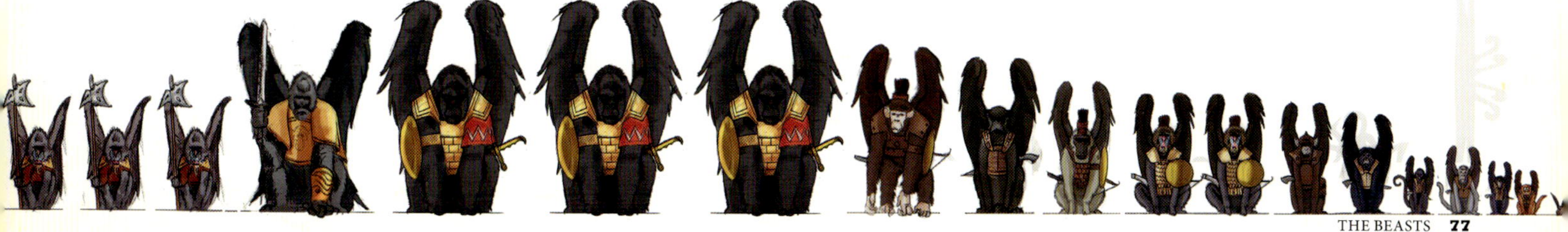

Winged Monkey Skeleton

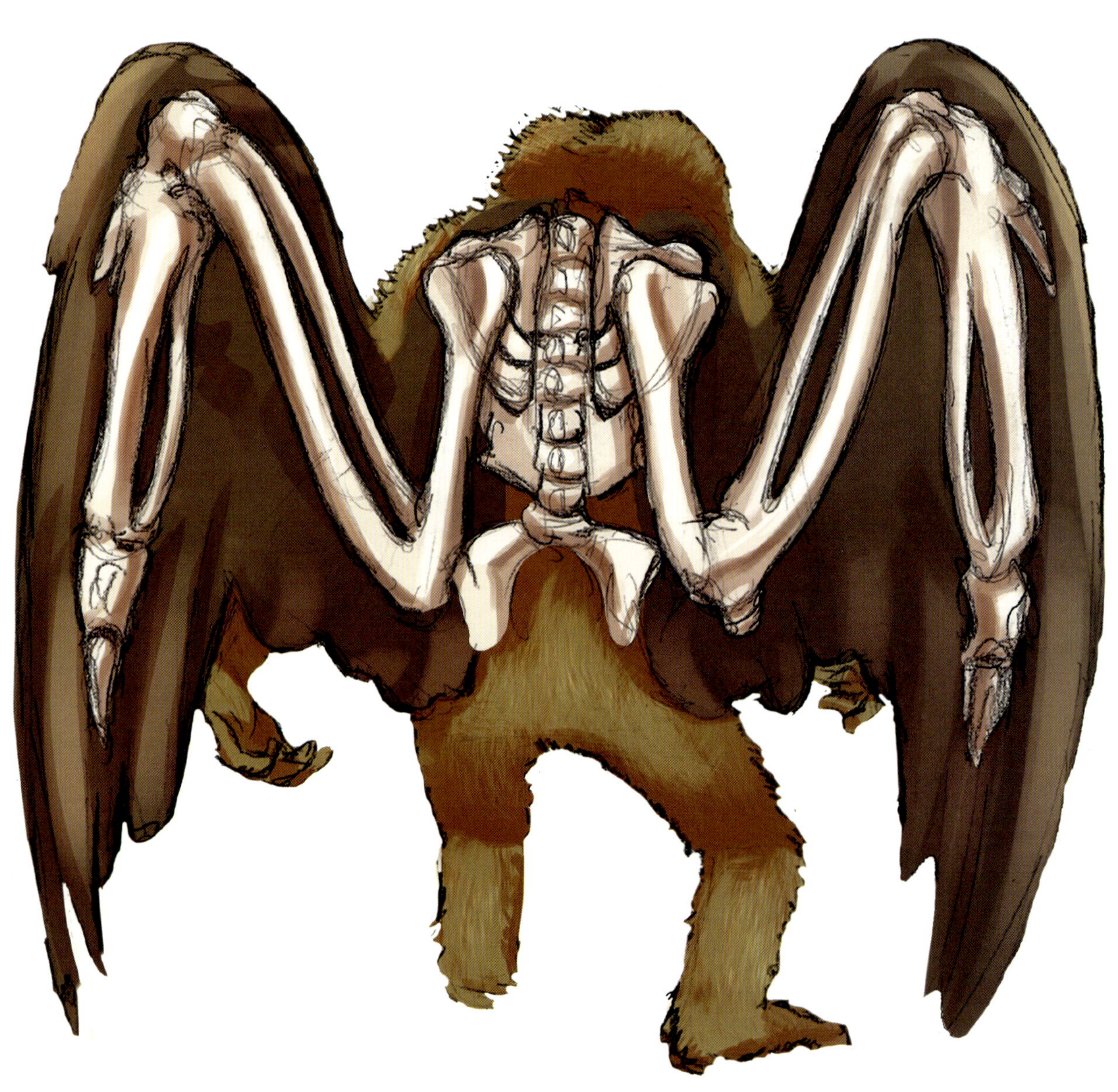

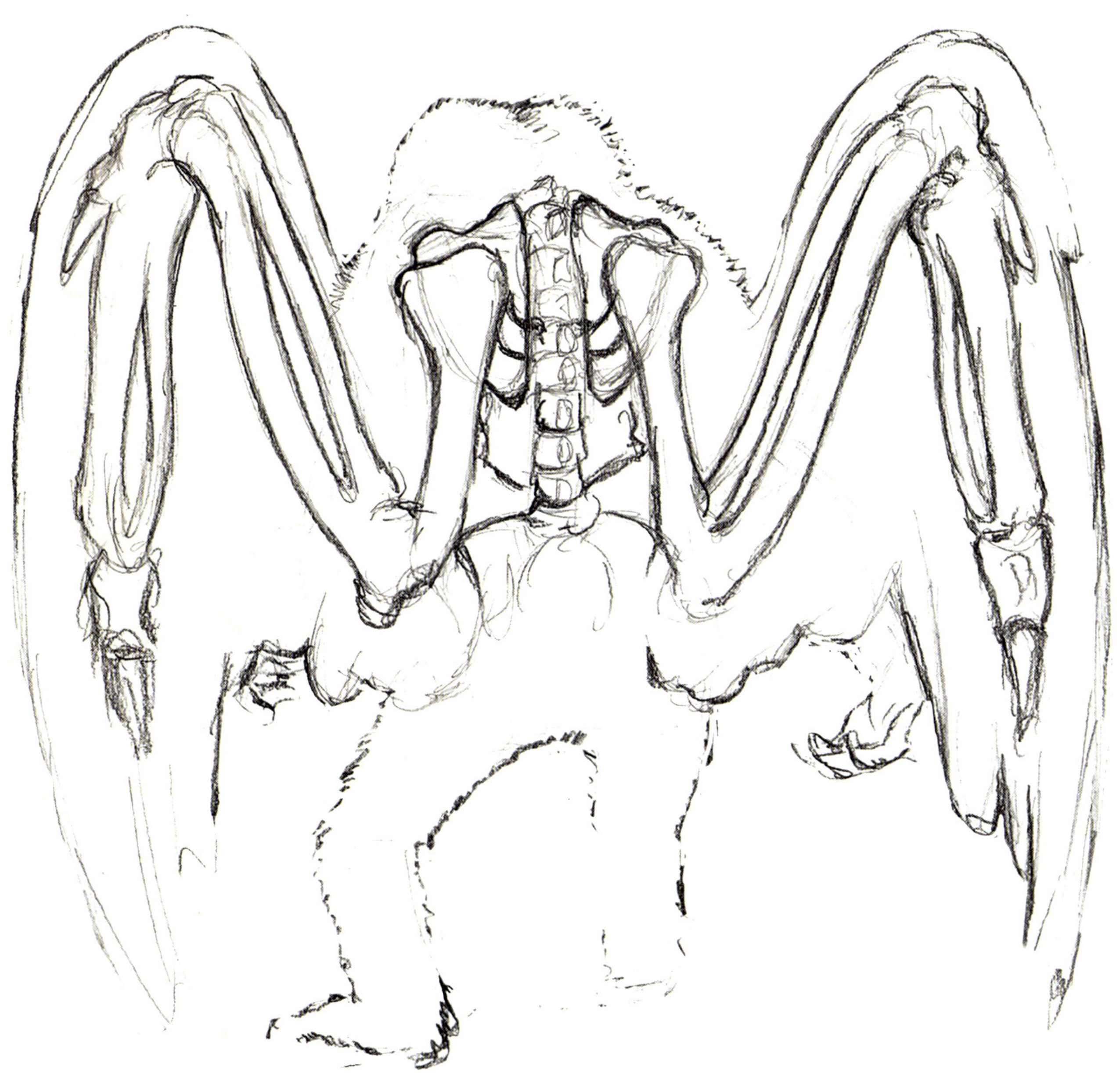

This drawing of the upper-body skeletal structure of the Winged Monkeys shows why they possess such flying power and strength.

The Curiosities

INTRODUCED BY THE SCARECROW

Here's a big "Hey! Hey!" from Oz—and what else could a stuffed Scarecrow offer in greeting? It had to be something involving hay! (Truthfully, though: fresh, golden straw is my filling of choice.) I imagine it's because of my own unique construction that I've been asked to write about Oz curiosities—those whose bodies are packed with cotton, constructed of furniture, built of wood, or have fruit for a head. After all, I myself was created from a set of old clothes, just chock-full of straw. Then the Munchkin farmer who assembled me added a pointed, broad-brimmed hat, roll-top boots, and painted my face on the sack he used to make my head. That certainly seems curious enough!

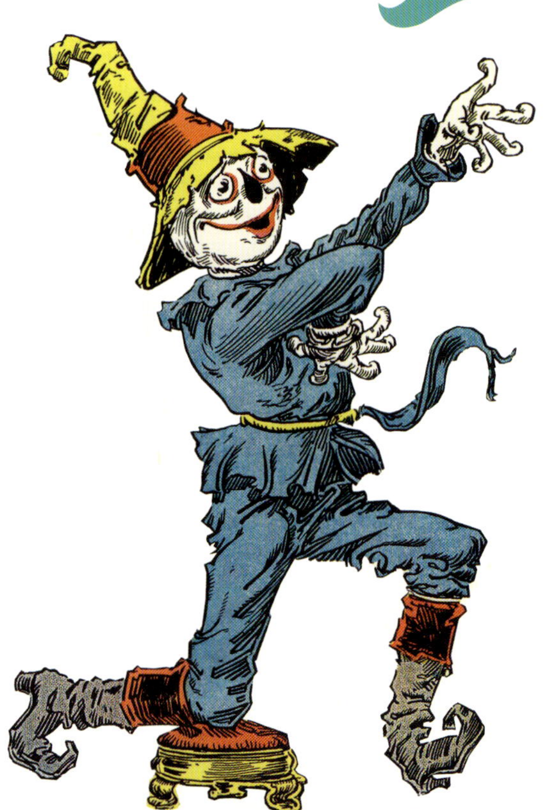

As I pondered what to tell you, however, the excellent brains given to me by my friend the Wizard suddenly made me realize that there are too many curiosities in Oz for us to consider them all. I also thought about those others who live in the countries surrounding Oz, in the lands underground, in the skies above, and in the

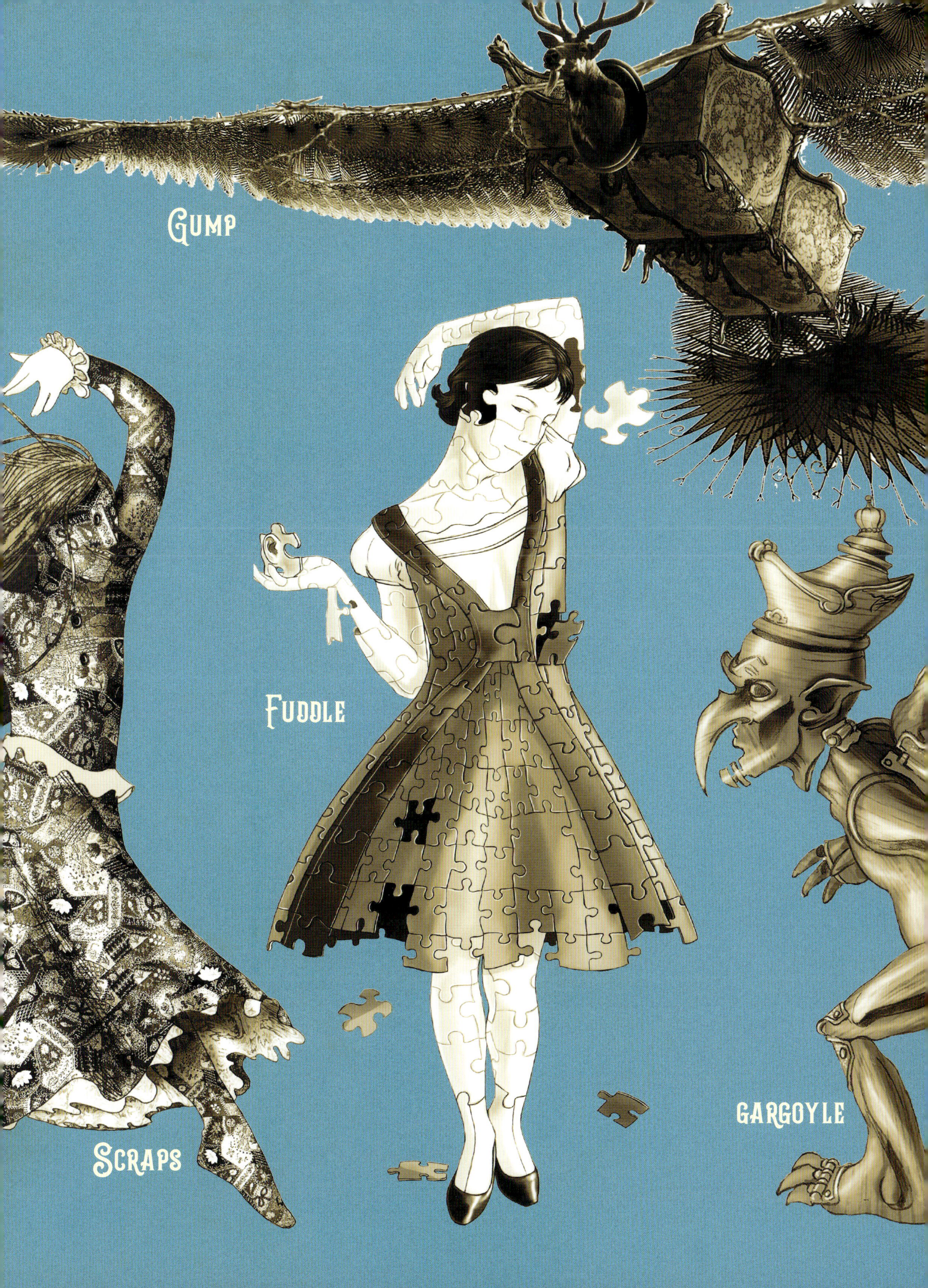
GUMP
FUDDLE
SCRAPS
GARGOYLE

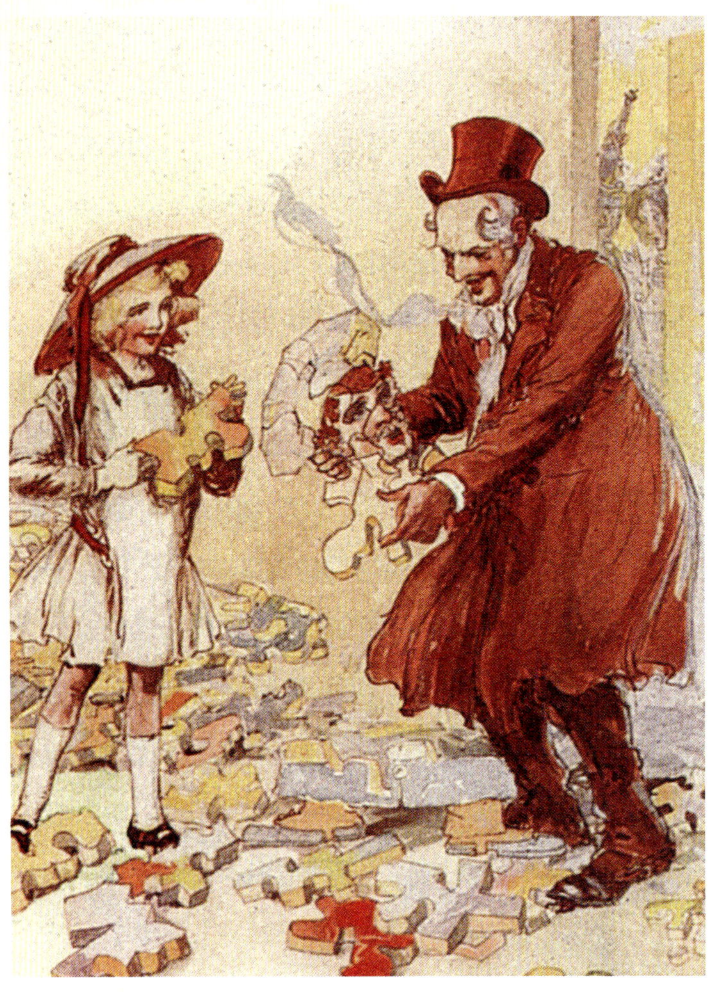

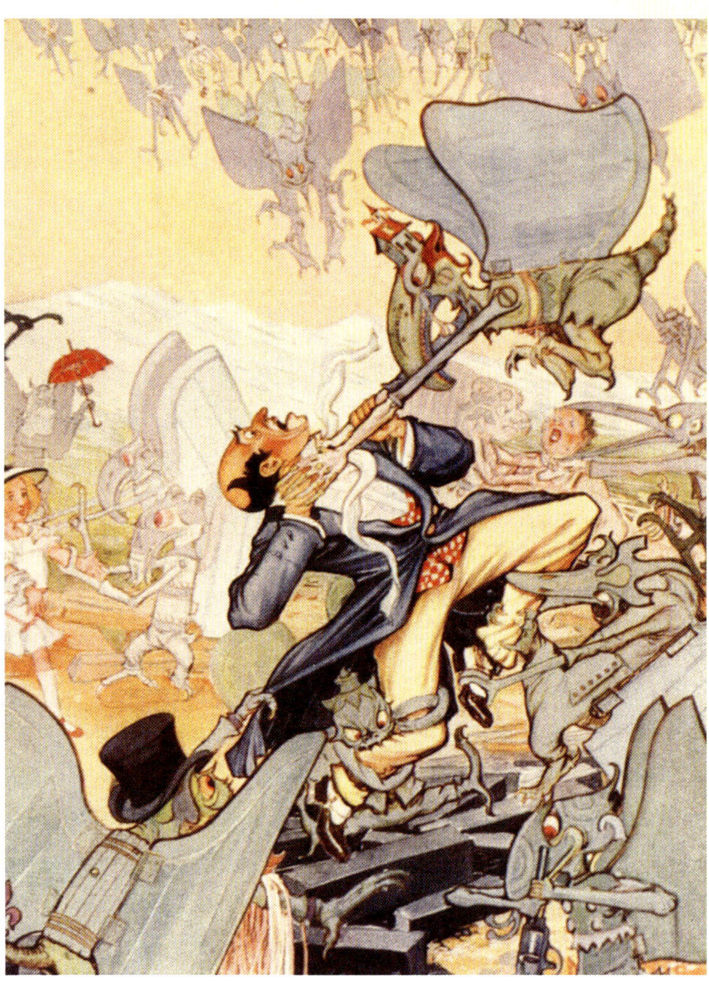

depths of the Nonestic Ocean and on its islands. By now you'll understand my dilemma; there are far too many characters to discuss in merely one chapter. (This is the reason there have been so many Oz books.) So, we'll be selective and examine just a few of the most interesting curiosities—or as we sometimes spell it, curi-OZ-ities!

The citizens of Fuddlecumjig, for example, are both fun and funny. They're made of living bits of wood, put together like individual and three-dimensional jigsaw puzzles. Yet when anyone approaches their village, it's the peculiarity of every Fuddle to scatter into dozens of pieces. As a result, visitors have to pick up all the beautifully painted fragments and completely reassemble those with whom they want to spend time. Regardless, this makes for a delightful challenge and a genuine joy. As Dorothy's Uncle Henry once said about the Fuddles, "They're more fun than playing solitaire or mumblety-peg!"

PAGE 80: The Scarecrow by Neill, *The Patchwork Girl of Oz*
ABOVE LEFT: Dorothy and the Wizard meet a Fuddle; Aunt Em and Uncle Henry look on. Art by Neill, *The Emerald City of Oz*.
ABOVE RIGHT: The Wizard, Dorothy, and cousin Zeb fight off the Gargoyles. Art by Neill, *Dorothy and the Wizard in Oz*.

Much less desirable are the Gargoyles. The Wizard, Dorothy, and their friends once ventured into the Gargoyles' all-wood Land of Naught on Pyramid Mountain, and only the Wizard's cleverness enabled them to escape certain death. The Gargoyles themselves are also made of invincibly strong wood, carved into hideous appearances. When anyone approaches them, they fiercely fly into battle with magical wooden wings that are hinged to their bodies.

A much happier creation is the Gump—or, as he was once defined, "a Thing with a Gump's head on it." When General Jinjur besieged the Emerald

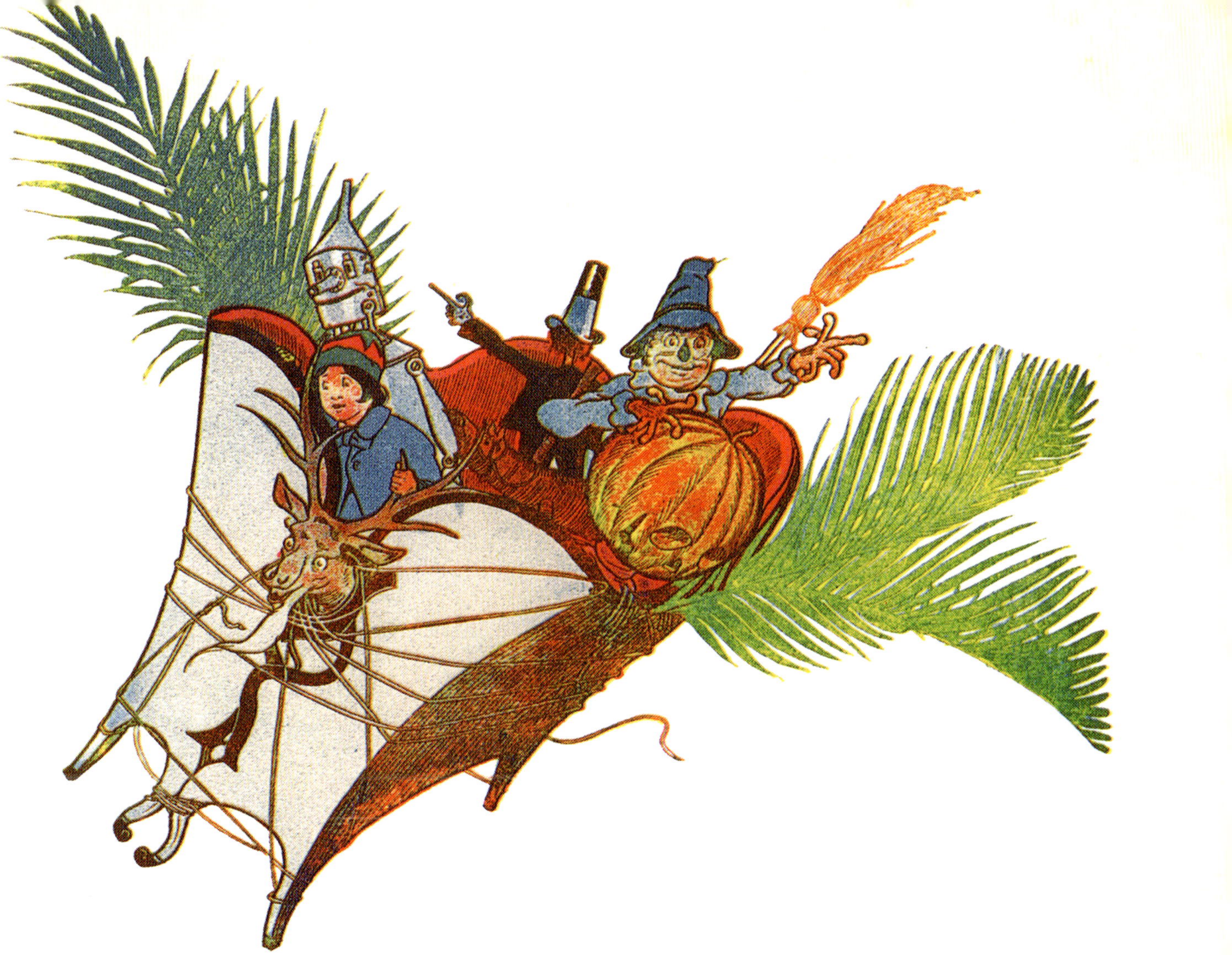

City with her Army of Revolt, it was my idea to manufacture a flying machine to allow me and my companions to escape imprisonment in the palace. We used rope to bind together two sofas, to which we then attached giant palm fronds as wings. Finally, the mounted head of a Gump was positioned at the front of our intended vehicle. Once sprinkled with the magical Powder of Life, this Ozian oddity was able to soar through the air, and we flew away to freedom!

A fine companion on that adventure was Jack Pumpkinhead, who was also brought to life by the same magic powder. Early in his existence, Jack worried that he might not survive after his carved head spoiled. He then proved, however, that the right sort

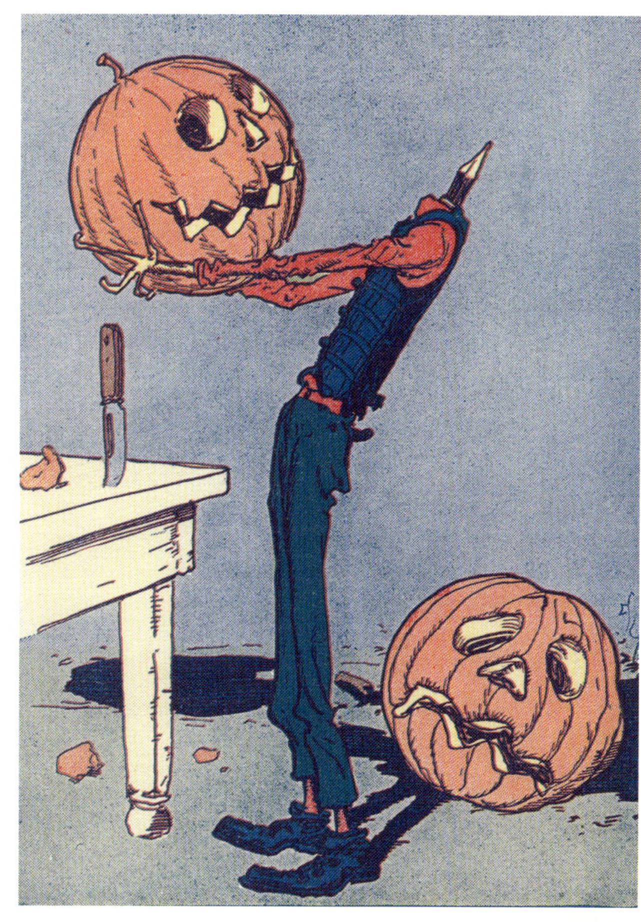

ABOVE: The Gump saves his friends. Art by Neill, *The Marvelous Land of Oz*.
RIGHT: Jack Pumpkinhead prepares his next head. Art by Neill, *Little Wizard Stories of Oz*.

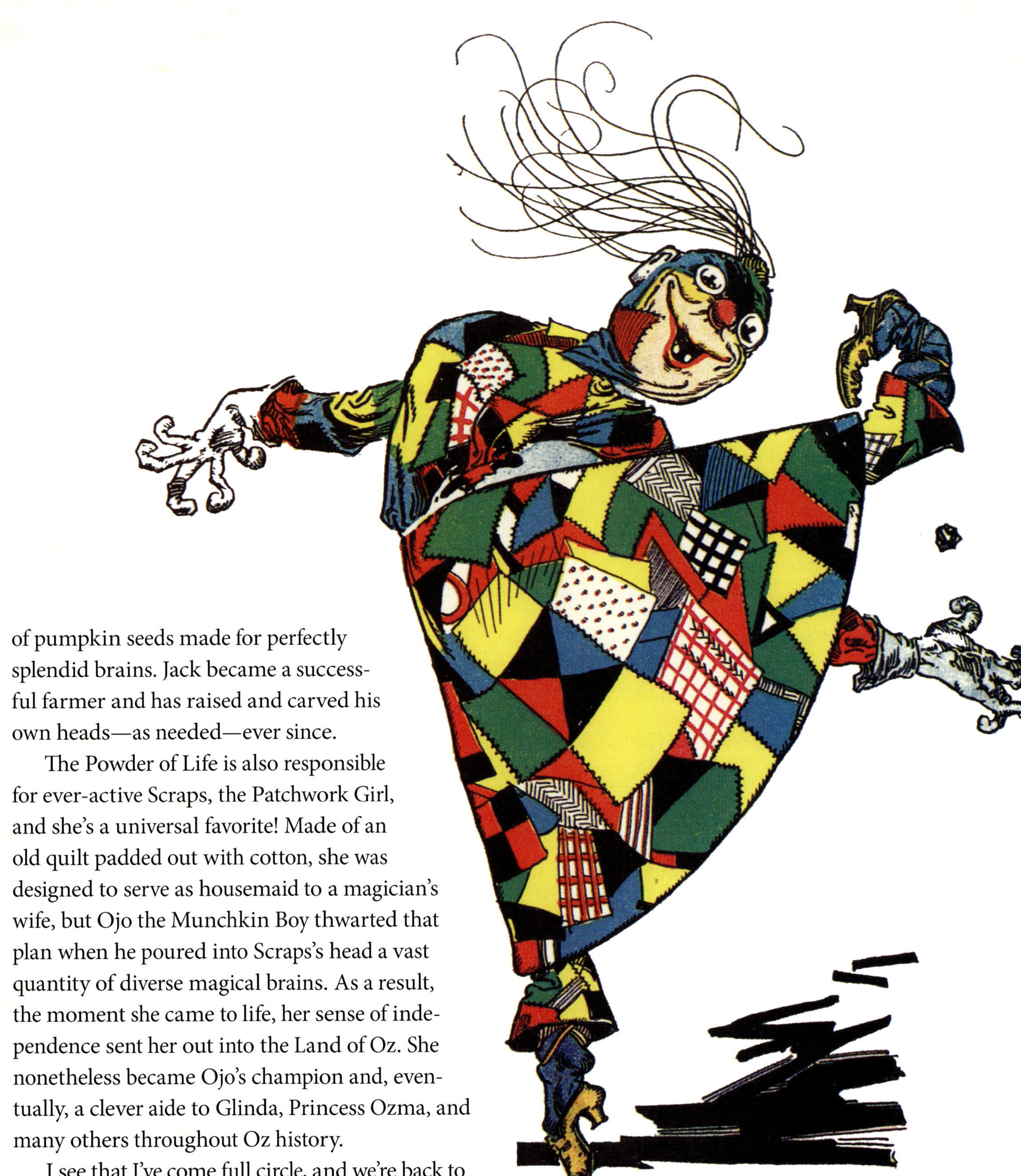

of pumpkin seeds made for perfectly splendid brains. Jack became a successful farmer and has raised and carved his own heads—as needed—ever since.

The Powder of Life is also responsible for ever-active Scraps, the Patchwork Girl, and she's a universal favorite! Made of an old quilt padded out with cotton, she was designed to serve as housemaid to a magician's wife, but Ojo the Munchkin Boy thwarted that plan when he poured into Scraps's head a vast quantity of diverse magical brains. As a result, the moment she came to life, her sense of independence sent her out into the Land of Oz. She nonetheless became Ojo's champion and, eventually, a clever aide to Glinda, Princess Ozma, and many others throughout Oz history.

I see that I've come full circle, and we're back to the topic of brains! One thing I've learned from my own adventures with some of our curiosities is that sorcery, wizardry, and pumpkin seeds aren't really necessary. All of us are created with brains, and every day we are given more and more opportunities to work with them. The *magic* comes when we use them well!

ABOVE: Scraps
OPPOSITE: Scraps, the Scarecrow, Dorothy, Toto, and Ojo encounter a Wall of Water. Both by Neill, *The Patchwork Girl of Oz.*

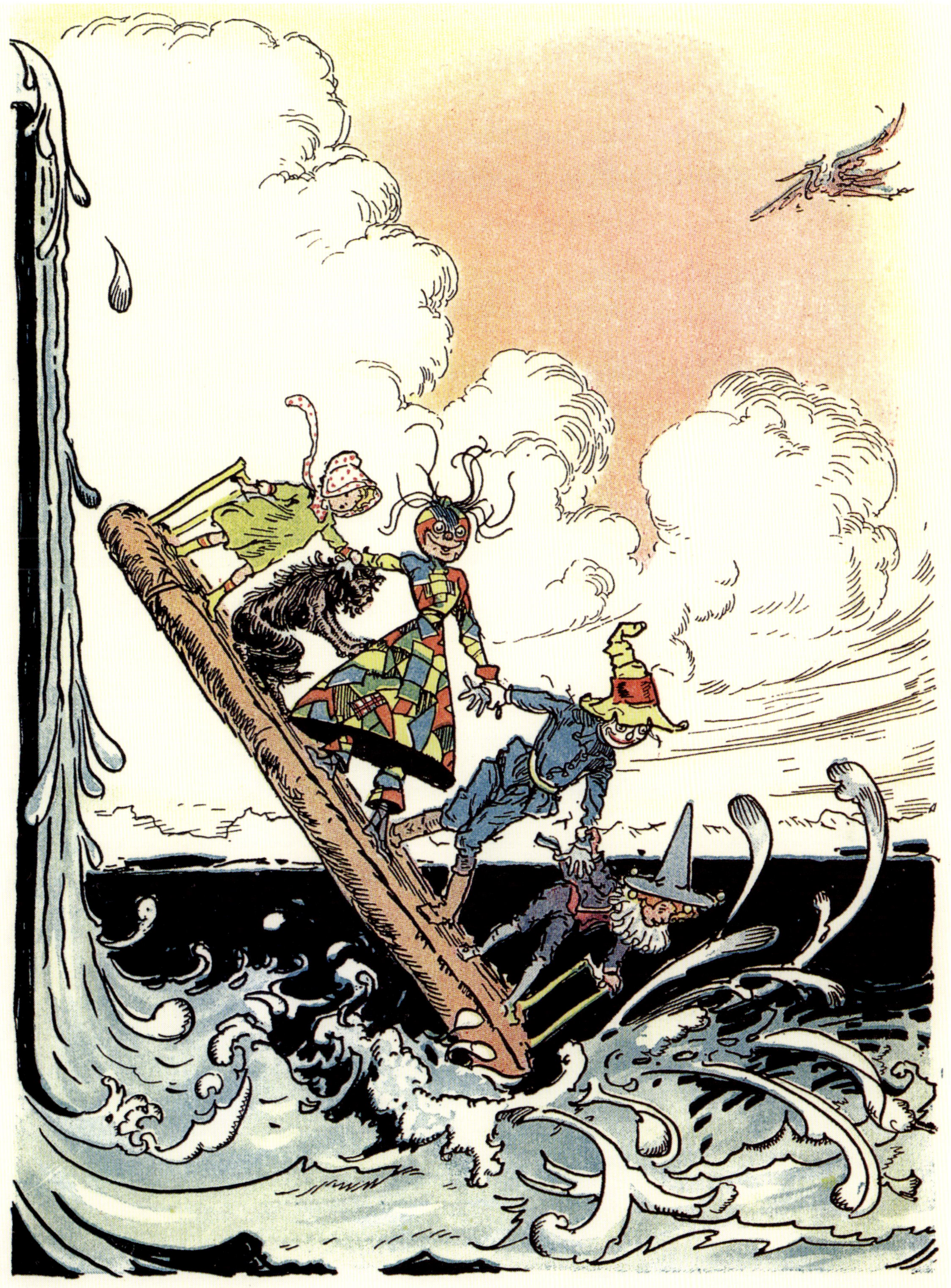

Fuddle

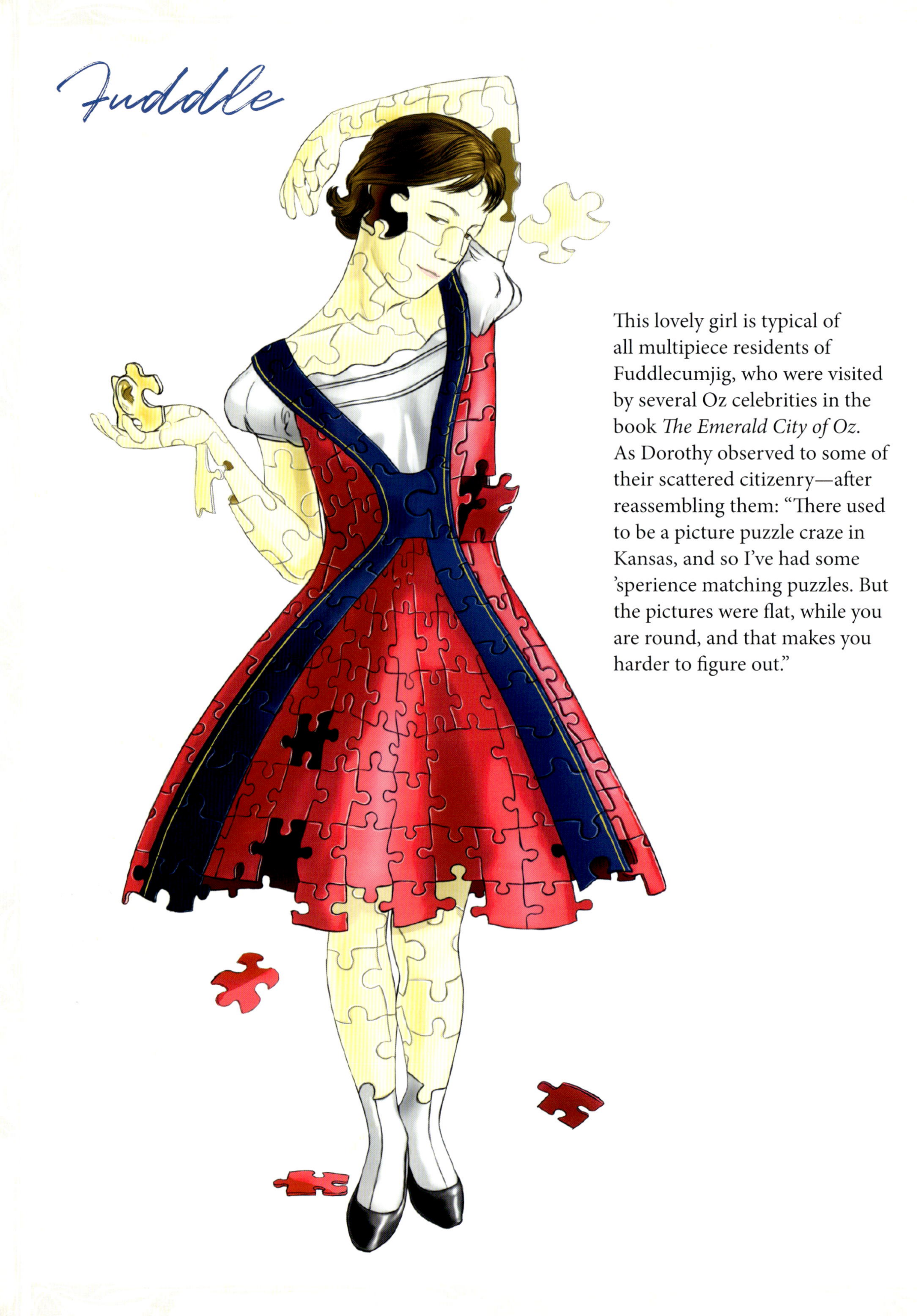

This lovely girl is typical of all multipiece residents of Fuddlecumjig, who were visited by several Oz celebrities in the book *The Emerald City of Oz*. As Dorothy observed to some of their scattered citizenry—after reassembling them: “There used to be a picture puzzle craze in Kansas, and so I’ve had some ’sperience matching puzzles. But the pictures were flat, while you are round, and that makes you harder to figure out.”

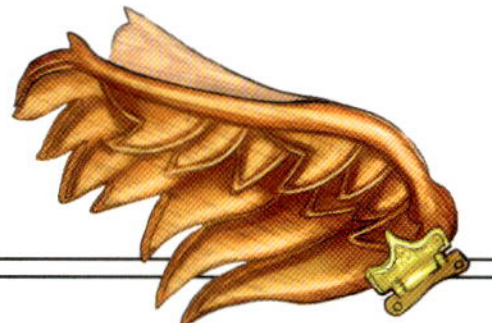

The Gargoyles were very small of stature, being less than three feet in height. Their bodies were round, their legs short and thick, and their arms extraordinarily long and stout. Their heads were too big for their bodies, and their faces were decidedly ugly to look upon. Some had long, curved noses and chins, small eyes, and wide, grinning mouths. Others had flat noses, protruding eyes, and ears that were shaped like those of an elephant. There were many types, indeed, scarcely two being alike. The tops of their heads had no hair, but were carved into a variety of fantastic shapes, some having a row of points or balls around the top, other designs resembling flowers or vegetables, and still others having squares that looked like waffles cut crisscross on their heads.

—DOROTHY AND THE WIZARD IN OZ

Gargoyle

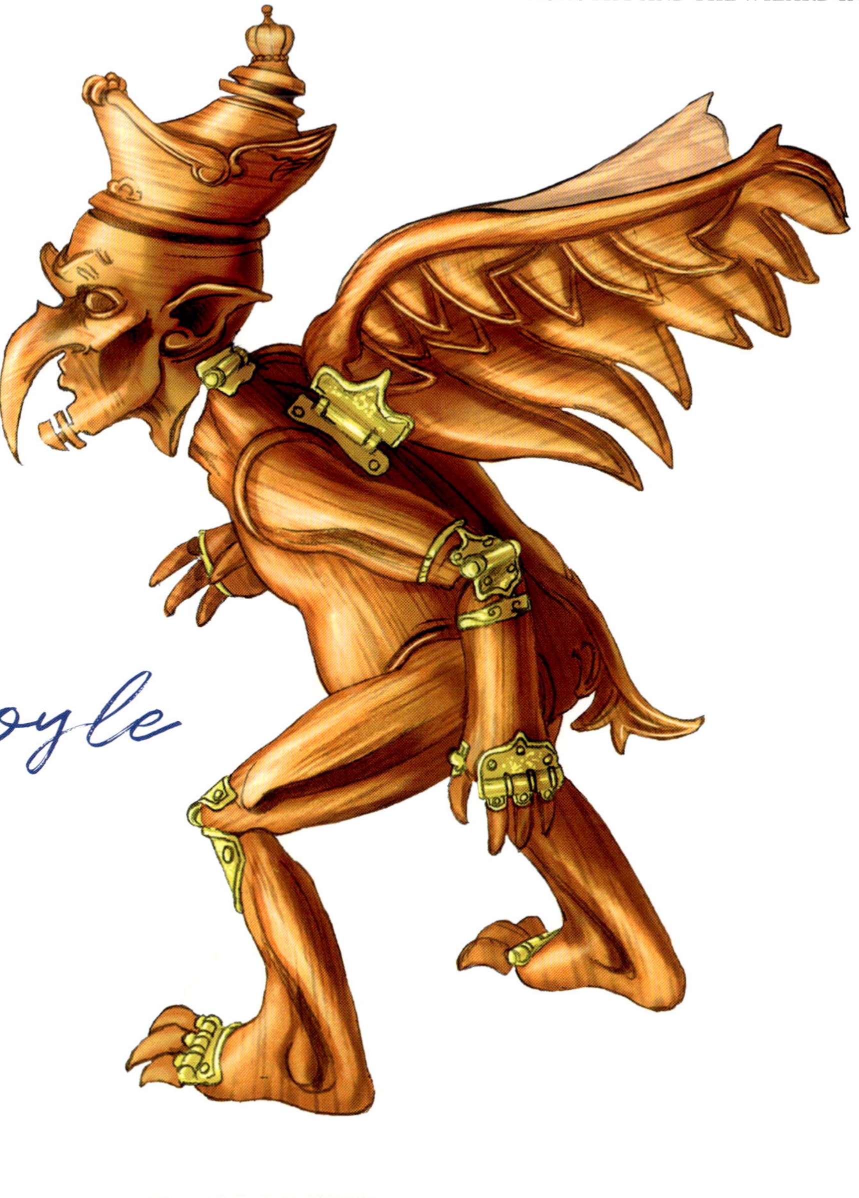

The Gumps

As can be seen here, the Gump's great spreading palm leaves were of enormous aid to the creature as it transported the Scarecrow and his friends away from the Emerald City. Indeed, the makeshift flying machine inadvertently flew completely out of Oz to the Great Outside World; thankfully, it got back on course and carried its passengers to the safety of the palace of Glinda the Good.

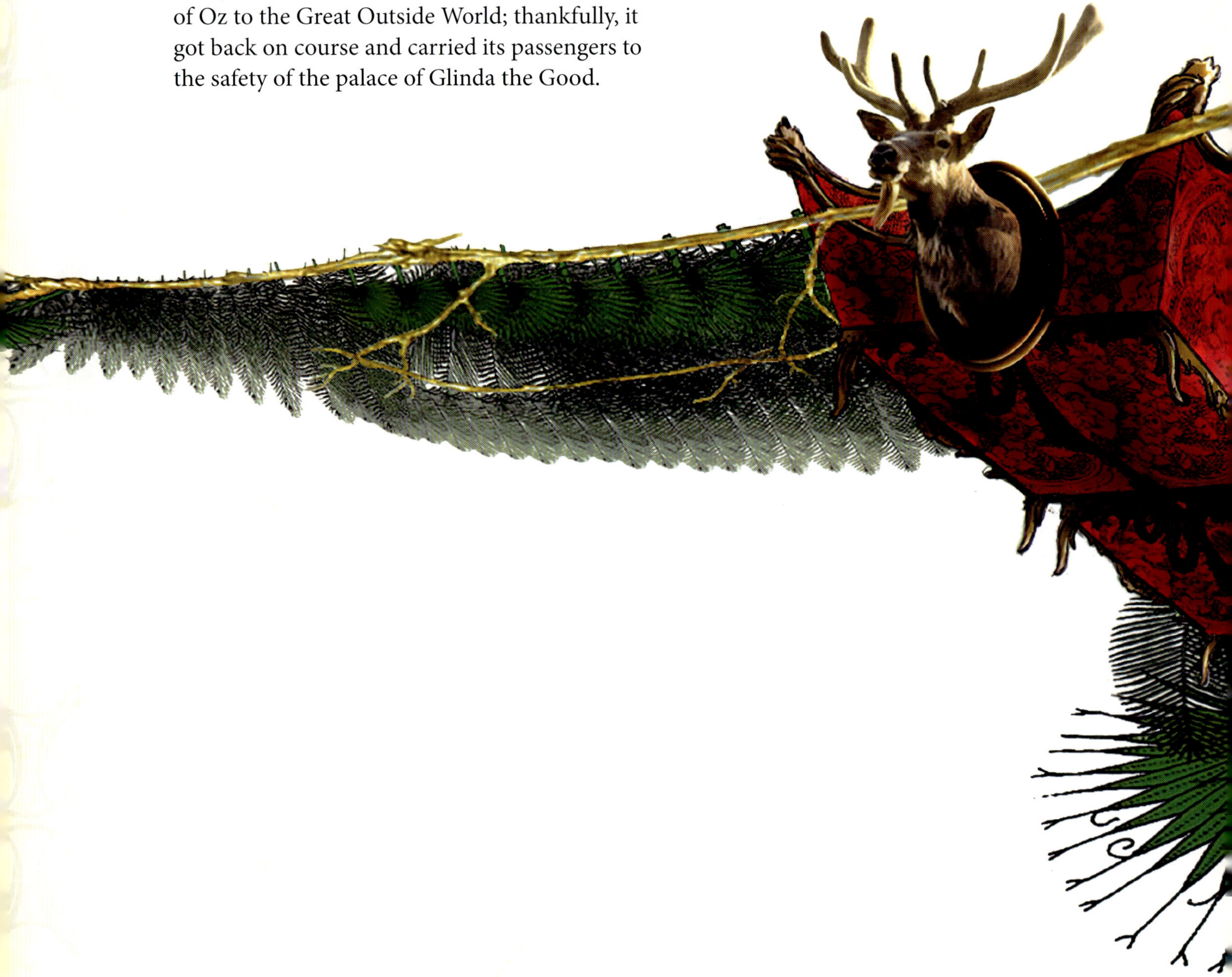

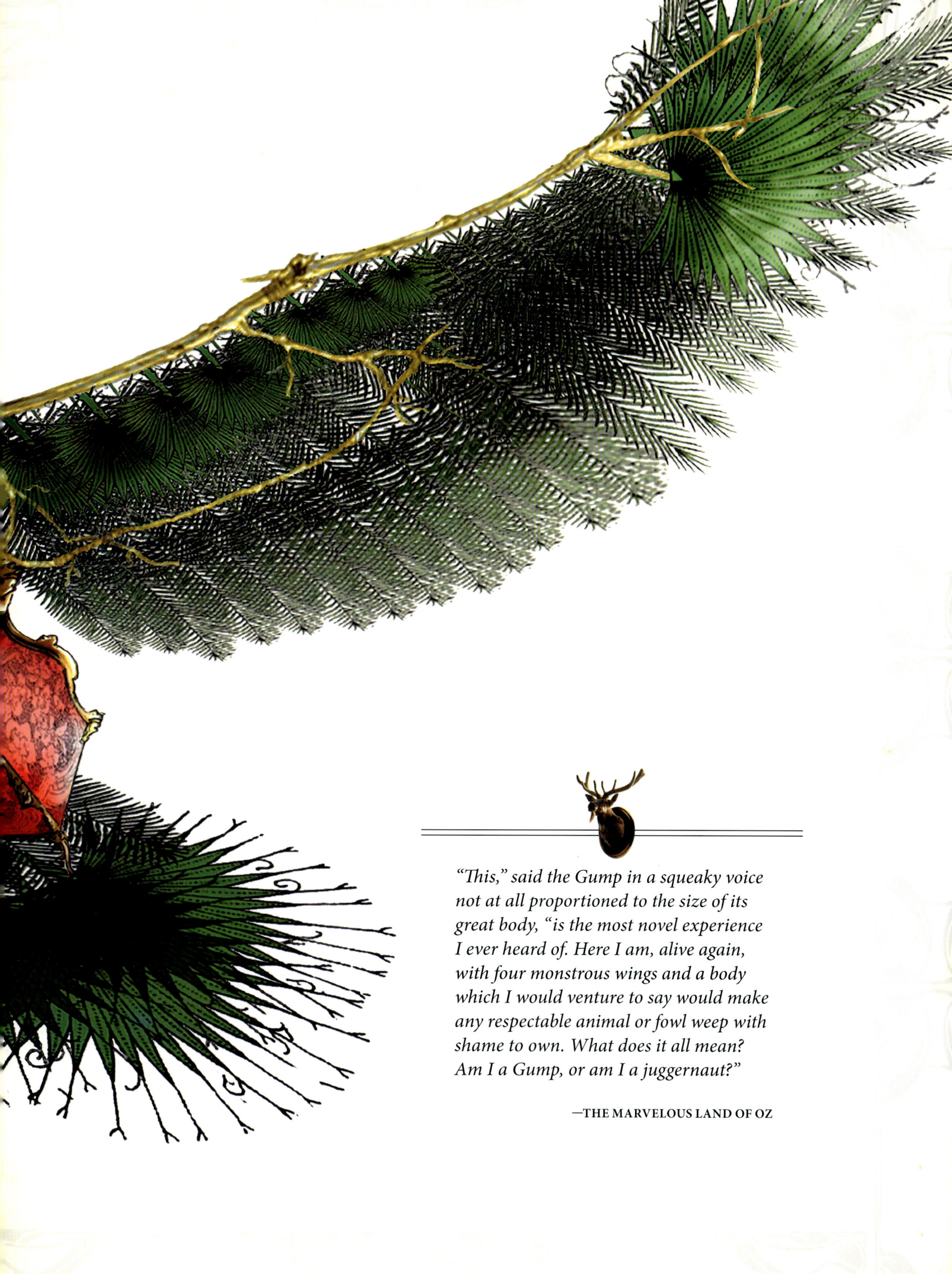

"This," said the Gump in a squeaky voice not at all proportioned to the size of its great body, "is the most novel experience I ever heard of. Here I am, alive again, with four monstrous wings and a body which I would venture to say would make any respectable animal or fowl weep with shame to own. What does it all mean? Am I a Gump, or am I a juggernaut?"

—THE MARVELOUS LAND OF OZ

Wingspan

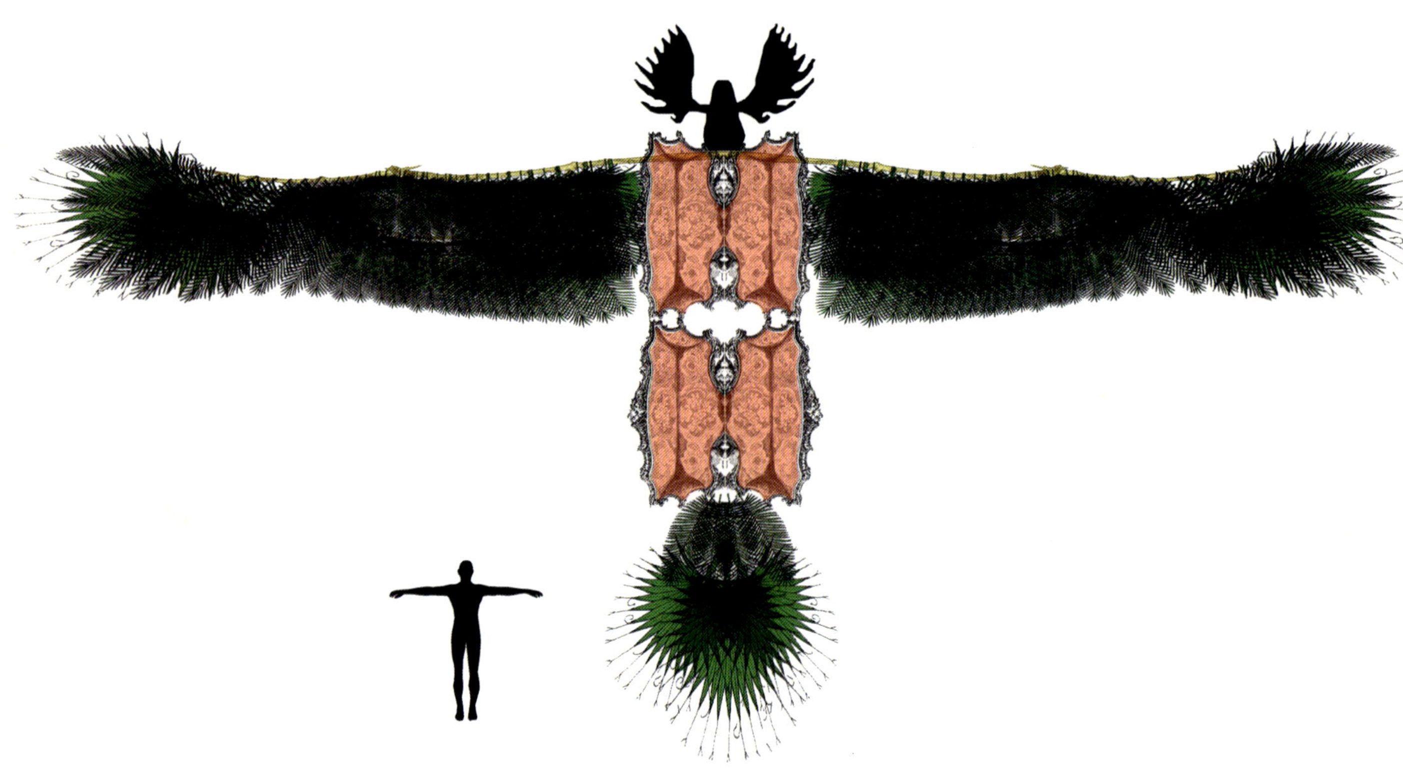

The above aerial view of the Gump displays its great and spreading palm-frond wings; their intricate, individual patterns are shown on the opposite page. The leaves on the Emerald City's royal palm tree grow in layers, and such intertwining gave the Gump the strength to take to the air.

Wing Layers

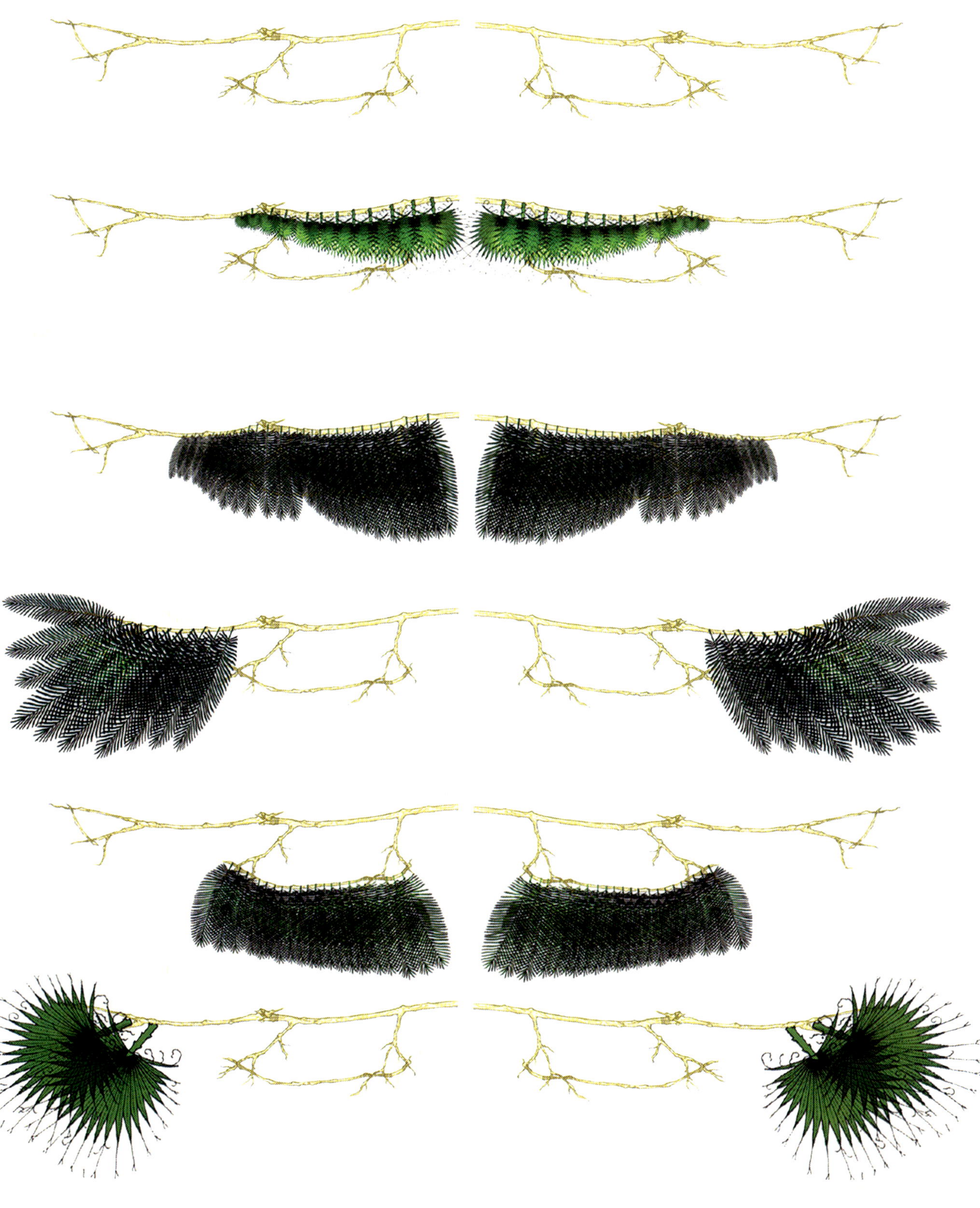

Jack Pumpkinhead

His body was merely sticks of wood, jointed clumsily together. On his neck was set a round, yellow pumpkin, with a face carved on it such as a boy often carves on a jack-lantern. Jack's face was jolly and smiling—being carved that way.

—THE ROAD TO OZ

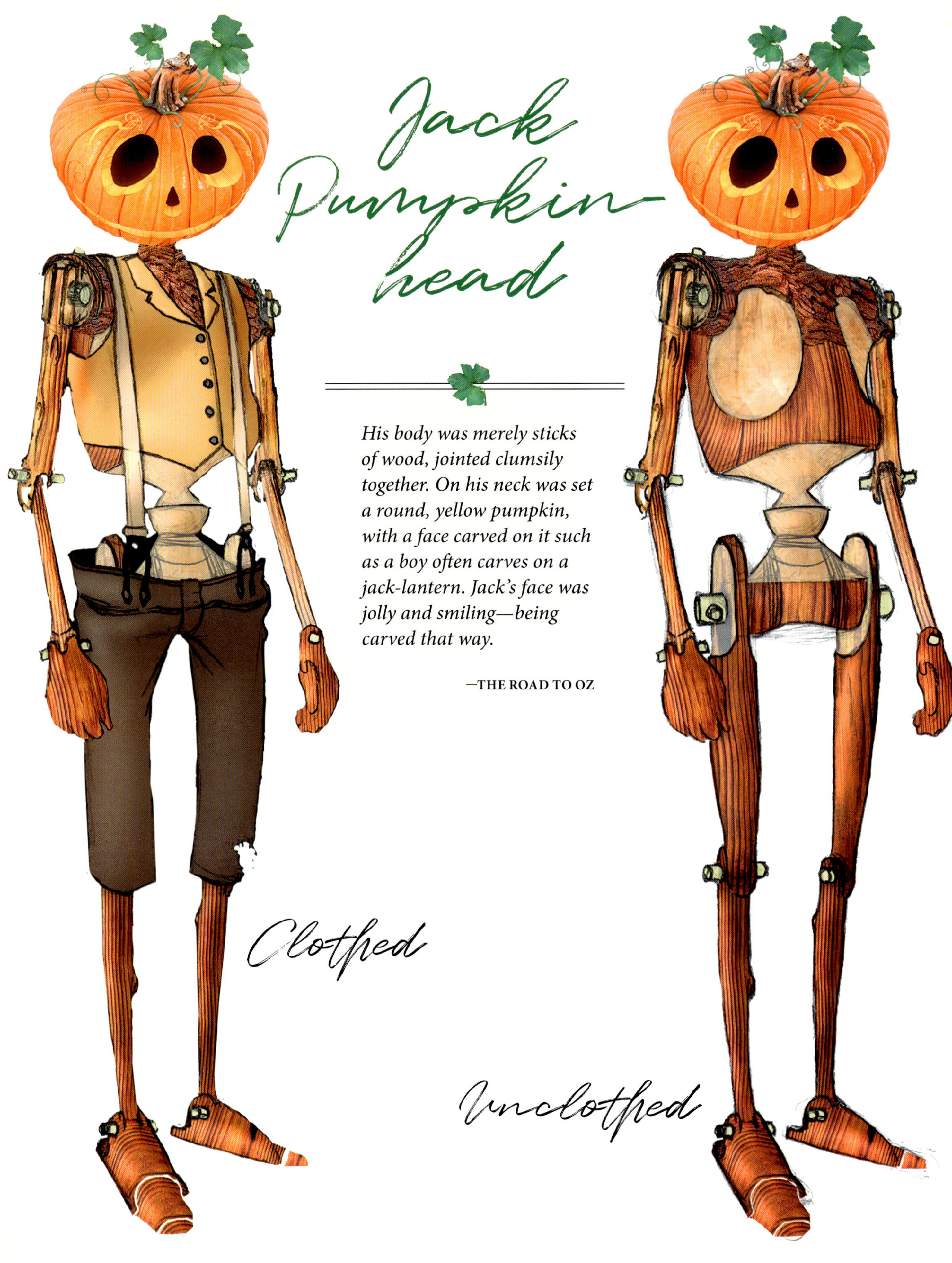

Clothed

Unclothed

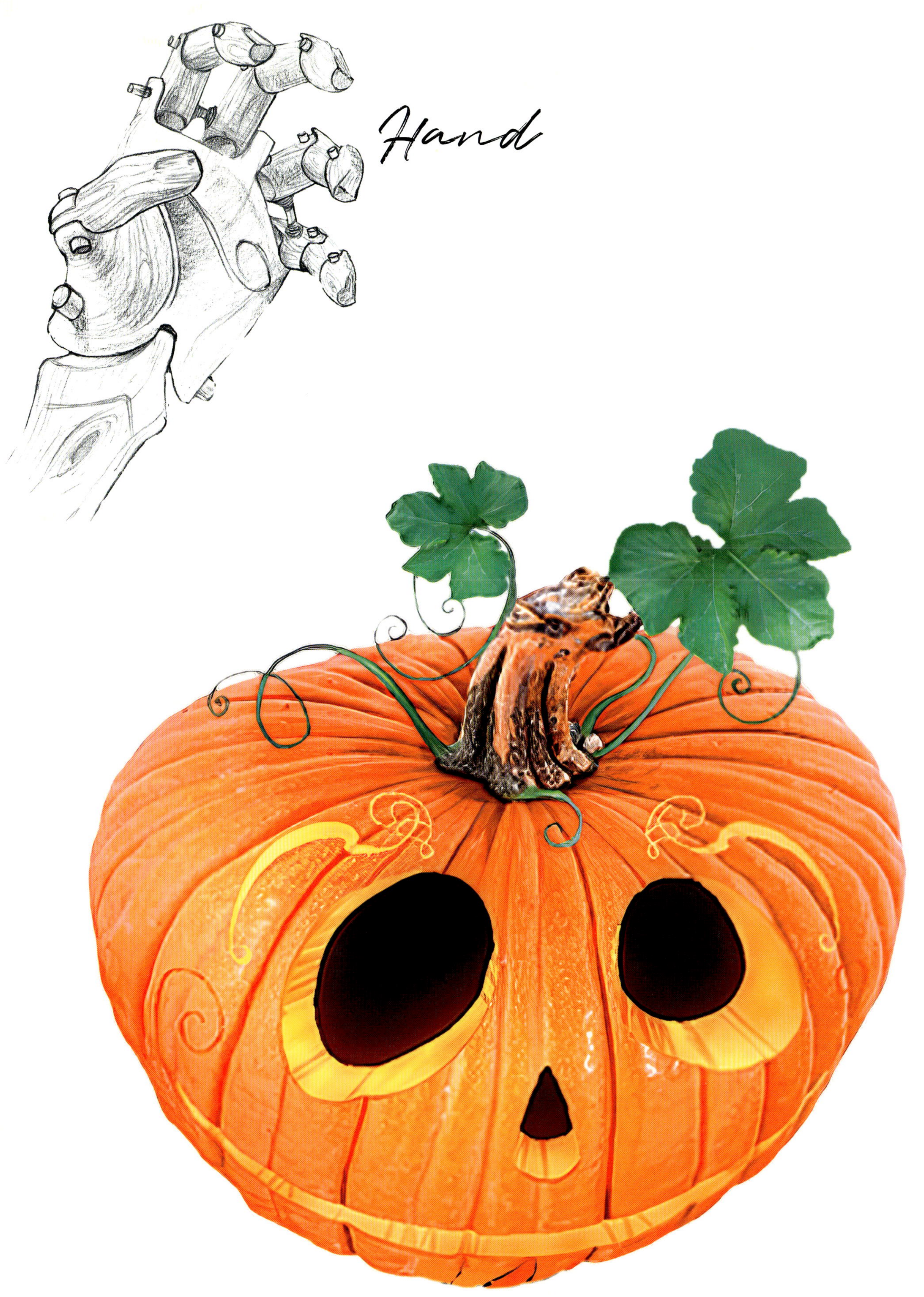
Hand

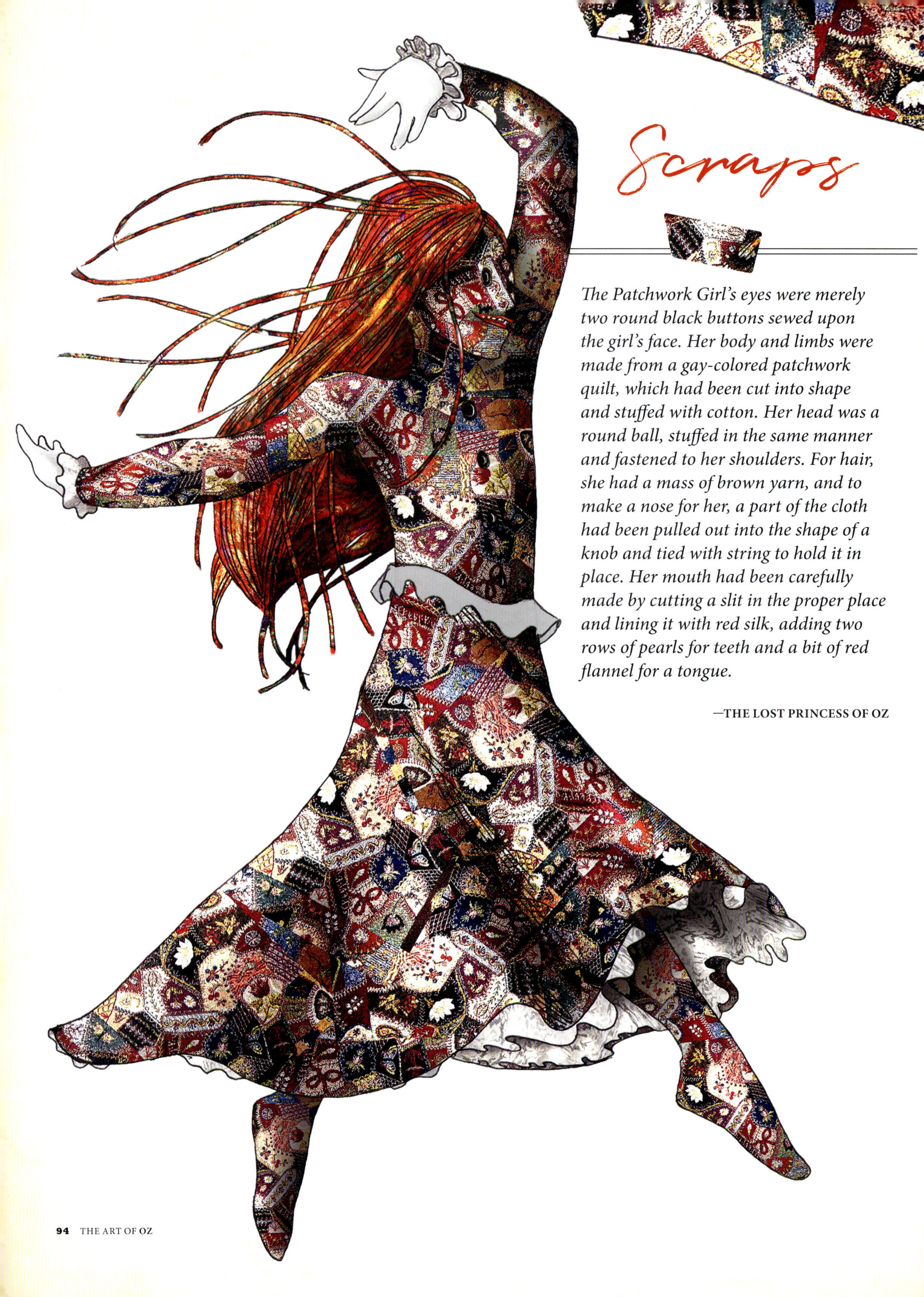

Scraps

The Patchwork Girl's eyes were merely two round black buttons sewed upon the girl's face. Her body and limbs were made from a gay-colored patchwork quilt, which had been cut into shape and stuffed with cotton. Her head was a round ball, stuffed in the same manner and fastened to her shoulders. For hair, she had a mass of brown yarn, and to make a nose for her, a part of the cloth had been pulled out into the shape of a knob and tied with string to hold it in place. Her mouth had been carefully made by cutting a slit in the proper place and lining it with red silk, adding two rows of pearls for teeth and a bit of red flannel for a tongue.

—THE LOST PRINCESS OF OZ

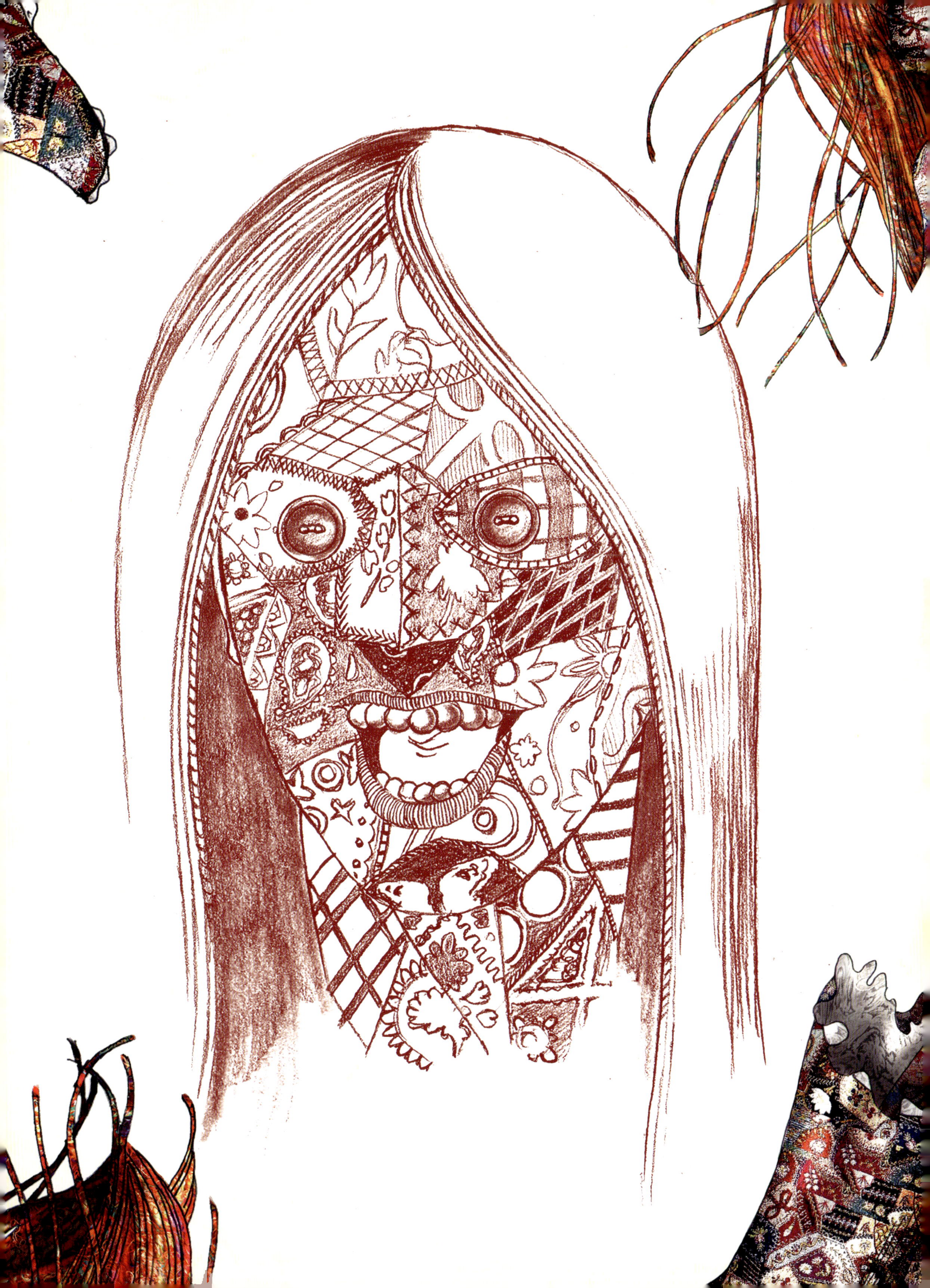

The Mechanicals

INTRODUCED BY THE TIN WOODMAN

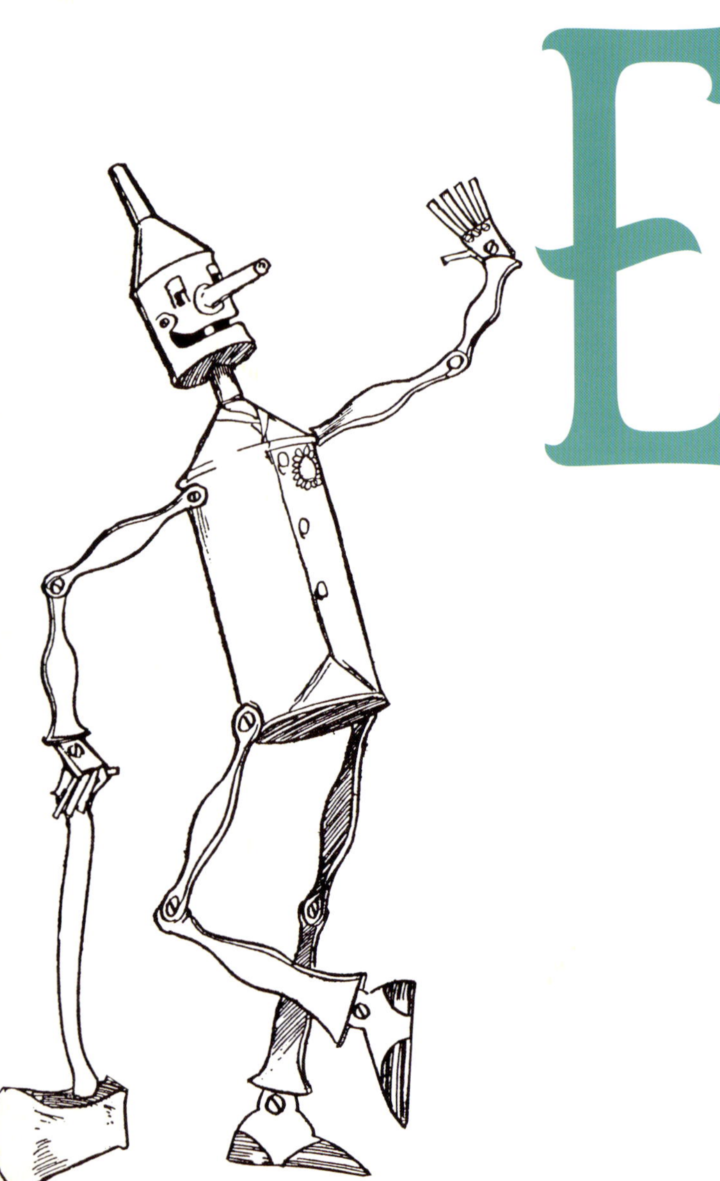

Except for the tender silk heart given to me by the Wonderful Wizard, I am a man made of tin—and the most likely "clinking-and-clattering" candidate to tell you about other mechanical citizens of our fair continent. The difference between these gentlemen and myself is that I was once a human resident of Oz, and you may read in Professor Woggle-Bug's introduction to this book about my magic transformation from Munchkin to mechanical. (Since then, of course—and as Mr. Baum once sensitively described it—I have been a soldered but wiser man.)

Of the eight mechanicals we'll consider, two are well-known: Tik-Tok the Clockwork Man and the Iron Giant—more familiarly known as the Giant with the Hammer. What is remarkable is that all eight were created by the same extraordinary technologists, Smith & Tinker of the Land of Ev. I want to express my thanks to Tik-Tok for sharing the stories of their innovations and especially the personal saga of such imaginative inventors; as he agrees, recognition for Smith & Tinker is decades overdue. Tik-Tok describes them as "very wonderful"

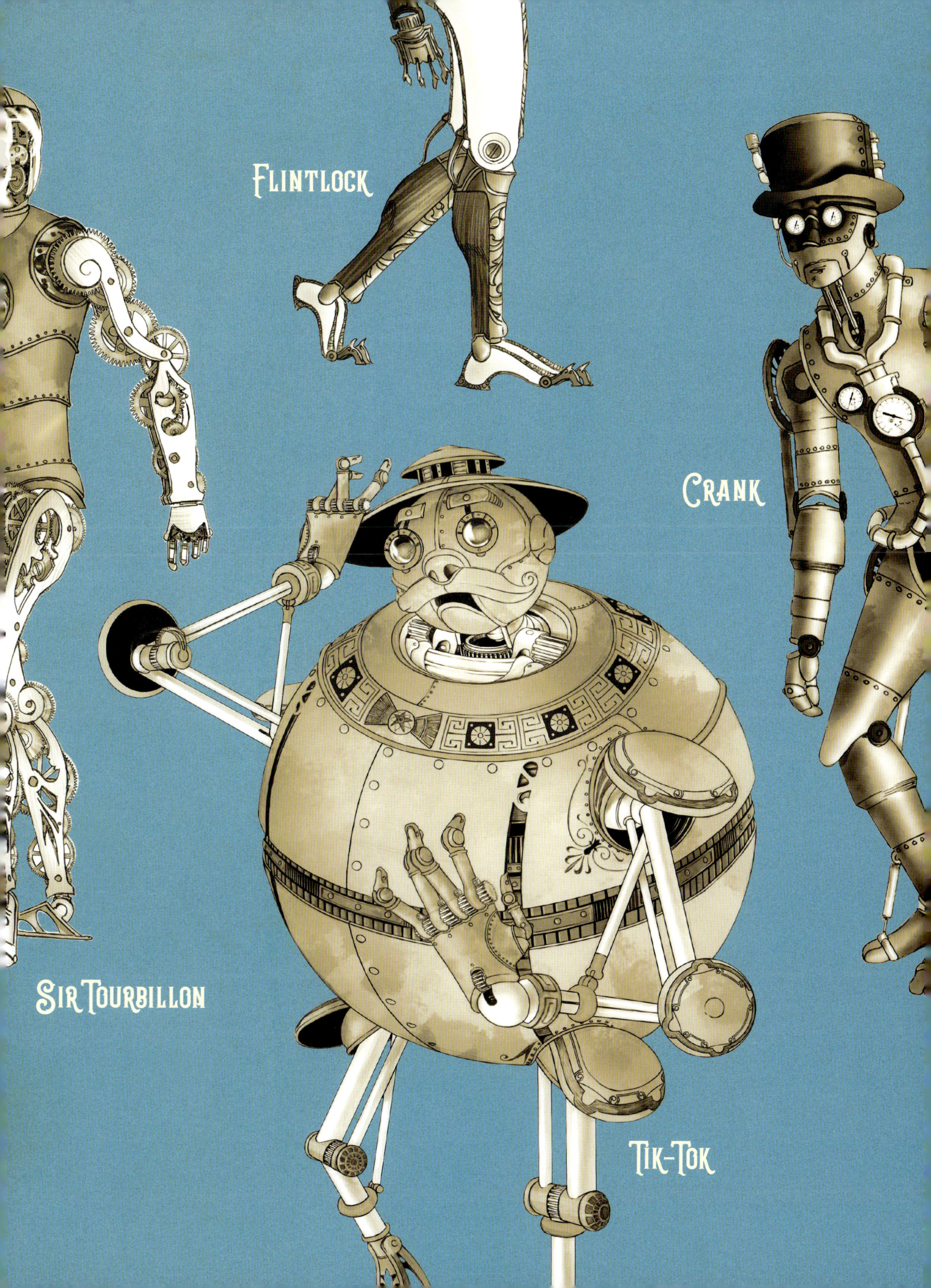
Flintlock
Crank
Sir Tourbillon
Tik-Tok

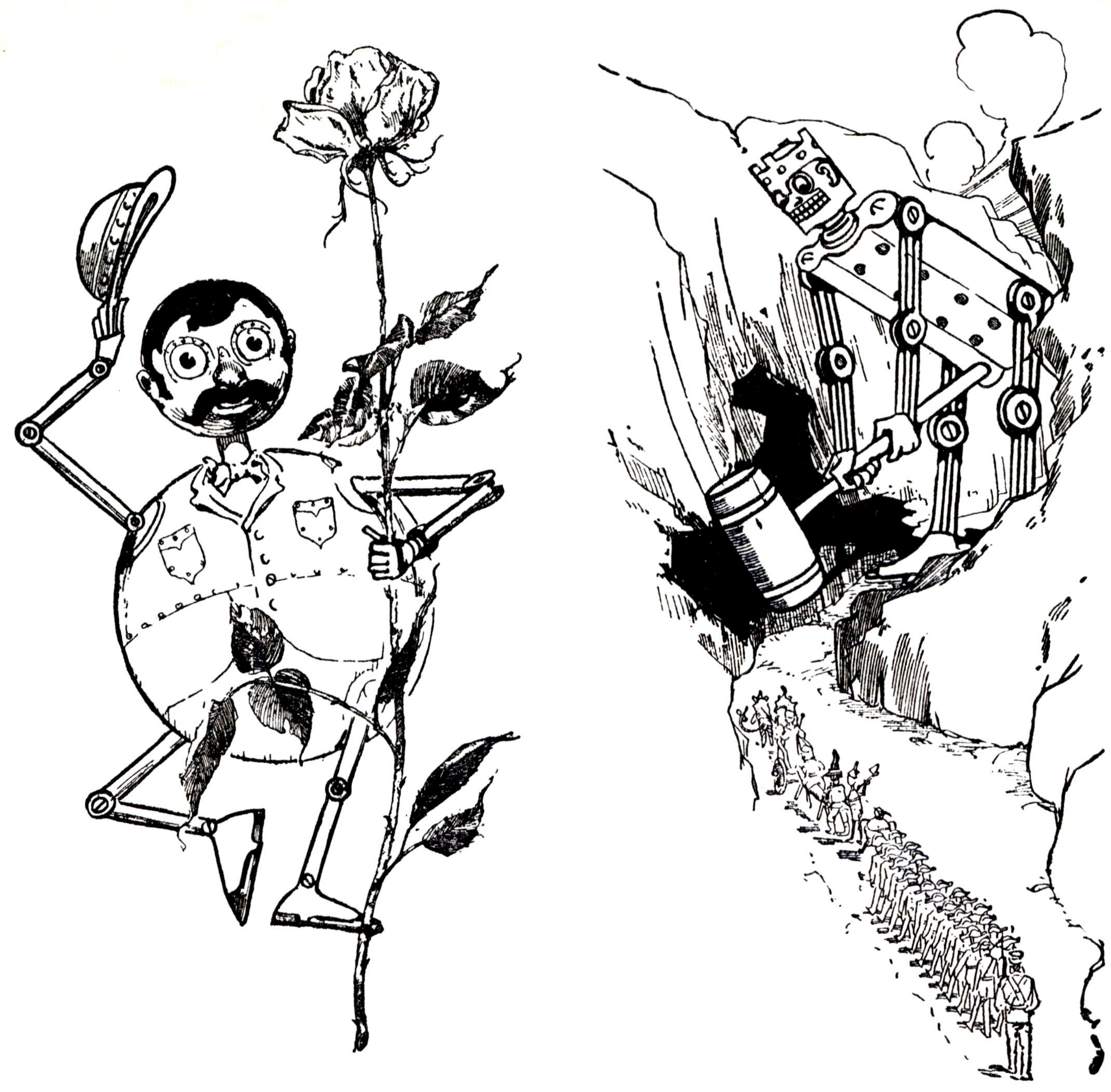

and "quite artistic in all they did," and I'm sure you will agree.

Unfortunately, their ingenious gifts were lost to us early on. Mr. Smith was also an adept illustrator, and as Tik-Tok relates, he once painted a picture of a river "which was so natural that, as he was reaching across it to paint some flowers on the opposite bank, he fell into the water and was drowned." (It is my heartfelt hope that Mr. Smith is now living at the bottom of that river and just too happy there to swim out.) Mr. Tinker used his astonishing gift for construction to build a ladder so long that he could rest one end of it against the moon. When he climbed to the highest rung, he found the moon so lovely that he decided to stay, "pulled up the ladder after him," and never returned!

Luckily, Smith & Tinker gave us Tik-Tok before they departed. Entirely composed of copper, his durable body encases a wondrous array of cogs and wheels. There is a key that hangs on a copper peg on his back, and Tik-Tok's inner mechanisms work like an old-fashioned clock: he can do whatever he is wound up to do. He was first discovered by little Dorothy and has been

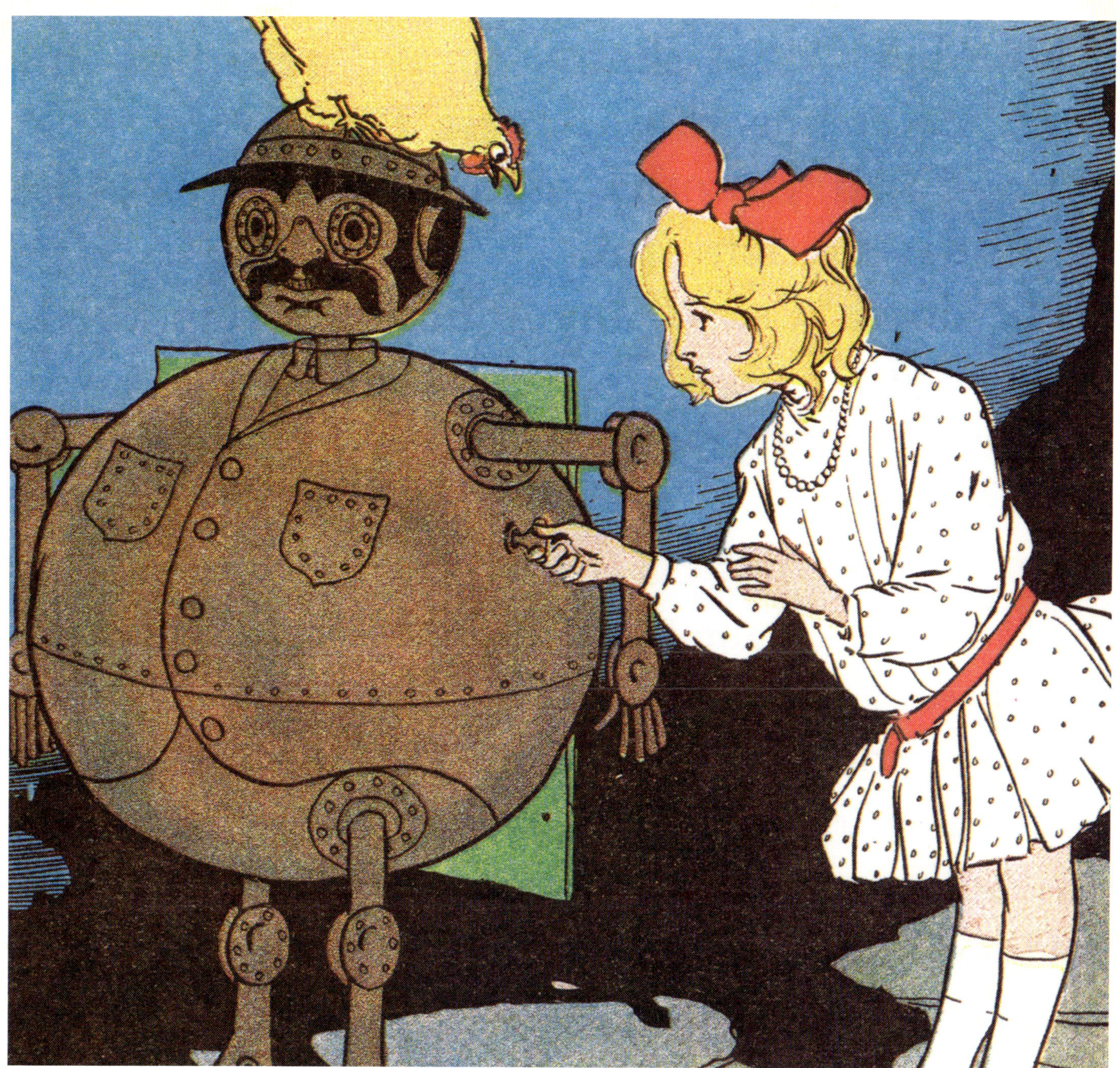

a valuable comrade to her, and to all of us, on many occasions.

Another awe-inspiring Smith & Tinker mechanical is their Iron Giant. This enormous machine, built of cast iron, stands near the entrance to the Nome Kingdom. In his hands, he holds a huge mallet with which he used to automatically and ceaselessly pound the center of the road, making it impossible for anyone to pass by to reach the Nome King's country. The Giant was a frightening barrier, to be sure, although the wise Scarecrow once thought of a way to thwart him: he and his

PAGE 96: The Tin Woodman by Neill, *The Tin Woodman of Oz*
OPPOSITE LEFT: Tik-Tok, the Clockwork Man by Neill, *Tik-Tok of Oz*
OPPOSITE RIGHT: The Giant with the Hammer blocks passage to the Nome Kingdom. Art by Neill, *Ozma of Oz*.
ABOVE: Dorothy discovers and winds Tik-Tok; Billina the Hen looks on. Art by Neill, *Ozma of Oz*.

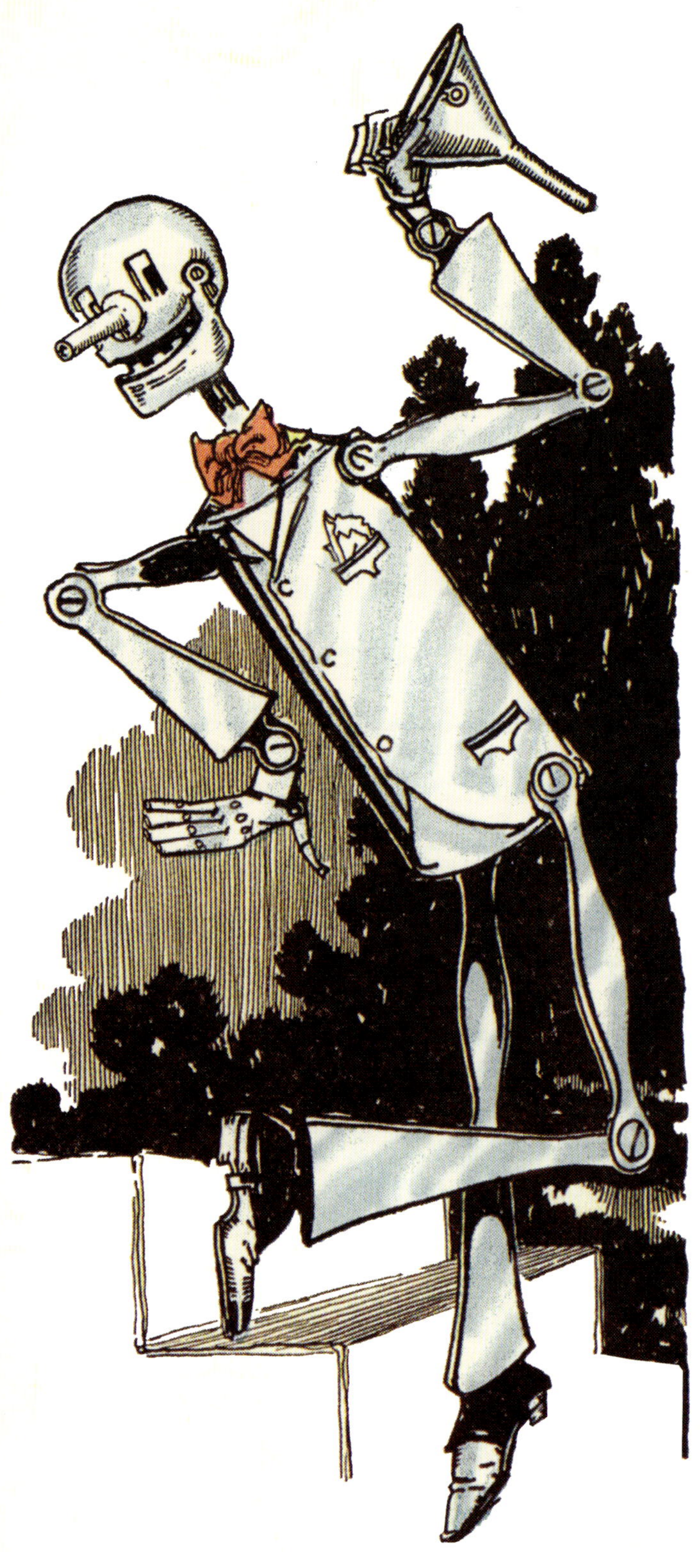

friends simply ran past, in between the blows of the hammer as it was hitting the ground! Later on, Dorothy used a magic belt to make the Giant pause and remain motionless with his weapon in the air; he now appears to be a gargantuan statue to anyone who dares to visit the Nomes.

Finally, Smith & Tinker experimented with six additional machine-driven versions of men, each automated by a different power source—and long before such things were imagined in the Great Outside World. These new concepts enabled the designers to work with steam, gunpowder, electricity, expanding bolts, and sophisticated clockwork instruments beyond those placed inside Tik-Tok. The inventors gave each creation a distinctive name as well, and Gabriel Gale has provided portraits of them in this chapter.

As Tik-Tok admits, however, he is the only automatic mechanical man that Smith & Tinker are known to have completed before they left us. (The Giant with a Hammer had no brains and was produced to simply pound and provide a roadblock, while the histories of the supplementary assemblages mentioned previously have yet to be learned.) Meanwhile, Tik-Tok remains proud of his heritage and once declared, "You have no idea how full of machinery I am." This is not a boast about himself or the others, but rather his tribute to the unique Smith & Tinker.

I hereby take off my funnel hat and bow to all of these mechanicals—to Smith and Tinker!—and to all of you!

Cross my heart.

ABOVE: Art by Neill, *The Patchwork Girl of Oz*
OPPOSITE: Tik-Tok once visited the Nome Kingdom to find replacements for some of his worn machinery. He was welcomed by Kaliko, the Chief Steward, but the evil Nome King was in a bad mood that day and destroyed Tik-Tok in anger. Fortunately, clever Kaliko secretly reassembled him, replacing any damaged parts. When Tik-Tok next met the King, the Nome was terrified; he thought Tik-Tok was a ghost! (The Clockwork Man's abundance of machinery is most evident in these pictures.) Art by Neill, *Little Wizard Storis of Oz.*

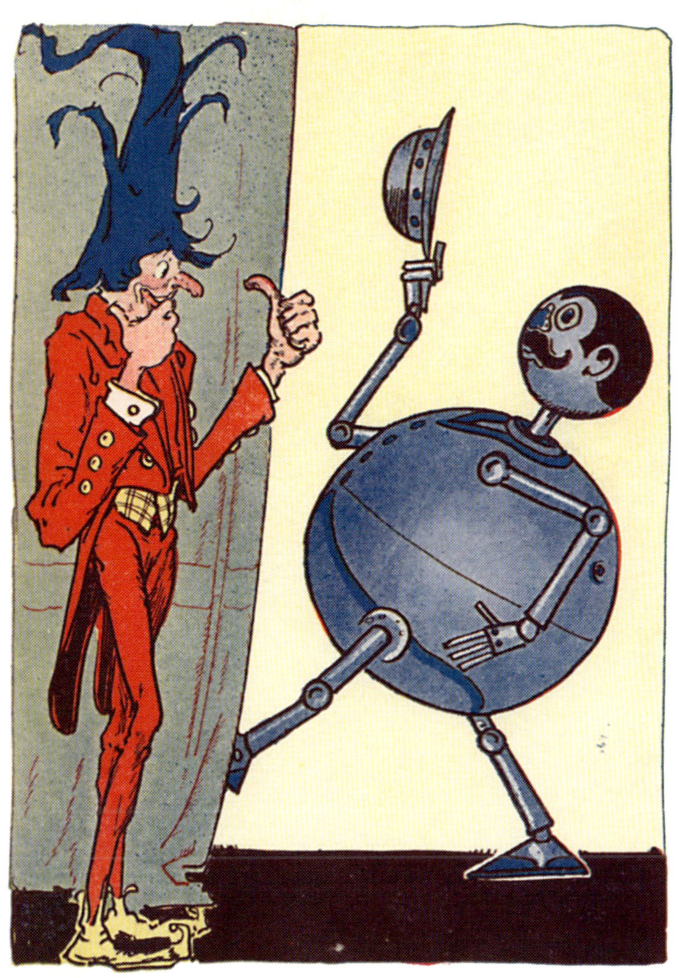
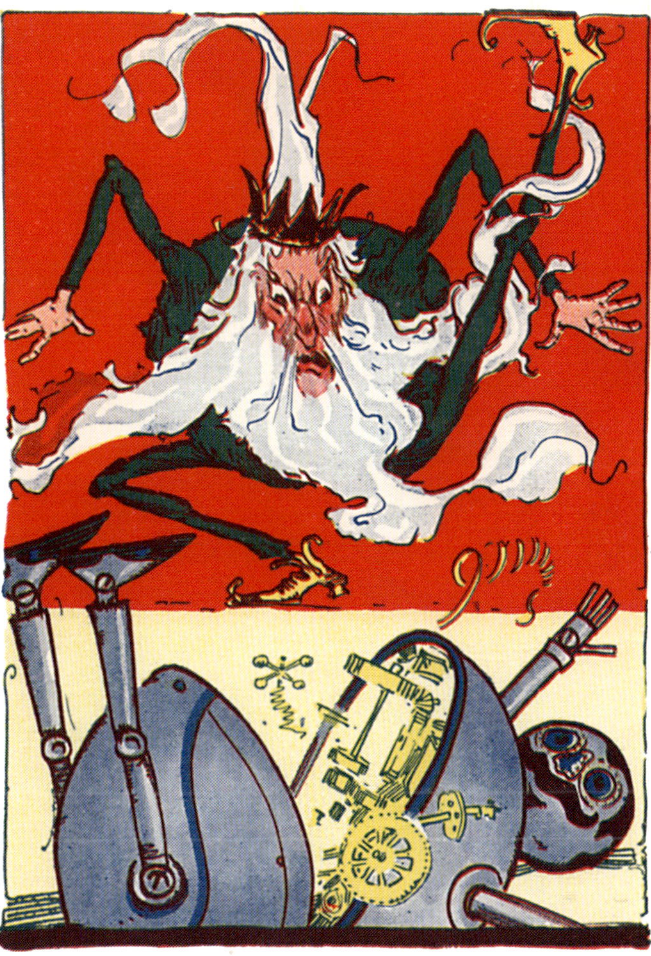
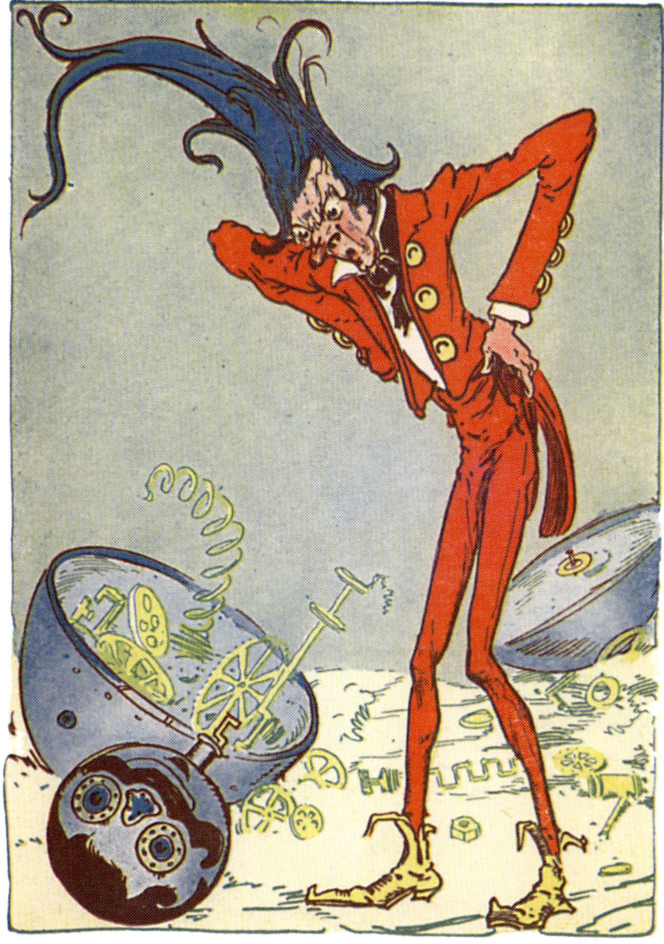
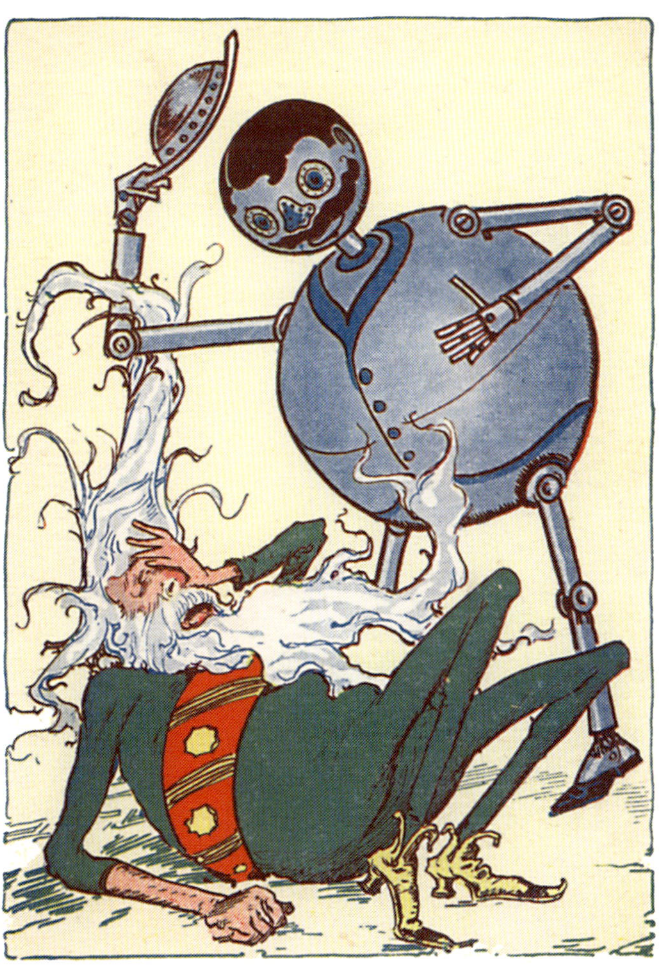

Tik-Tok

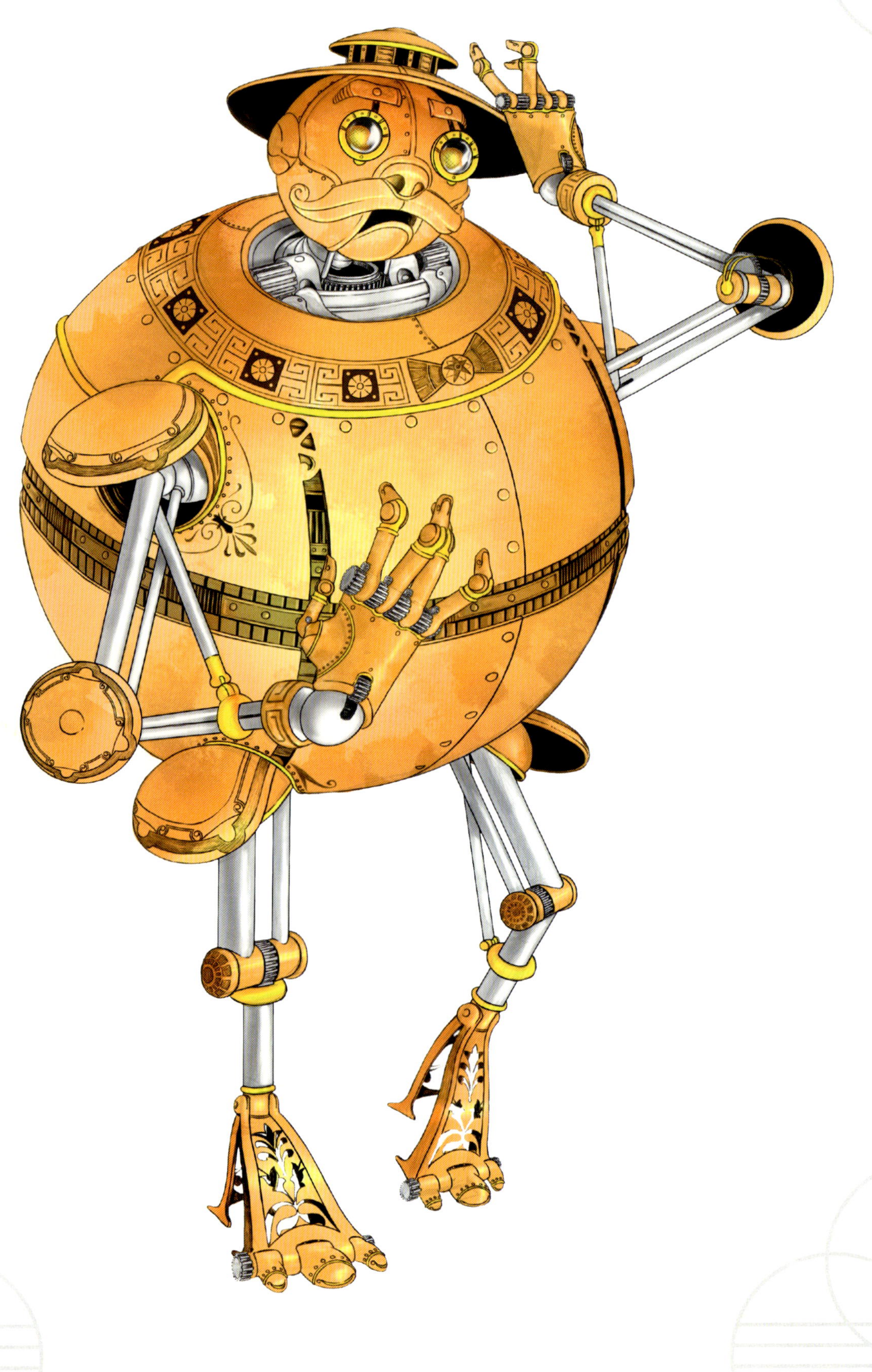

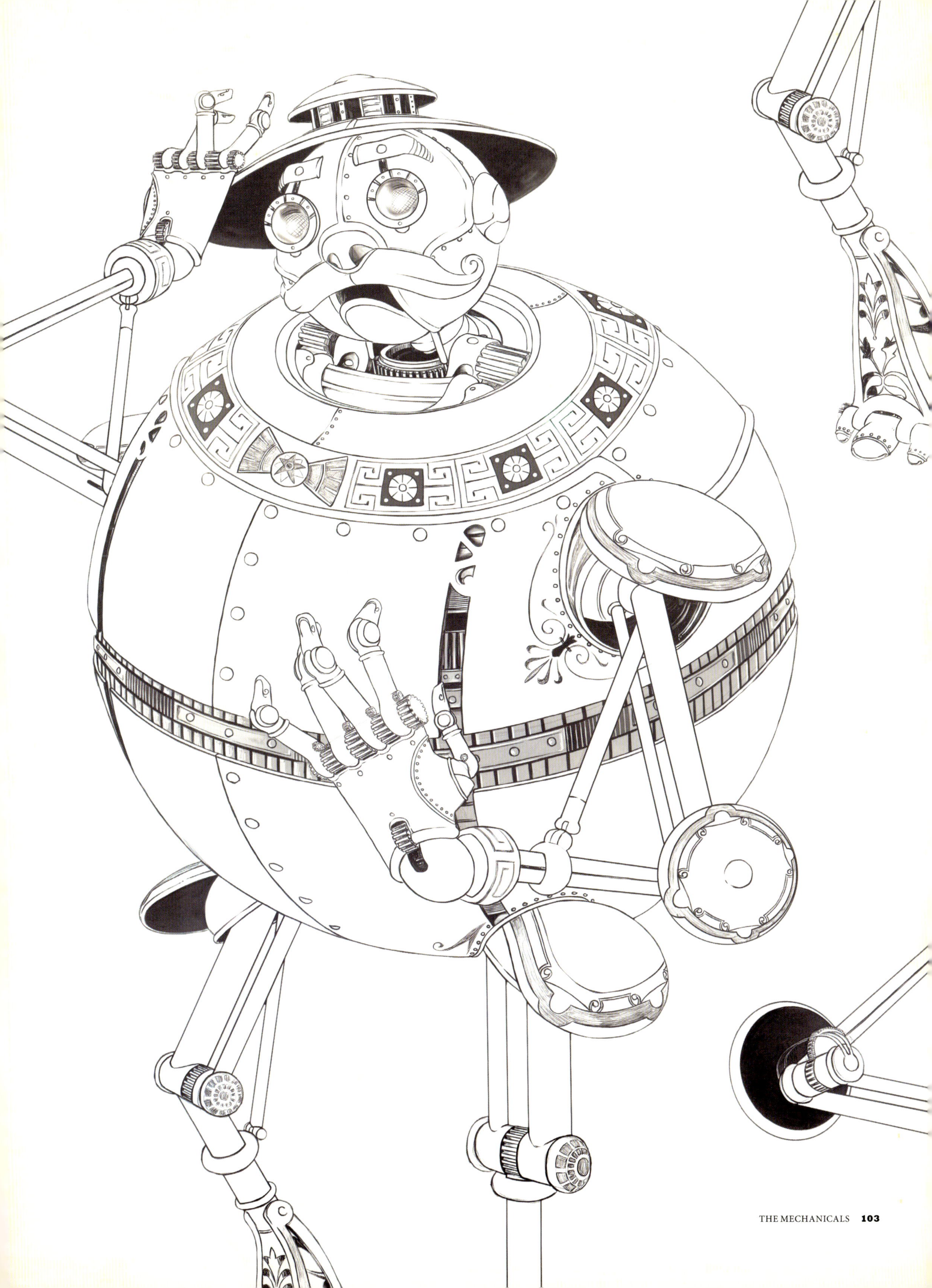

Windmill Giant

The Windmill Giant was created by Smith & Tinker as a possible foil for the Iron Giant.

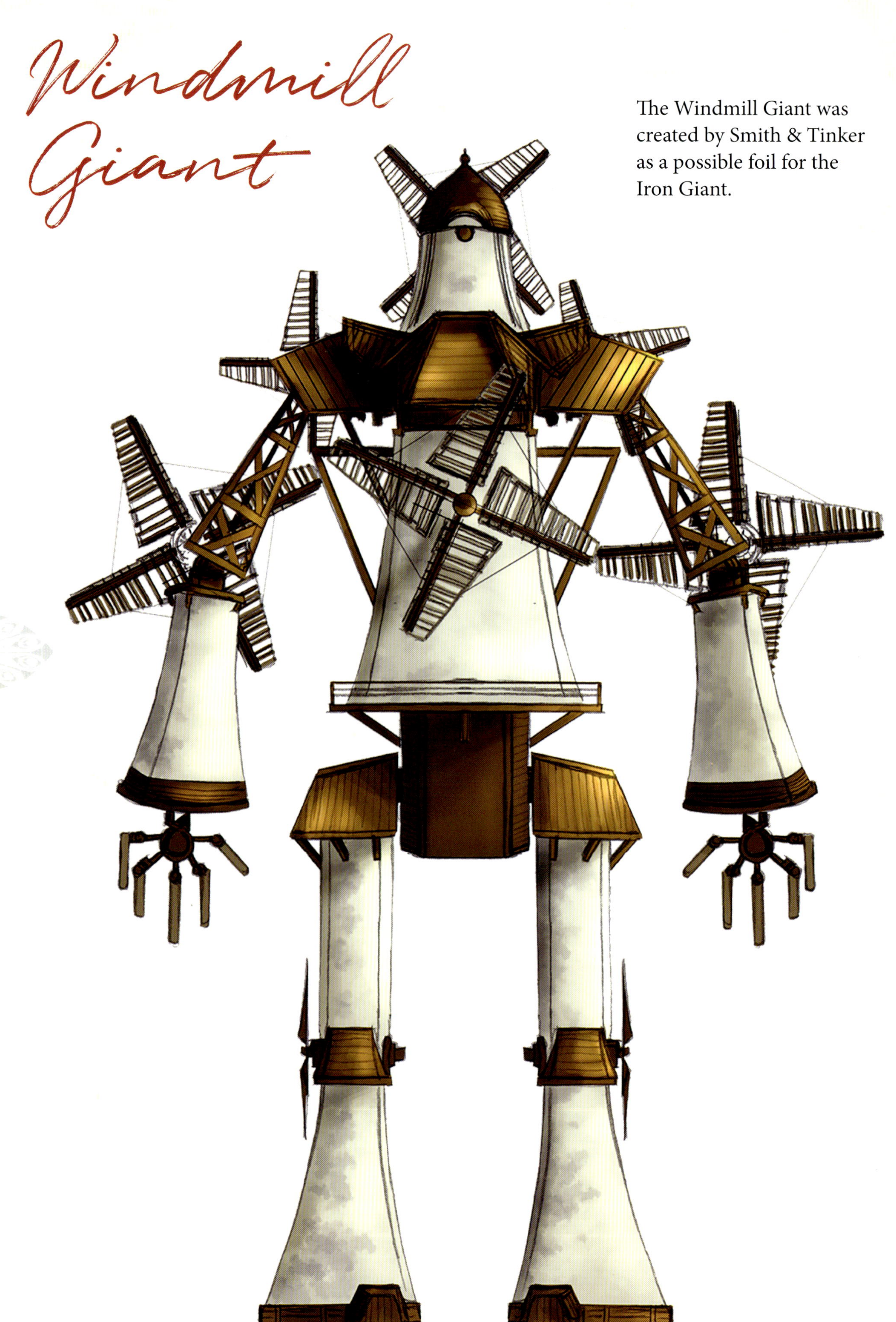

Breech

Breech is considered a bolt-action device. His knobs may be turned to extend or lengthen his neck, arms, or legs in an "expanding bolt" fashion, and this gives him the ability to see above and beyond, to reach out at length, or to move forward with greater strides.

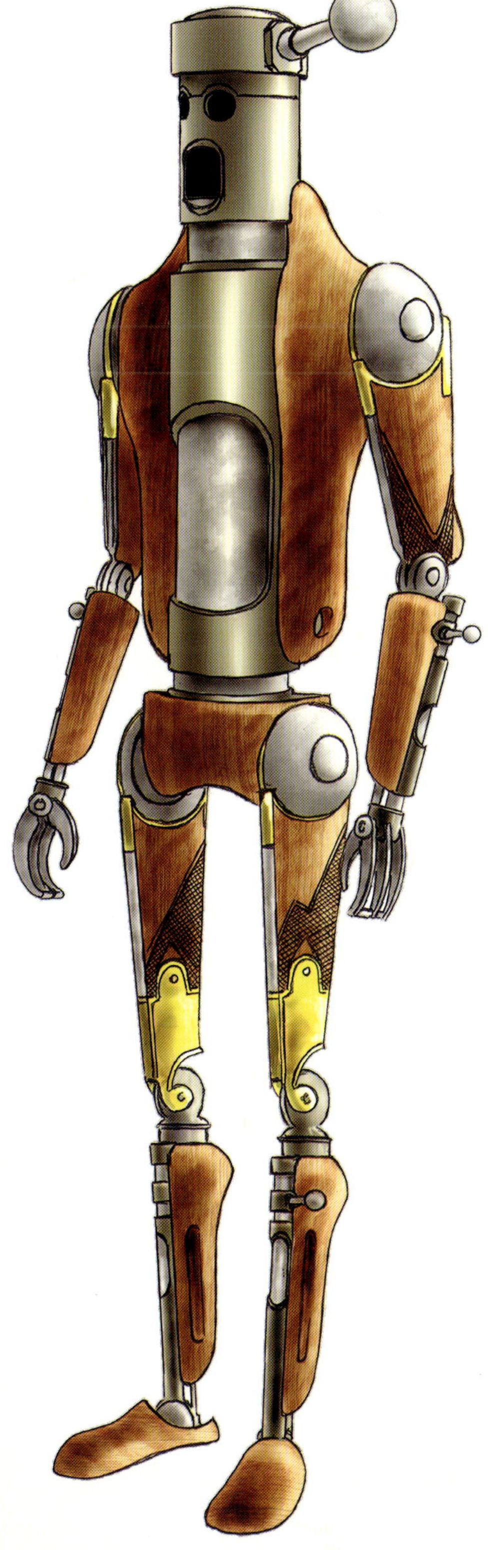

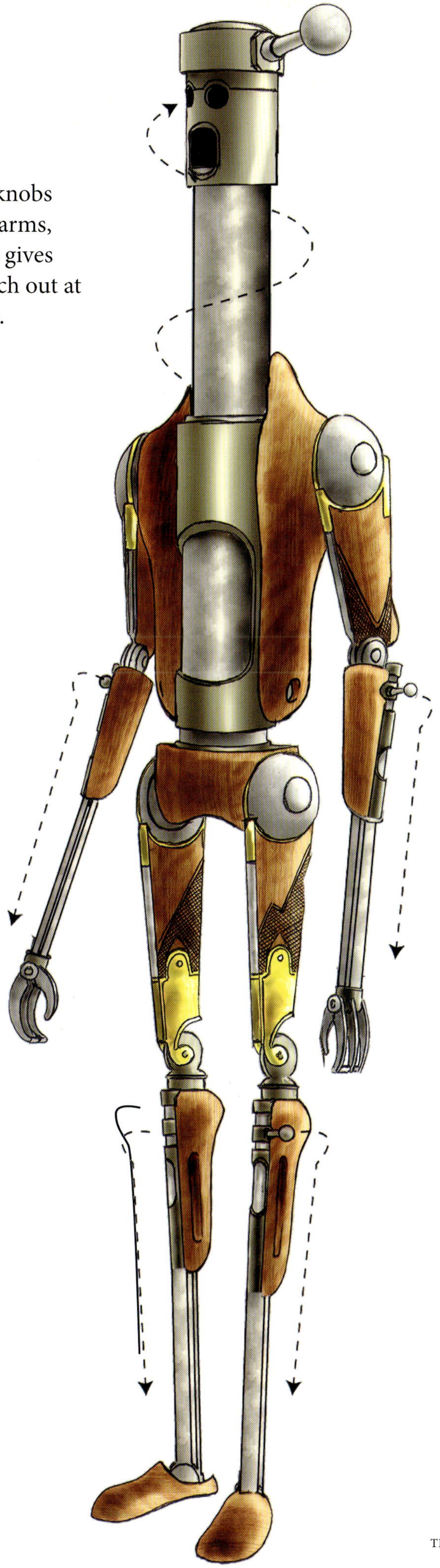

Crank

An interior furnace provides Crank with all the motivating force he requires; he is steam propelled.

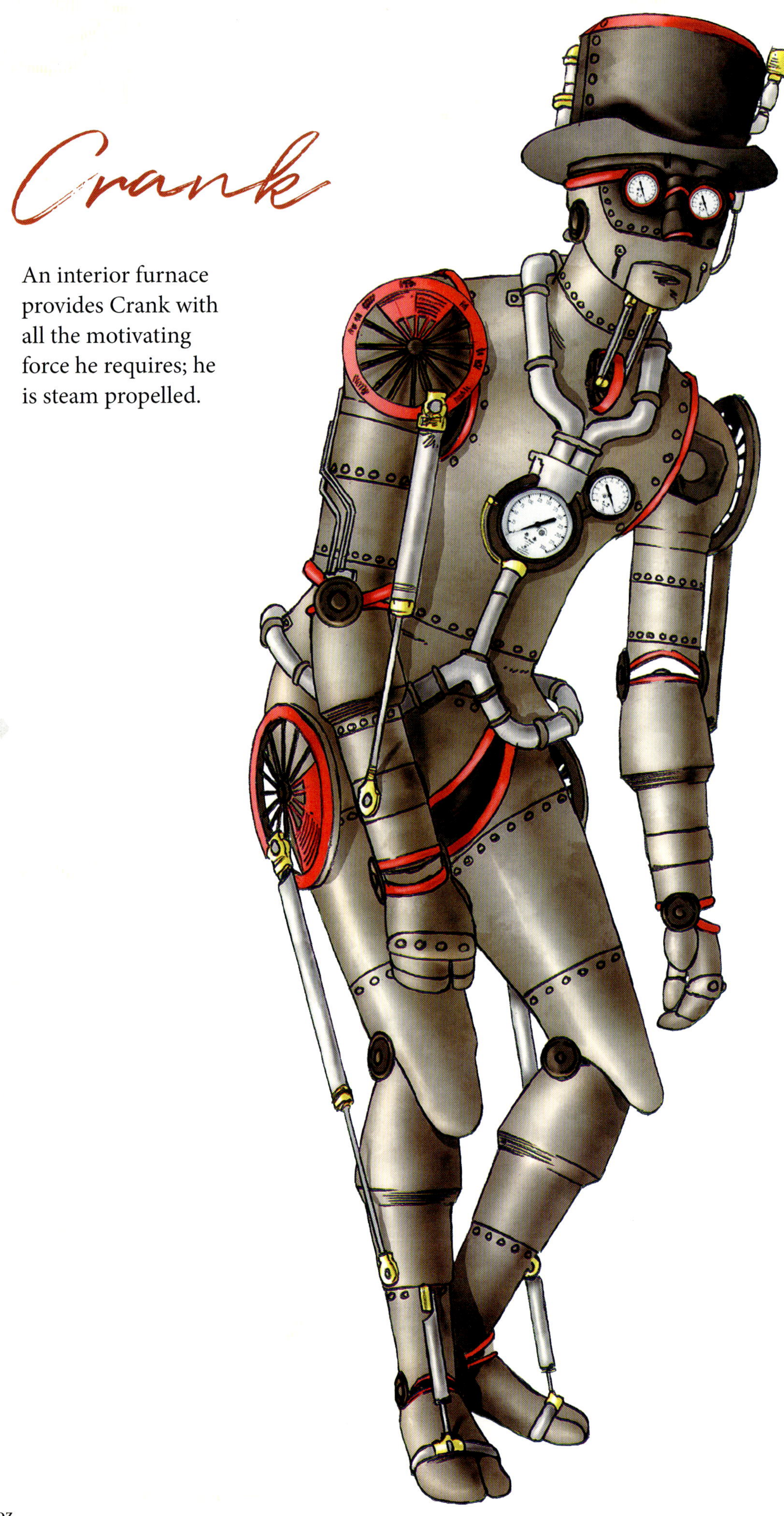

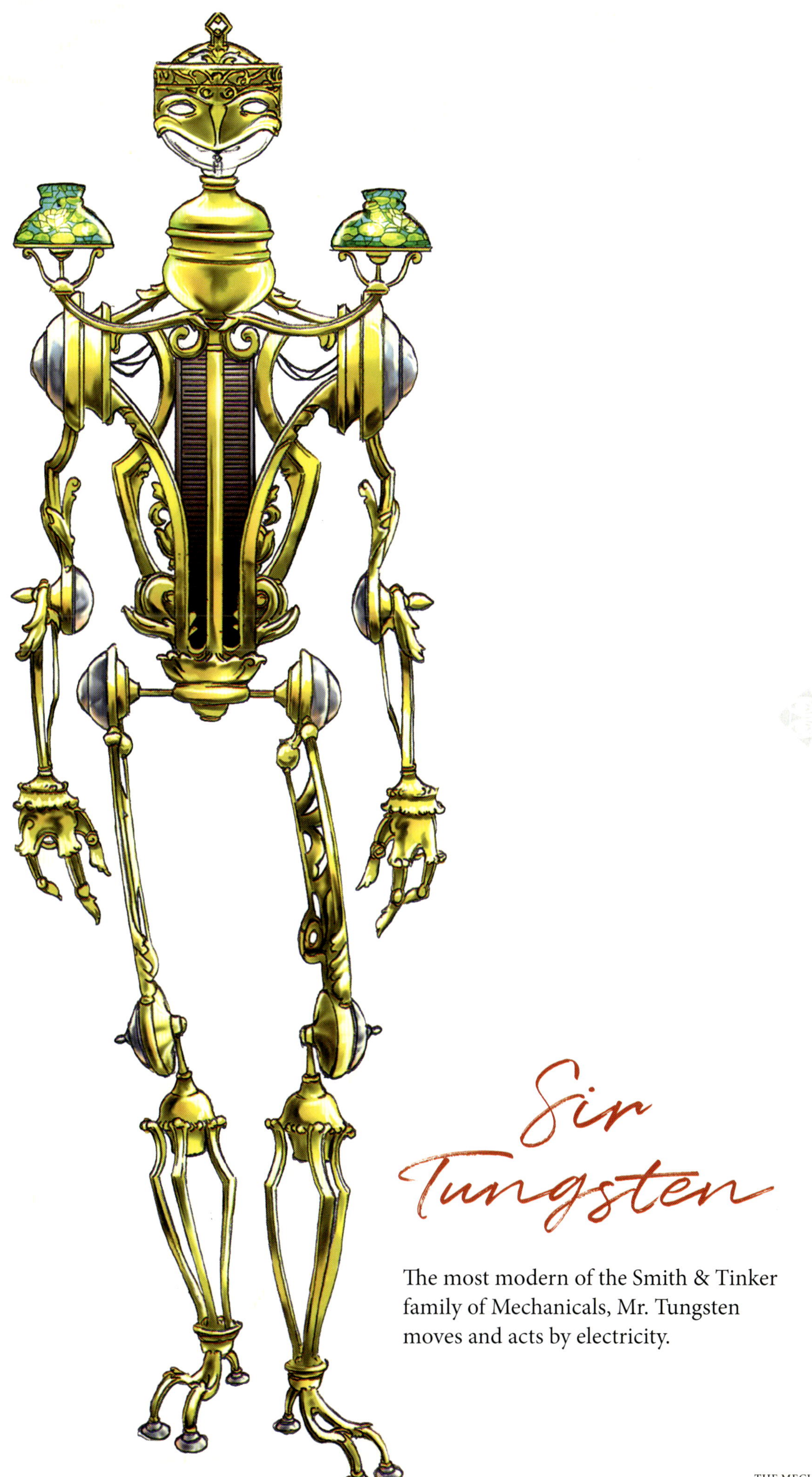

Sir Tungsten

The most modern of the Smith & Tinker family of Mechanicals, Mr. Tungsten moves and acts by electricity.

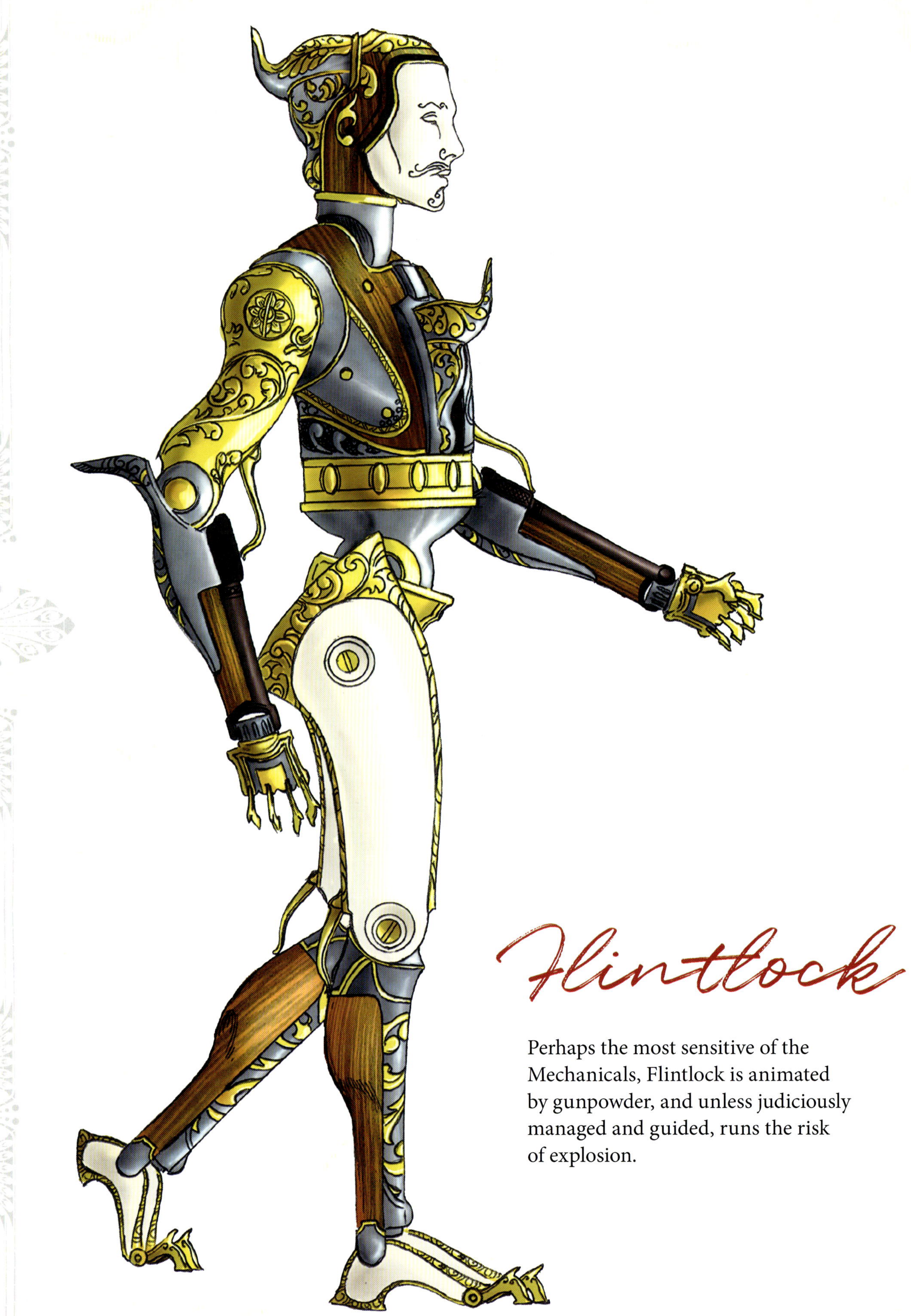

Flintlock

Perhaps the most sensitive of the Mechanicals, Flintlock is animated by gunpowder, and unless judiciously managed and guided, runs the risk of explosion.

Sir Tourbillon

Like Tik-Tok before him, Sir Tourbillon is a clockwork man but created from a more contemporary point of view. He is sleeker, more physically manlike in appearance—and always on time.

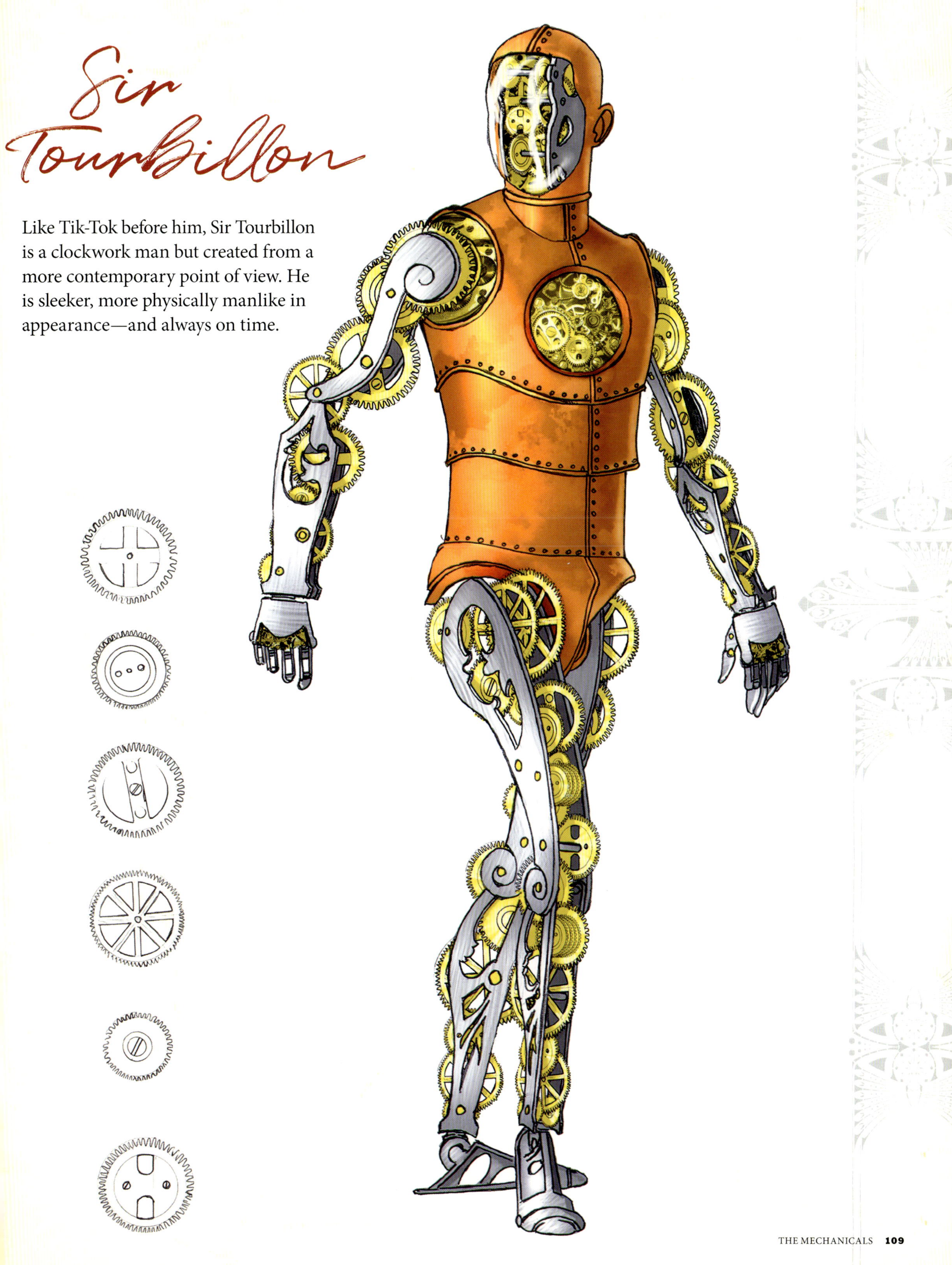

Iron Giant

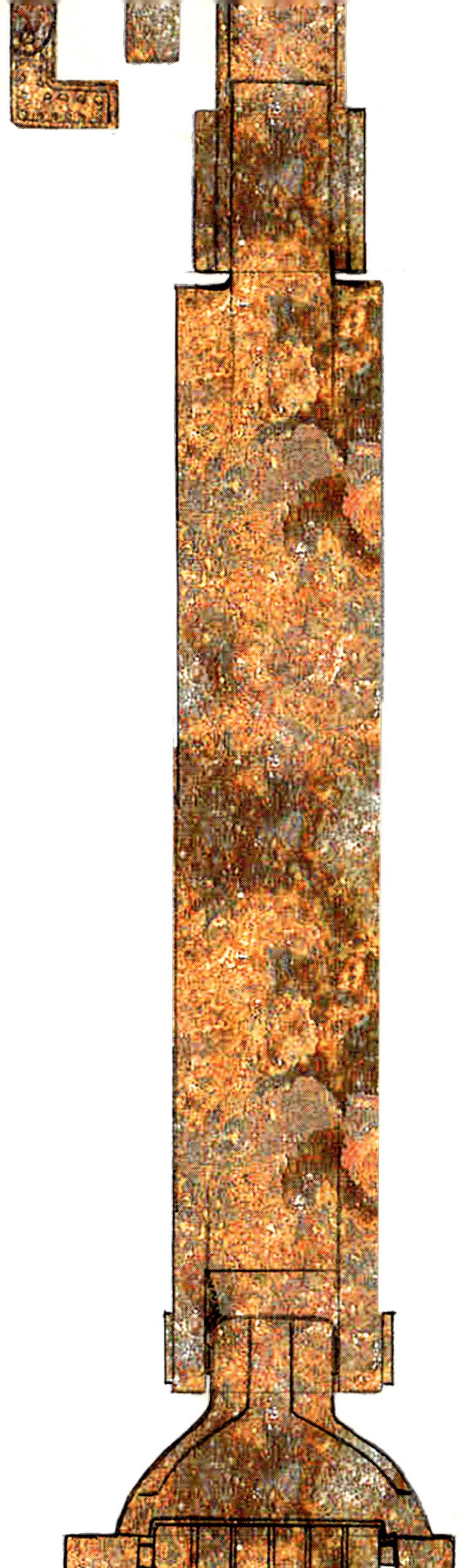

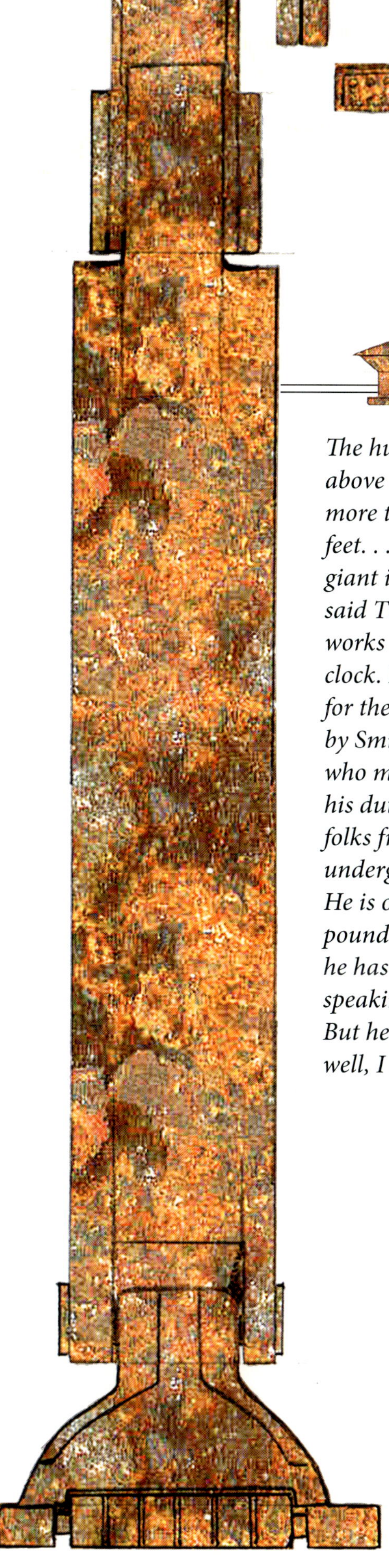

The huge man towered above the path for more than a hundred feet. . . . "The iron giant is a fine fellow," said Tik-Tok, "and works as steadily as a clock. He was made for the Nome King by Smith & Tinker, who made me, and his duty is to keep folks from finding the underground palace. He is only made to pound the road, and he has no thinking or speaking attachment. But he pounds very well, I think."

—OZMA OF OZ

The Ethereals

INTRODUCED BY GLINDA THE GOOD

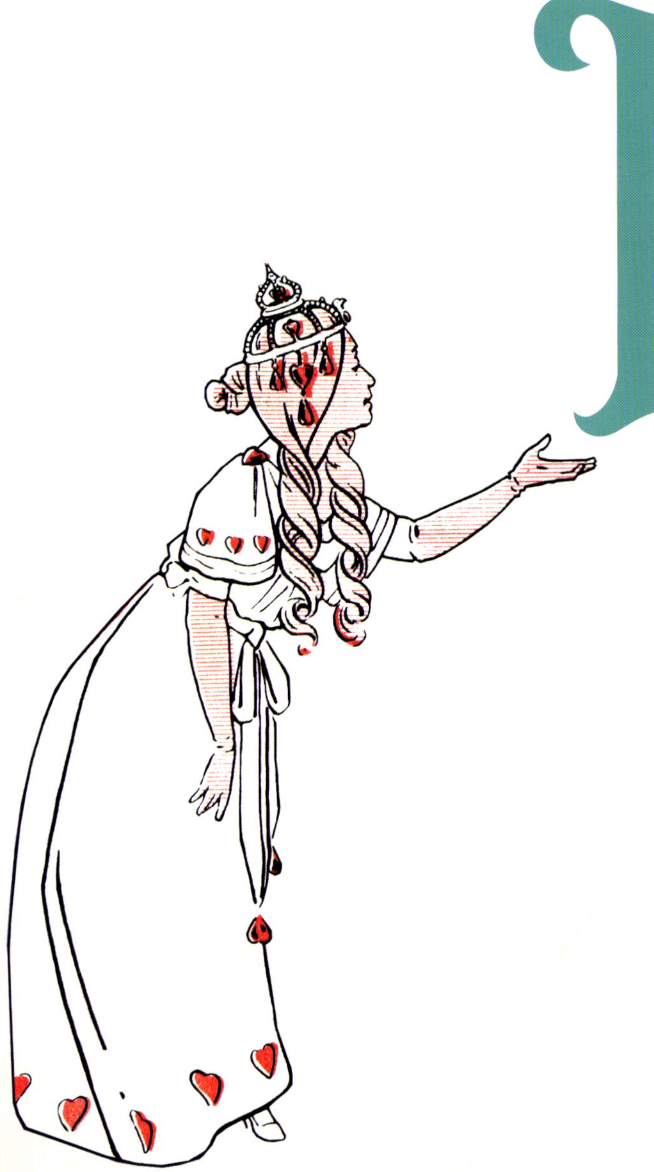

It has been observed that "people come and go so quickly here" in Oz, and this is especially true of our ethereals—the magically empowered residents of the land. Whether their mysterious arts or benevolent hearts have been used for good or bad, they have made a remarkable and sometimes historical impact on our beloved country. It is safe to say that no deeds have been more beneficial—or more threatening—than those wonders and terrors attempted by the ethereals.

As the Good Witch of the South, my own sorcery is always used to benefit Oz and its people. I learned at age thirteen that this would be my life's work; hundreds of years have since passed, but the pleasure of this privilege has never wavered. There are many others, as well, whose powers for joy are equally valuable in their own way; certainly Polychrome, daughter of the Rainbow, is at the forefront of these. Although her many sisters of the sky are content to remain with their father as he and his colorful arc continually bless the world, Polly occasionally has danced

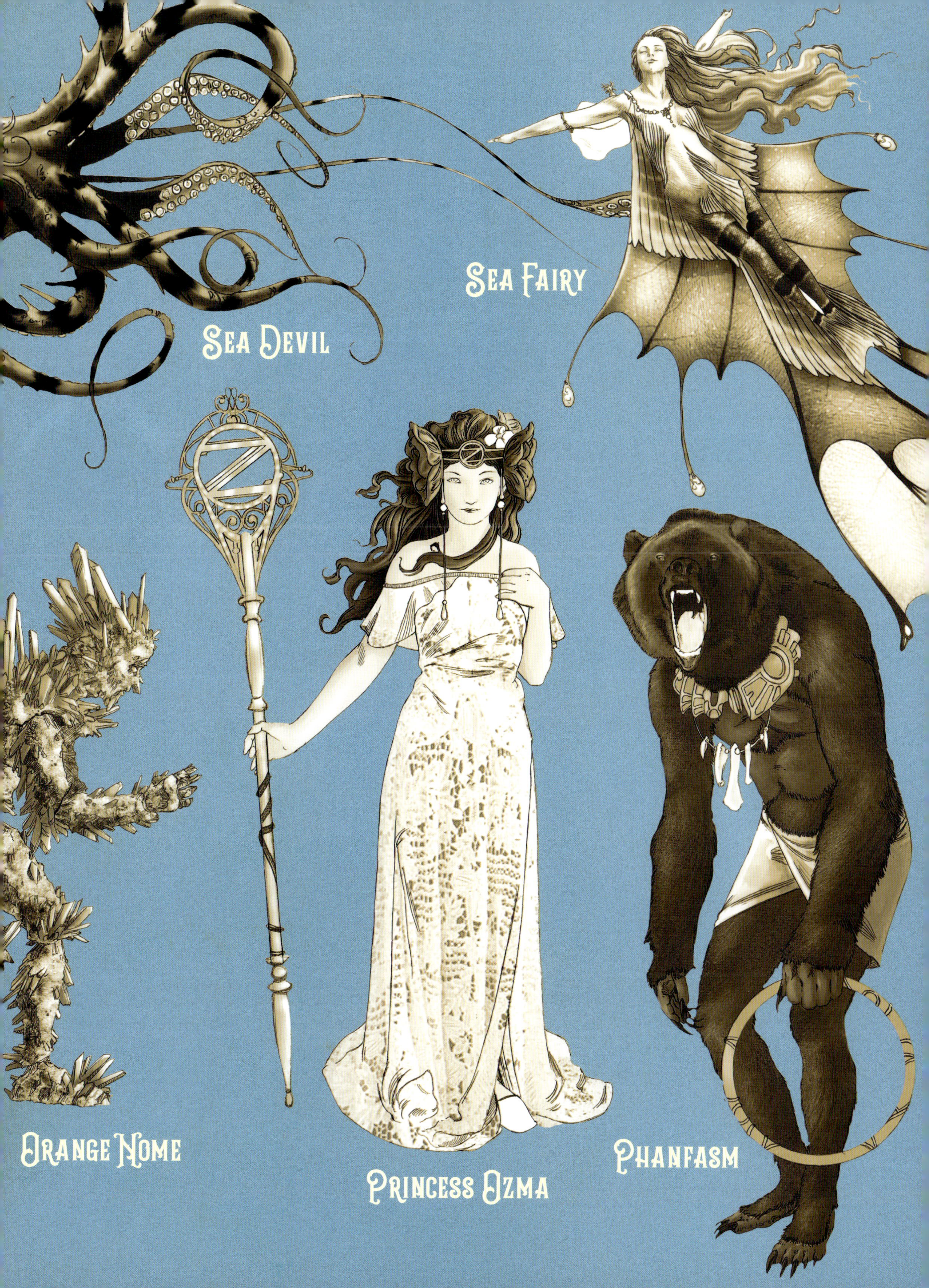
Sea Fairy
Sea Devil
Orange Nome
Princess Ozma
Phanfasm

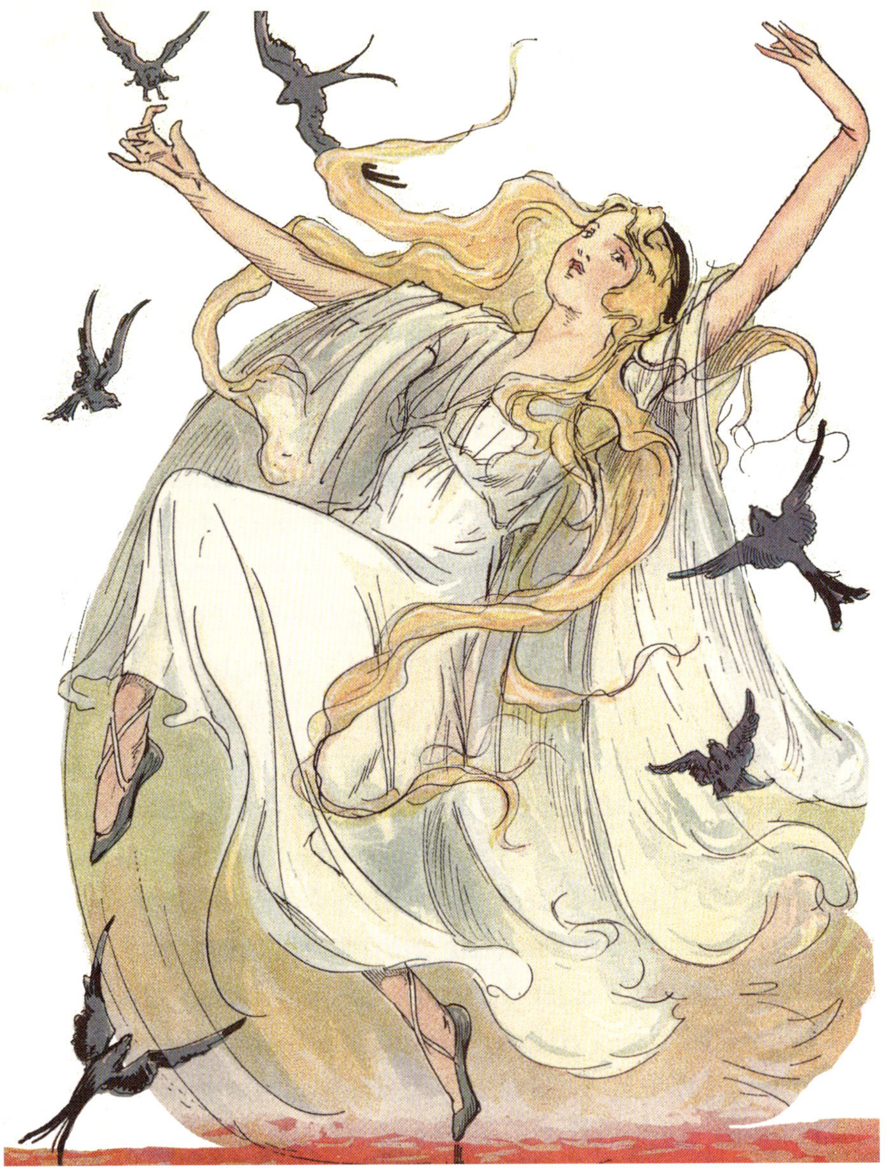

PAGE 112: Glinda the Good by Denslow, *The Wonderful Wizard of Oz*
ABOVE: Polychrome, the Rainbow's Daughter, by Neill, *The Tin Woodman of Oz*
OPPOSITE LEFT: The First and Foremost of the Phanfasms "entertains" General Guph of the Nomes; the eyes of countless invisible Phanfasms look on. Art by Neill, *The Emerald City of Oz*.

off the end of the Rainbow and spent time on earth, sharing splendor and gladness with whomever she meets. Dorothy first introduced her to the Emerald City, and on every subsequent visit, Polychrome has brought the radiance of the Rainbow with her.

Where Polly is of the air and clouds, the Nomes are rock fairies of the underground, and their behavior is a curious mix. They demonstrate amazing ability and agility as they shape-shift and slink through stone—all the while creating the gold, silver, and gems they then hide. (The many precious jewels that have found their way to the Great Outside World are but a tiny percentage of those collected, buried, and protected by their jealous makers.) The Nomes themselves are basically good, industrious individuals, but they are sometimes forced into cruel conduct and war

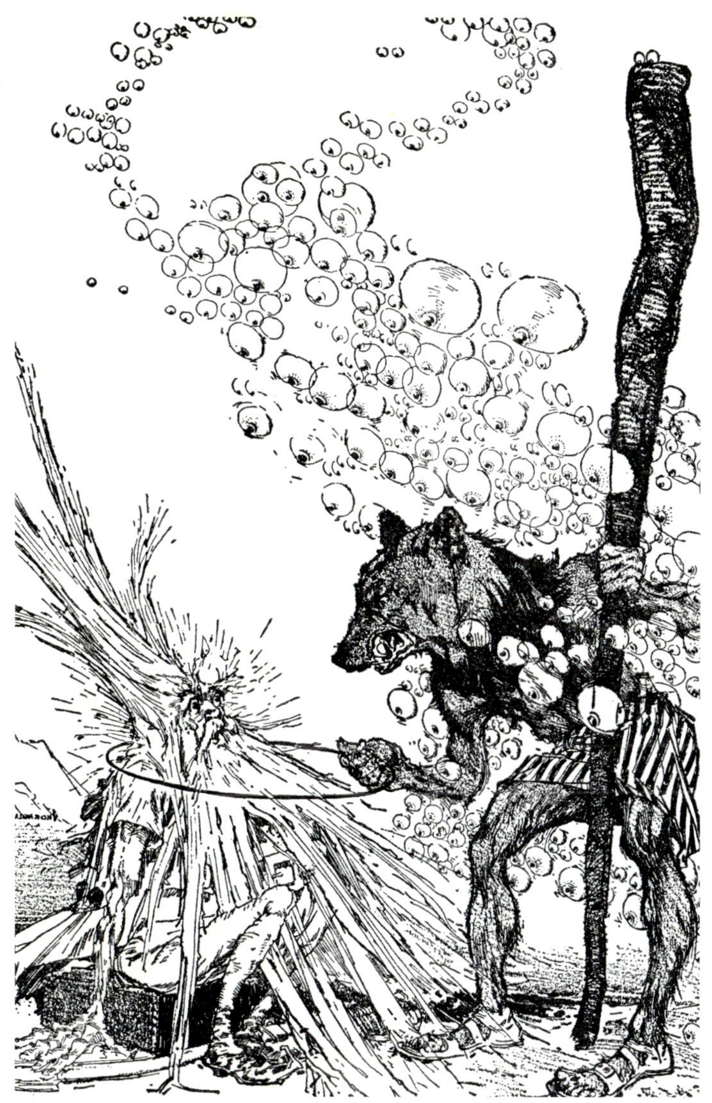

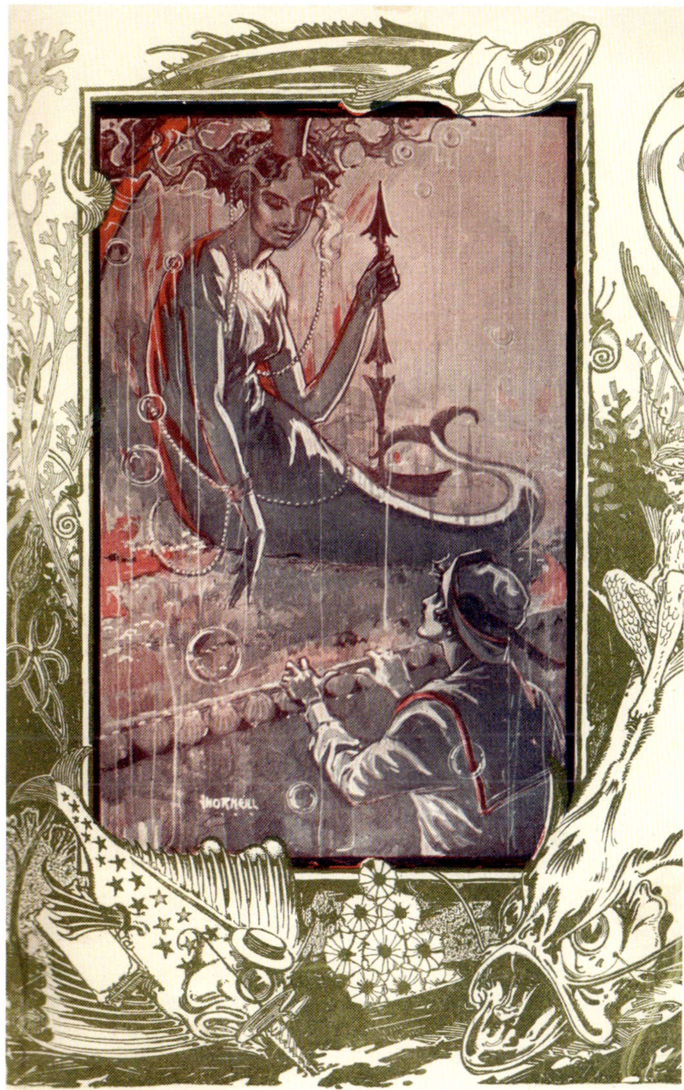

by their greedy and ignorant kings and officials. Ruggedo, a long-term ruler, was ultimately deposed because of his crazed desires for riches and revenge.

Of all the ethereals, however, the Erbs are perhaps the most terrible and unredeemable. This massive mountain band of evildoers includes the Phanfasms and Mimics, whose powers of transformation allow them to take on countless terrifying forms every day. They live only to destroy the happiness of others, and Erb tribes have twice attempted to turn Oz into a wasteland. Only the sharp thinking of the Scarecrow and Dorothy's dog, Toto, saved us on those occasions.

Meanwhile, underwater, few inhabitants are more dangerous than the Sea Devils. These fiends possess the ability to entrap anyone by caging them in their long, "feeler"-like arms; it is wise for undersea travelers to avoid the dismal caverns the Devils call home. Fortunately, their activities these days are much controlled by benevolent Anko, the serpent King of the Ocean, and it is much more pleasant to think instead of his other subjects, the Sea Fairies. The most stunning of these are the Mermaids, and their world is made exquisite by their care for fellow creatures, by the marvels of the ocean-floor palaces they've created, and by their own loveliness of deed, face, and garb.

ABOVE RIGHT: Mermaid Queen Aquareine welcomes young Trot from California to her undersea realm. Art by Neill, *The Sea Fairies*.

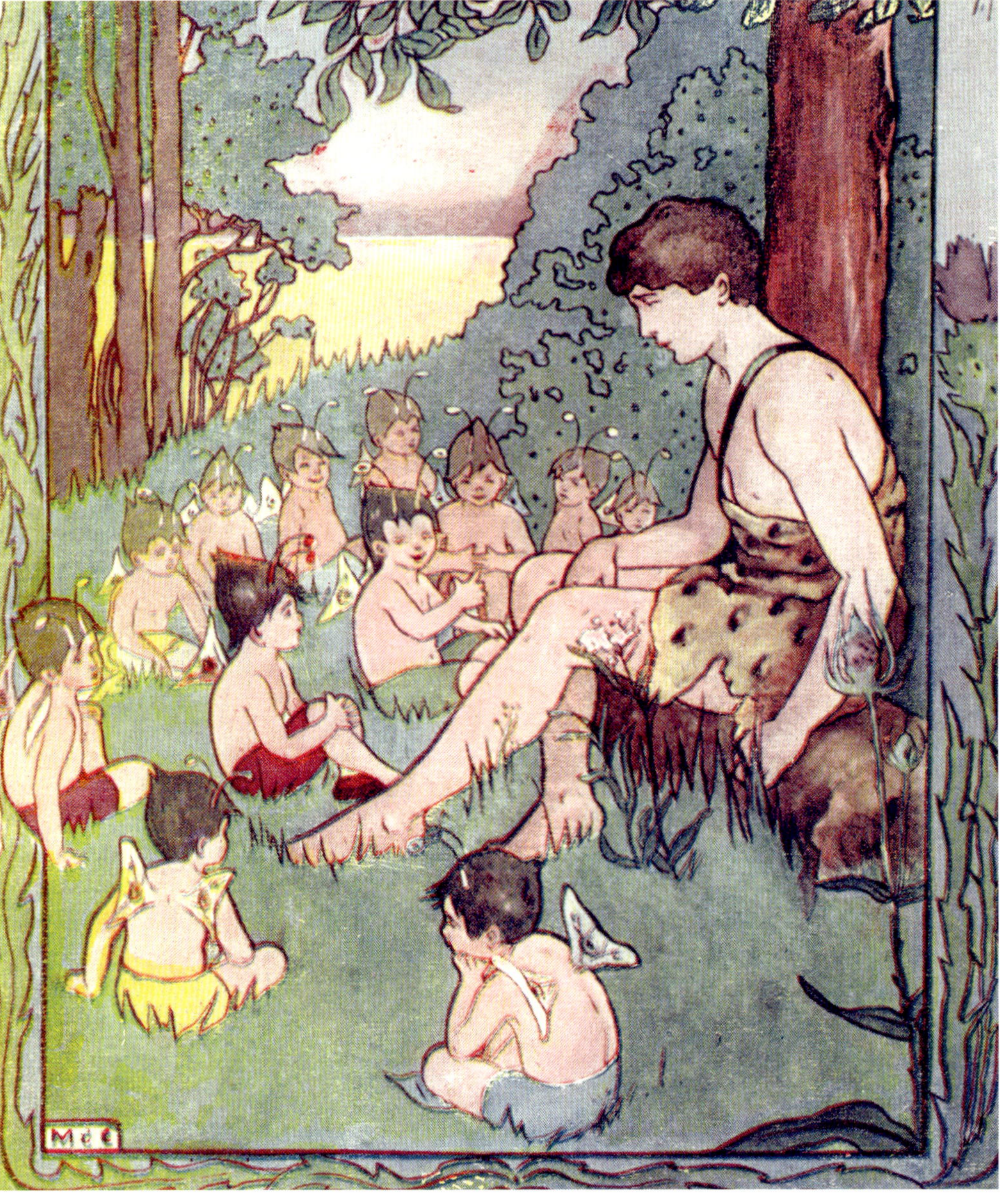

RIGHT: The Ryls counsel the boy who became every child's best friend; Mr. Baum told his story in *The Life and Adventures of Santa Claus*. Art by Mary Cowles Clark. **OPPOSITE**: At top, the vanquished Nome King, who was prevented from conquering Oz many times by Glinda, Ozma, and Dorothy, among others. Dorothy's hair was shorter when she returned to Oz, and the Kansas sunshine had turned it to gold. Art by Neill, *The Emerald City of Oz*.

Back on land, there are The Ryls, who live in the Forest of Burzee across the Deadly Desert from Oz. They are elvish and childlike in appearance, and their job is to care for all flowers, providing them with the diverse colors that glorify many a garden. Ryls are actually members of a much larger group of ethereals called Sprites, and these pixie compatriots are composed of the essential elements of water, wind, fire, and earth-growing greenery.

Finally, and unquestionably, the most beautiful, important, and magically gifted of all Oz ethereals is Ozma, who has ruled our kingdom wisely for many years. She is a fairy descendant of the greatest ensemble of wonderworkers known to history, and it was their Queen Lurline who first decided that our desert-bordered terrain should become a fairyland. Lurline enchanted the entire realm and left the baby Ozma behind to grow up to be our royal princess. Countless ethereals—good and evil—have been impacted by her reign across the decades; Ozma herself has persevered through threats of war and invasion, through magical kidnappings and transformations. Yet her inherent good magic, and her unfailing wisdom and benevolence, have grown with such experiences. She is incomparable.

There has been space here to discuss only a few of our ethereals. As for me, I am proud to be one of them—and ever grateful to be of service to Ozma and Oz!

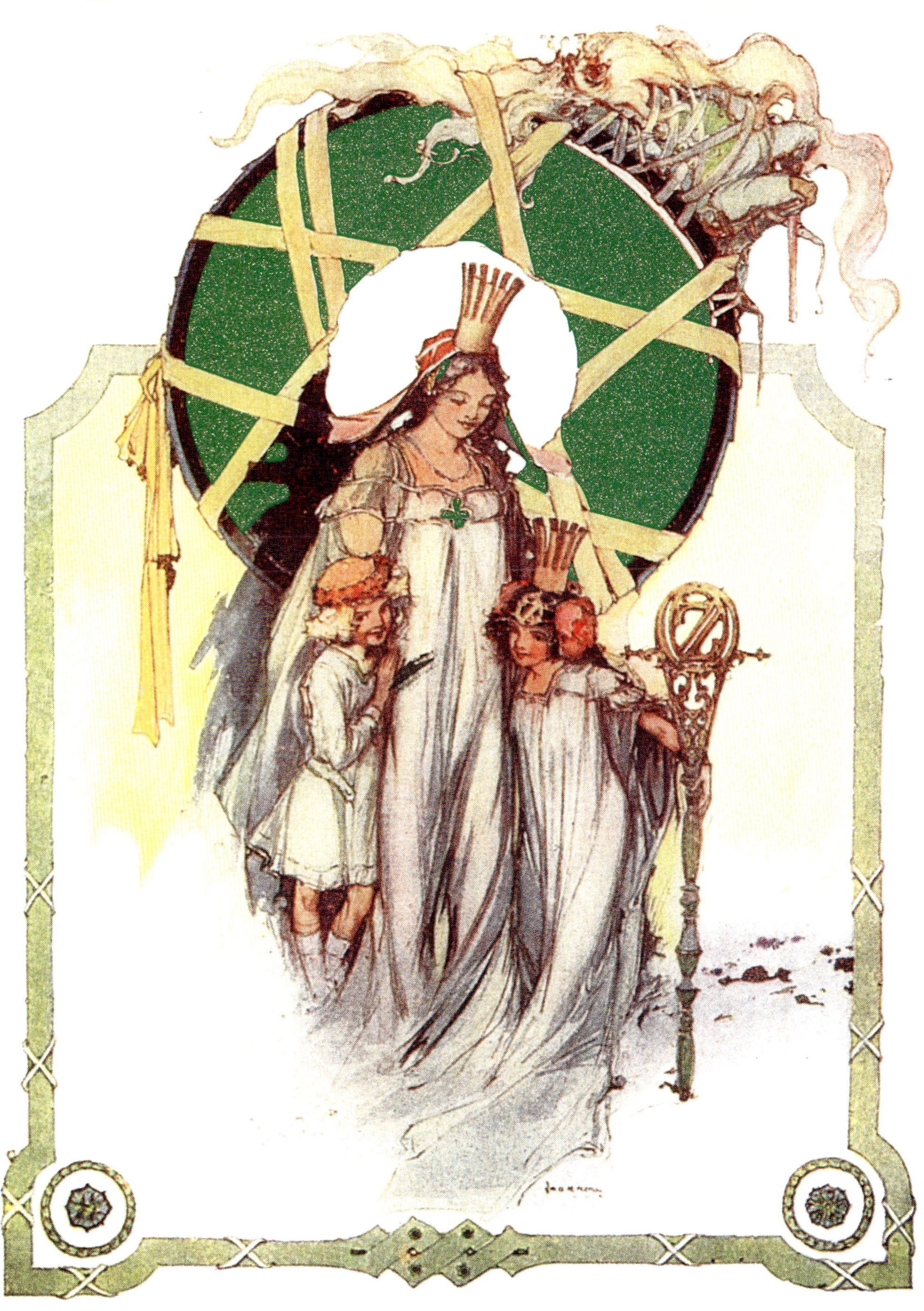

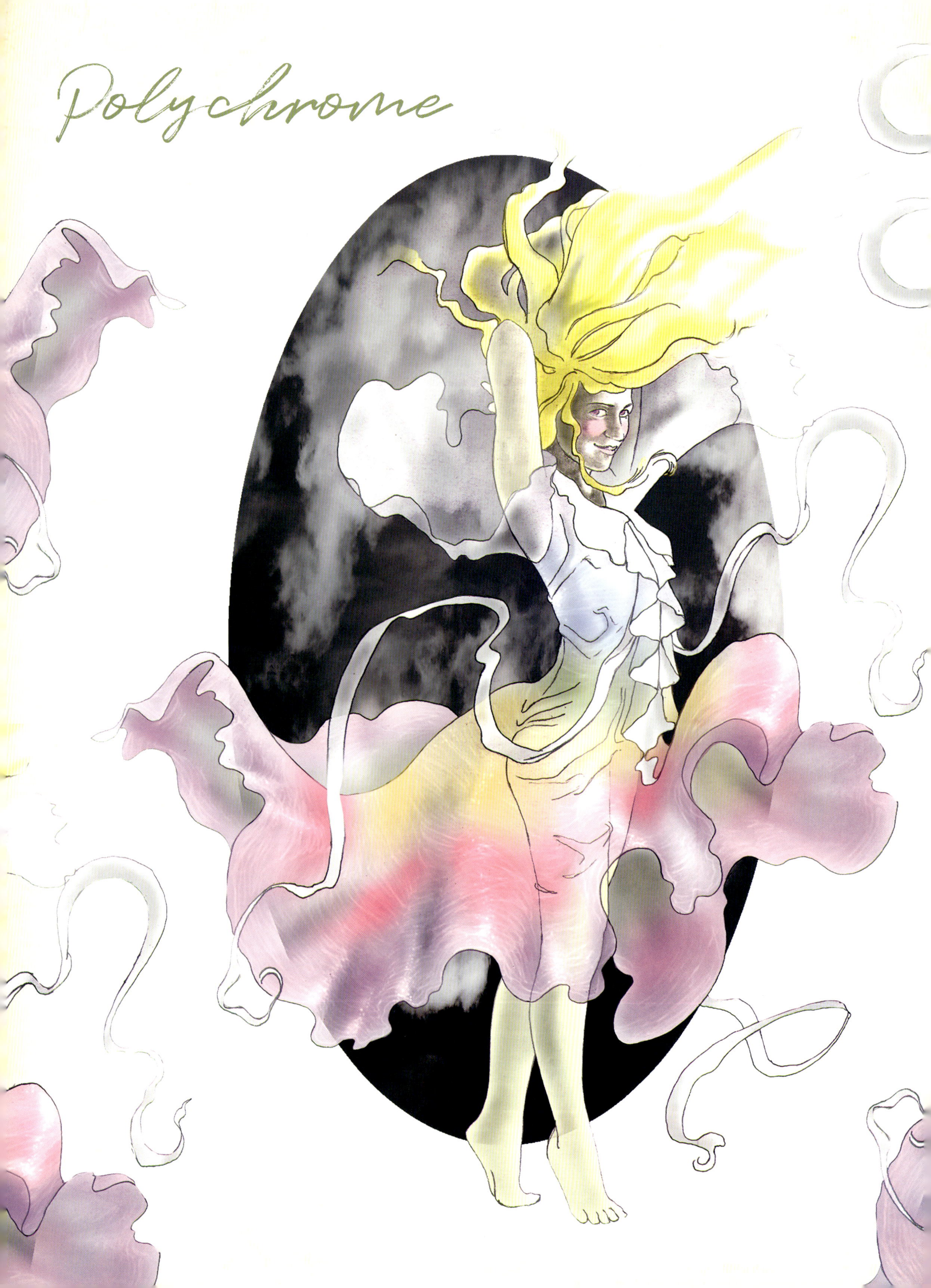
Polychrome

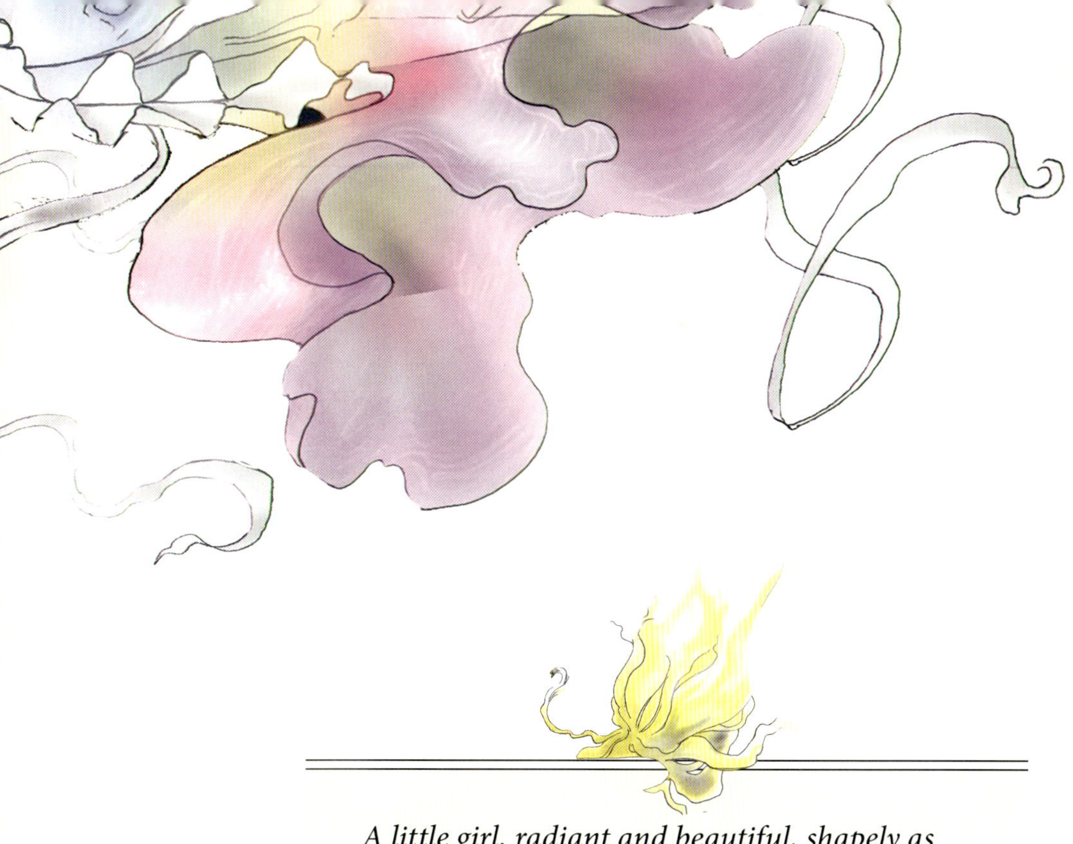

A little girl, radiant and beautiful, shapely as a fairy and exquisitely dressed, was dancing gracefully in the middle of the lonely road, whirling slowly this way and that, her dainty feet twinkling in sprightly fashion. She was clad in flowing, fluffy robes of soft material that reminded Dorothy of woven cobwebs, only it was colored in soft tintings of violet, rose, topaz, olive, azure, and white, mingled together most harmoniously in stripes which melted one into the other with soft blendings. Her hair was like spun gold and flowed around her in a cloud, no strand being fastened or confined by either pin or ornament or ribbon.

—THE ROAD TO OZ

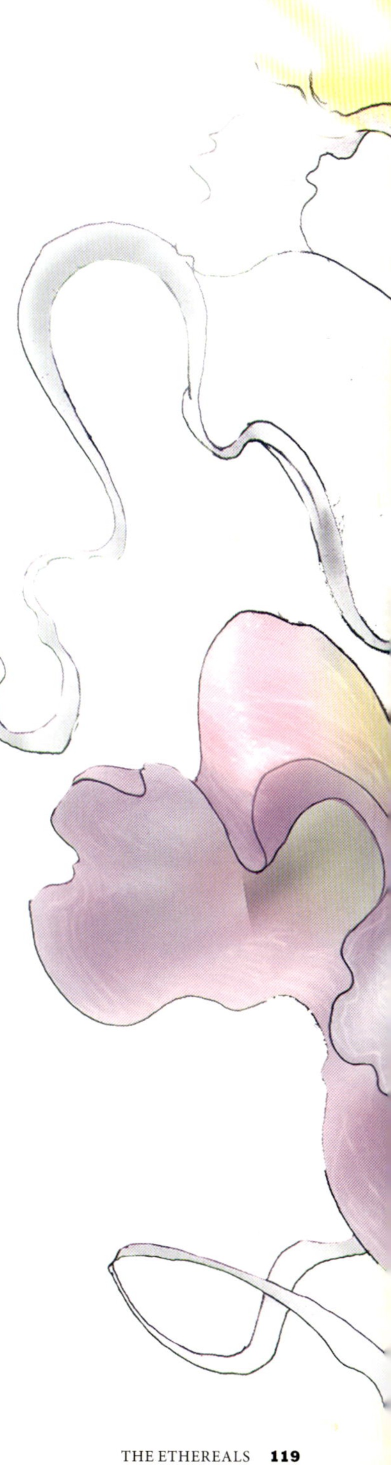

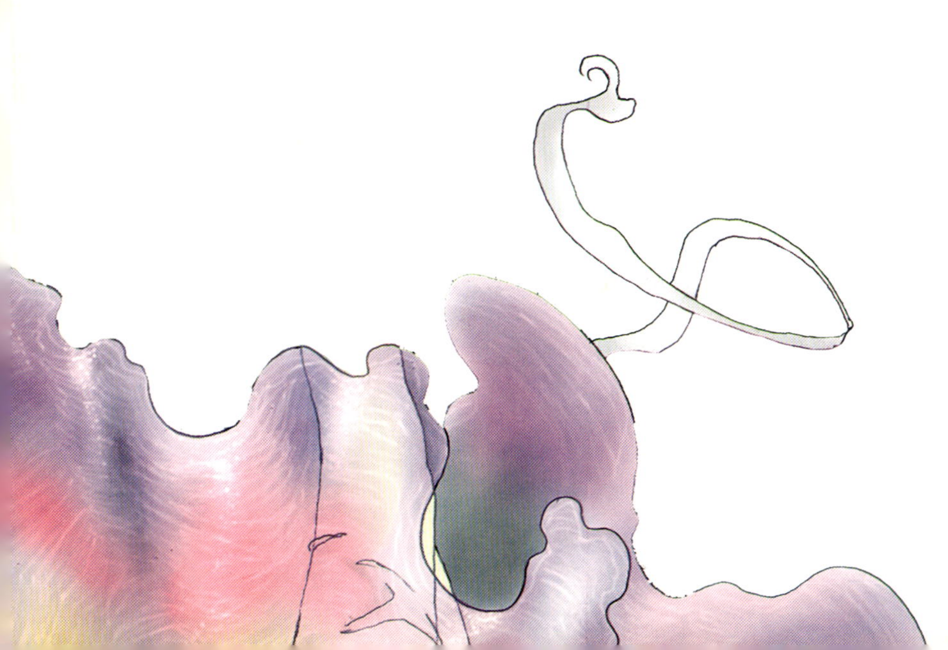

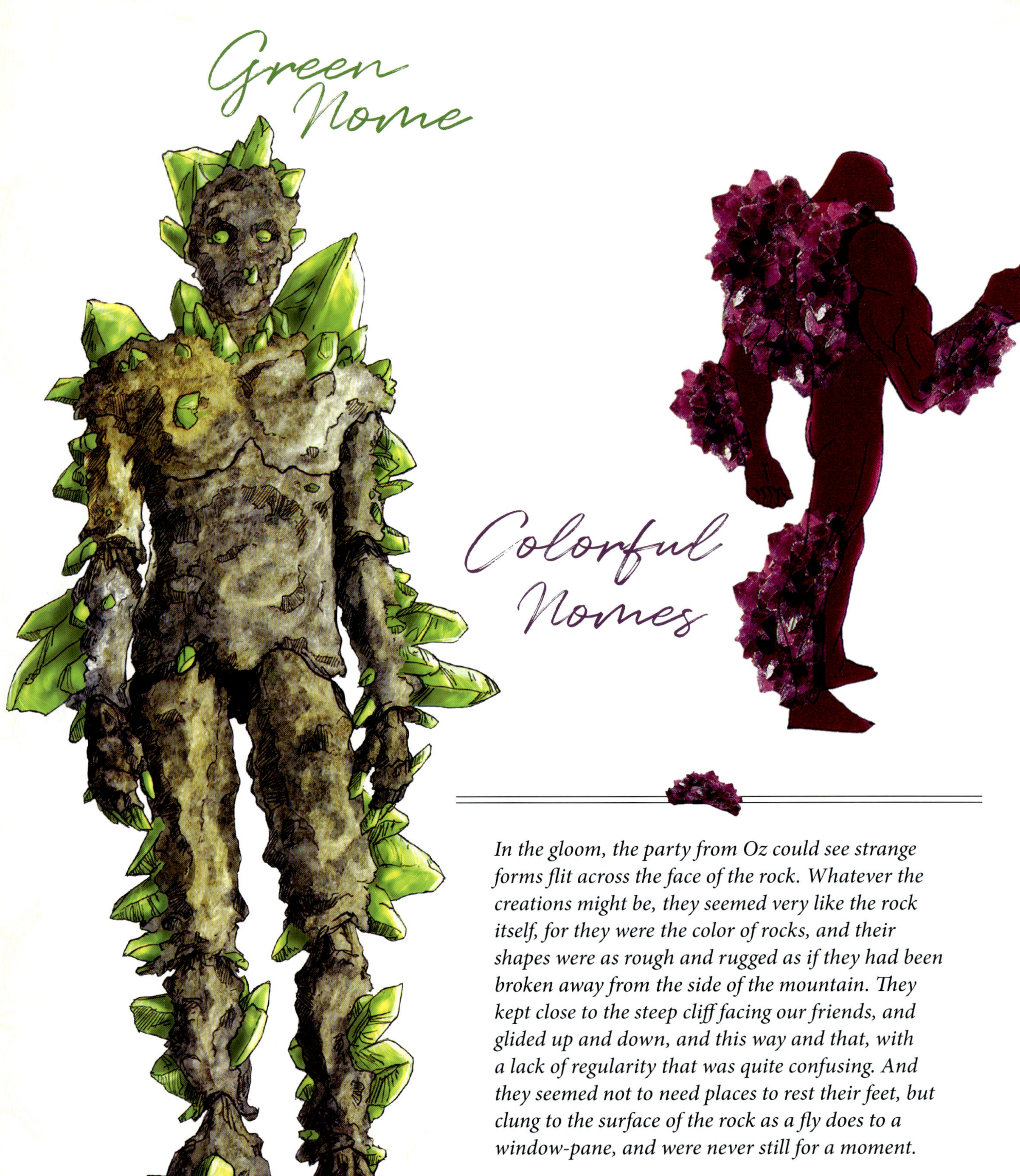

In the gloom, the party from Oz could see strange forms flit across the face of the rock. Whatever the creations might be, they seemed very like the rock itself, for they were the color of rocks, and their shapes were as rough and rugged as if they had been broken away from the side of the mountain. They kept close to the steep cliff facing our friends, and glided up and down, and this way and that, with a lack of regularity that was quite confusing. And they seemed not to need places to rest their feet, but clung to the surface of the rock as a fly does to a window-pane, and were never still for a moment.

—OZMA OF OZ

Mr. Baum has told us that the Nomes create all the precious metals and stones found anywhere in the world. As they themselves resemble and imitate rock, these portraits offer a quartet of the creatures whose stony surfaces are in the process of manifesting colorful and valuable gems.

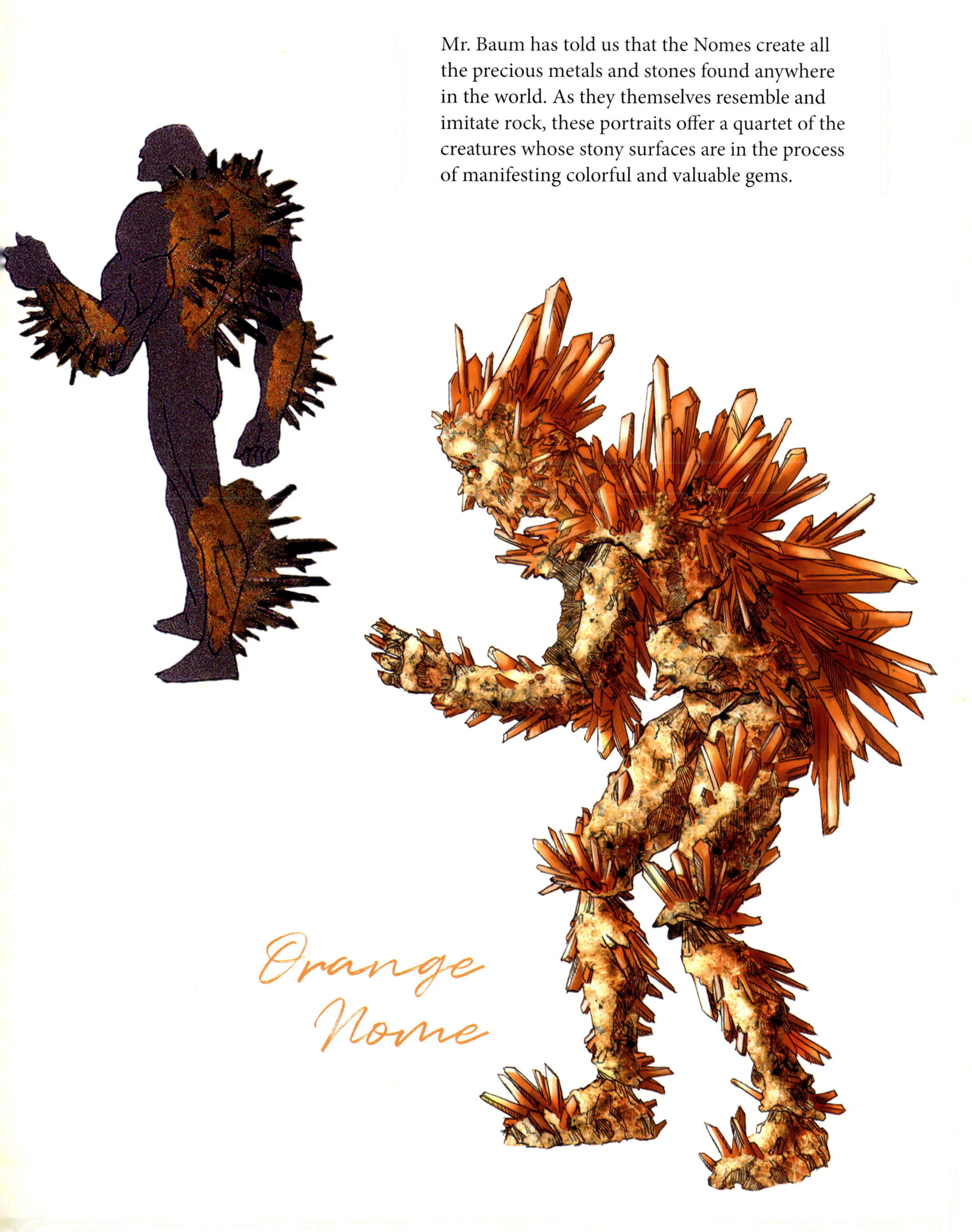

Orange Nome

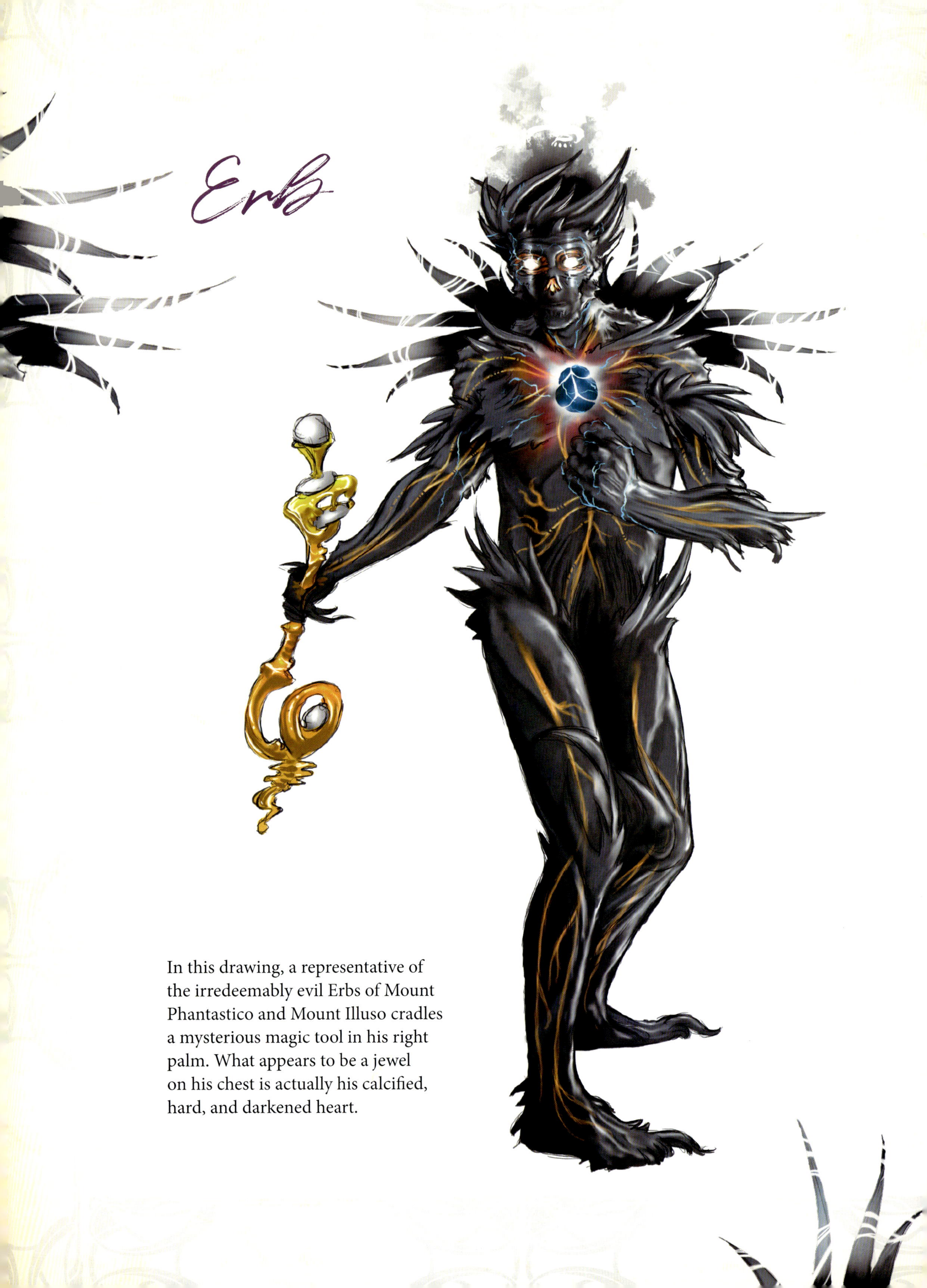

Erb

In this drawing, a representative of the irredeemably evil Erbs of Mount Phantastico and Mount Illuso cradles a mysterious magic tool in his right palm. What appears to be a jewel on his chest is actually his calcified, hard, and darkened heart.

Phanfasm

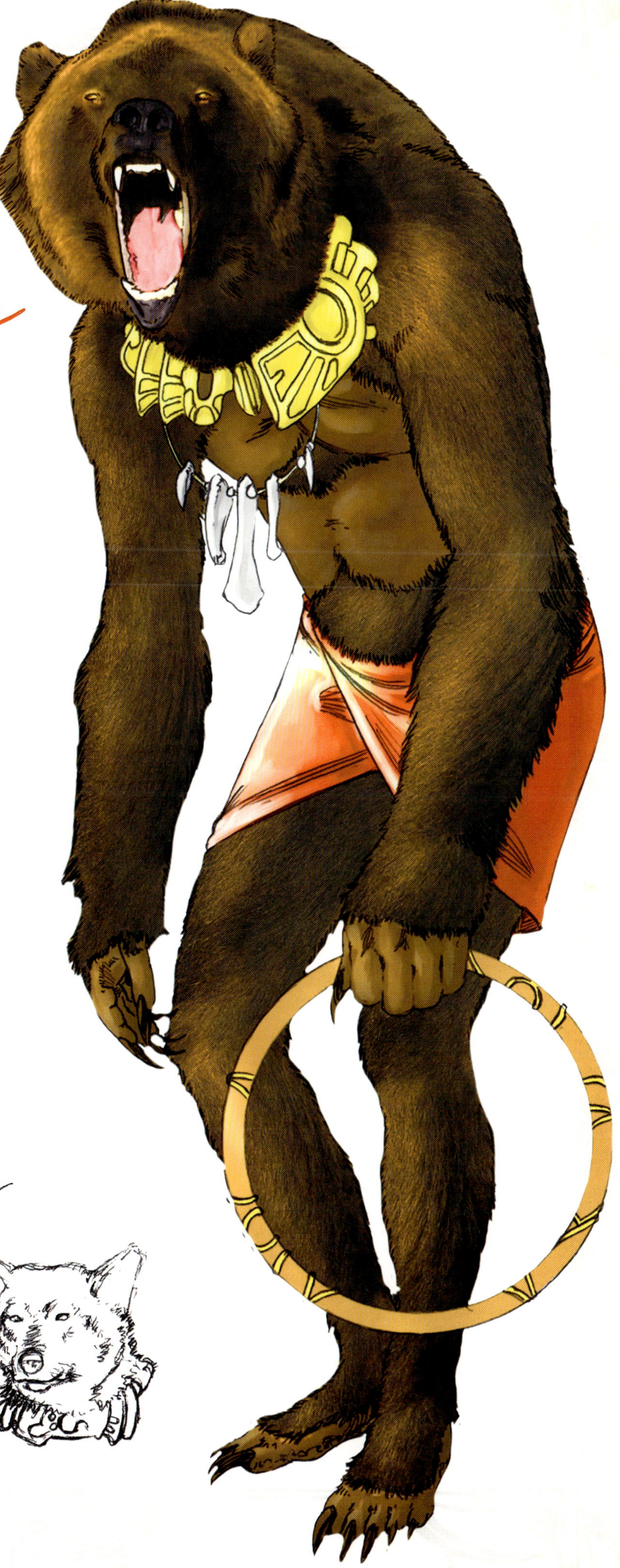

As Mr. Baum tells us in *The Emerald City of Oz*, all Erbs and their descendants are able to change appearance at will. When General Guph of the Nome Army met with the Phanfasms to discuss the utter destruction of Oz, the Erbs around him took the form of hairy beasts wearing the heads of birds, animals, and reptiles. They next became howling wolves and crawling lizards. At the same time, their leader, the First and Foremost Phanfasm, evolved from a bear to a beautiful woman to a huge butterfly. This portrait of his bearlike guise includes the brass hoop by which he cavalierly caught General Guph around the neck and yanked him away for interrogation.

Phanfasm Types

Ryl

As Mr. Baum explains in *The Life and Adventures of Santa Claus*, the Ryls are first cousins to the wood-nymphs. The latter care for the forest trees, while the Ryls are entrusted with feeding the plants and providing all color for the flowers. To achieve the various hues, the Ryls place dyes in the soil; these are then drawn through the little veins in the plant roots and directly up into the bodies of the plants as they reach maturity.

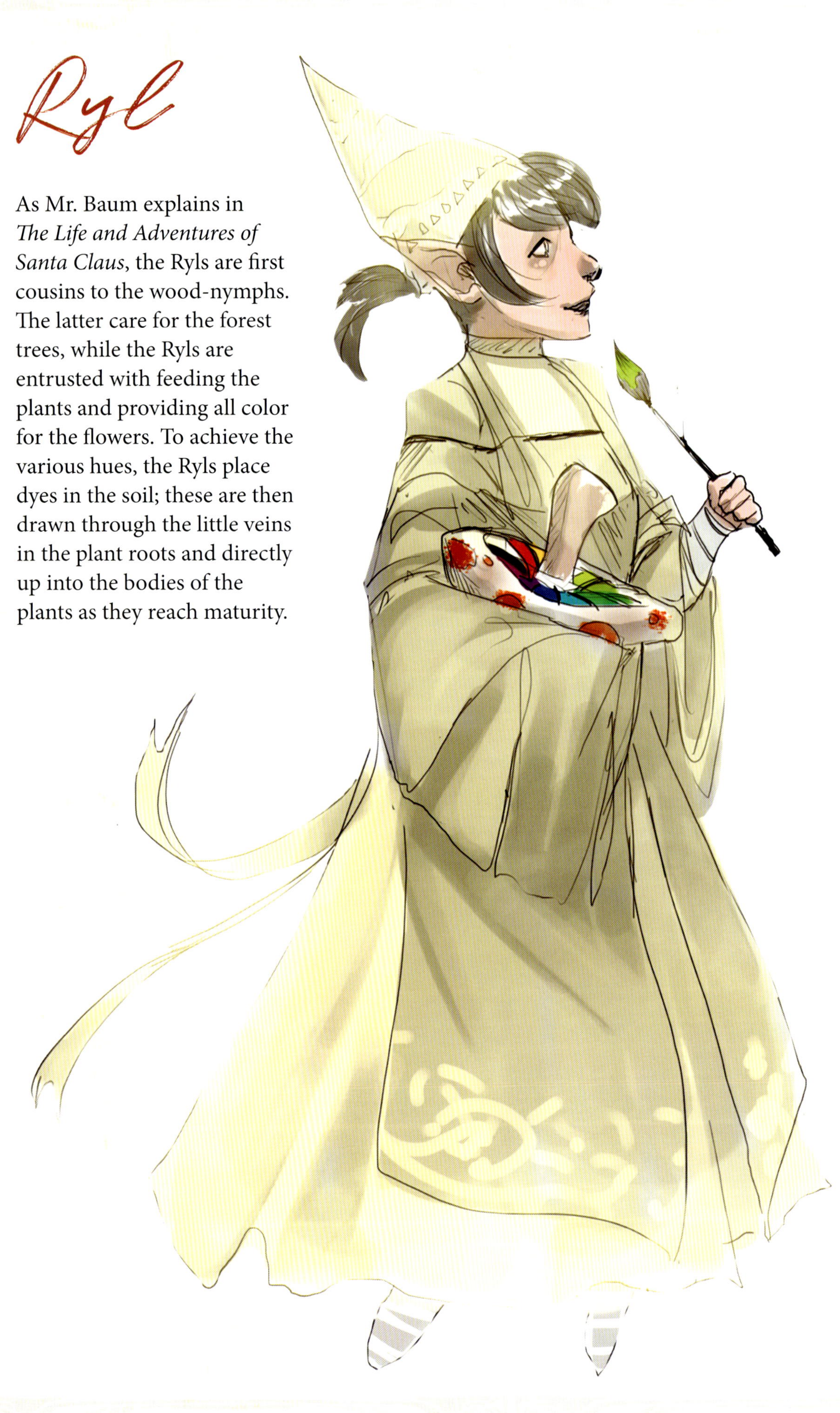

Elemental Sprites

These four playful sprites represent the elements of water, fire, wind, and plant-producing earth.

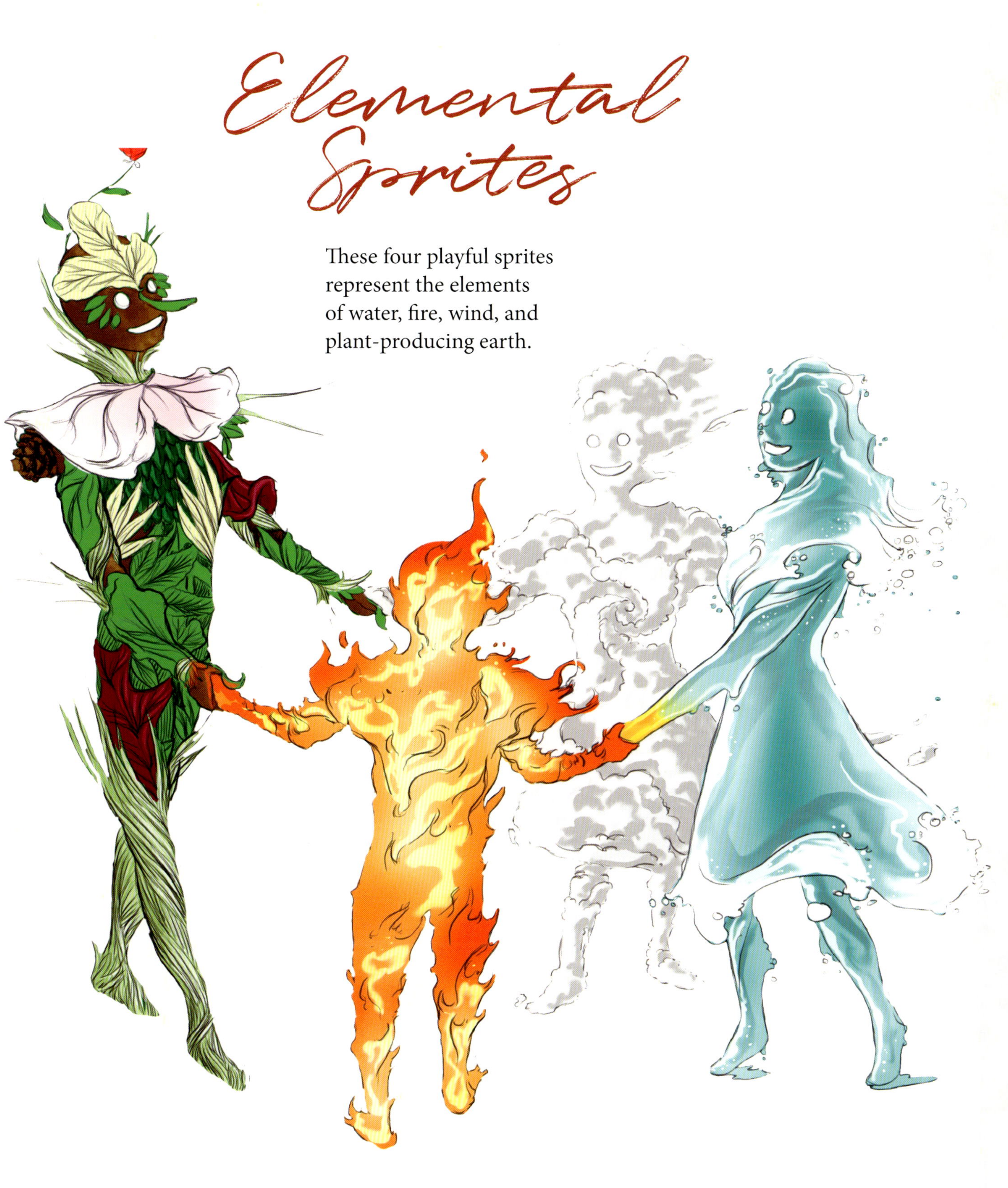

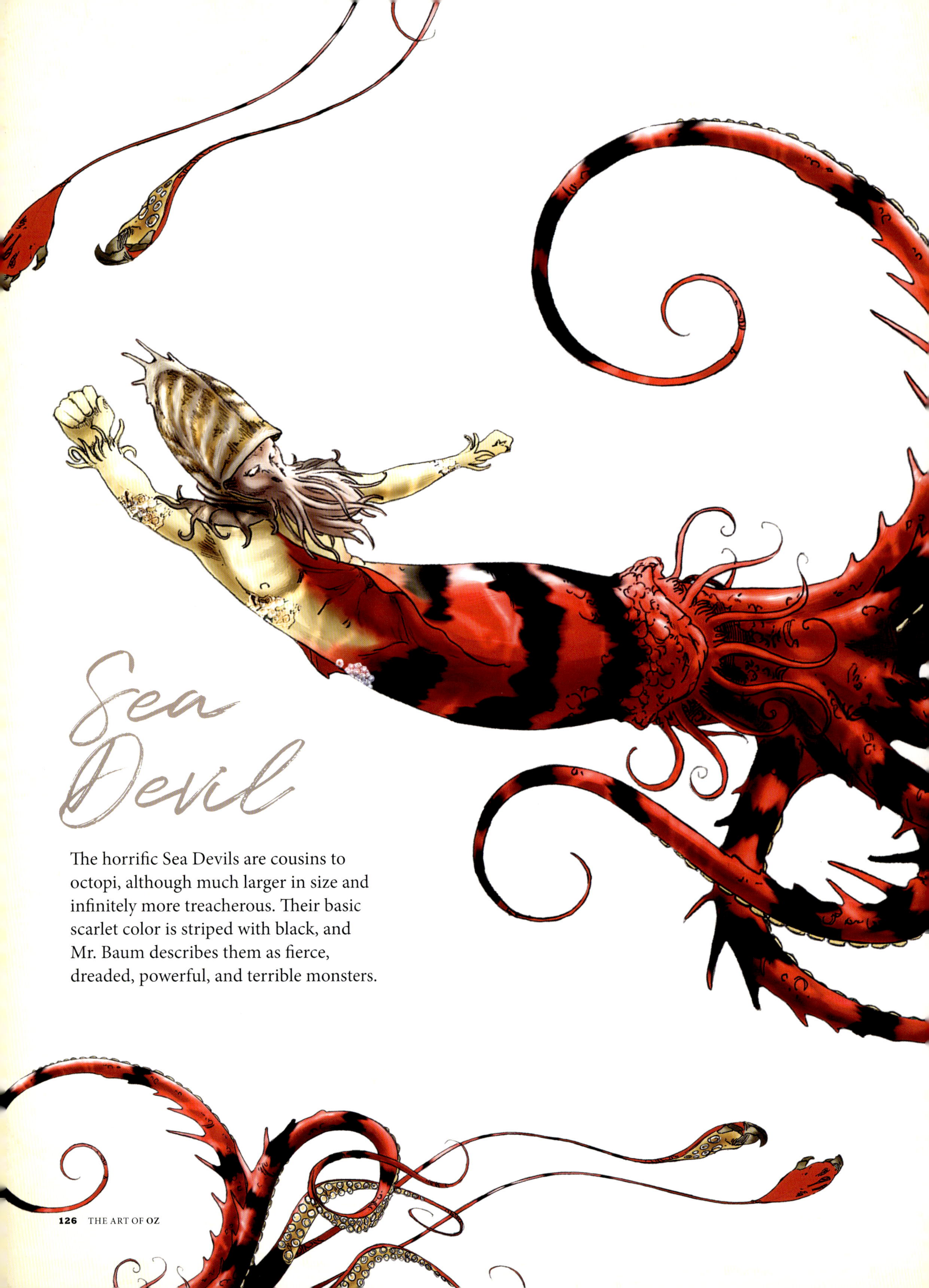

Sea Devil

The horrific Sea Devils are cousins to octopi, although much larger in size and infinitely more treacherous. Their basic scarlet color is striped with black, and Mr. Baum describes them as fierce, dreaded, powerful, and terrible monsters.

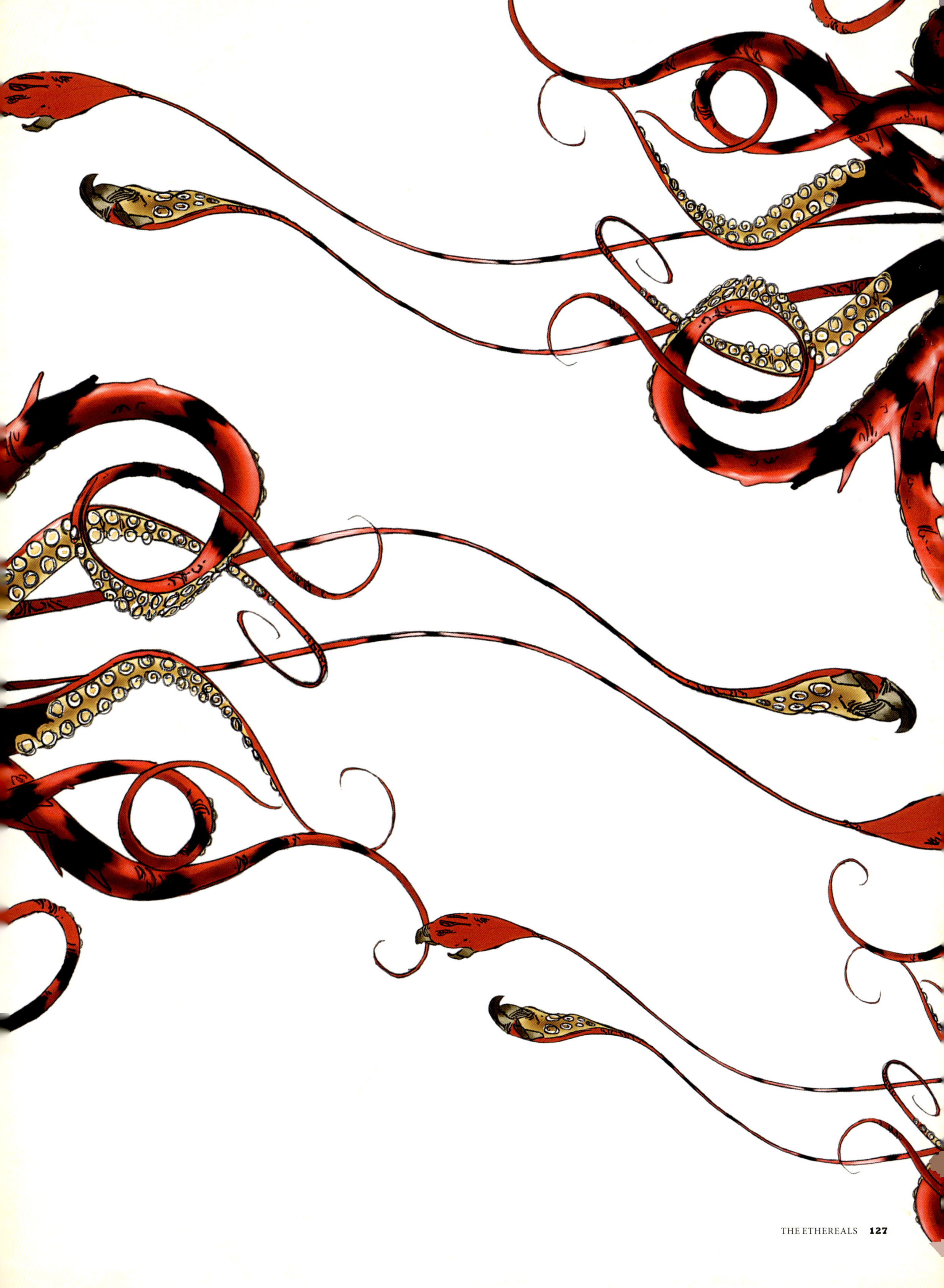

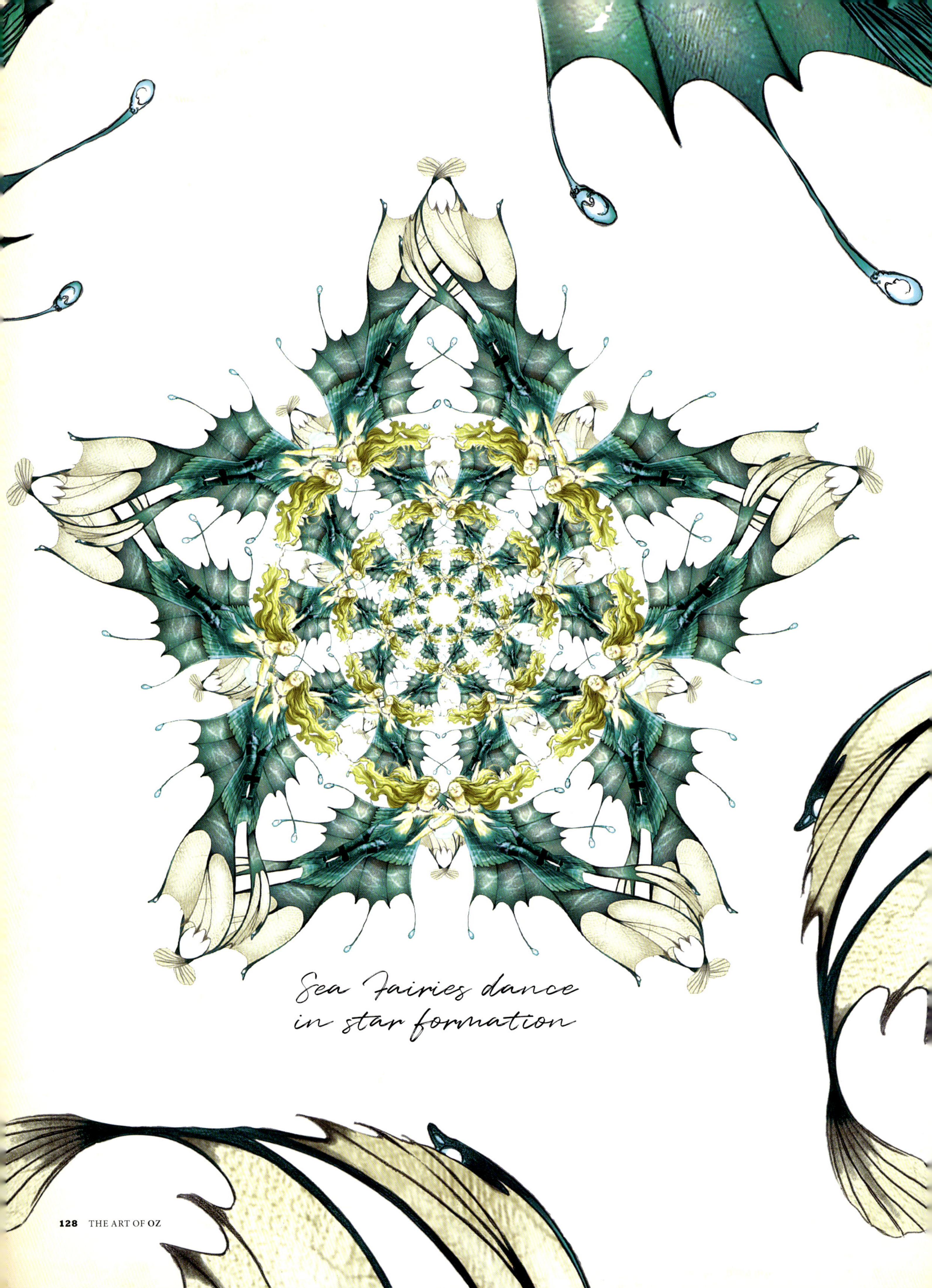

Sea Fairies dance in star formation

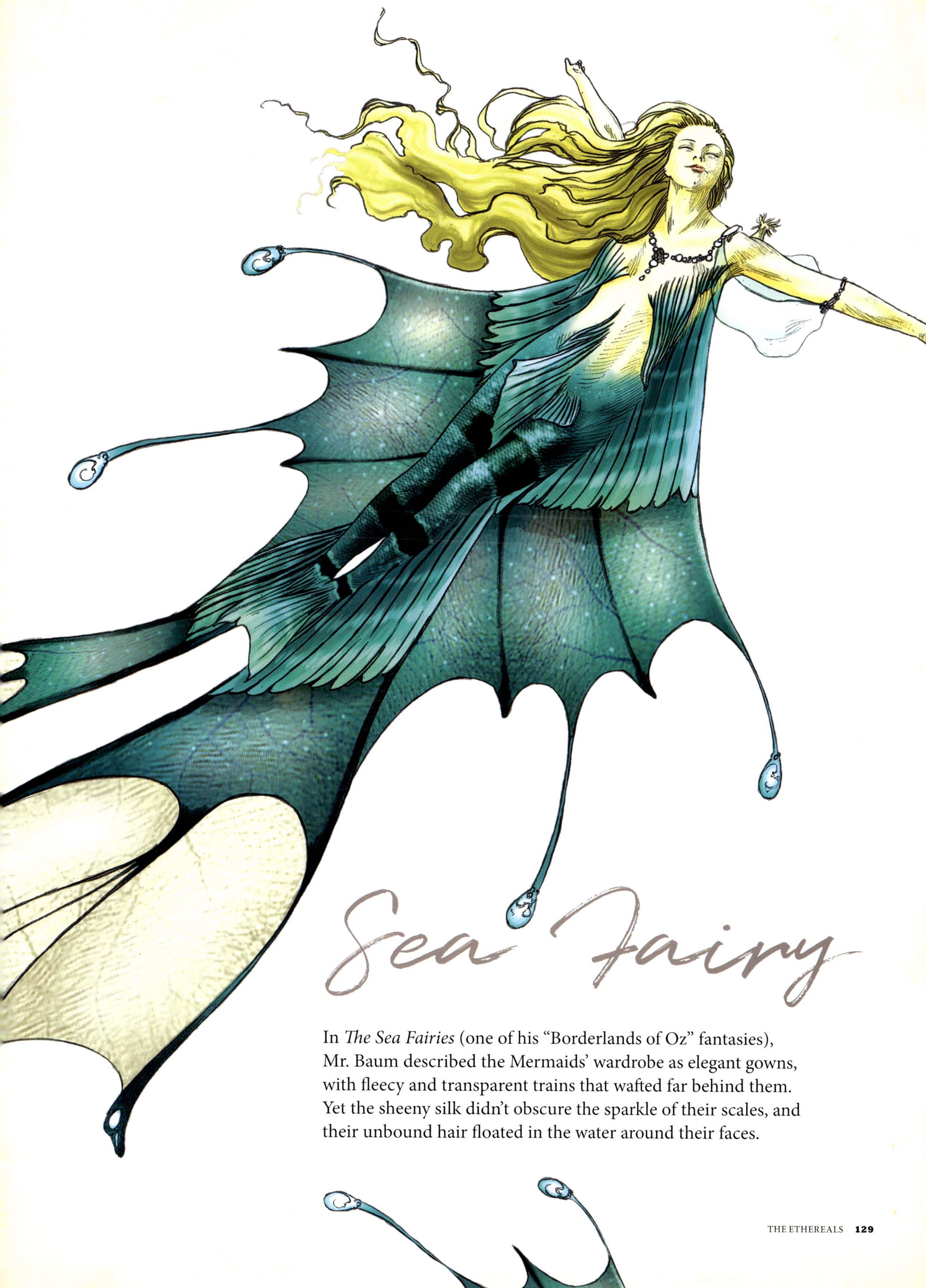

Sea Fairy

In *The Sea Fairies* (one of his "Borderlands of Oz" fantasies), Mr. Baum described the Mermaids' wardrobe as elegant gowns, with fleecy and transparent trains that wafted far behind them. Yet the sheeny silk didn't obscure the sparkle of their scales, and their unbound hair floated in the water around their faces.

Princess Ozma

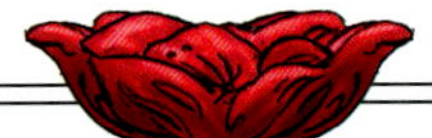

The royal historians of Oz, who are fine writers and know any number of big words, have often tried to describe the rare beauty of Ozma and failed because the words were not good enough. So of course, I cannot hope to tell you how great was the charm of this little Princess, or how her loveliness put to shame all the sparkling jewels and magnificent luxury that surrounded her in . . . her royal palace. Whatever else was beautiful or dainty or delightful of itself faded to dullness when contrasted with Ozma's bewitching face, and it has often been said by those who know that no other ruler in all the world can ever hope to equal the gracious charm of her manner. Everything about Ozma attracted one, and she inspired love and the sweetest affection rather than awe or ordinary admiration.

—THE ROAD TO OZ

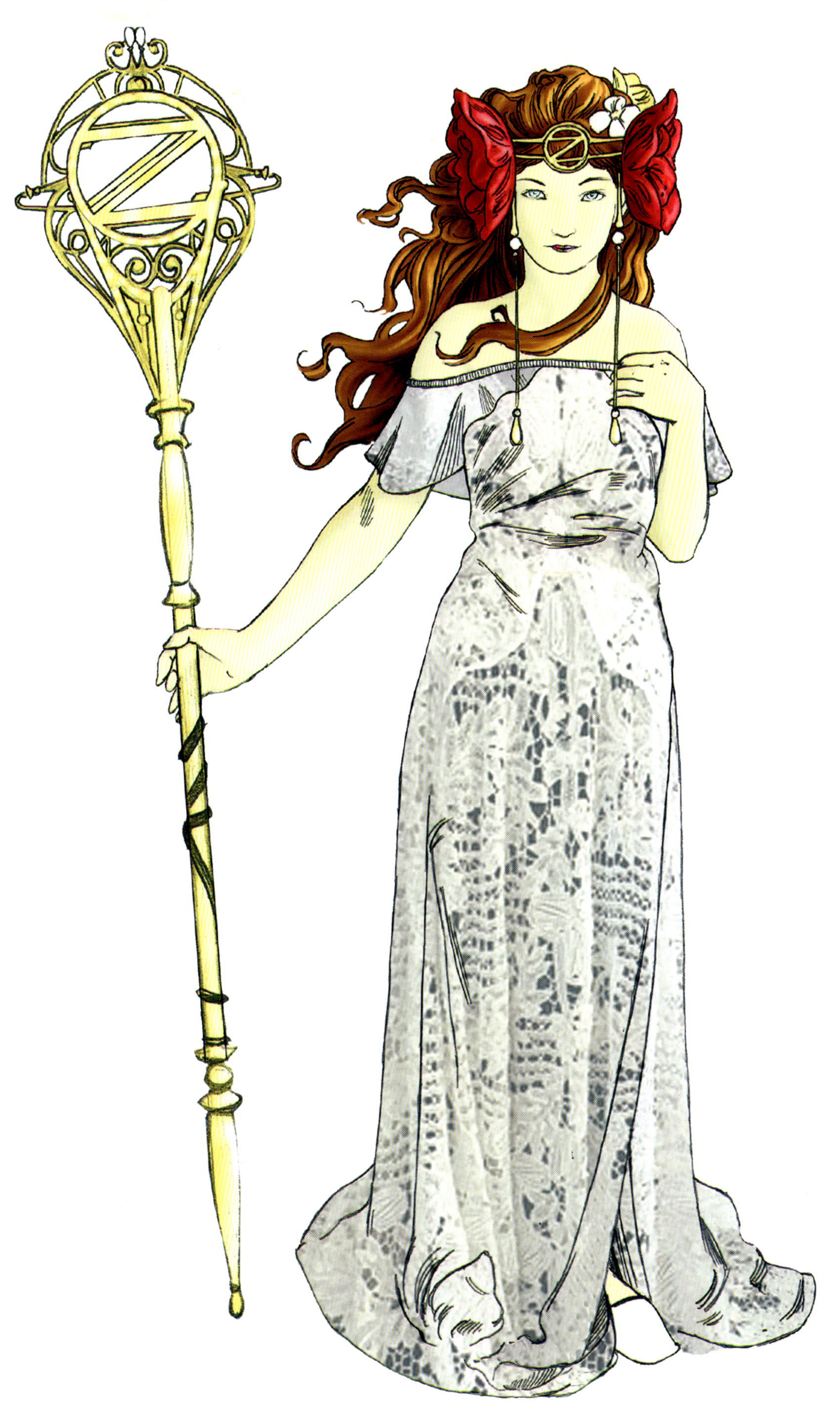

The Phantasms

INTRODUCED BY TOTO

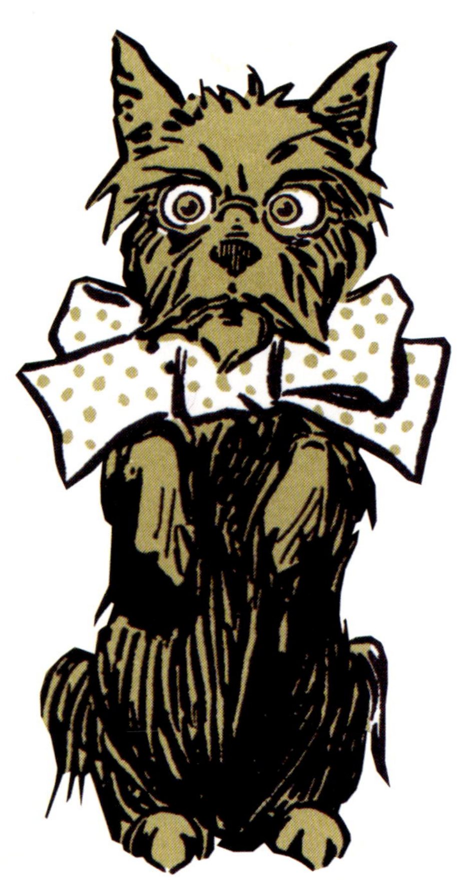

Are you surprised I can write? I can talk, too! Oz animals have that ability, although I lived in the Emerald City for years before anyone knew it about me. Until then, I communicated with my bark and tail . . . and charm!

One day, however, Princess Ozma told Dorothy that any animal who "came under the spell of" Oz could talk. So, Dorothy encouraged me "to be more sociable," and after teasing her with bow-wows, woofs, and wagging, I agreed. I've been speaking ever since!

Before writing this chapter, I asked Professor Woggle-Bug to clarify the meaning of "Phantasm." He explained that there are many definitions, although the characters here fall into two classifications: "nightmare" and "fantasy." He added that most Phantasms are figments of the imagination—except in Oz, where they're real! It's as if good or bad dream characters suddenly appear in your life.

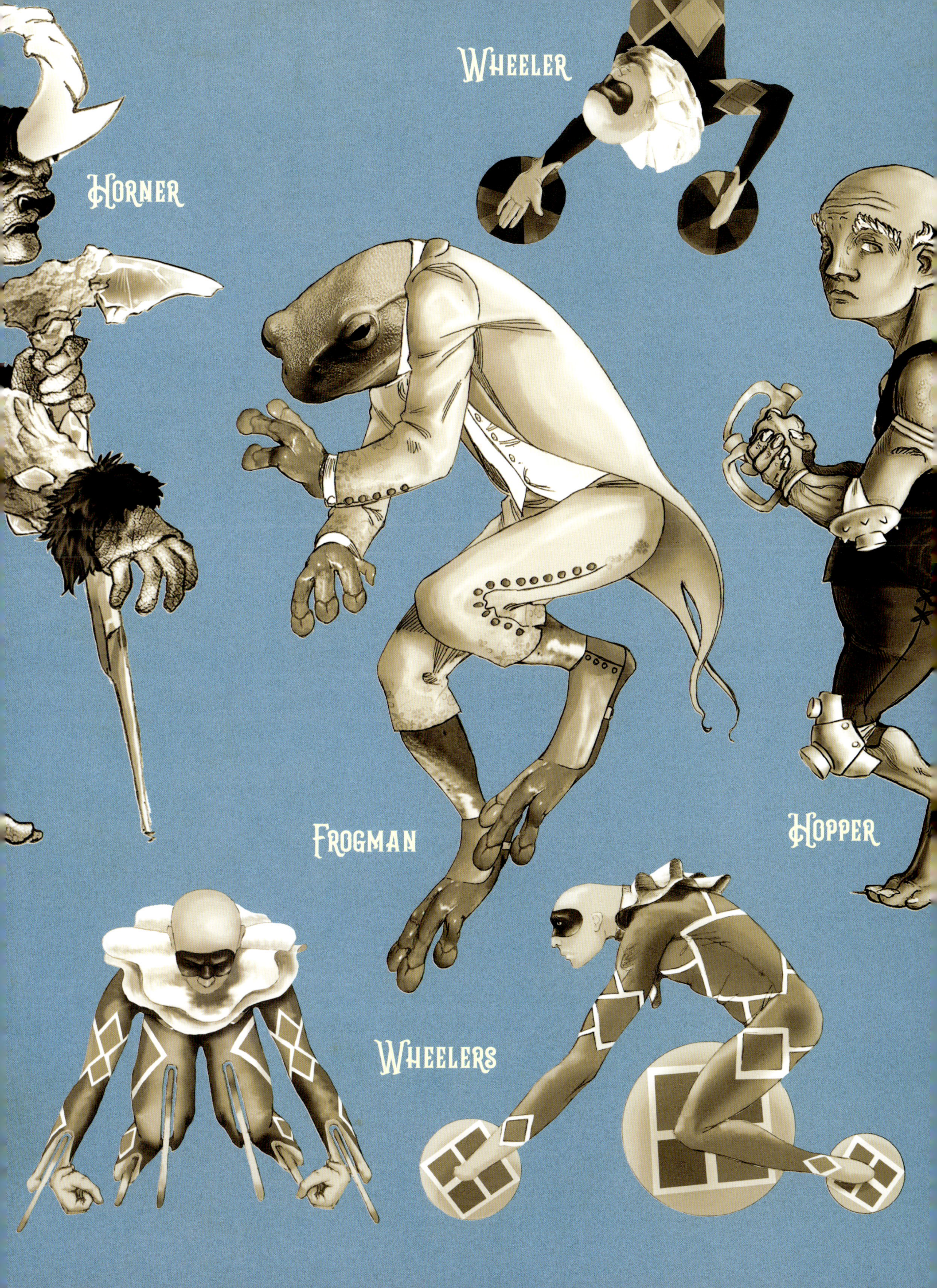

Wheeler
Horner
Frogman
Hopper
Wheelers

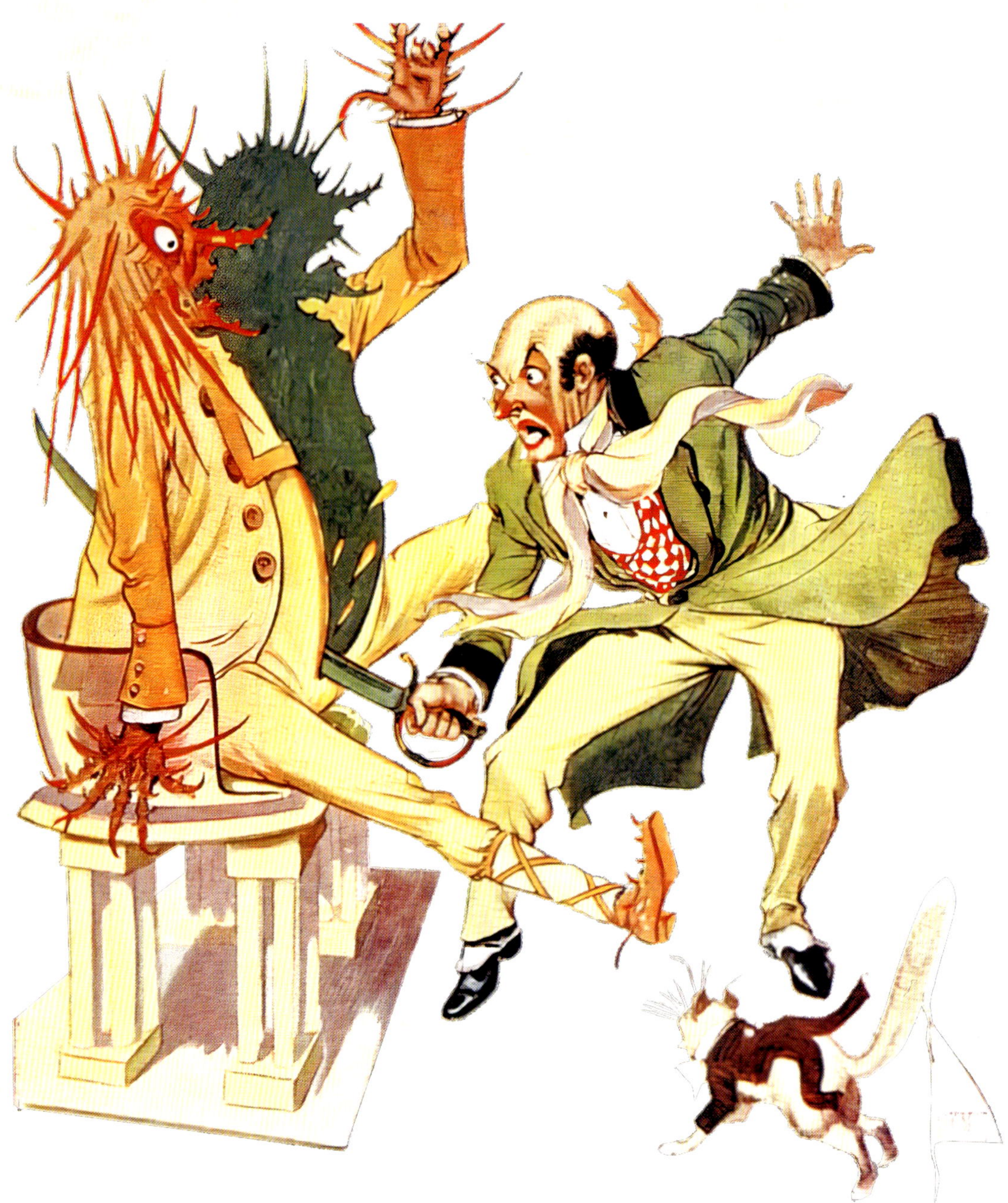

To start, let's discuss some creatures who tried to hurt Dorothy, because I heard about them—firsthand—from her. During a terrible earthquake, Dorothy and the Wizard fell into deep cracks in the ground and met the Mangaboos, who live far beneath the earth's surface. They are vegetable people: they grow in gardens, are "picked" when ripe, and planted again when they spoil. They never smile or frown, as they have no hearts, and they and their wicked sorcerer Gwig wanted to destroy Dorothy and her friends. Gwig almost stopped the Wizard from breathing, so in self-defense, the Wizard took a sword and sliced Gwig in half—like a potato! Then he, Dorothy, and their companions escaped.

The Wheelers were bullies who chased Dorothy up a hill in the Land of Ev, but they have wheels for hands and feet and couldn't follow her through rocky terrain. Fortunately, she discovered Tik-Tok the Clockwork Man in a cave there, wound him up, and he scared the Wheelers away. As Tik-Tok remarked, all they could do was yell and shout, which "does not hurt anyone at all."

The Flatheads look exactly like their name. They lived stupidly for years, as there was no

PAGE 132: Toto by Denslow, *The Wonderful Wizard of Oz*
ABOVE: The Wizard dispatches Gwig, as Eureka the kitten reacts! Art by Neill, *Dorothy and the Wizard in Oz*.
OPPOSITE: The famous Frogman by Neill, *The Lost Princess of Oz*

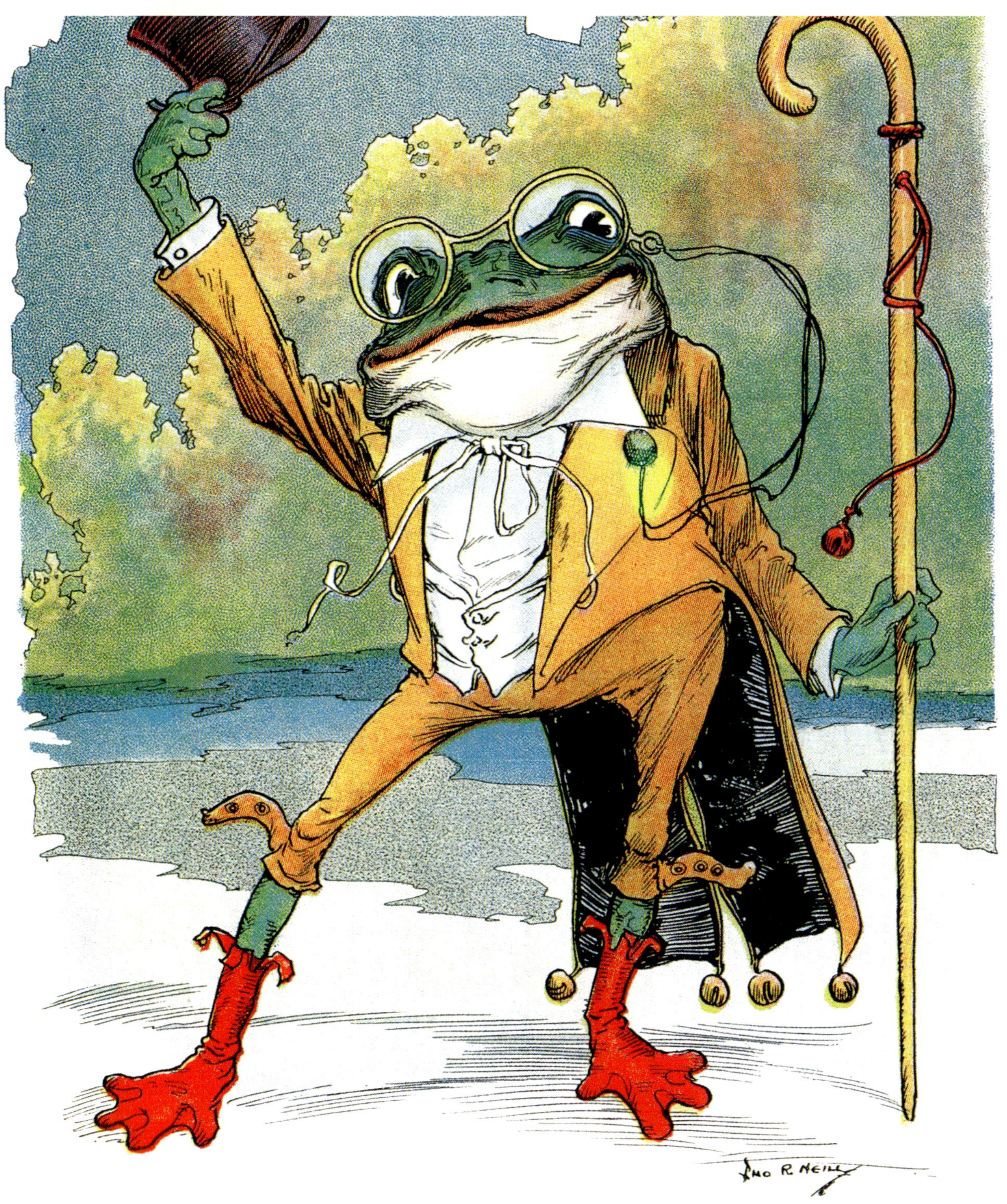

place in their heads for brains. Finally, a Fairy Queen took pity on them and gave each Flathead a can of brains to carry in his or her pocket. Yet some didn't use their cans, and they even declared war on their neighbors. It was left to Dorothy and Ozma to travel to the Flatheads' mountain home to arrange peace; instead, they got trapped in a sunken city in the nearby Lake of the Skeezers. It took Glinda, the Wizard, and the Three Adepts at Magic to save them, although I'm proud to say it was Dorothy who figured out the mystical words to raise the city out of the lake.

In describing other Phantasms, I can do better than firsthand; I can provide "firstpaw"—for I was there! I only caught a glimpse of the Growleywogs when they attempted to conquer Oz, as they forgot their evil after one drink from the Fountain of Oblivion, and Ozma instantly sent

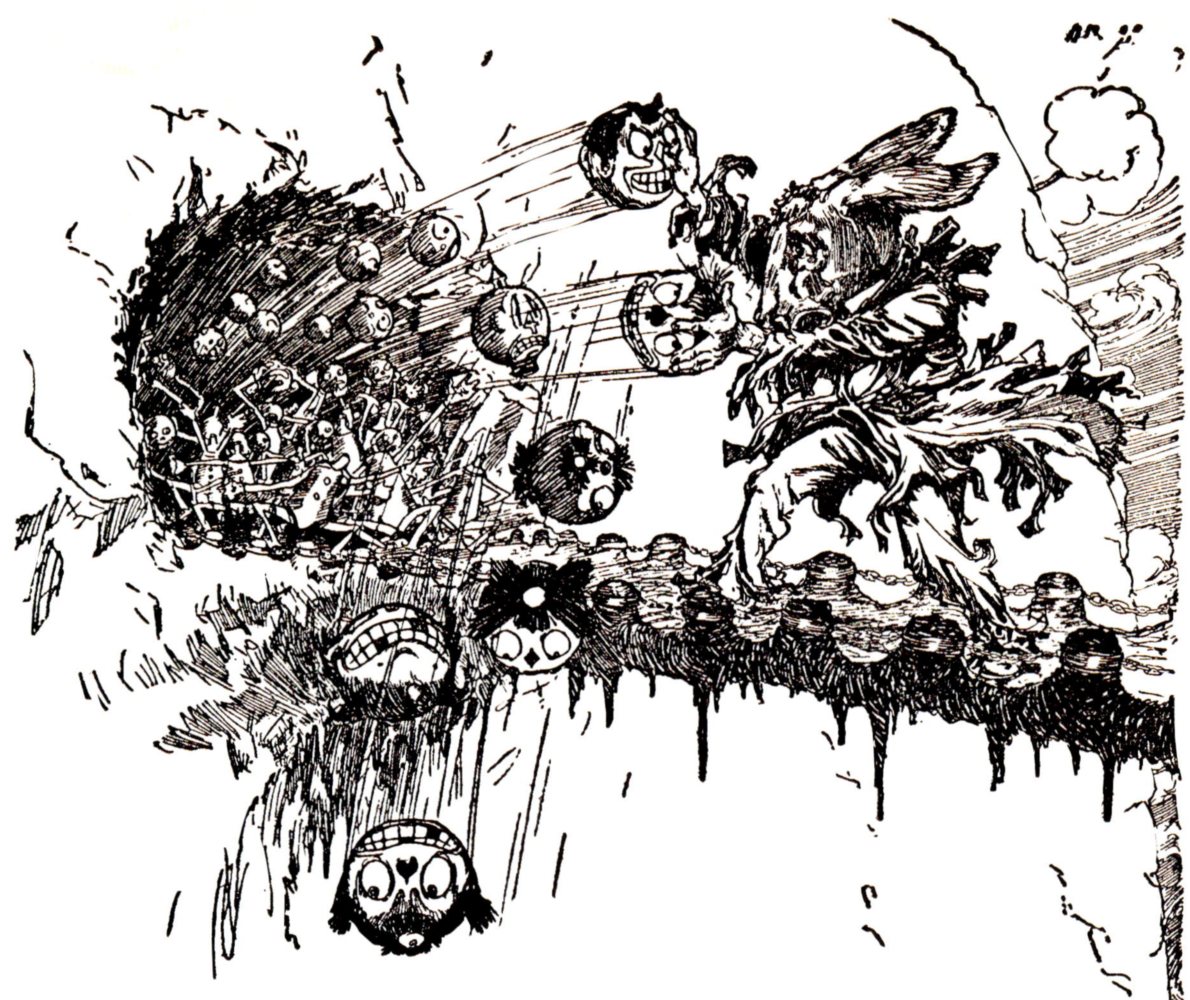

them home. On an earlier adventure, however, Dorothy and I and our friends encountered the Hammer-Heads, and they tried to prevent us from climbing their mountain to reach Glinda's palace on the other side. We nevertheless got past them, as Dorothy summoned the Winged Monkeys to fly us over the hill—and those expanding Hammer-Head necks couldn't reach us up in the sky!

The Scoodlers, however, actually captured Dorothy, me, and our friends—to make us into soup! Only the Shaggy Man's baseball talents rescued us. You see, Scoodlers take off their heads and throw them at their enemies; then they retrieve their heads and put them back on. When we ran to escape, their heads came at us from every direction, but the Shaggy Man caught them all and threw them down a deep gulf where they couldn't be recovered!

Of course, there are *good* Phantasms, too. The Hoppers and Horners occupy side-by-side countries and sometimes argue among themselves. But they were playful with us and helped Ojo the Munchkin find an ingredient he needed for a magic compound. Finally, the Frogman was a good friend from the moment we met him. He was originally a normal-sized amphibian (I looked it up!) who, by chance, ate some magic skosh. It made him intelligent and enormous in size; he was excellent help on our search for the lost princess of Oz.

I guess it's lucky I *can* talk; nightmare or fantasy, the Phantasms give me plenty to say!

ABOVE: The Shaggy Man's baseball skills ultimately defeated the evil Scoodlers. Art by Neill, *The Road to Oz*. **OPPOSITE**: The Hammer-Heads gave the Scarecrow a difficult time. Art by Denslow, *The Wonderful Wizard of Oz*.

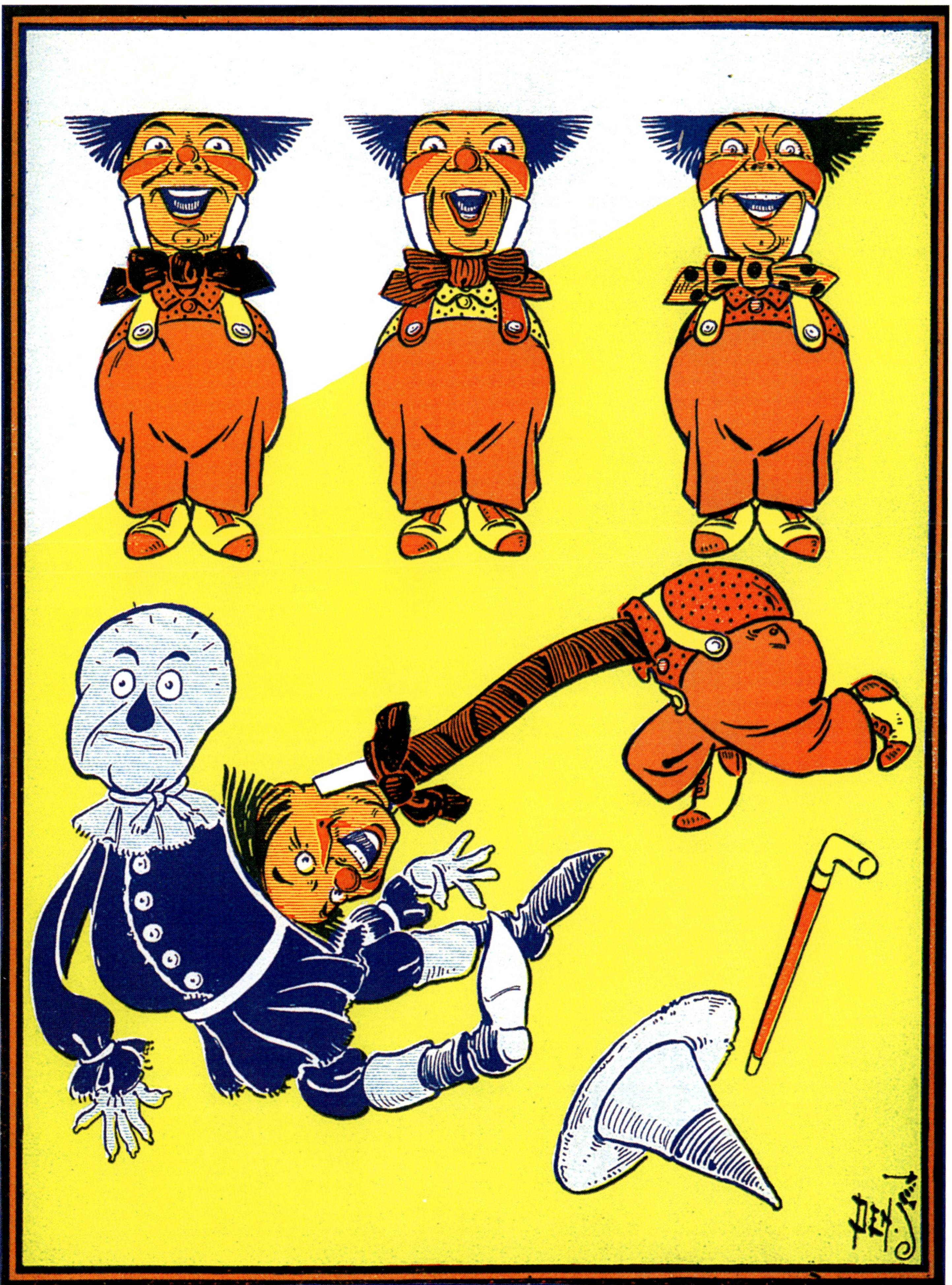

Mangaboos

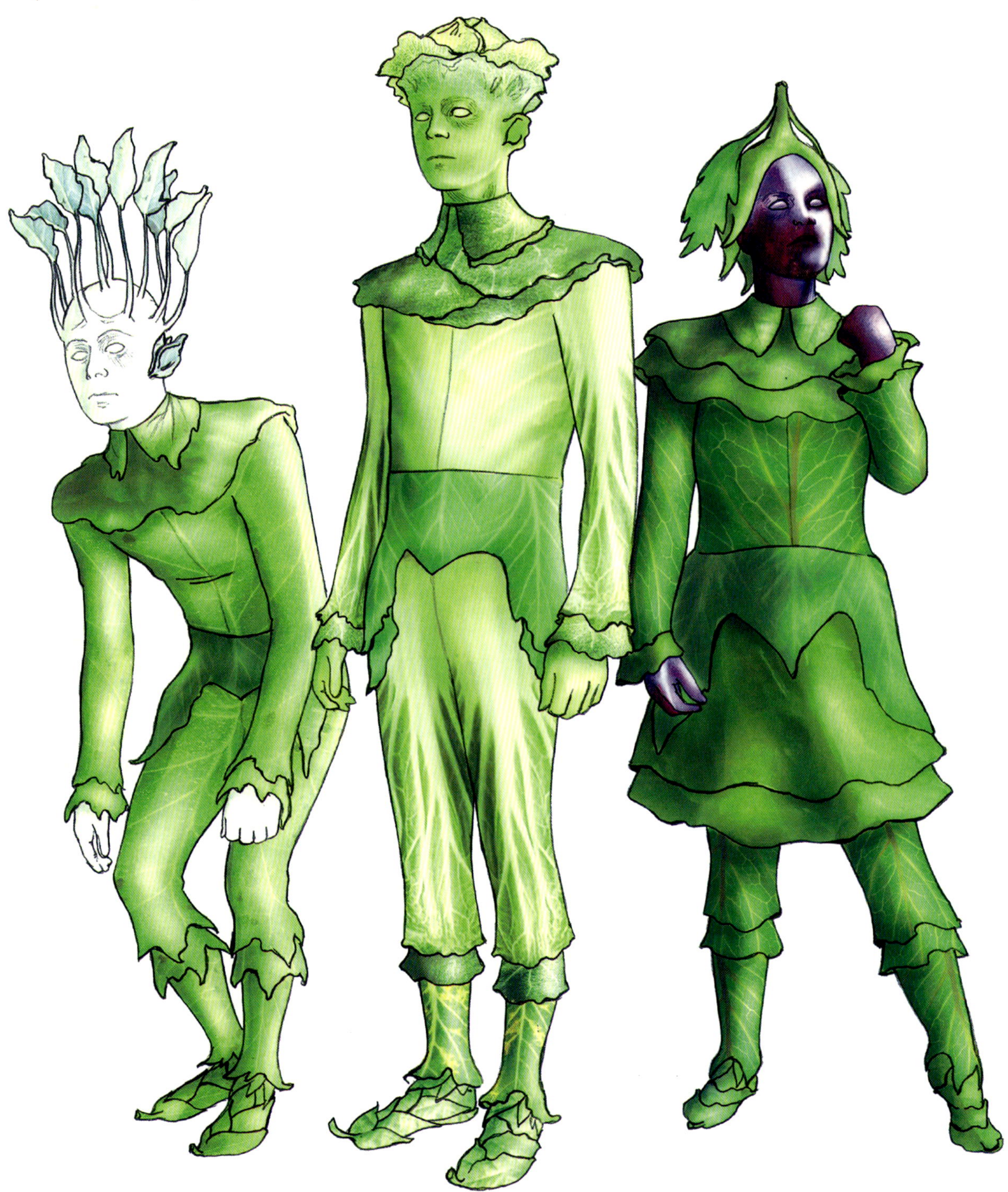

As the Mangaboo vegetable people are not picked from their gardens until fully grown, there are no children among them, only men and women. They are handsome and beautiful in appearance, yet as Dorothy discovered, they weren't pleasant to see because they never displayed any joy or sorrow. They had the faces of motionless dolls.

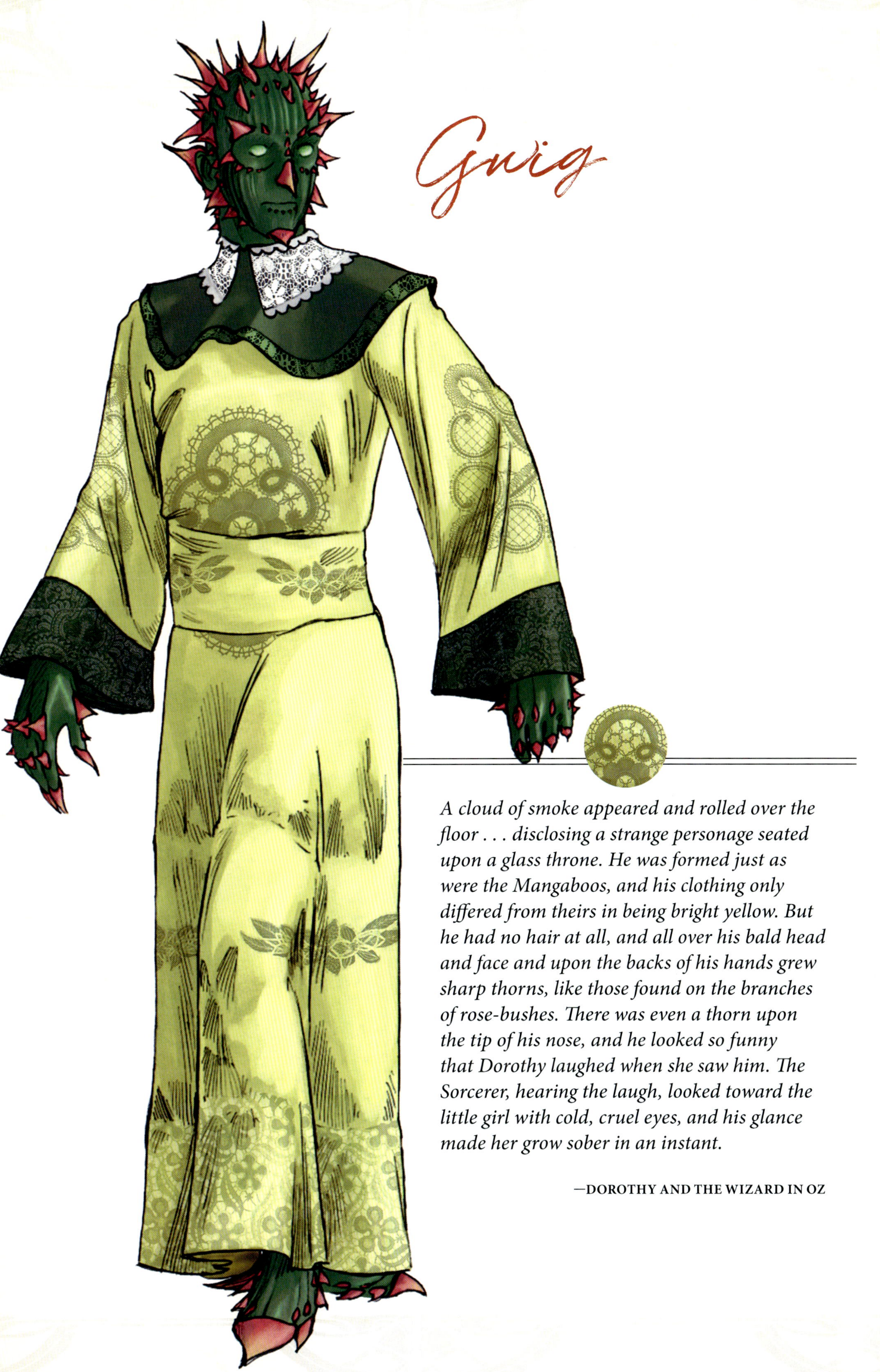

Gwig

A cloud of smoke appeared and rolled over the floor . . . disclosing a strange personage seated upon a glass throne. He was formed just as were the Mangaboos, and his clothing only differed from theirs in being bright yellow. But he had no hair at all, and all over his bald head and face and upon the backs of his hands grew sharp thorns, like those found on the branches of rose-bushes. There was even a thorn upon the tip of his nose, and he looked so funny that Dorothy laughed when she saw him. The Sorcerer, hearing the laugh, looked toward the little girl with cold, cruel eyes, and his glance made her grow sober in an instant.

—DOROTHY AND THE WIZARD IN OZ

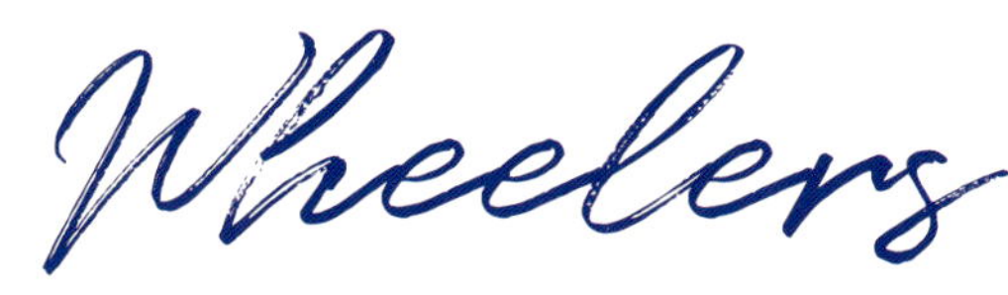

Wheelers

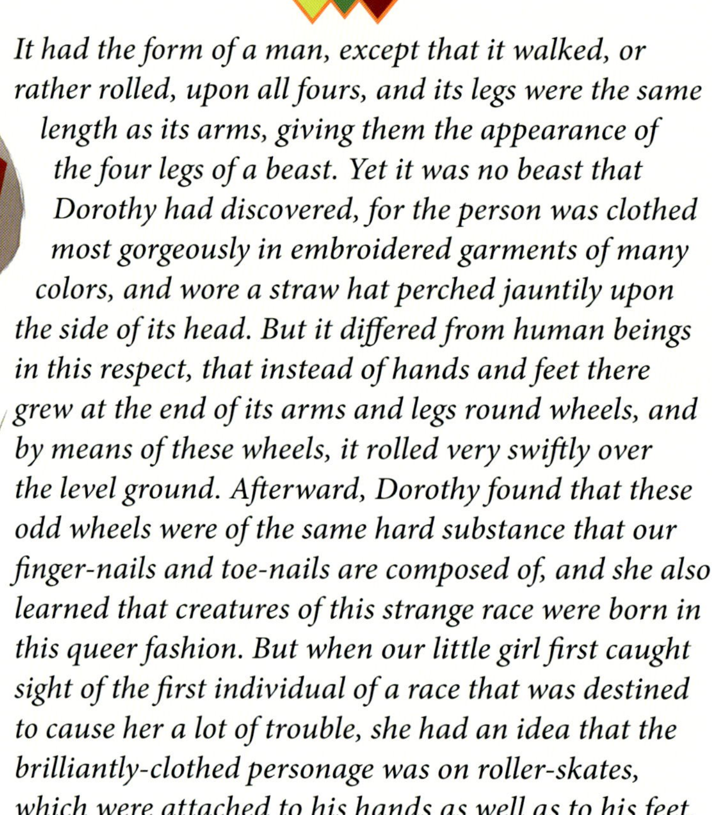

It had the form of a man, except that it walked, or rather rolled, upon all fours, and its legs were the same length as its arms, giving them the appearance of the four legs of a beast. Yet it was no beast that Dorothy had discovered, for the person was clothed most gorgeously in embroidered garments of many colors, and wore a straw hat perched jauntily upon the side of its head. But it differed from human beings in this respect, that instead of hands and feet there grew at the end of its arms and legs round wheels, and by means of these wheels, it rolled very swiftly over the level ground. Afterward, Dorothy found that these odd wheels were of the same hard substance that our finger-nails and toe-nails are composed of, and she also learned that creatures of this strange race were born in this queer fashion. But when our little girl first caught sight of the first individual of a race that was destined to cause her a lot of trouble, she had an idea that the brilliantly-clothed personage was on roller-skates, which were attached to his hands as well as to his feet.

—OZMA OF OZ

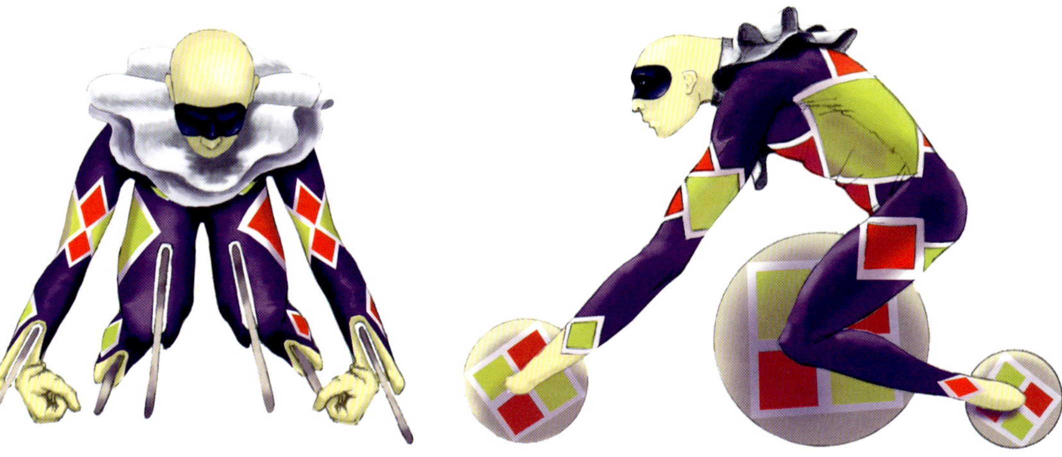

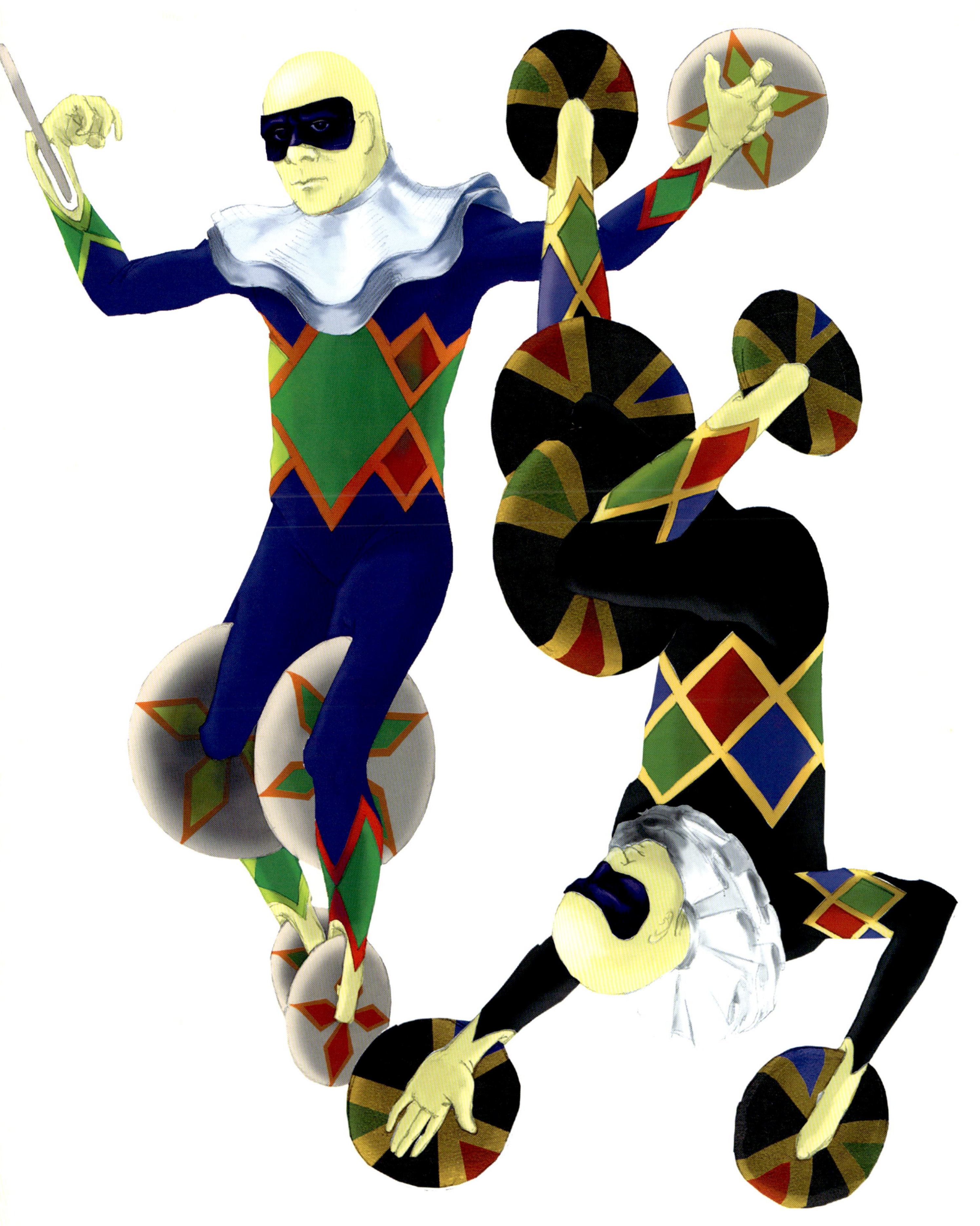

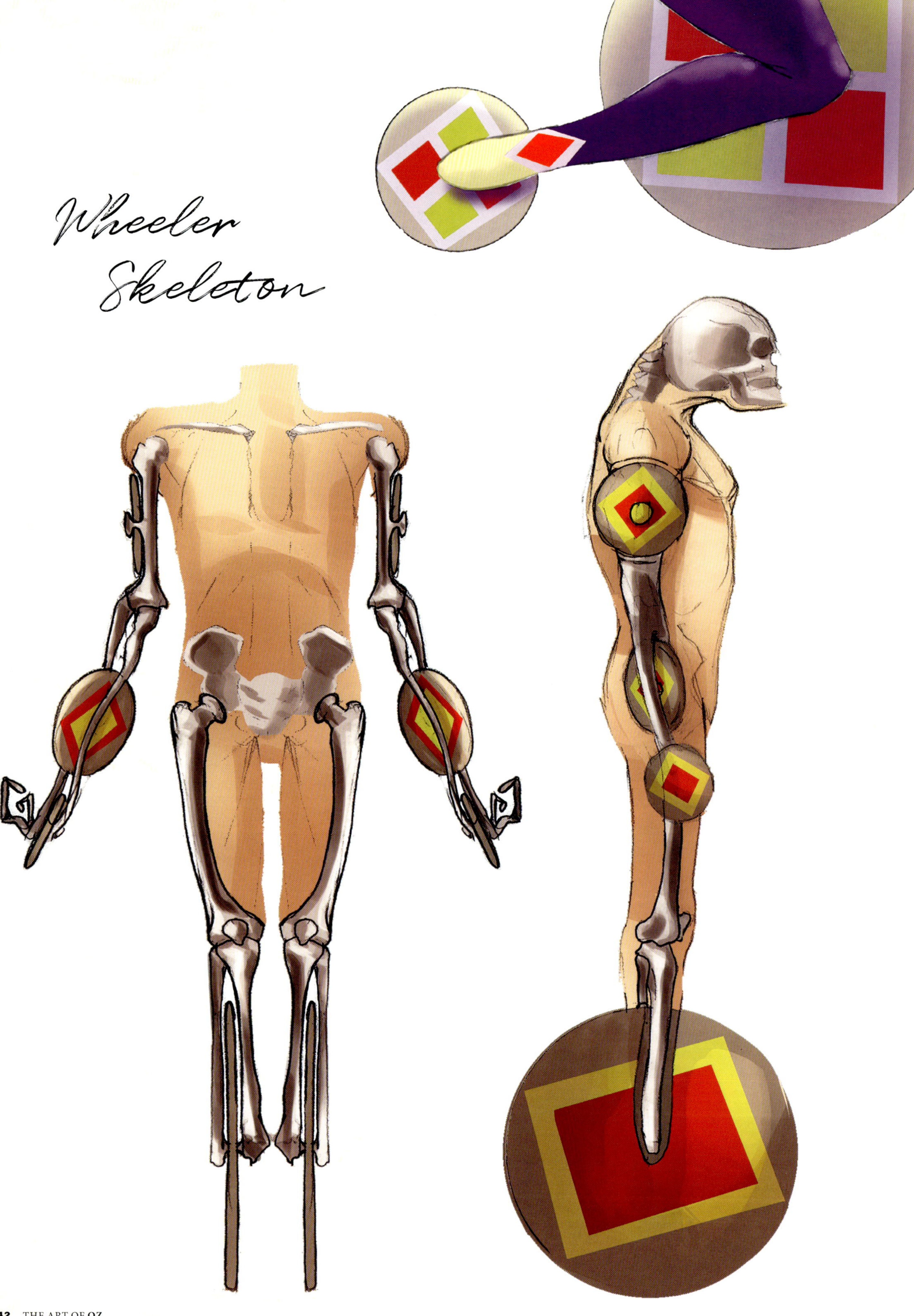
Wheeler
Skeleton

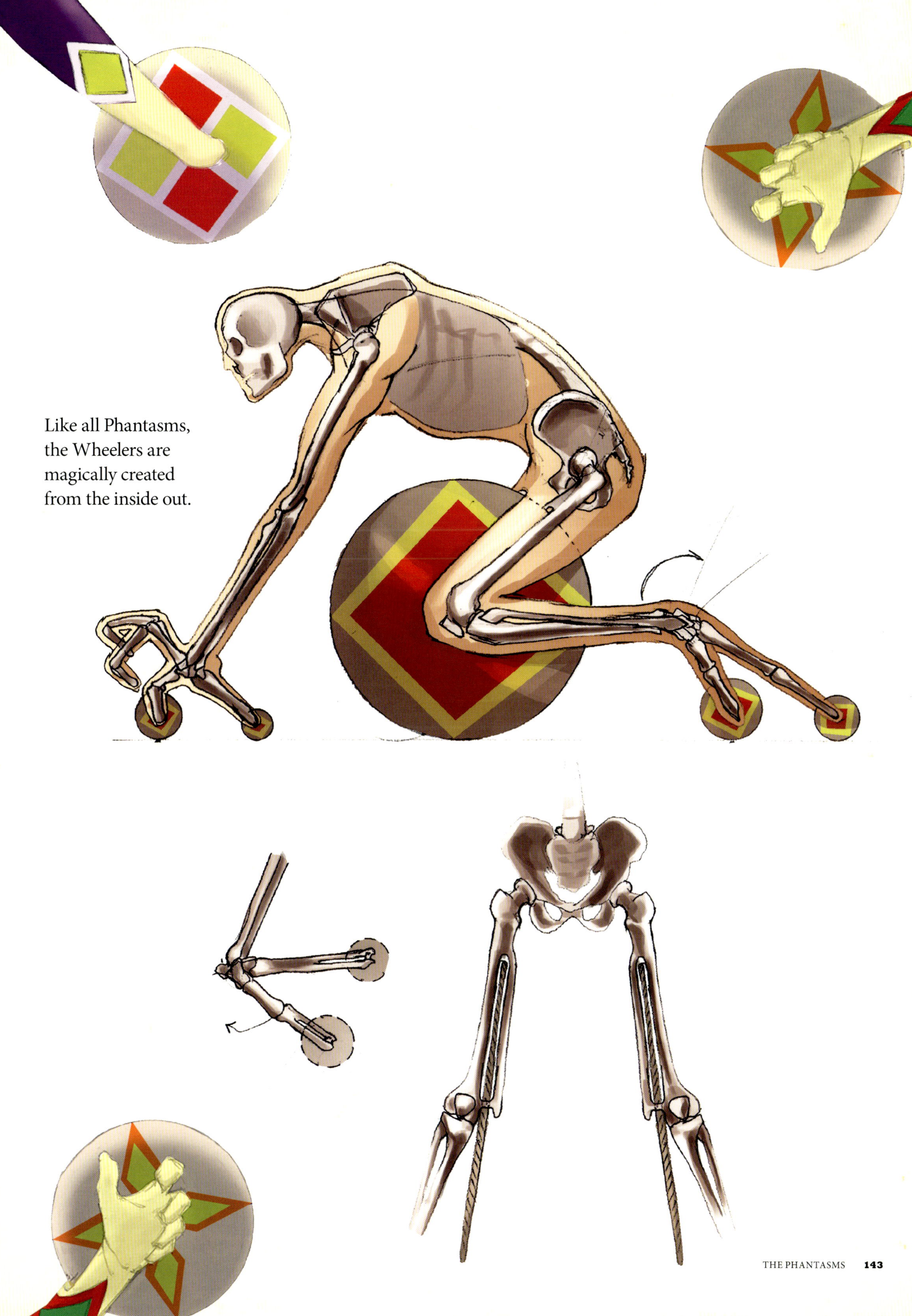

Like all Phantasms, the Wheelers are magically created from the inside out.

Flatheads

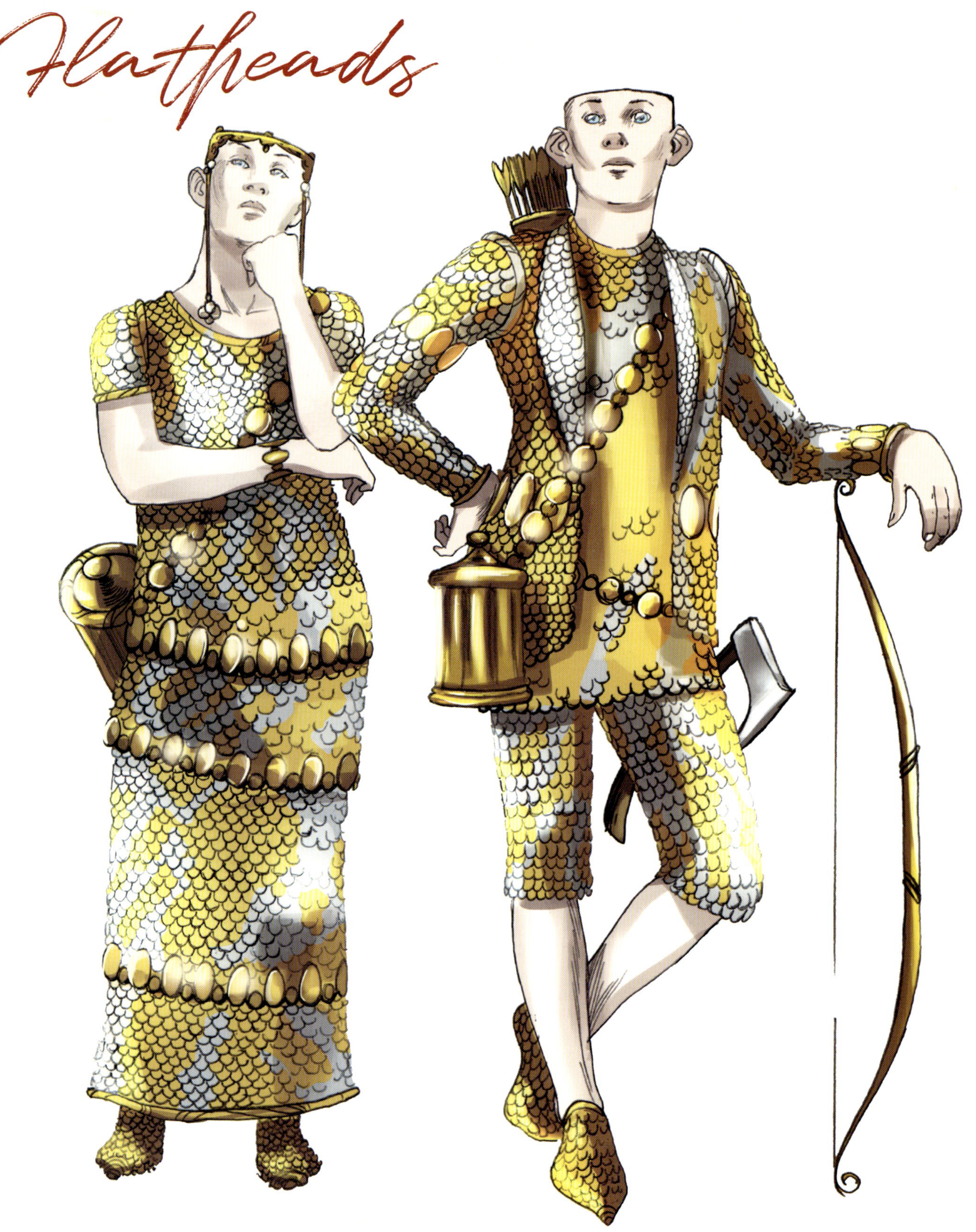

Until Glinda transformed them, the heads of the Flatheads were genuinely flat (as seen here) and looked as if they had stopped growing just above their eyes. Their clothes were also unique—made of precious metals that they mined and formed into discs. When wired together, the discs created their trousers, shirts, and skirts.

Growleywog

The monstrous Growleywogs are gigantic and all bone and skin and muscle. According to Mr. Baum, “the weakest Growleywog was so strong that he could pick up an elephant and toss it seven miles away.” Such strength made them feared, which pleased them. These hateful, disagreeable creatures are discussed in *The Emerald City of Oz*, when they join the Nomes, the Phanfasms, and the Whimsies in an effort to conquer and destroy Oz and make all the citizens their slaves.

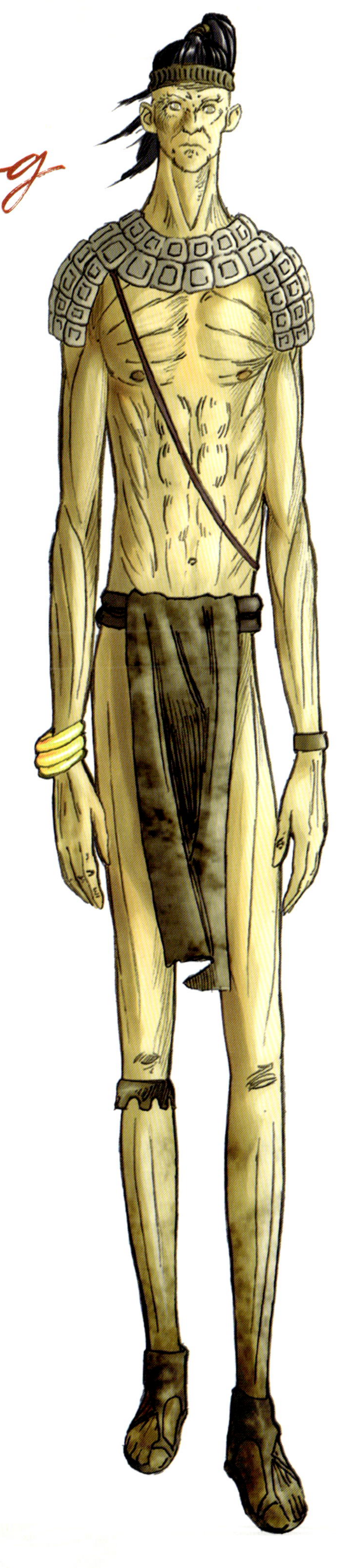

Hammer-Head

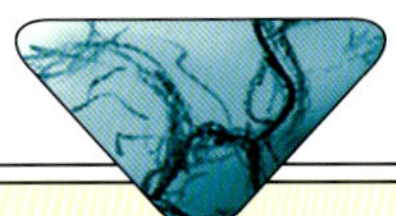

There stepped from behind the rock the strangest man the travelers had ever seen. He was quite short and stout and had a big head, which was flat at the top and supported by a thick neck full of wrinkles. But he had no arms at all, and seeing this, the Scarecrow did not fear that so helpless a creature could prevent them from climbing the hill . . . and he walked boldly forward. As quick as lightning, the man's head shot forward and his neck stretched out until the top of the head, where it was flat, struck the Scarecrow in the middle and sent him tumbling, over and over, down the hill. Almost as quickly as it came, the head went back to the body. . . . A chorus of boisterous laughter came from the other rocks, and Dorothy saw hundreds of the armless Hammer-Heads upon the hillside, one behind every rock.

—THE WONDERFUL WIZARD OF OZ

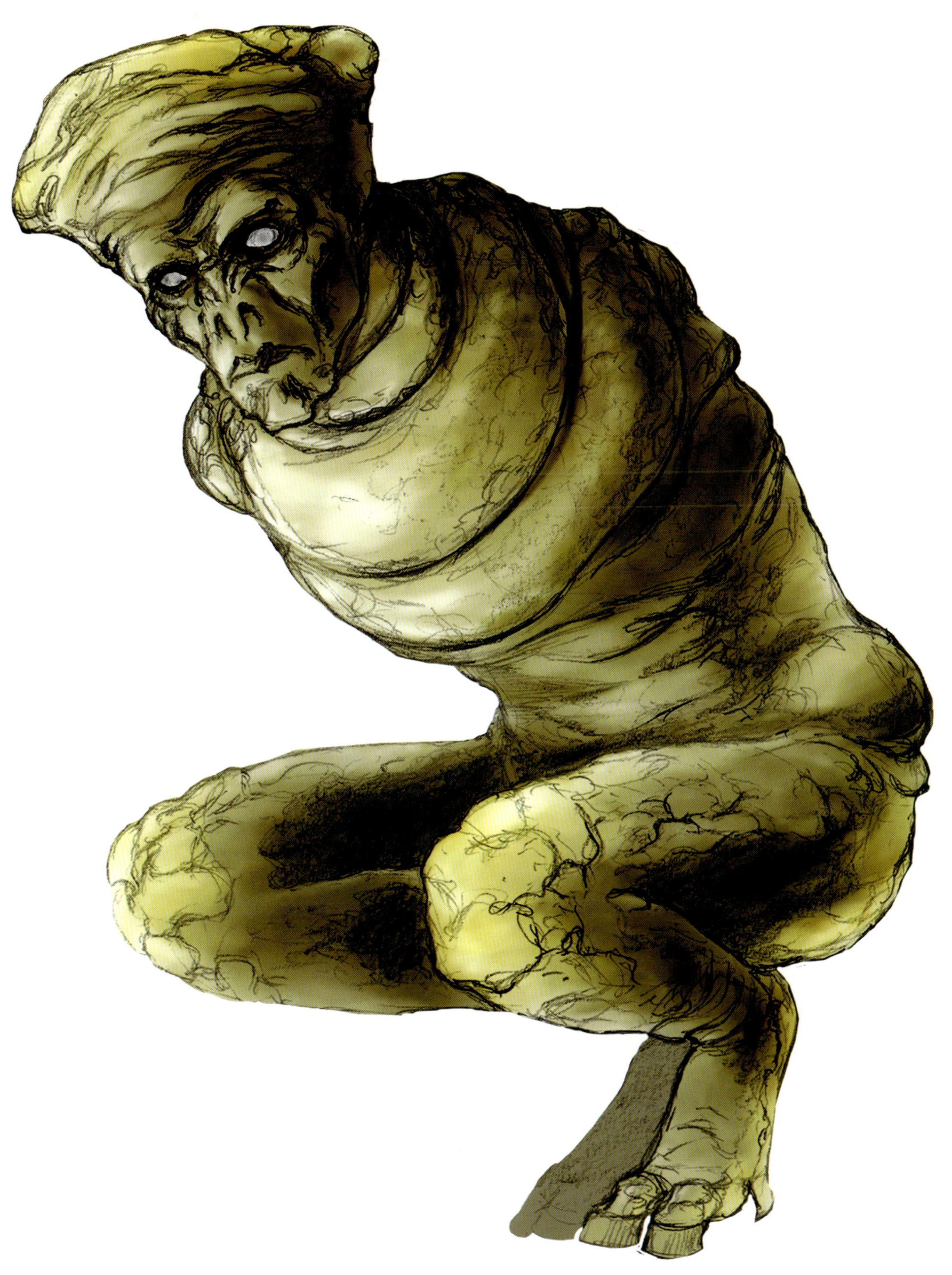

Hammer-Head Types

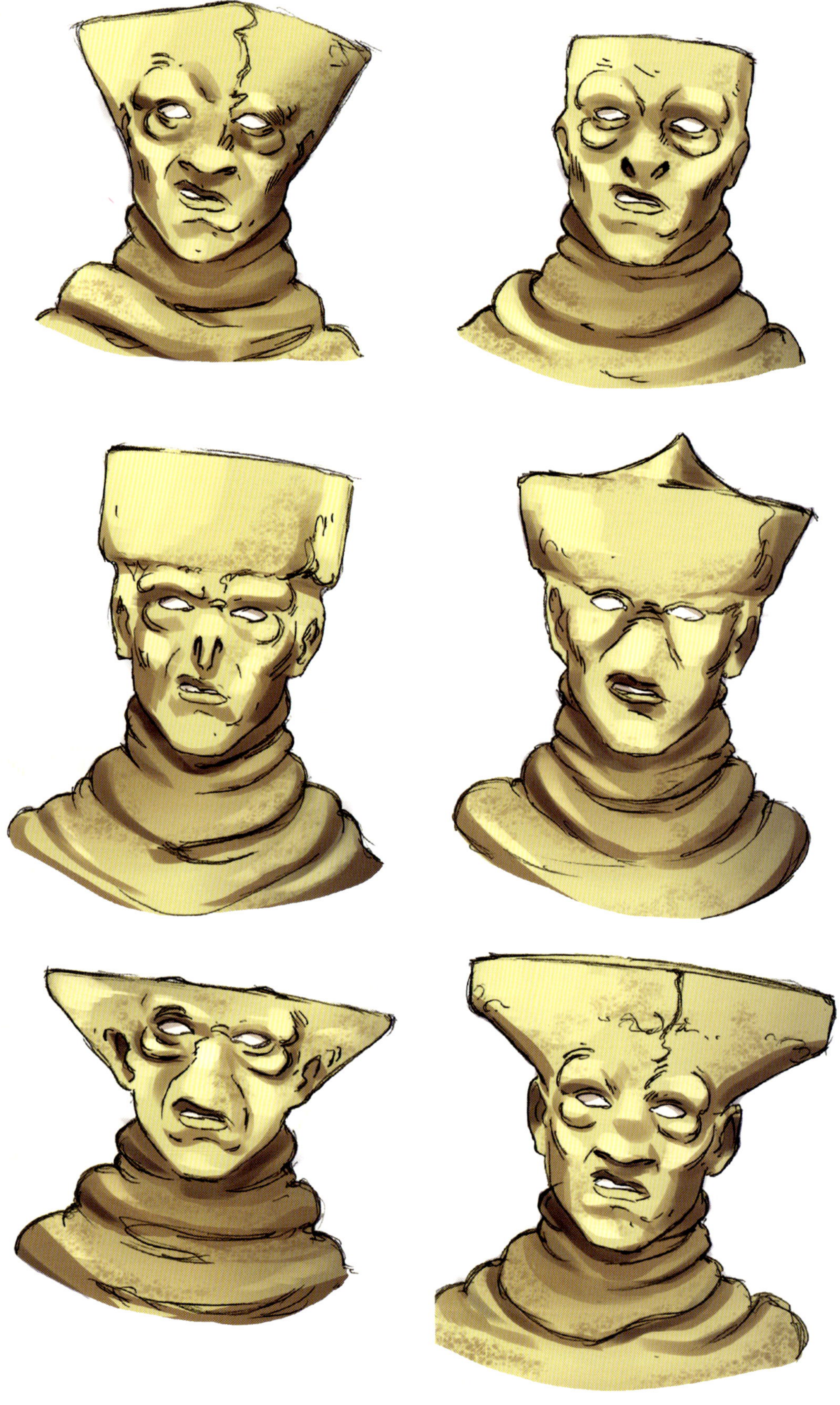

Hammer-Head Skeletons

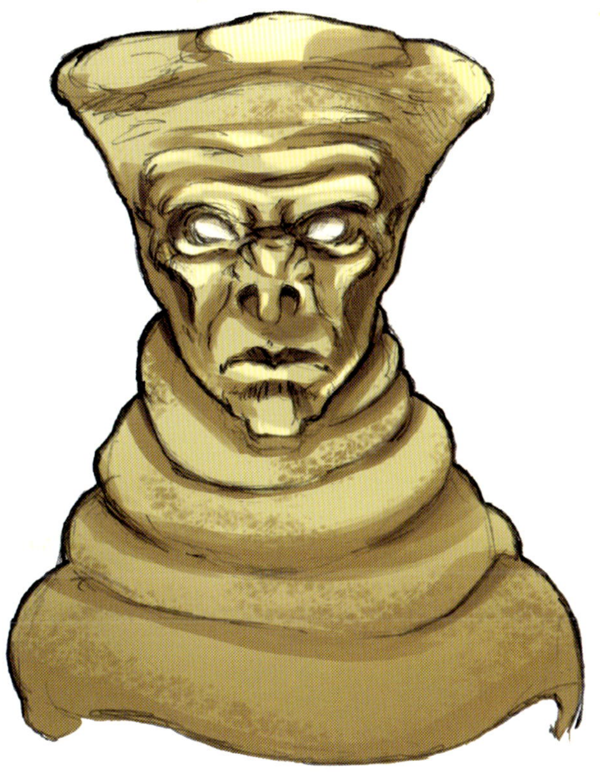

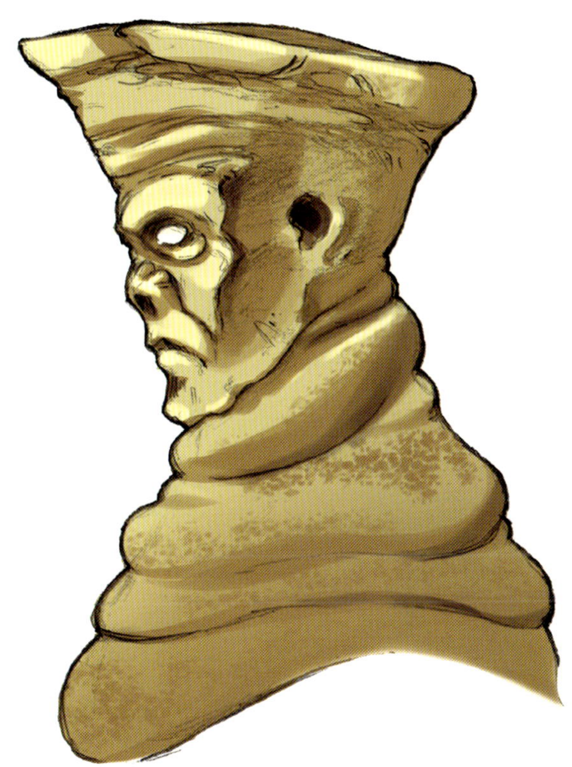

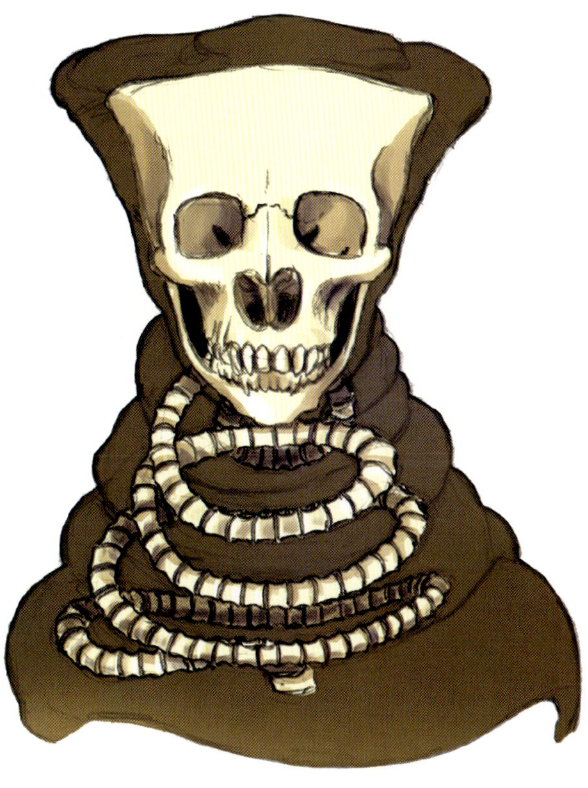

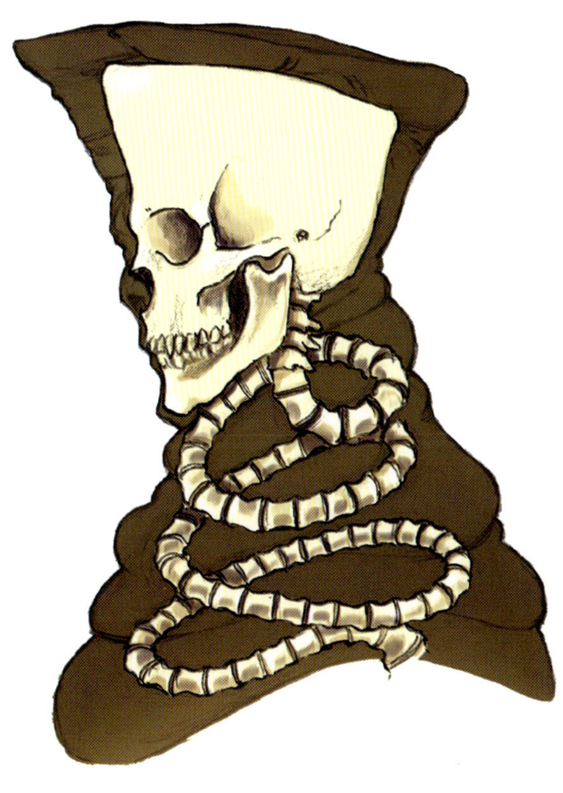

Scoodler

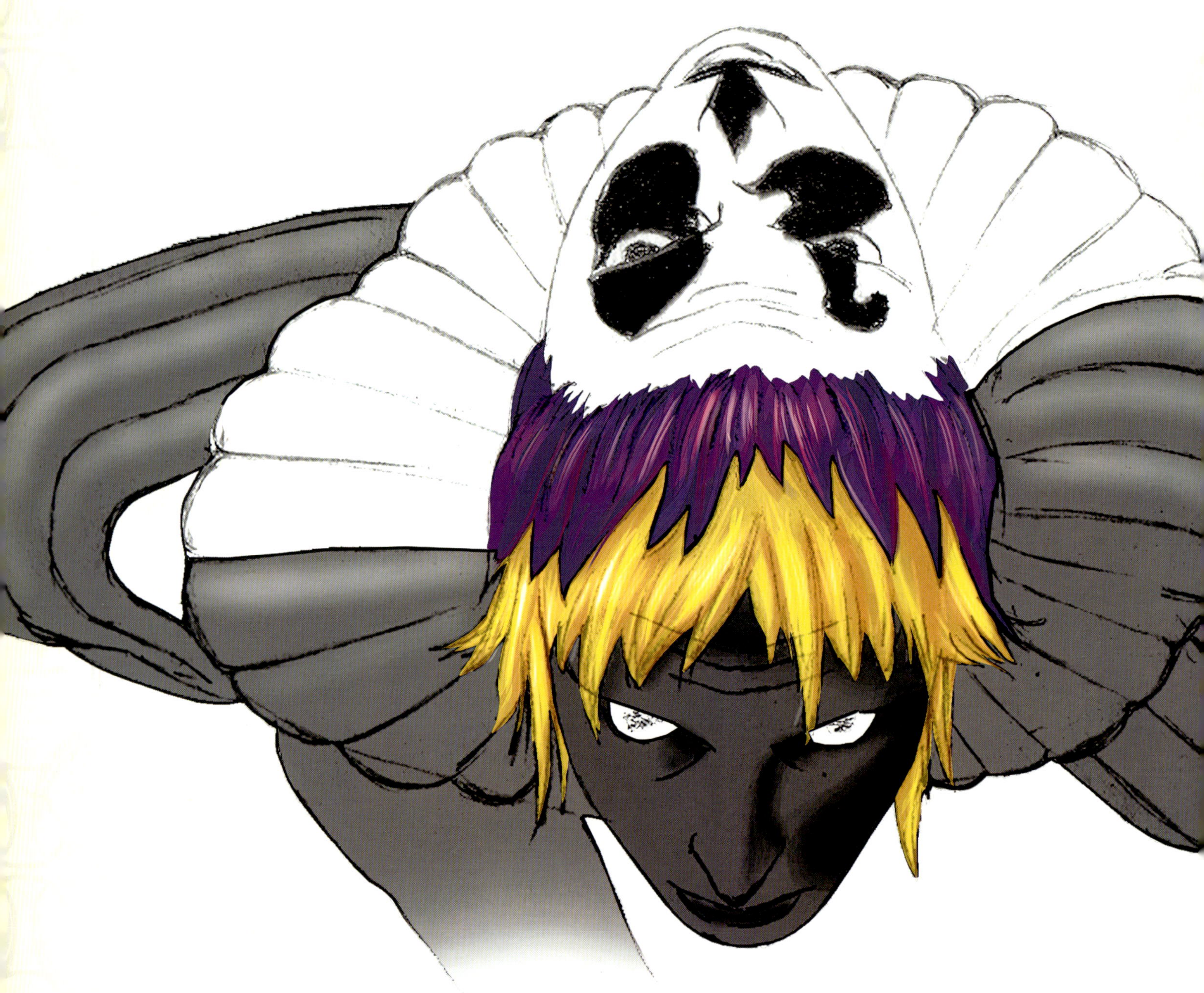

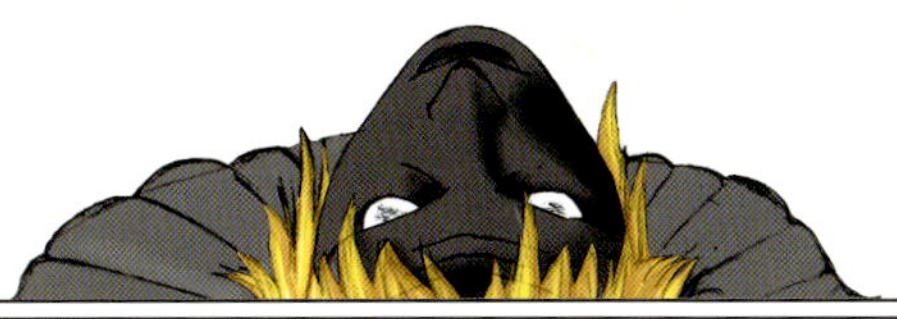

[The] curious creature had the form of a man, middle-sized and rather slender and graceful. . . . [Its] face was black as ink, and it wore a black cloth costume made like a union suit and fitting tight to its skin. Its hands were black, too, and its toes curled down, like a bird's. The creature was black all over except its hair, which was fine and yellow, banged in front across the black forehead and cut close at the sides. The eyes, which were fixed steadily upon Toto [Note from Toto: He knew to be wary of me!], *were small and sparkling and looked like the eyes of a weasel. The thing gave a jump and turned half around, sitting in the same place but with the other side of its body facing them. Instead of being black, it was now pure white, with a face like that of a clown in a circus and hair of a brilliant purple. The creature could bend either way, and its white toes now curled the same way the black ones on the other side had done. "It has a face both front and back," whispered Dorothy, wonderingly, "only there's no back at all, but two fronts."*

—THE ROAD TO OZ

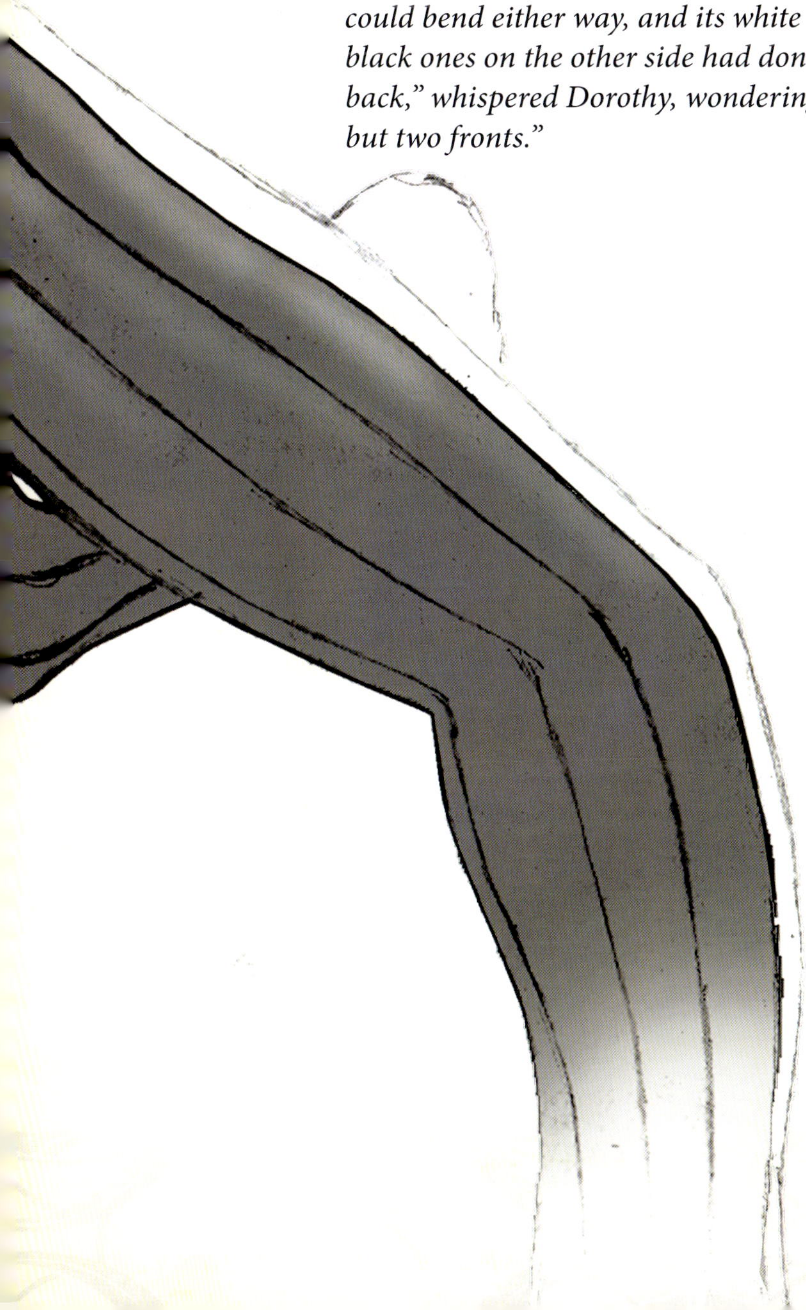

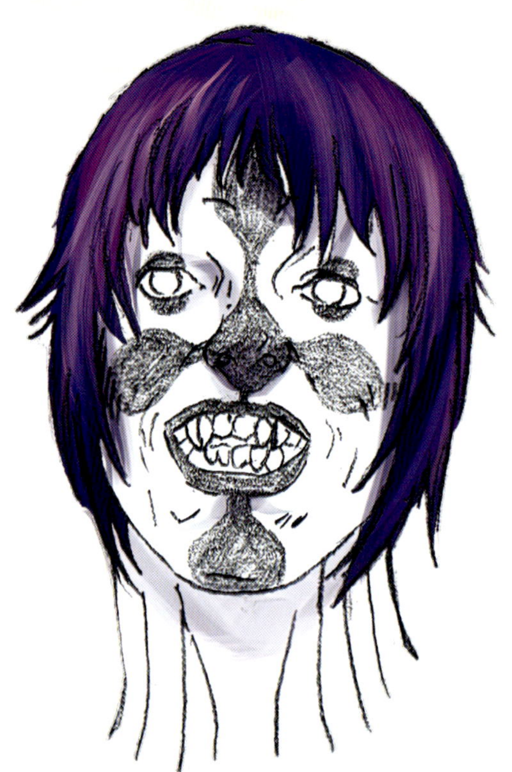

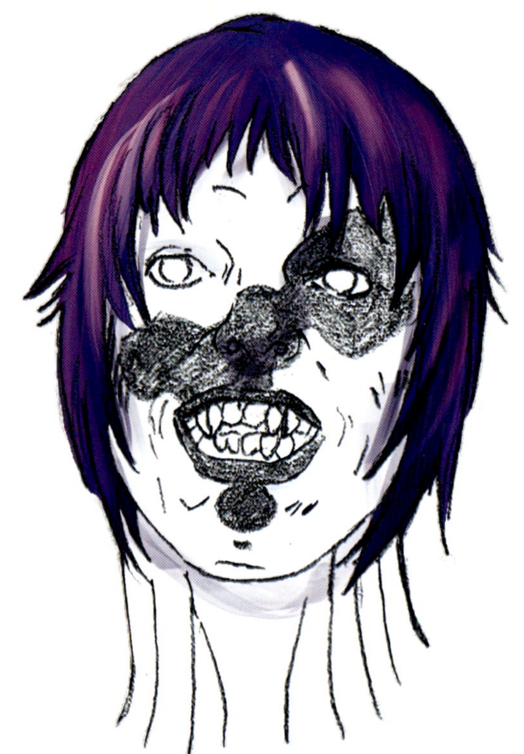

Scoodler Faces

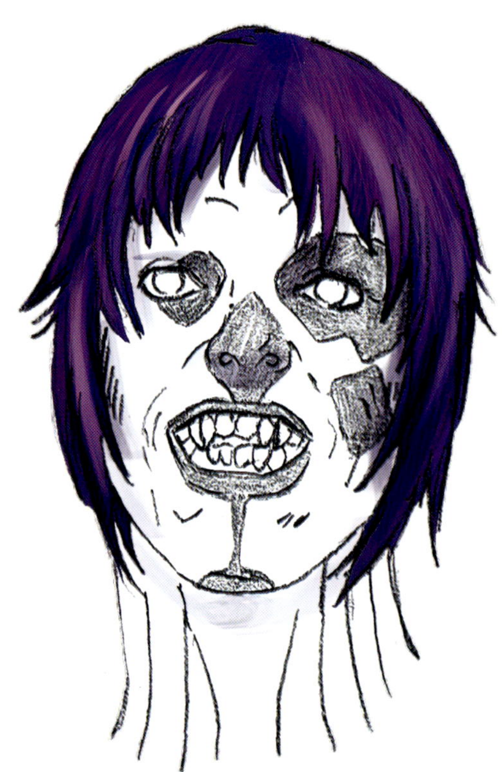

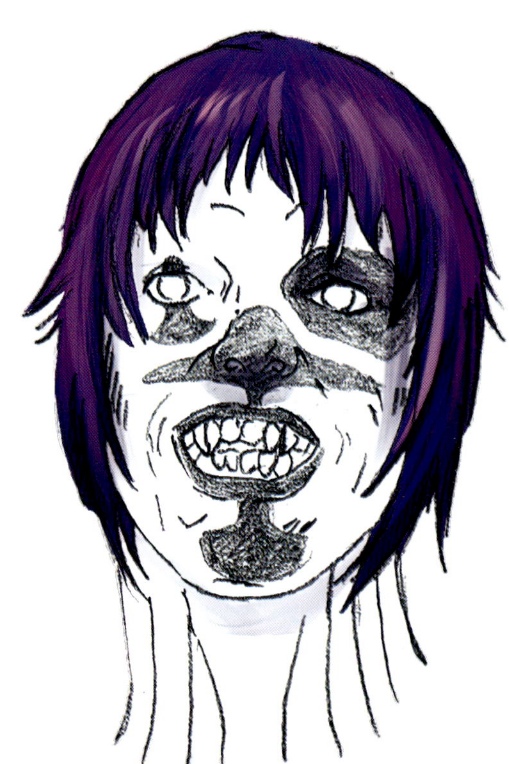

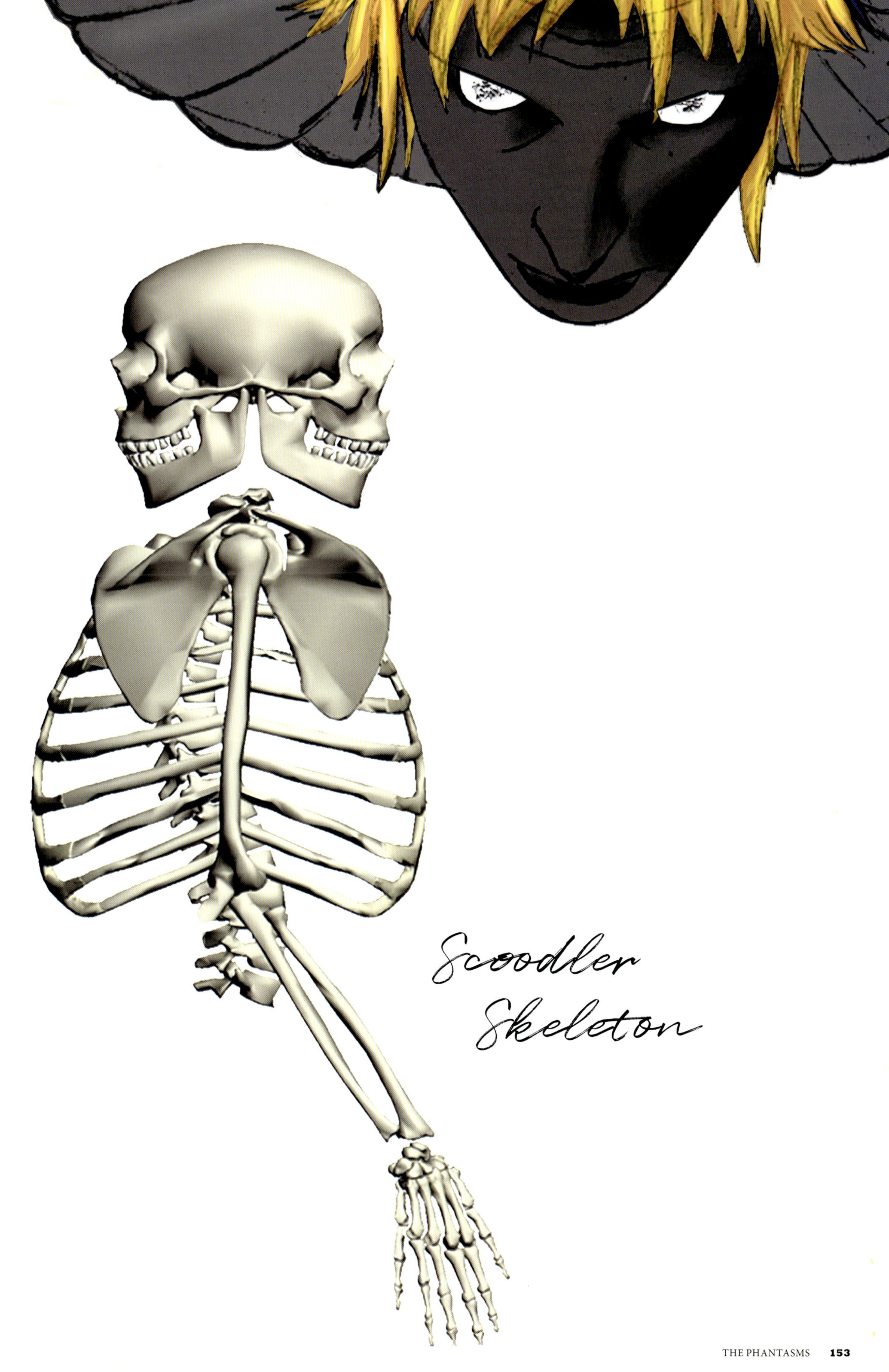
Scoodler
Skeleton

Hopper

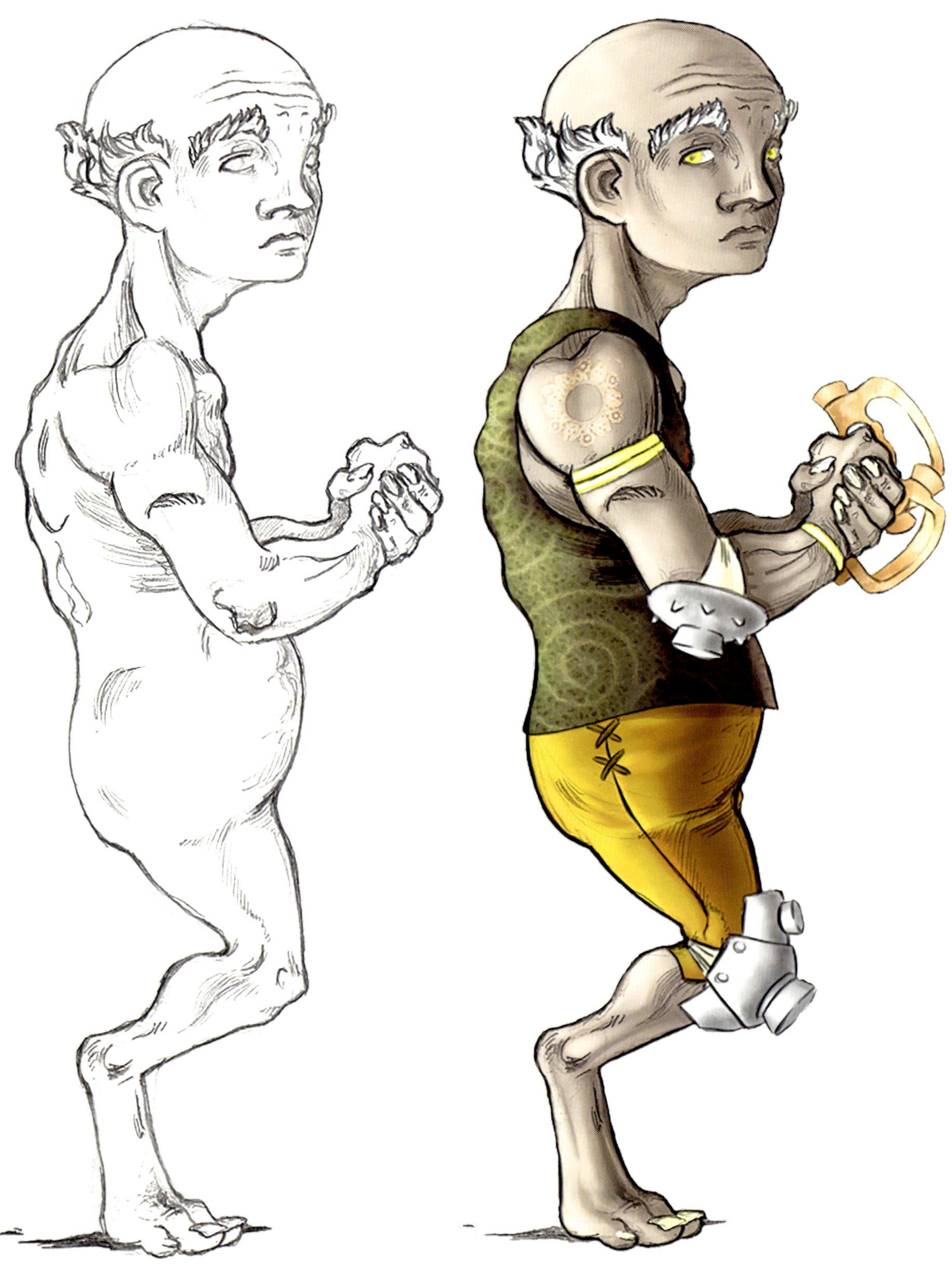

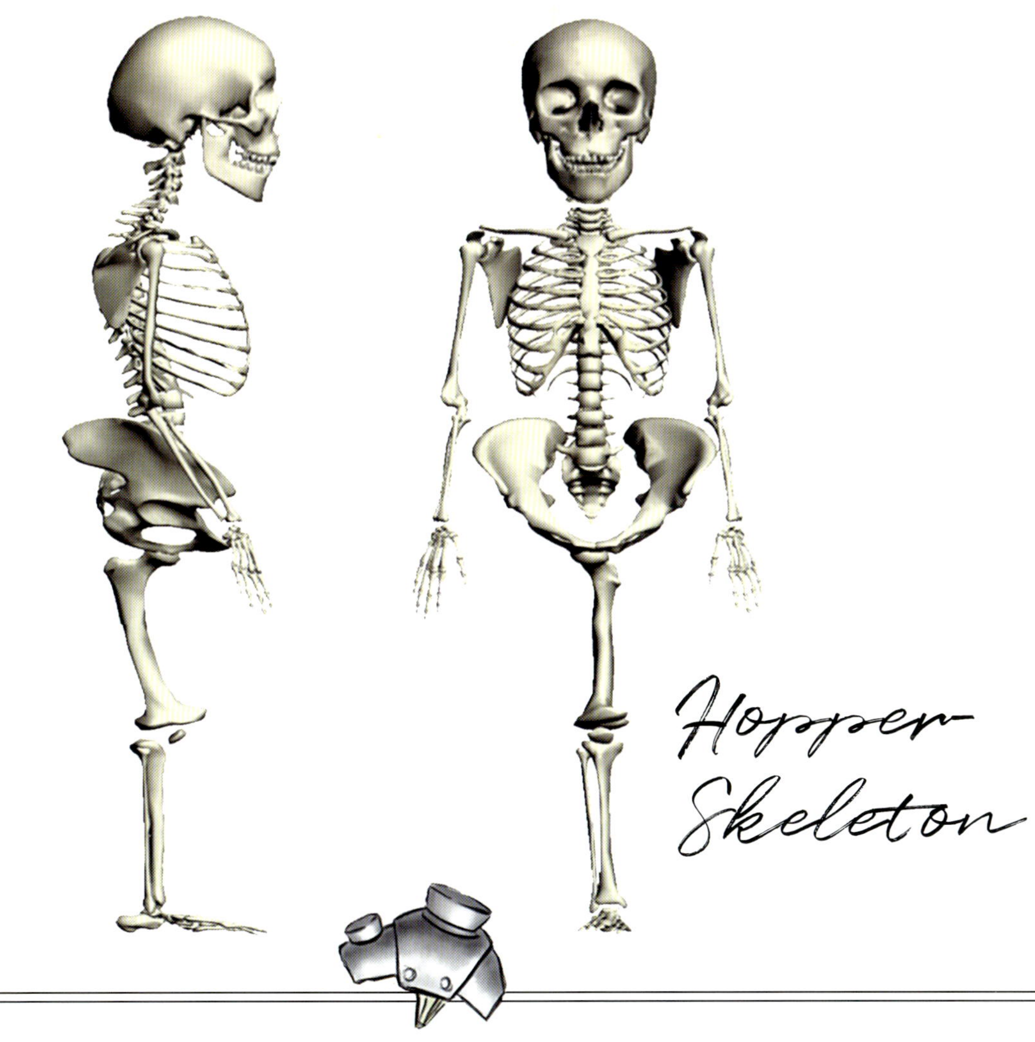

Toto, who had gone on ahead, began to bark loudly. [Dorothy, Ojo, Scraps the Patchwork Girl, and the Scarecrow] ran around a bend and found a man sitting on the floor of the passage. . . . There was something about this man that Toto objected to, and when he slowly rose to his foot, they saw what it was. He had but one leg, set just below the middle of his round, fat body; but it was a stout leg and had a broad, flat foot at the bottom of it, on which the man seemed to stand very well. He had never had but this one leg, which looked something like a pedestal, and when Toto ran up and made a grab at the man's ankle, he hopped first one way and then another in a very active manner, looking so frightened that Scraps laughed aloud. Toto was usually a well-behaved dog [Note from Toto: Thank you, Mr. Baum!], *but this time he was angry and snapped at the man's leg again and again. This filled the poor fellow with fear, and in hopping out of Toto's reach, he suddenly lost his balance and tumbled heel-over-head upon the floor. When he sat up, he kicked Toto on the nose and made the dog howl angrily, but Dorothy now ran forward and caught Toto's collar, holding him back.*

—THE PATCHWORK GIRL OF OZ

Horner

They were little folks in size and had bodies round as balls and short legs and arms. Their heads were round, too, and they had long, pointed ears and a horn set in the center of the forehead. The horns did not seem very terrible, for they were not more than six inches long; but they were ivory white and sharp pointed, and no wonder the Hoppers feared them. The skins of the Horners were light brown, [and] they were bare-footed.

—THE PATCHWORK GIRL OF OZ

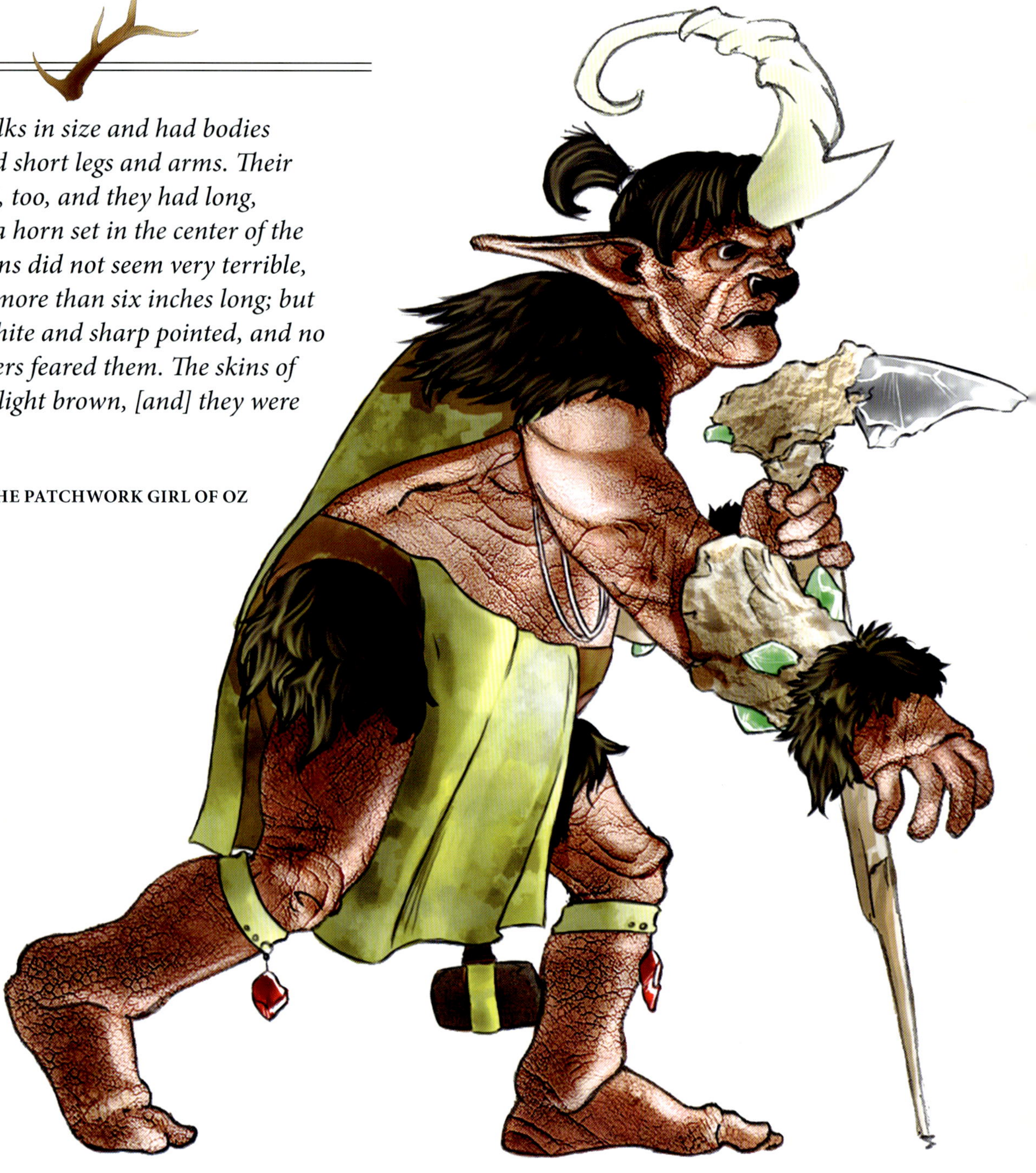

Horner Horns

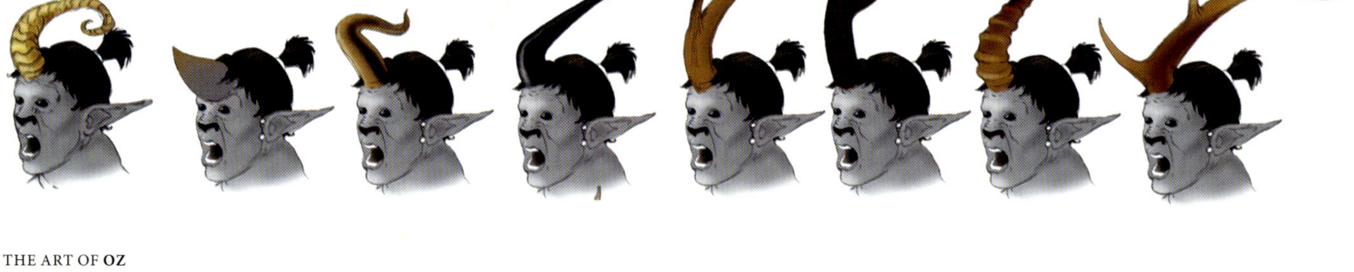

Frogman

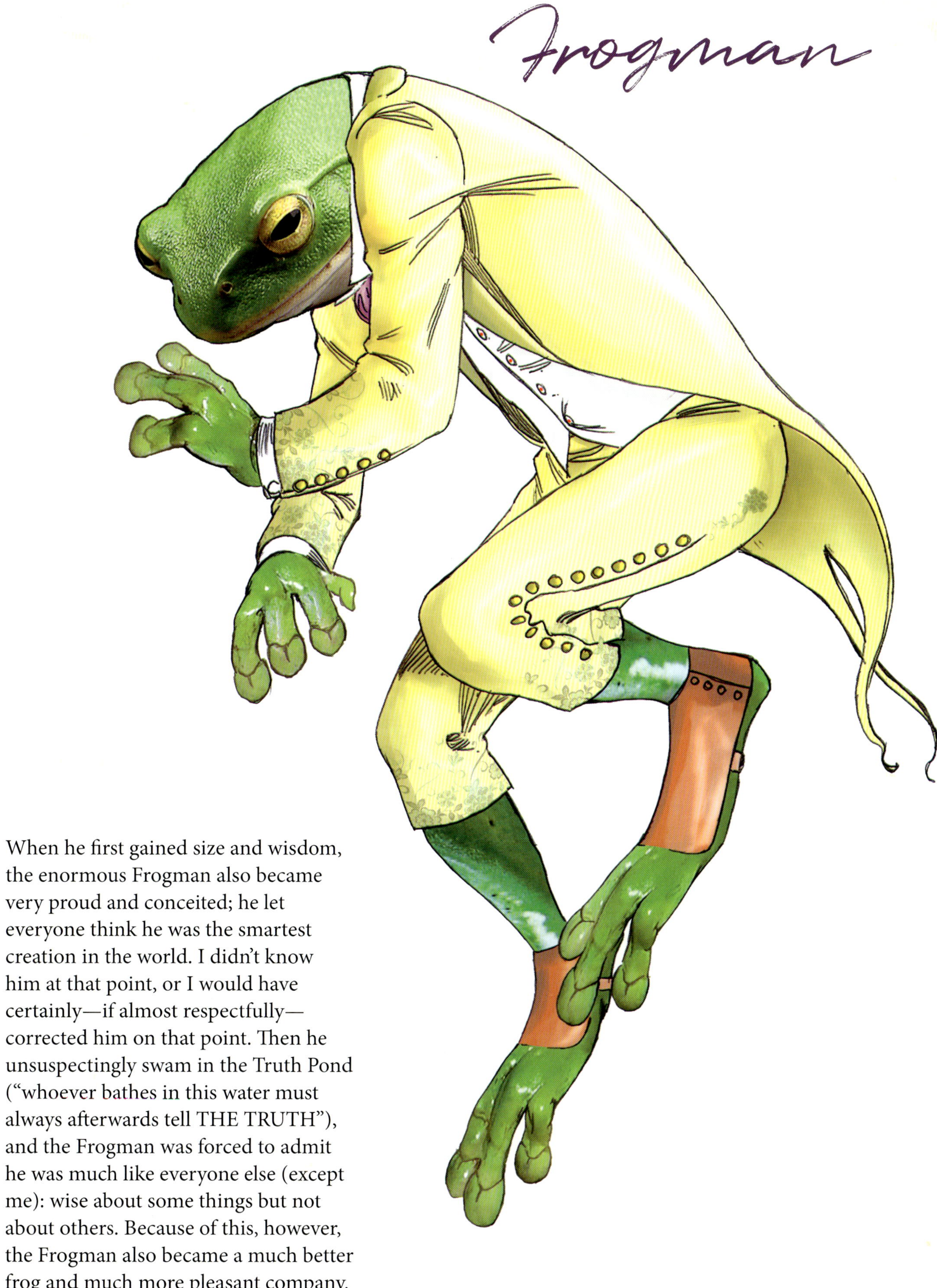

When he first gained size and wisdom, the enormous Frogman also became very proud and conceited; he let everyone think he was the smartest creation in the world. I didn't know him at that point, or I would have certainly—if almost respectfully—corrected him on that point. Then he unsuspectingly swam in the Truth Pond ("whoever bathes in this water must always afterwards tell THE TRUTH"), and the Frogman was forced to admit he was much like everyone else (except me): wise about some things but not about others. Because of this, however, the Frogman also became a much better frog and much more pleasant company.

The Emerald City

INTRODUCED BY THE WIZARD

"I am Oz, the Great and Terrible. . . ."

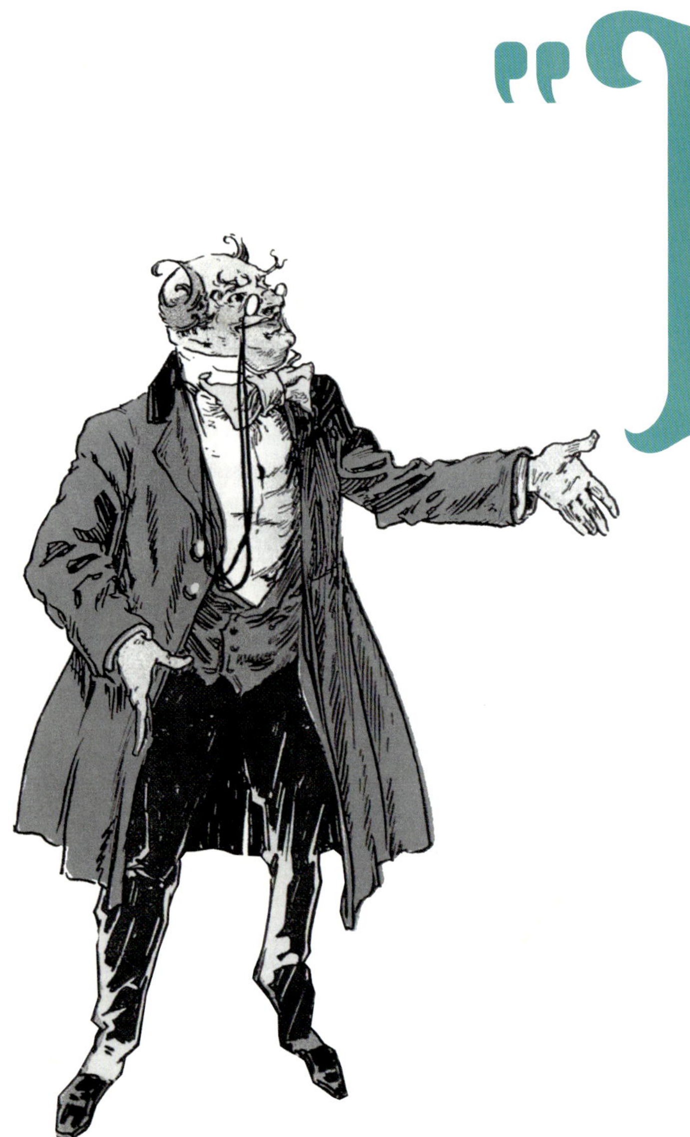

Those were the first words I spoke to Dorothy Gale, as recorded by L. Frank Baum in his book *The Wonderful Wizard of Oz*. A bit later, however, I had to admit to her and her friends that I wasn't great, terrible, or wonderful. I was, instead, "making believe"—and "a humbug." That last was the declaration of the Scarecrow, and he realized this about me even before receiving his highly superior brains.

Though I was a very bad wizard, I did try to be a very good man and to aid those I could. Soon after helping Dorothy's friends, I left the Emerald City in my balloon, but I eventually returned to Oz to stay. Since then, I have become a genuine Wizard, thanks to the remarkable training of Glinda the Good. Only she and I and Princess Ozma are now permitted to perform magic to benefit Oz and its people.

There is one achievement from back in my humbug days of which I am proud: It was my idea to build the Emerald City. On that first

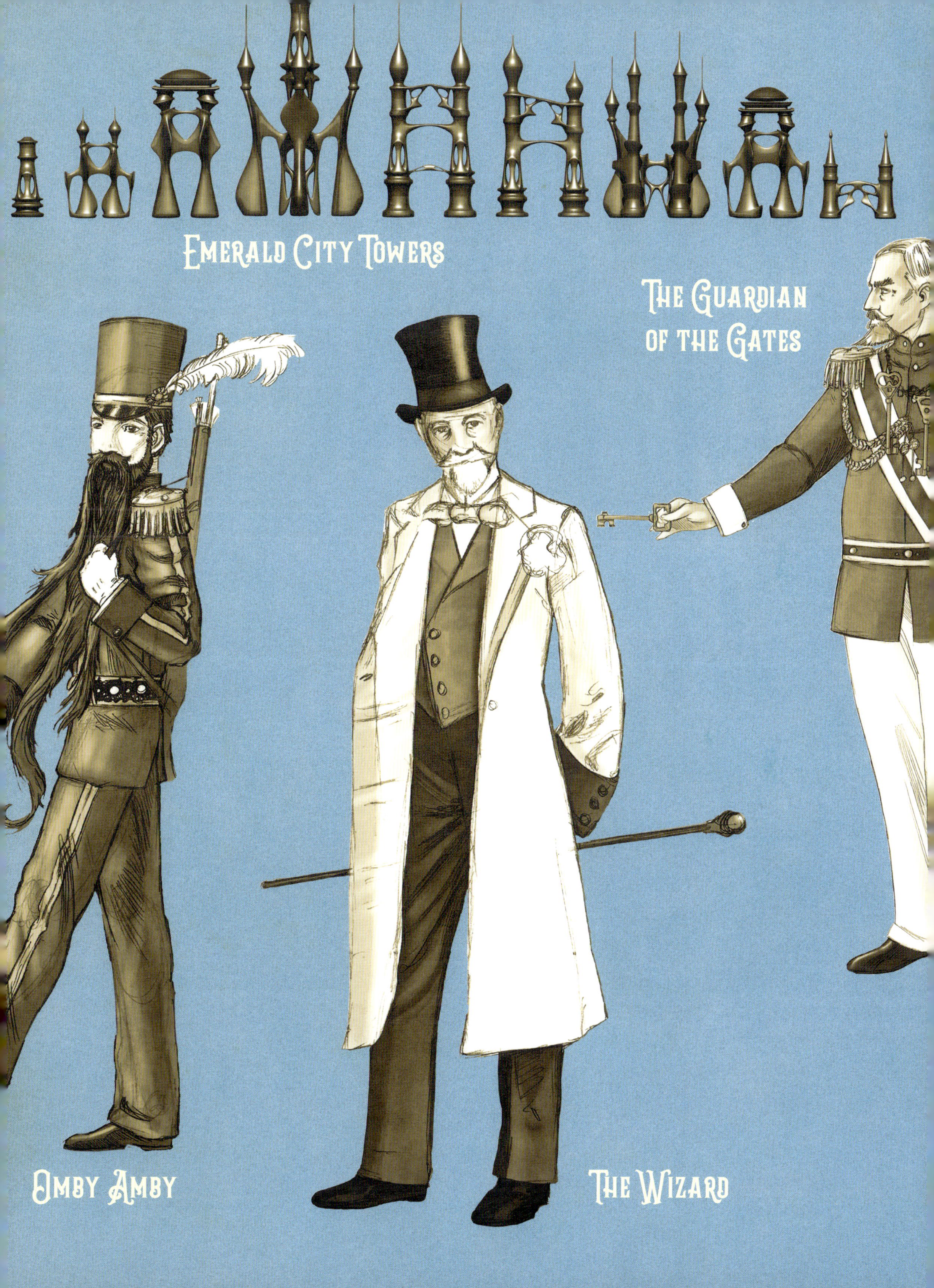
Emerald City Towers
The Guardian
of the Gates
Omby Amby
The Wizard

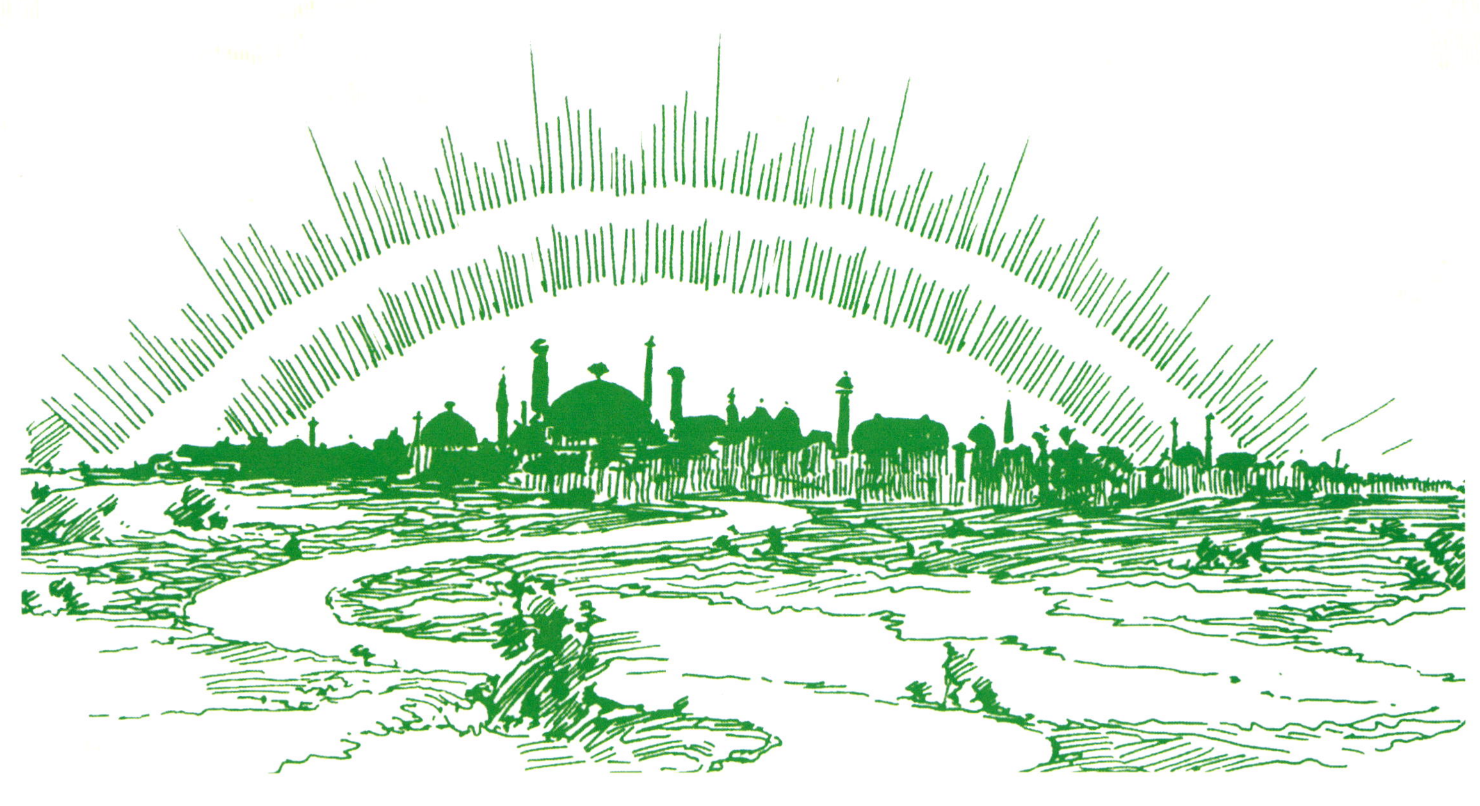

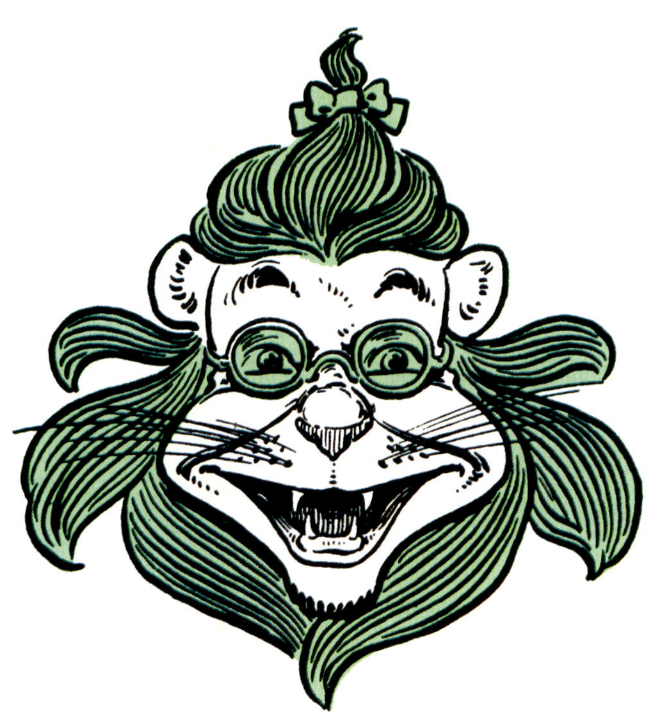

visit—when a windstorm blew me here from the United States—I was acclaimed by the Ozites as a Wizard, and there were two reasons for this. First, I chanced to come out of the sky in the exact center of the country, precisely (if coincidentally) where the castle of the long-lost "King Oz" had stood. Second, my balloon had the letters "OZ" painted on it, as those are my first two initials; my name is Oscar Zoroaster Diggs. Yet those who welcomed me thought "OZ" meant I was their new, rightful ruler, and when they explained this, I decided to both take the job and earn their kindness. Together, we created the capital city, primarily as protection from the Wicked Witches who back then ruled the four countries around us.

I supremely appreciated such safety and such a home, although to tell the truth, the people did the work. (As we used to say in my native Omaha, I "only bossed the job.") The populace brought together luminous marble and bushes of jewels—mostly emeralds—which enabled the construction of a shimmering city surrounded by gem-encrusted walls. These workers paved the streets with additional marble and rare metals,

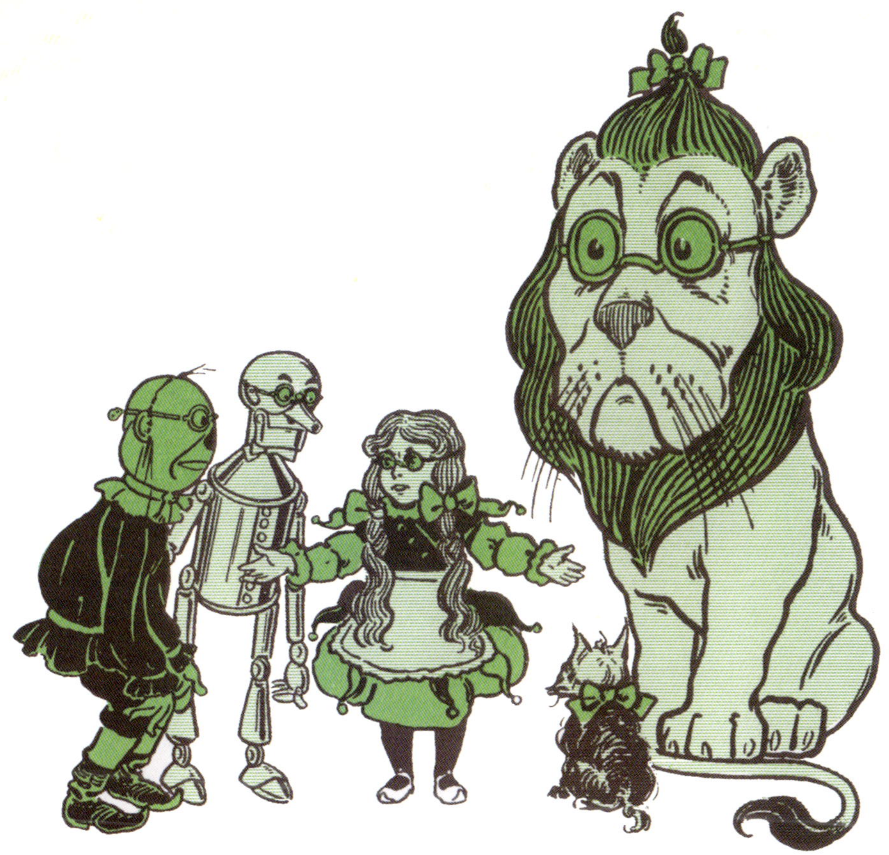

and studded them with other precious stones. They built Ozian homes—everything from amiable single dwellings (that look like they're smiling!) to emerald-covered skyscrapers. Finally, in the middle of the City, we erected the Royal Palace; its radiance sparkles in the sun and lights the skies for miles around.

I have many trusted companions among the people of the Emerald City, including two gentlemen who befriended me early on; their loyalty has meant much to me and to the town. One is our Guardian of the Gates, who is the first person that visitors meet when they arrive here. For years, it was at his careful insistence that all who entered must wear spectacles to protect their eyes from the brightness of our innumerable jewels. These glasses were fitted with green lenses, which also heightened the hues of lime-, avocado-, jade-, olive-, and turquoise-shaded emeralds everywhere on display. Eventually, we discovered that the enchanted quality of these gems was such that any damage to the eyes was precluded, so we abandoned the use of such spectacles. Also—and to be honest—I didn't completely understand the growing magic of Oz in

PAGE 158: The Wizard by Neill, *The Patchwork Girl of Oz*
OPPOSITE TOP: The glow of the Emerald City may be seen from miles away.
OPPOSITE BOTTOM: I think it's apparent that the Cowardly Lion had just received his courage from the Wizard when this portrait was made!
ABOVE: On Dorothy's first visits to the Emerald City, she and her companions had to wear green spectacles—just like all the other residents at that time.
All art by Denslow, *The Wonderful Wizard of Oz*

those years, and I thought the glasses were needed so as to make everything appear to be green. It *was* green (and getting greener!) all the time.

My other faithful confidant is Omby Amby, the Soldier with the Green Whiskers. Through the years, he graduated from private to captain general of the Army of Oz (he is now its sole member); he also serves as Ozma's official bodyguard. As a firm believer in peace, he brandishes a musket that has flowers growing out of its barrel and is quite the most benevolent protector we could desire.

There are many more in my "extended family" here, and I am more content and in demand than at any point in my past careers with Bailum & Barney's Great Consolidated Shows or the Miracle Wonderland Carnival Company. How extraordinary it is to have secured a home in the city I helped build.

And how awed and grateful I am to be . . . the Wizard of Oz.

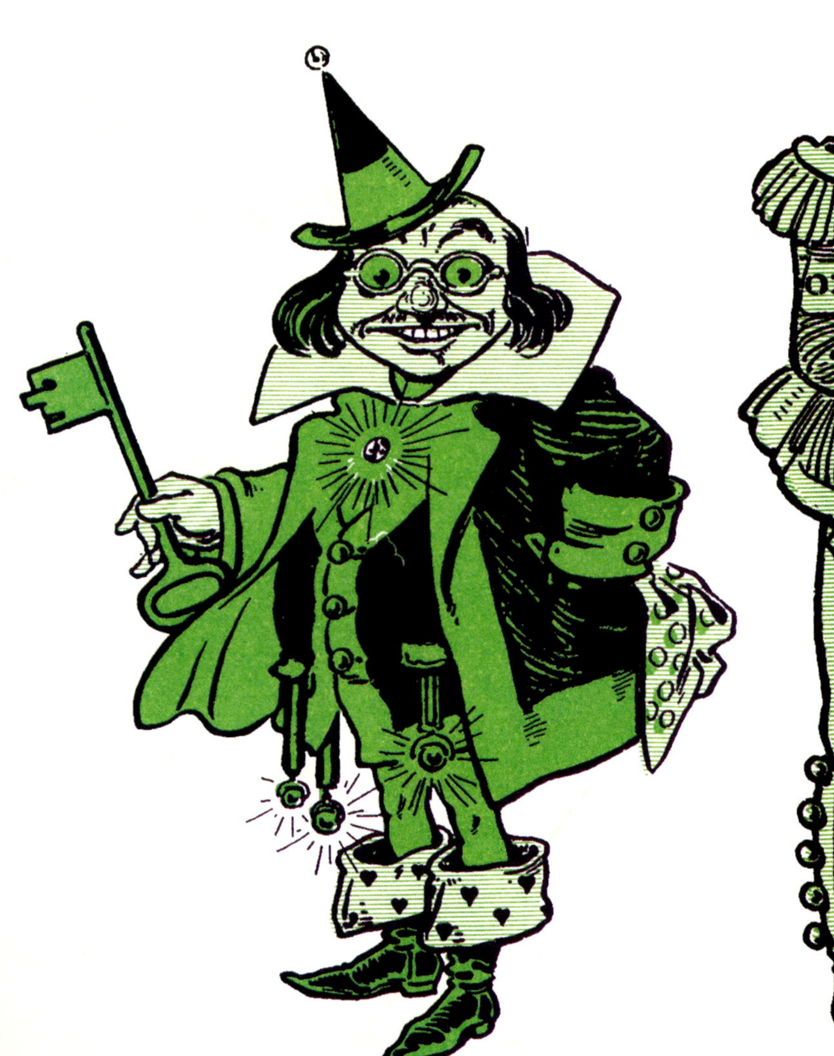

LEFT: The Guardian of the Gates and the Soldier with the Green Whiskers have been Emerald City officials ever since the Wizard built our capital. Art by Denslow, *The Wonderful Wizard of Oz*. **OPPOSITE**: Both on duty! The Guardian and the Soldier (whose name is Omby Amby) welcome newcomers—little knowing that Jack Pumpkinhead and the Sawhorse would be instrumental in bringing Princess Ozma to the throne as our Rightful Ruler. Art by Neill, *The Marvelous Land of Oz*.

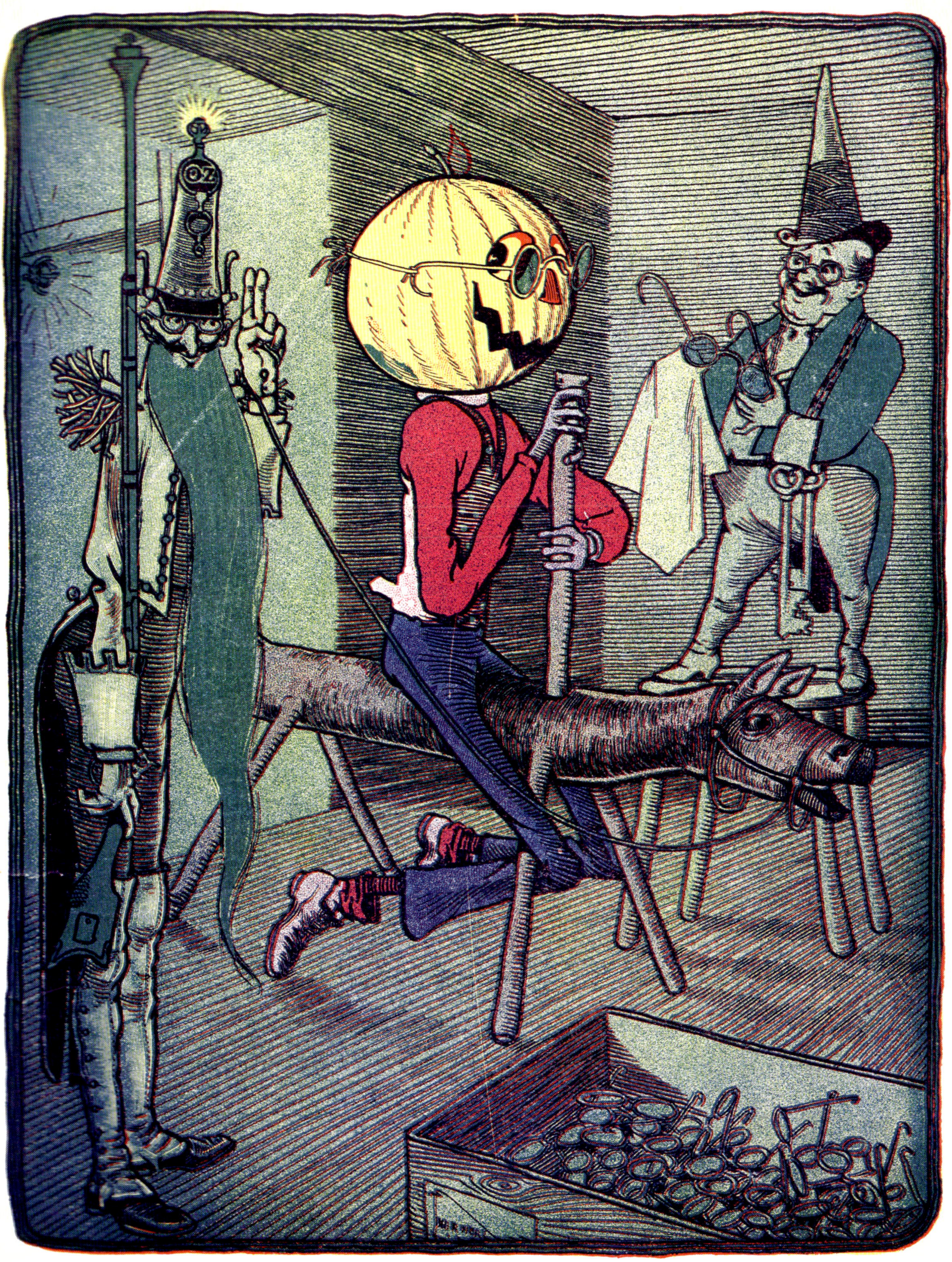
OZ

The Wizard

[The Wizard told them:] My father, who was a politician, named me Oscar Zoroaster Phadrig Isaac Norman Henkle Emmannuel Ambroise Diggs, Diggs being the last name because he could think of no more to go before it. Taken altogether, it was a dreadfully long name to weigh down a poor innocent child, and one of the hardest lessons I ever learned was to remember my own name. When I grew up, I just called myself O. Z., because the other initials were P-I-N-H-E-A-D; and that spelled "pinhead," which was a reflection on my intelligence.

—DOROTHY AND THE WIZARD IN OZ

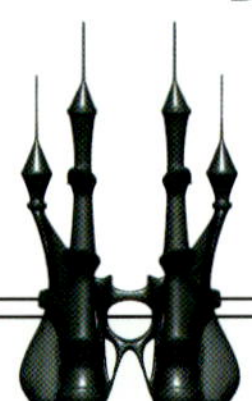

The Wizard of Oz . . . had a room fitted up in one of the high towers of the palace, where he studied magic so as to be able to perform such wizardry as Ozma commanded him to do for the welfare of her subjects. The Wizard and Dorothy were firm friends and had enjoyed many strange adventures together. He was a little man with a bald head and sharp eyes and a round, jolly face, and because he was neither haughty nor proud, he had become a great favorite with the Oz people.

—THE MAGIC OF OZ

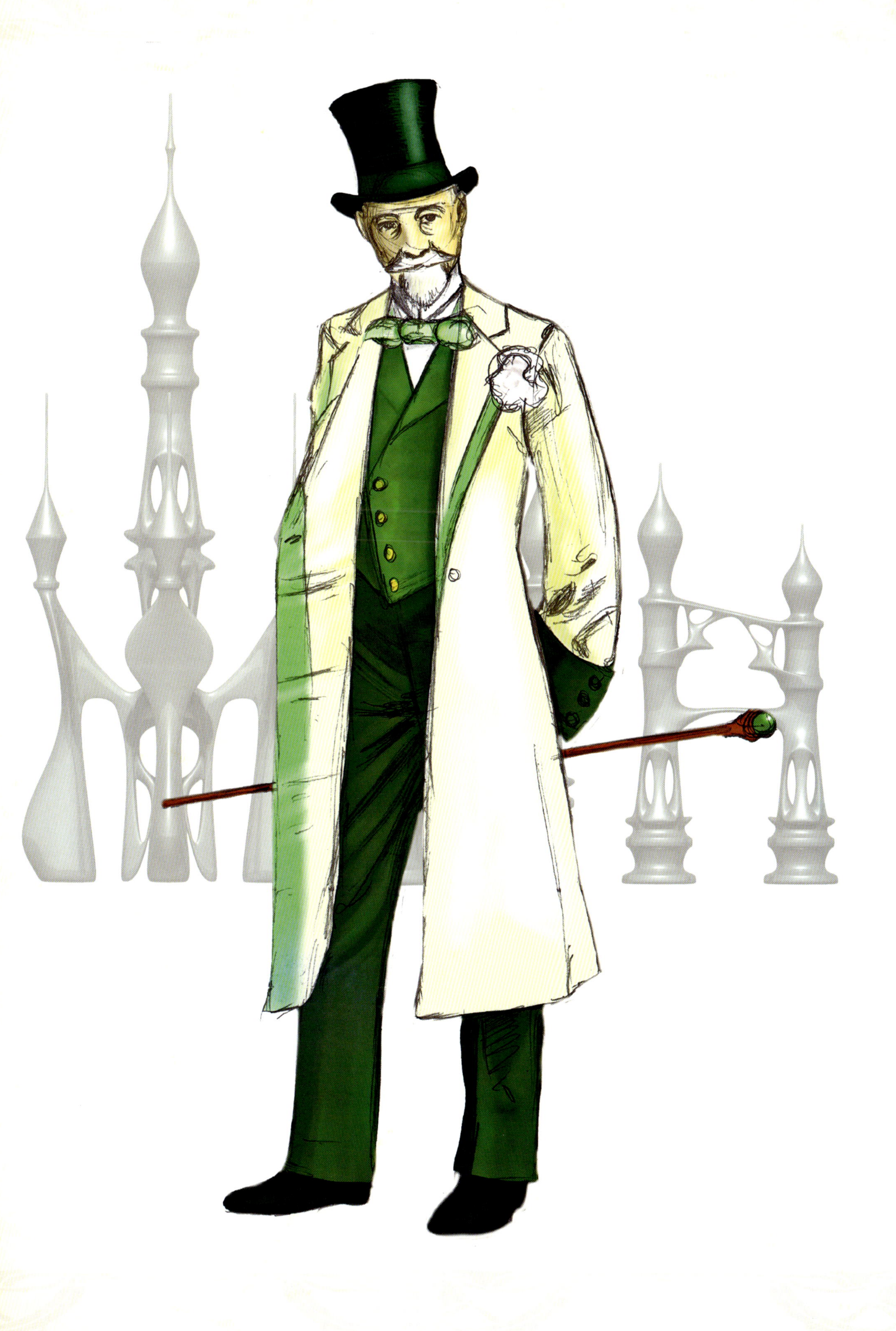

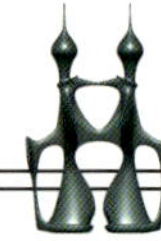

The next morning, as soon as the sun was up, they started on their way and soon saw a beautiful green glow in the sky just before them. As they walked on, the green glow became brighter and brighter, and it seemed that at last they were nearing the end of their travels. [When] they came to the great wall that surrounded the City, it was high and thick and of a bright green color. In front of them, and at the end of the road of yellow brick, was a big gate, all studded with emeralds that glittered so in the sun that even the painted eyes of the Scarecrow were dazzled by their brilliancy.

—THE WONDERFUL WIZARD OF OZ

Emerald City Towers

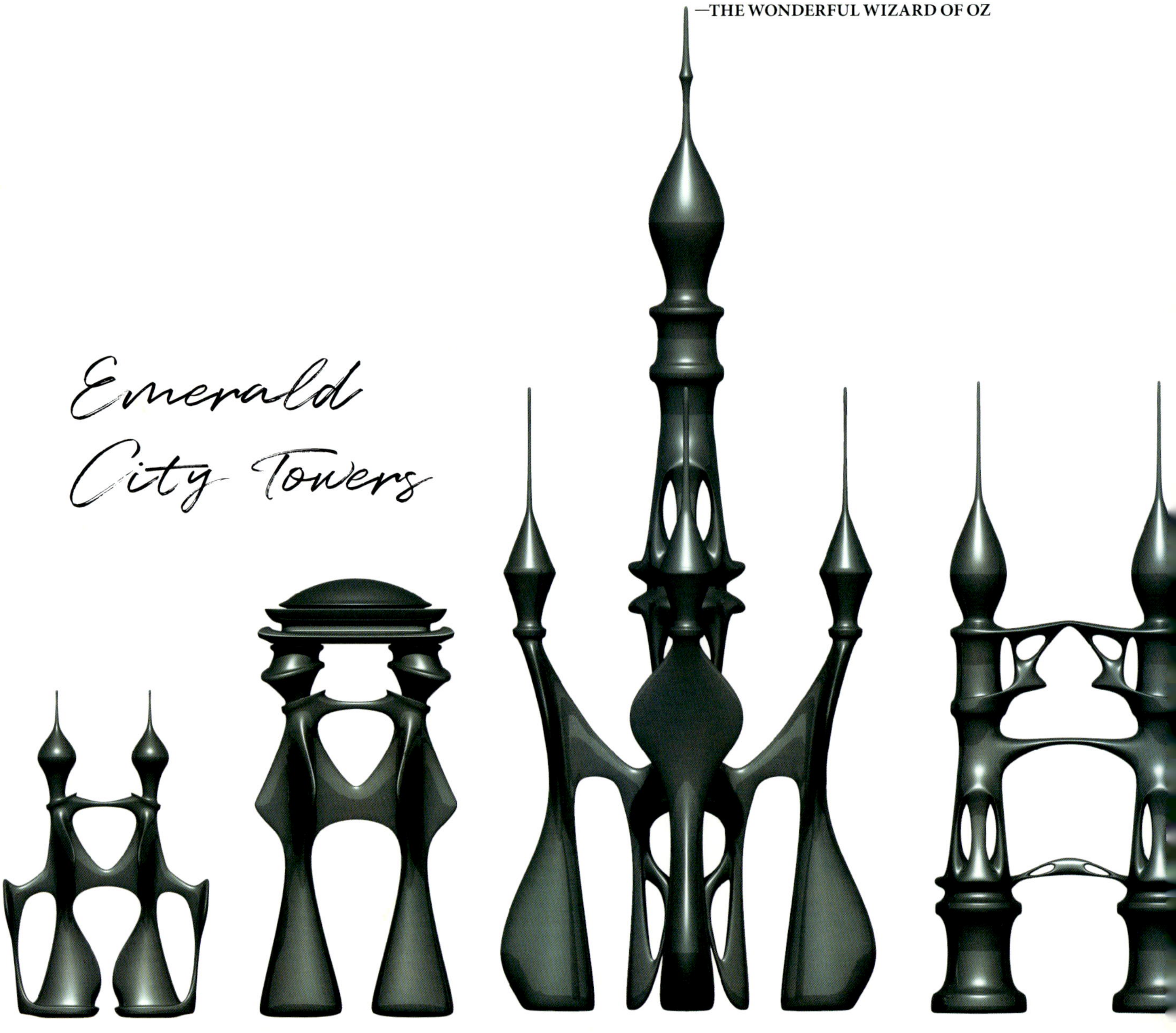

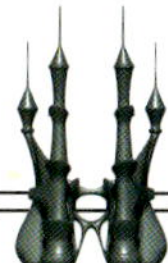

The Emerald City lies directly in the center of [the] four important countries of Oz. The gates had bars of pure gold, and on either side of each gateway were built high towers, from which floated gay banners. Other towers were set at distances along the walls, which were broad enough for four people to walk abreast upon. . . . Beyond the wall was the vast city it surrounded, and hundreds of jeweled spires, domes and minarets, flaunting flags and banners, reared their crests far above the towers of the gateways. In the center of the city, [one] could see the tops of many magnificent trees, some nearly as tall as the spires of the buildings . . . these trees were in the royal gardens of Princess Ozma.

—THE PATCHWORK GIRL OF OZ

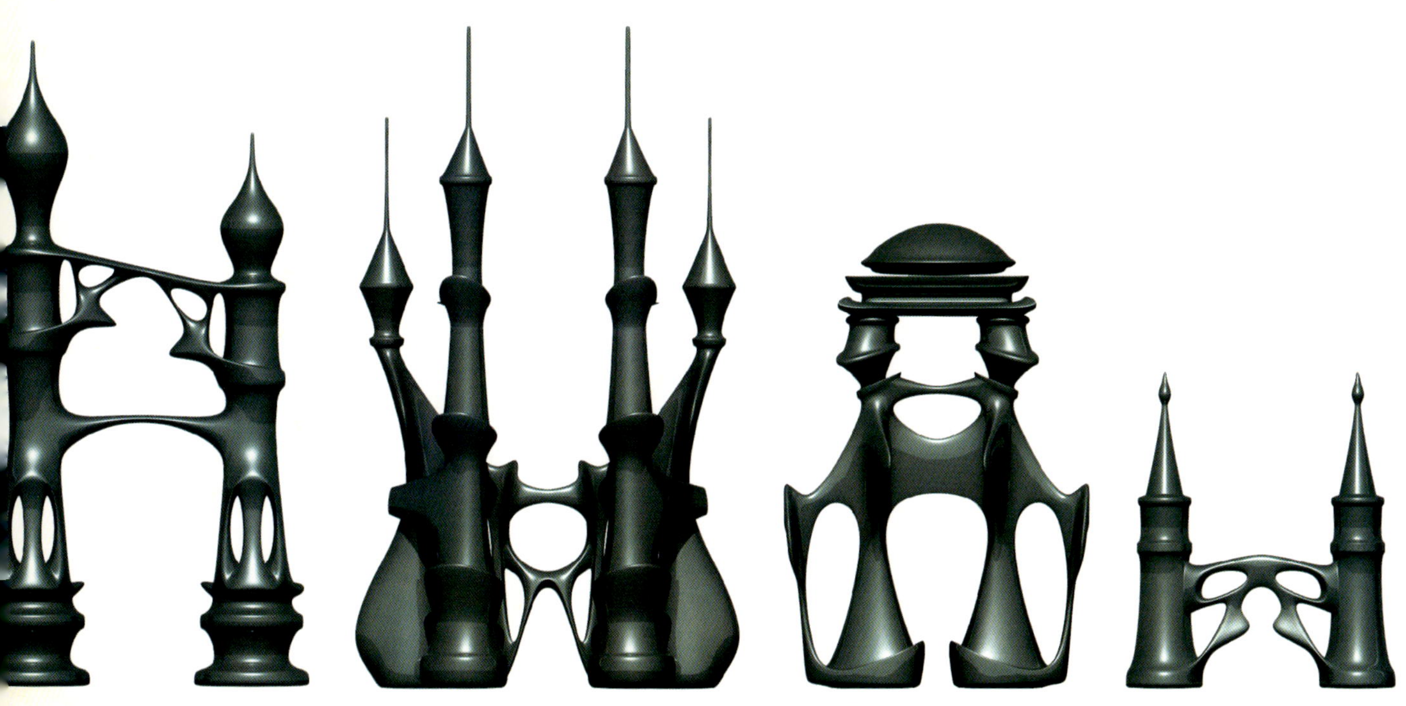

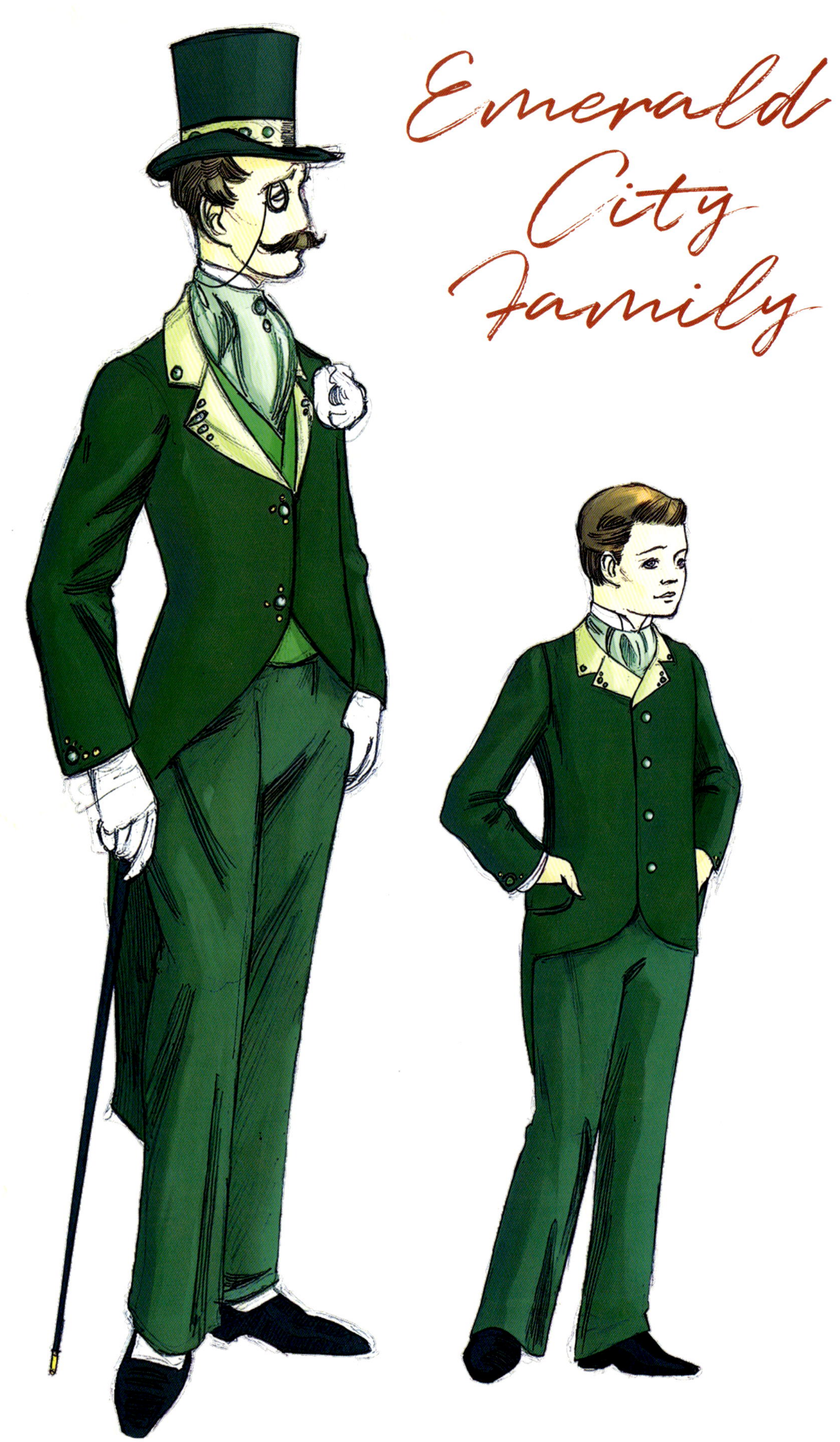
Emerald
City
Family

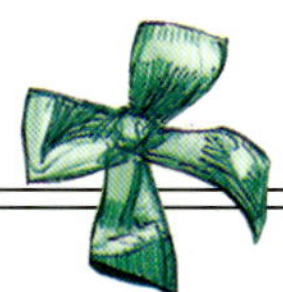

There are no other people so happy and contented and prosperous as the Oz people. They have all they desire; they love and admire their beautiful girl Ruler, Ozma of Oz, and they mix work and play so justly that both are delightful and satisfying and no one has any reason to complain.

—THE MAGIC OF OZ

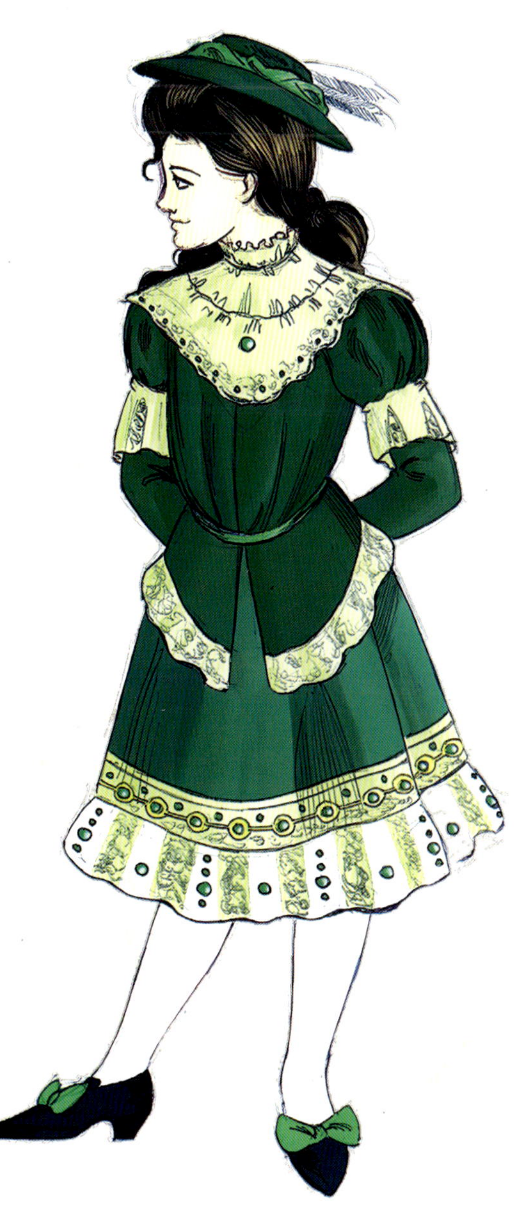

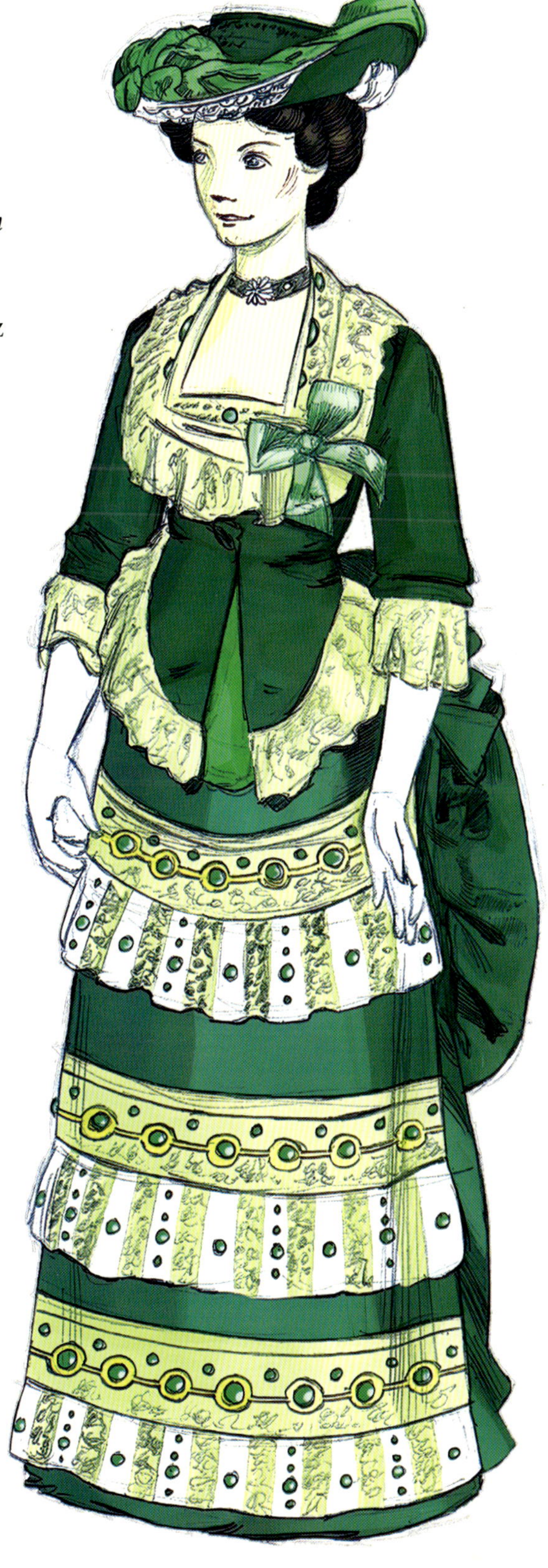

The Guardian of the Gates

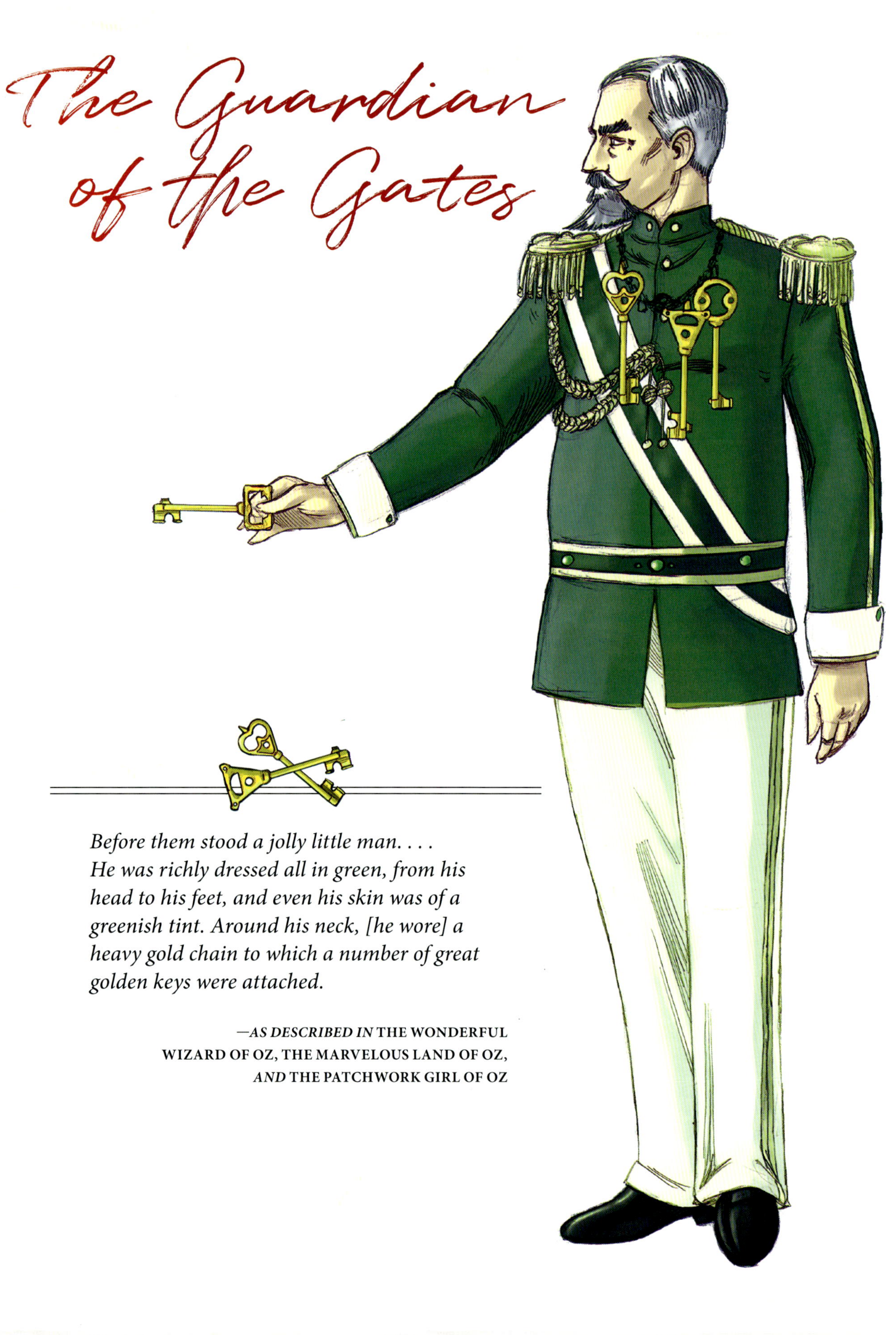

Before them stood a jolly little man. . . . He was richly dressed all in green, from his head to his feet, and even his skin was of a greenish tint. Around his neck, [he wore] a heavy gold chain to which a number of great golden keys were attached.

—*AS DESCRIBED IN* THE WONDERFUL WIZARD OF OZ, THE MARVELOUS LAND OF OZ, *AND* THE PATCHWORK GIRL OF OZ

Omby Amby

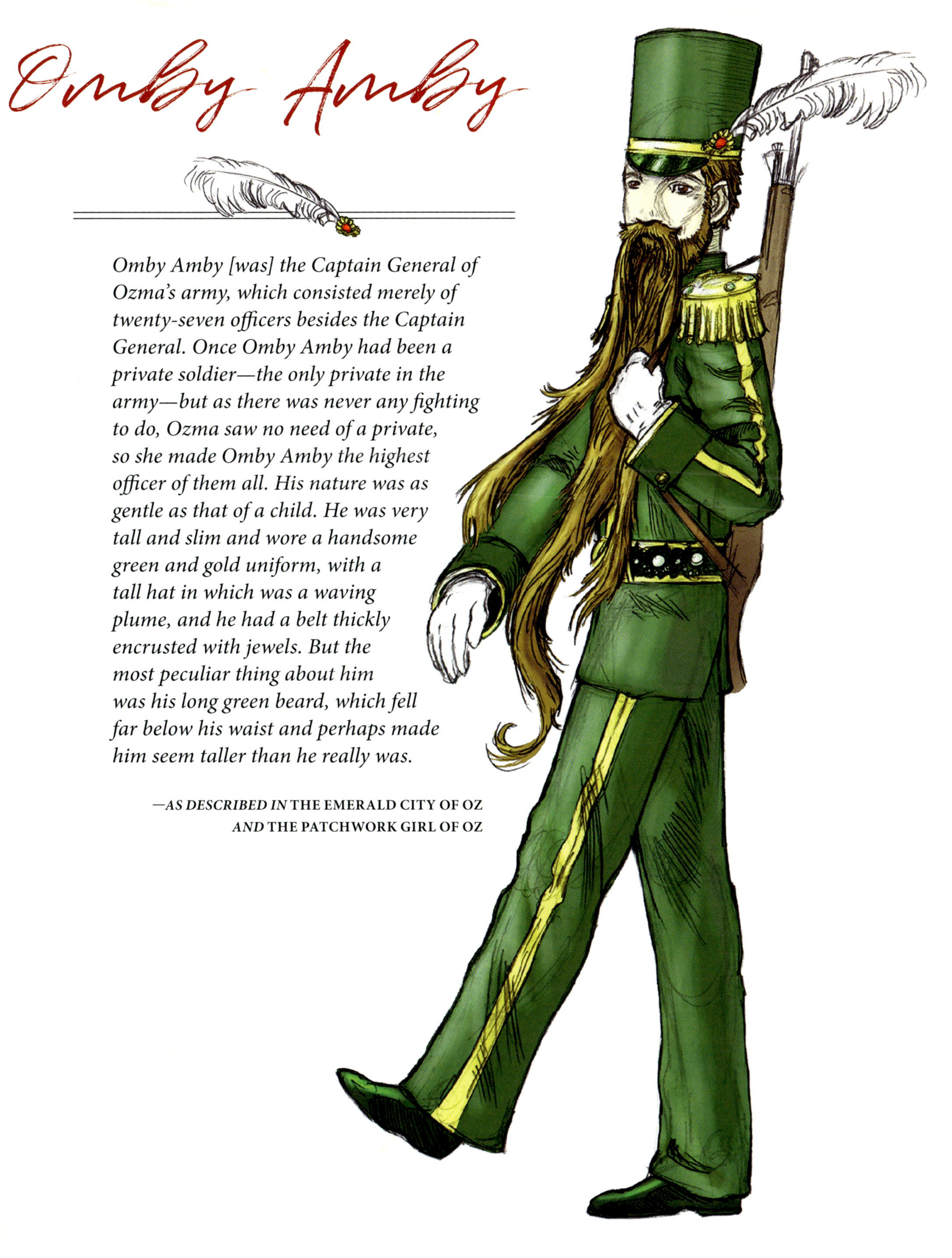

Omby Amby [was] the Captain General of Ozma's army, which consisted merely of twenty-seven officers besides the Captain General. Once Omby Amby had been a private soldier—the only private in the army—but as there was never any fighting to do, Ozma saw no need of a private, so she made Omby Amby the highest officer of them all. His nature was as gentle as that of a child. He was very tall and slim and wore a handsome green and gold uniform, with a tall hat in which was a waving plume, and he had a belt thickly encrusted with jewels. But the most peculiar thing about him was his long green beard, which fell far below his waist and perhaps made him seem taller than he really was.

—*AS DESCRIBED IN* THE EMERALD CITY OF OZ *AND* THE PATCHWORK GIRL OF OZ

The Maps of Oz

INTRODUCED BY PROFESSOR H. M. WOGGLE-BUG, T. E.

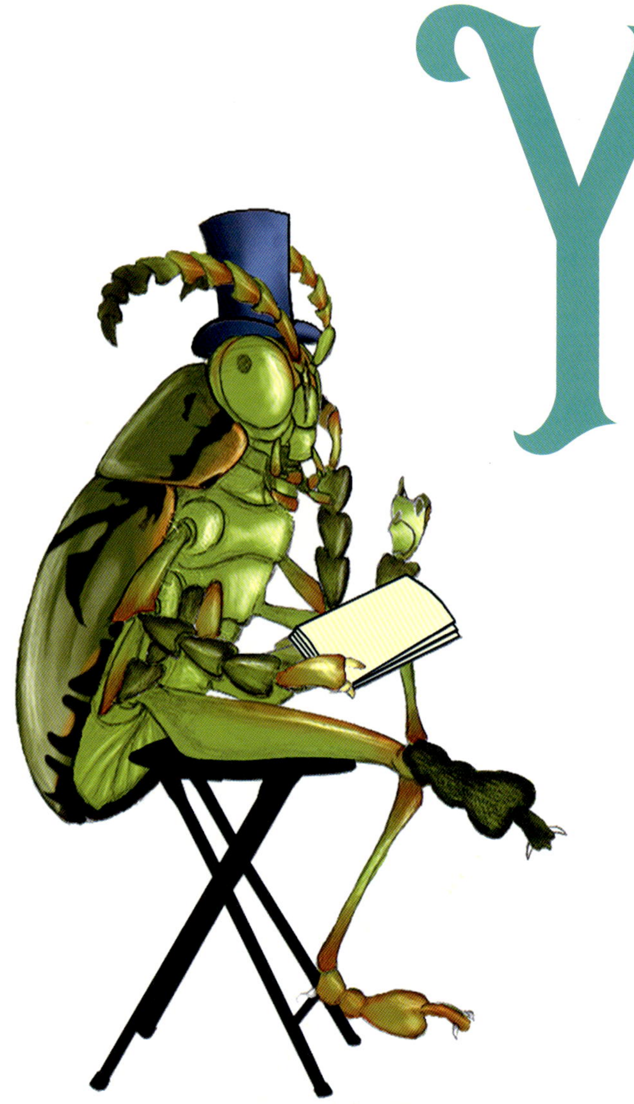

Years ago, his Royal Writeness, L. Frank Baum, requested that we work together to create maps of Oz. One of these showed our kingdom as explored by Mr. Baum up to that time; the other charted realms across the desert that surrounds us. (He had chronicled earlier adventures in those places, and these countries became known as the "Borderlands of Oz.") To my deserved pleasure—but not, of course, to my surprise—the maps were highly esteemed by Oz readers, and I'll always believe Mr. Baum was crediting me when he later wrote his publishers, "Nothing we ever did made such a hit . . . as the maps of Oz."

Given my superior intellect and overwhelming humility, I have since been amused to hear that students in the Great Outside World have found inconsistencies in my cartography and have tried to rationalize such variations, explaining my "mistakes"! They primarily consider the fact that the Munchkin and Winkie Countries have

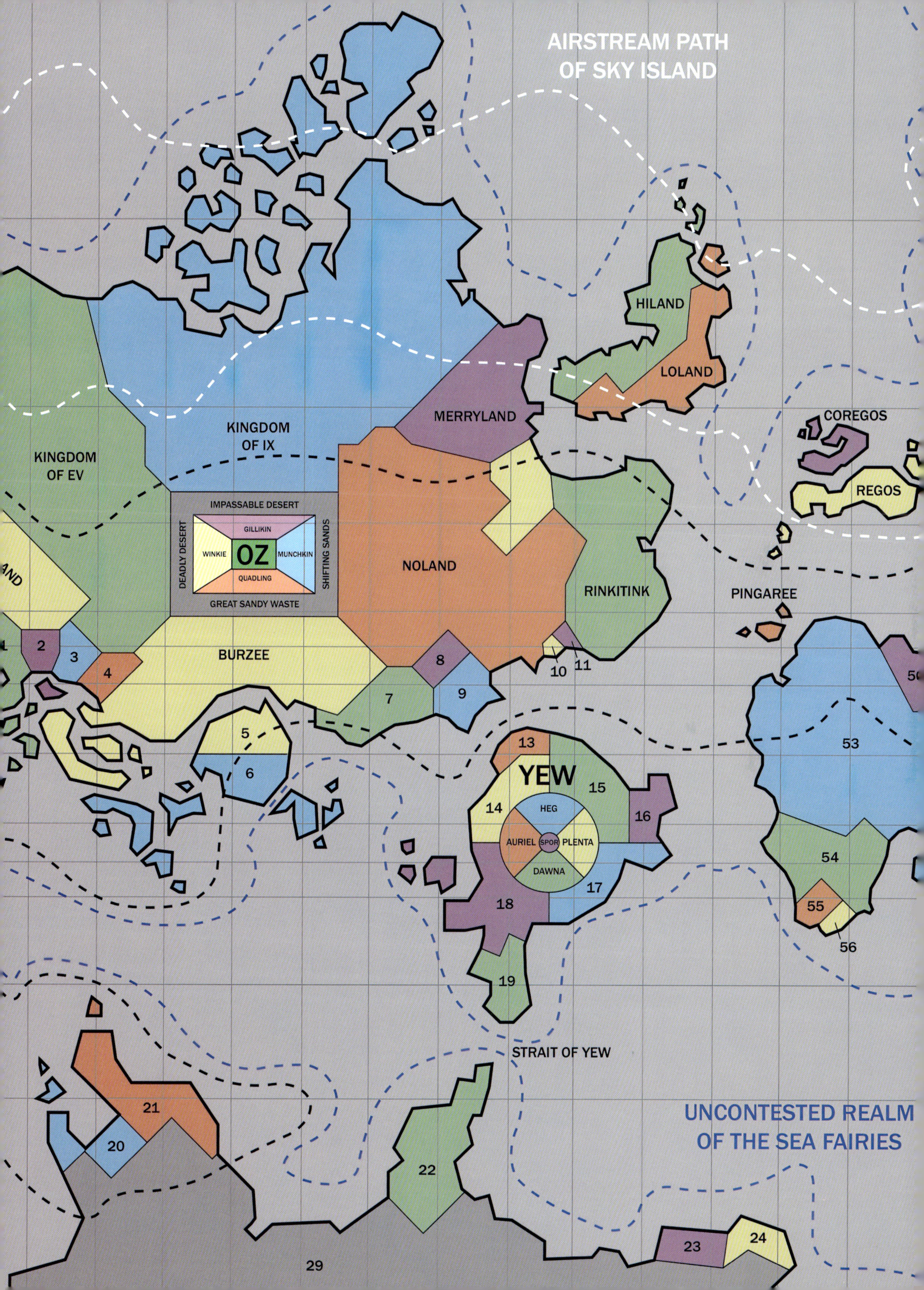

AIRSTREAM PATH OF SKY ISLAND
HILAND
LOLAND
COREGOS
REGOS
MERRYLAND
KINGDOM OF IX
KINGDOM OF EV
IMPASSABLE DESERT
GILLIKIN
WINKIE
OZ
MUNCHKIN
QUADLING
DEADLY DESERT
SHIFTING SANDS
GREAT SANDY WASTE
NOLAND
RINKITINK
PINGAREE
BURZEE
2
3
4
5
6
7
8
9
10
11
13
YEW
14
15
16
HEG
AURIEL
SPOR
PLENTA
DAWNA
17
18
19
53
54
55
56
STRAIT OF YEW
21
20
22
UNCONTESTED REALM OF THE SEA FAIRIES
23
24
29

switched places on the maps, being shown as—respectively—West and East of the Emerald City, when the facts in Mr. Baum's books say the opposite.

Well! There is no means by which any non-Ozian can justify this seeming "error"! With my outstanding advanced thinking, however, I will now provide logical self-vindication. The directionals in our Land of Oz (north, south, east, and west) are not nearly so static as those in other nations. Earlier in this book, you read that Oz became a wonderland through the resplendent powers of the Fairy Queen Lurline. Her far-reaching enchantment pervades to this day, and the amount of magic she wove into her spell leads to constant changes in our geography. Oz somehow continues to expand, an easily comprehended fact when one notes the new peoples, territories, mountains, rivers, lakes, and forests that are regularly discovered. What I must underscore (in keeping with my gloriously elevated aptitude) is that such variety extends at times even to the alternating indications of our East (E)/West (W) directional—*and* to the infrequent but actual fluctuating locations of entire countries. This effect perplexes map readers (ahem!), but I assure you it is a basically well-ordered system and works quite finely for our residents. Glinda, Princess Ozma, and our Wizard may even adjust these characteristics as preference or expediency demands!

In summation: The Munchkins are always in the East, and the Winkies are always in the West. Except when they're not.

I would do well to indicate that such mystical, massive (and, I graciously concede, confusing) land movement is not an accident. It is an example of Lurline's foresight as she contemplated the defense Oz might someday require from any enemies. Her concept of protection—one cannot find a moving target!—was later augmented when Glinda placed a Barrier of Invisibility all around us. In Glinda's own words, "We cannot be seen, and therefore we cannot be found." (I could say it only a trifle better myself.)

Lurline also ensured our safety by mixing deterrent magic into the sands of our desert. A mess of superheated soil and grit, it was a life-destroying boundary from the onset; on her first visit here, Dorothy was told by the Munchkins, "None could live to cross it." As its bewitchment heightened, however, that wasteland became ever more a fortified shield, and even I could find no more pungent words than did Mr. Baum, who classified it as fearful, dismal, awful, and everywhere gray. Most citizens inside and outside Oz are ever aware of the desert's danger, and in some places, signs have been erected to warn any who might not suspect its fatal impact.

Since those early charting efforts made by Mr. Baum and myself, hundreds of additional Oz stories have been written. Yet this merry old land shows no sign of overcrowding, and today's technology makes it possible to grid, graph, and diagram us as never before. Mr. Baum firmly endorsed the fact that "magic is a science," and for this book, Gabriel Gale has used scientific methods to picture the world in which Oz coexists with other fantasylands. Some are locations discovered by Mr. Baum; others are places in Mr. Gale's *Ages of Oz* tales.

Mr. Gale has also made use of today's from-the-air approach in order to "Google Map" the four strips of the desert, as well as Oz itself. Naturally, with my incomparable eyesight and powers of perception, I've had no difficulty in identifying myself, even from above.

I am, after all, a Very Big Bug.

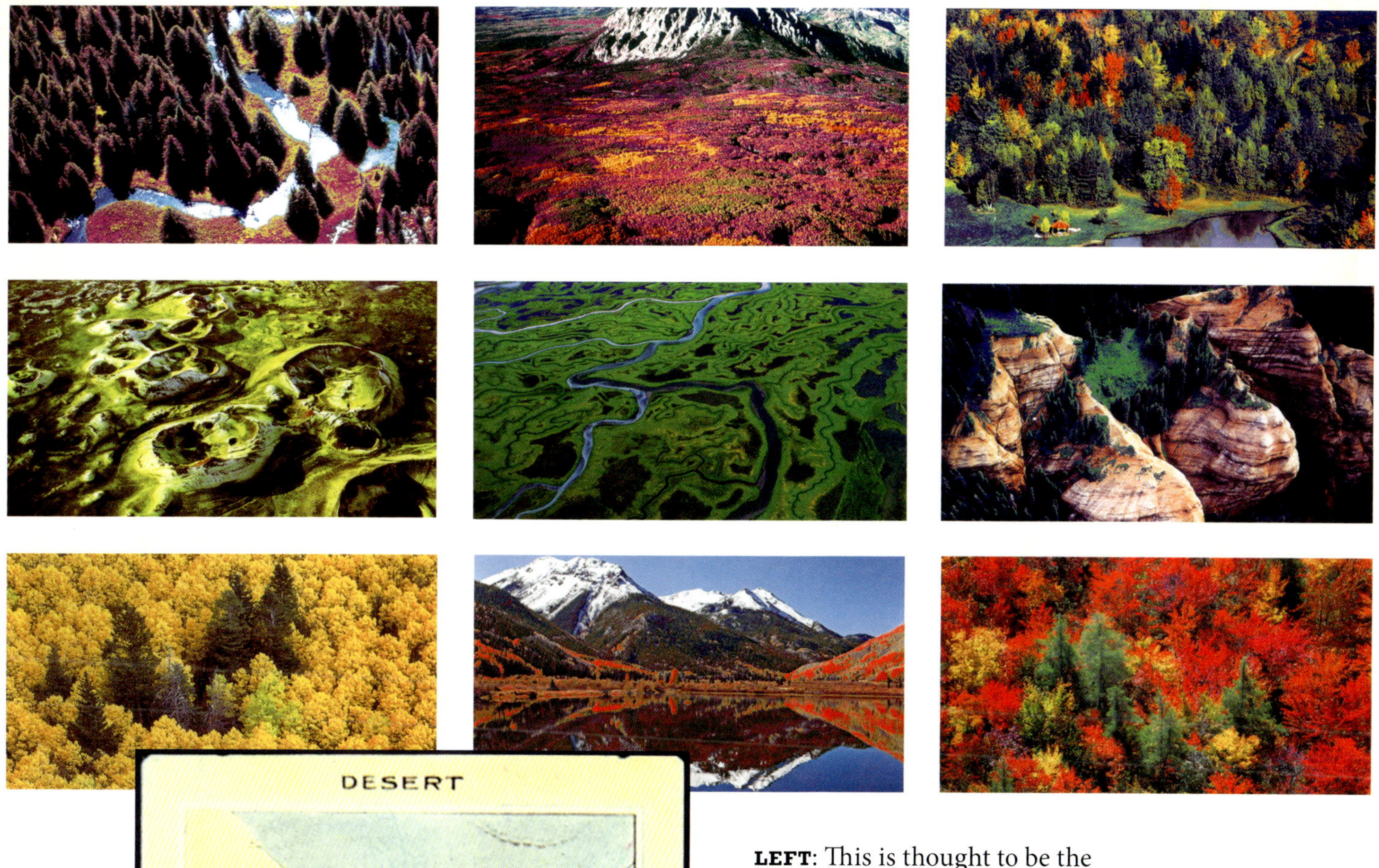

LEFT: This is thought to be the first Oz map created by Mr. Baum. It was shown during his touring multimedia stage show, *Fairylogue and Radio-Plays.*

Oz itself is a huge oblong country divided into four parts, the North being the purple Gillikin country, the East the blue Munchkin country, the South the red lands of the Quadlings, and the West the pleasant yellow country of the Winkies. In the very center of Oz, as almost every boy and girl knows, is the wonderful Emerald City, and in its gorgeous green palace lives Ozma, the lovely little Fairy Princess. . . . Oz is so large and inhabited by so many strange and singular peoples that although [many] books of history have been written about it, only half the story has been told.

—KABUMPO IN OZ
RUTH PLUMLY THOMPSON (SECOND "ROYAL HISTORIAN OF OZ")

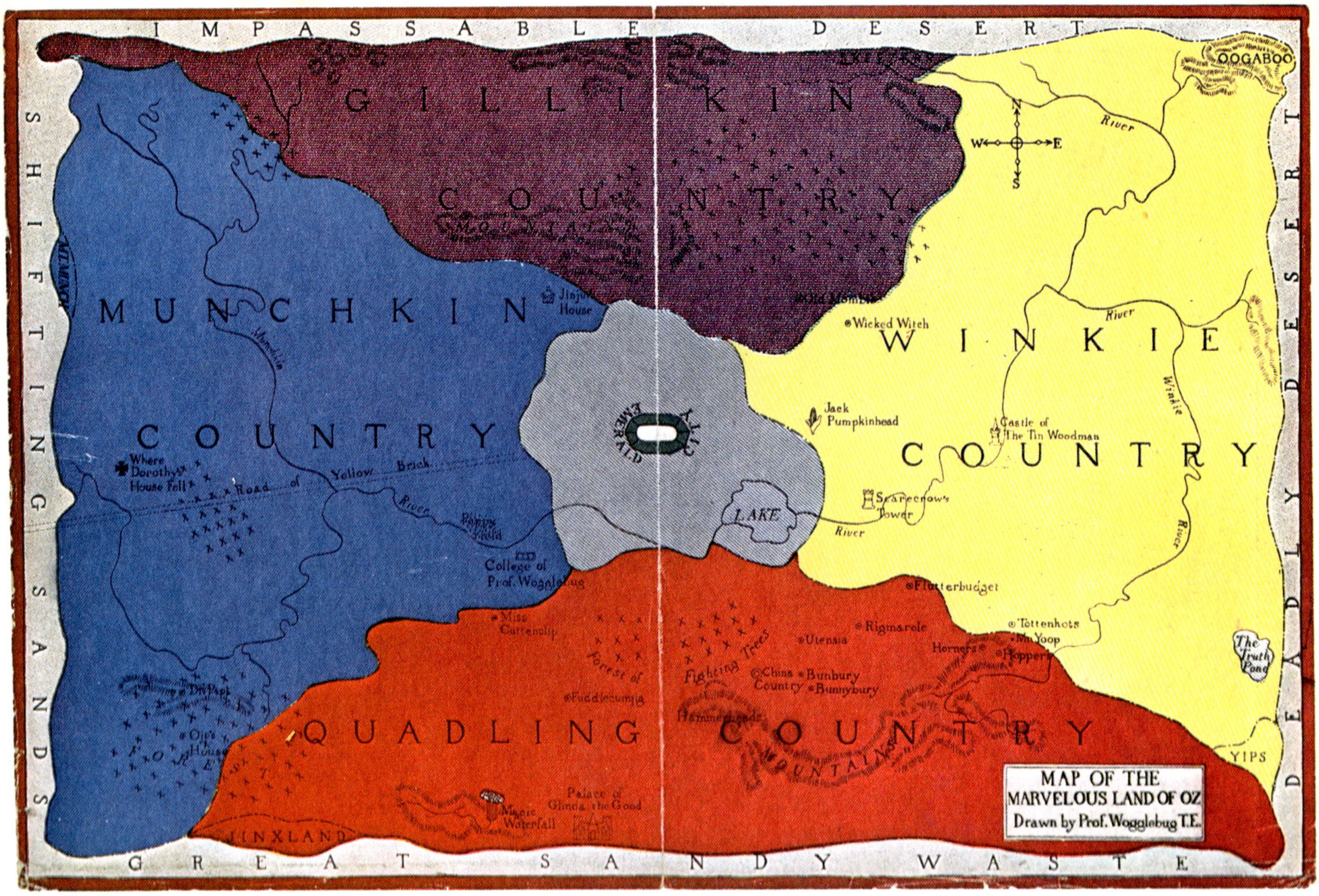

ABOVE AND OPPOSITE: These are the detailed maps Mr. Baum and I collaborated to create. Some may detect that the Munchkin Country and Winkie Country are here reversed in location. To them, I will smugly (Bug-ly) note: So are the compass directionals on one of the maps!

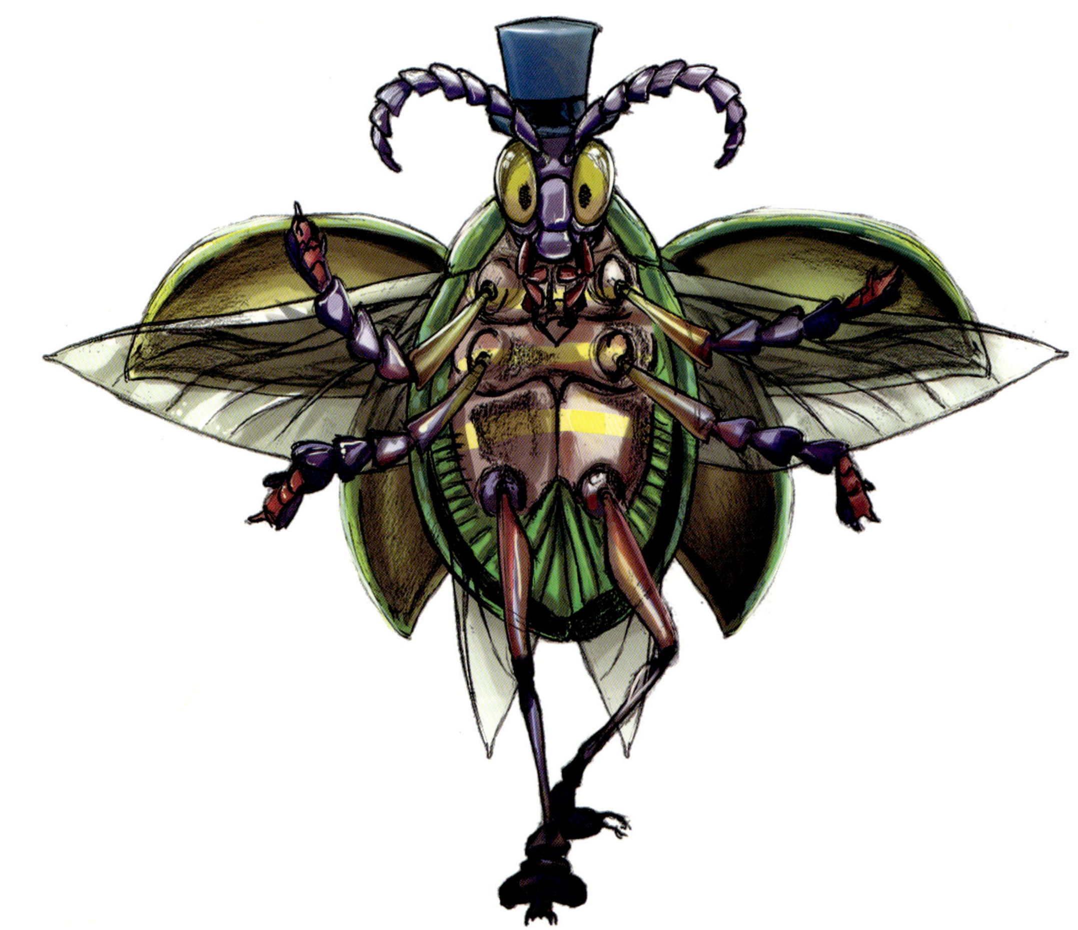

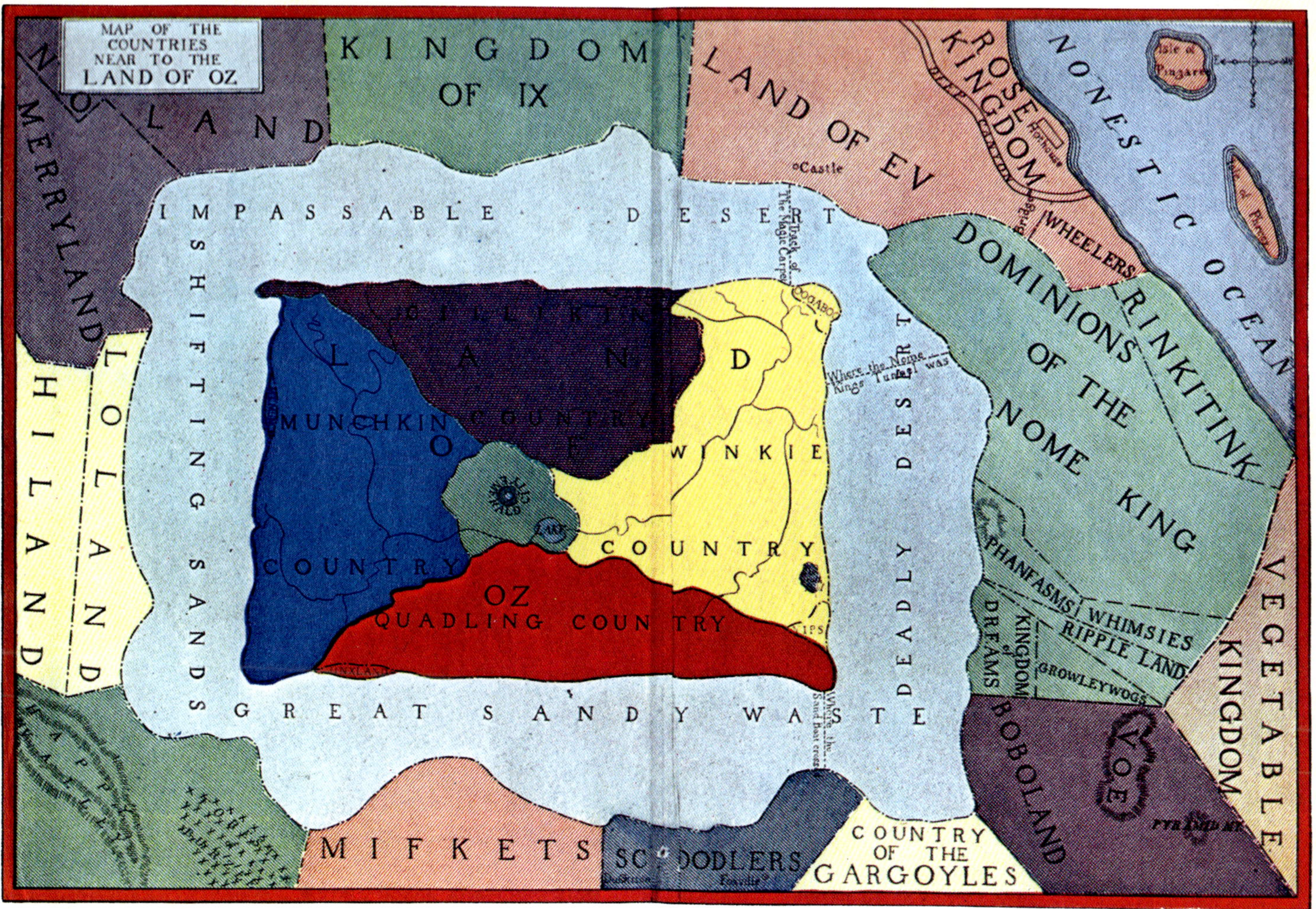

In the above map, you see the Borderlands of Oz, on the other side of our protective Deadly Desert. Mr. Baum wrote about some of these territories and peoples in his Oz books: the Land of Ev, the Wheelers, and the Dominions of the Nome King in *Ozma of Oz*; the Vegetable Kingdom, Voe, Pyramid Mountain, and the Country of the Gargoyles (all of these locations exist beneath the surface of our earth) in *Dorothy and the Wizard in Oz*; the Scoodlers in *The Road to Oz*; the Whimsies, the Ripple Lands, the Growleywogs, and the Phanfasms in *The Emerald City of Oz*; the Rose Kingdom in *Tik-Tok of Oz*; and the Isle of Pingaree, Rinkitink, and Boboland in *Rinkitink in Oz*. His other fantasy realms, residents, and books represented here include Merryland (*Dot and Tot of Merryland*); the Happy Valley and the Forest of Burzee (*The Life and Adventures of Santa Claus*); the kingdoms of Ix and Noland (*Queen Zixi of Ix*); and the Isle of Phreex, the Mifkets, Hiland, and Loland (*John Dough and the Cherub*). Not shown on the map are the Baum-discovered countries of Mo (*The Magical Monarch of Mo*) and Yew (*The Enchanted Island of Yew*); the under-ocean residences of *The Sea Fairies*; and *Sky Island*, which floats through the atmosphere above the earth. The only charted setting about which Mr. Baum himself never wrote is the Kingdom of Dreams. It has been speculated that this is the home of the Sand Man, as he appears near that locale in a brief but pivotal role in Ruth Plumly Thompson's *Kabumpo in Oz*. One of the fundamental characters in the story—Peg Amy, the wooden doll who is really a transformed princess—comments that she had heard that the Sand Man lived in that vicinity.

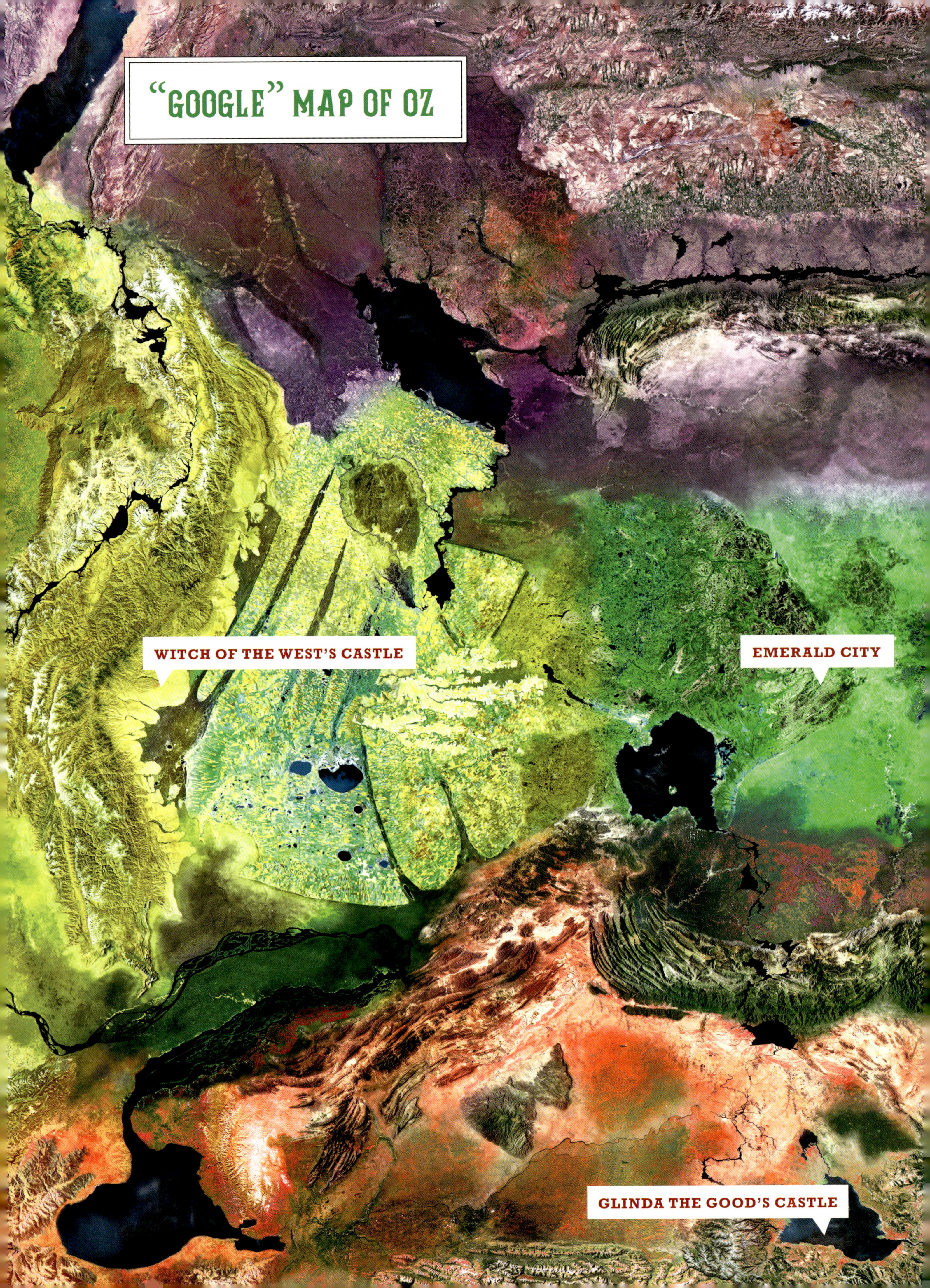

"GOOGLE" MAP OF OZ
WITCH OF THE WEST'S CASTLE
EMERALD CITY
GLINDA THE GOOD'S CASTLE

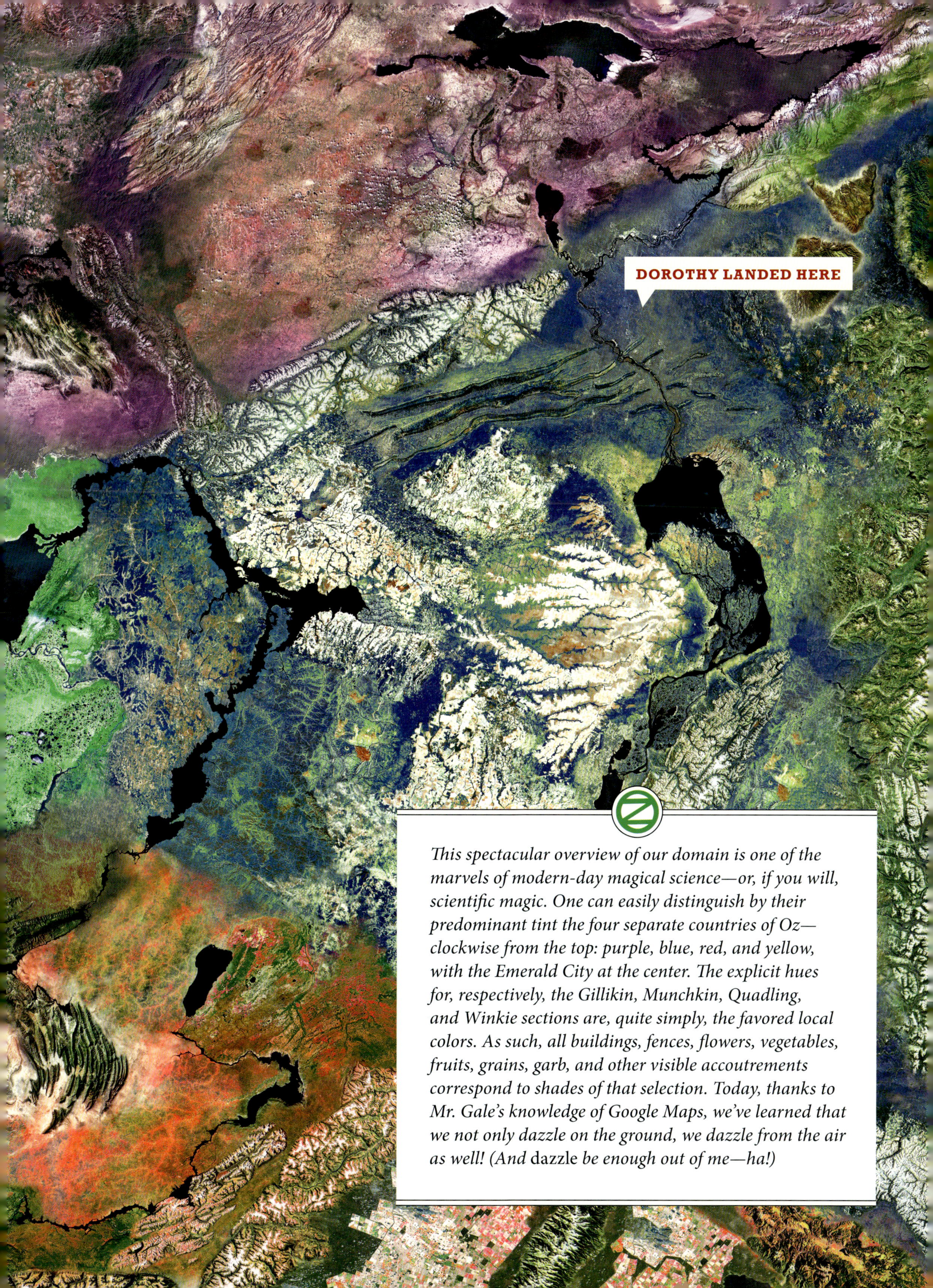

This spectacular overview of our domain is one of the marvels of modern-day magical science—or, if you will, scientific magic. One can easily distinguish by their predominant tint the four separate countries of Oz—clockwise from the top: purple, blue, red, and yellow, with the Emerald City at the center. The explicit hues for, respectively, the Gillikin, Munchkin, Quadling, and Winkie sections are, quite simply, the favored local colors. As such, all buildings, fences, flowers, vegetables, fruits, grains, garb, and other visible accoutrements correspond to shades of that selection. Today, thanks to Mr. Gale's knowledge of Google Maps, we've learned that we not only dazzle on the ground, we dazzle from the air as well! (And dazzle *be enough out of me—ha!)*

There are four strips of arid, poisonous, and fatal territory that form the boundaries of Oz. They surround and protect us from alien invasion—and possibly, as well, from floods of tourists. Yet each expanse of wasteland is far from a joking matter: they are individually and collectively a living horror.

Each portion has its own distinctive name. At the far side of the Winkie Country, one confronts the Deadly Desert (which also serves as a generic designation for the entire barren wilderness). On the opposite side of Oz, you'll find the Shifting Sands as the outer boundary of the Munchkin Country. The Great Sandy Waste edges the southern Quadling Country, and finally, the Impassable Desert tops off the northern Gillikin Country.

Mr. Baum summarized the heinous powers of the Deadly Desert by including, in *The Road to Oz*, one of the signs posted to warn travelers of the nearby danger (at right):

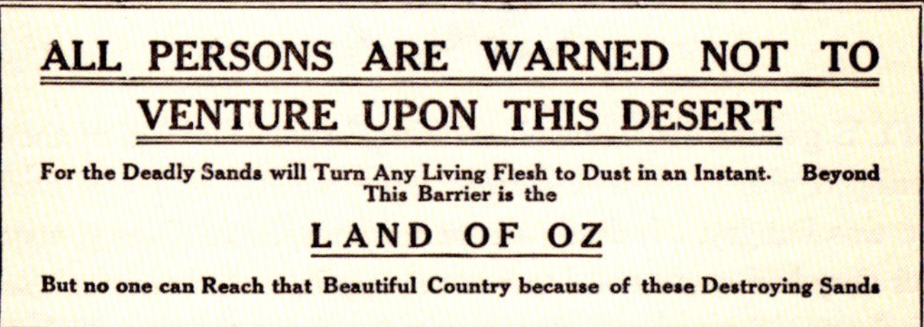

Oz historians have used many other frightening phrases to describe the Deadly Desert, as the ground there is far from static. Mr. Baum noted that, at times and in some areas of the Great Sandy Waste, the silt piles up in sultry, treacherous billows and is very uneven. Miss Thompson designated a spot in the Impassable Desert where "the seething sand smoked, churned, and tumbled, sending up sulfurous waves of heat that made . . . travelers cough and splutter." Indeed, Mr. Neill's depiction of that sector in *The Silver Princess of Oz* resembles the content of a boiling witch's cauldron or a roiling bed of lava.

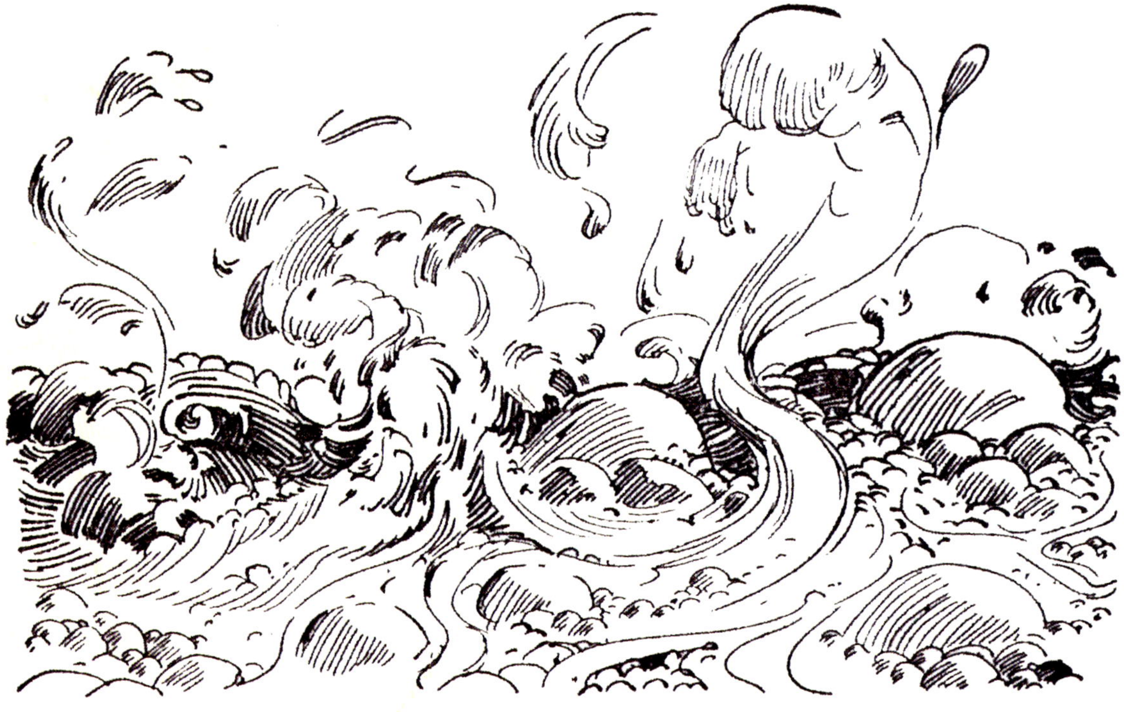

For his book *The Shaggy Man of Oz*, Jack Snow—another of the "Royal Historians"—discovered and reported on the only known "Dwellers of the [Deadly] Desert." These despicable living beings live on the shifting sands, and as their bodies are entirely made of fire, they are more familiarly termed the Flame Folk.

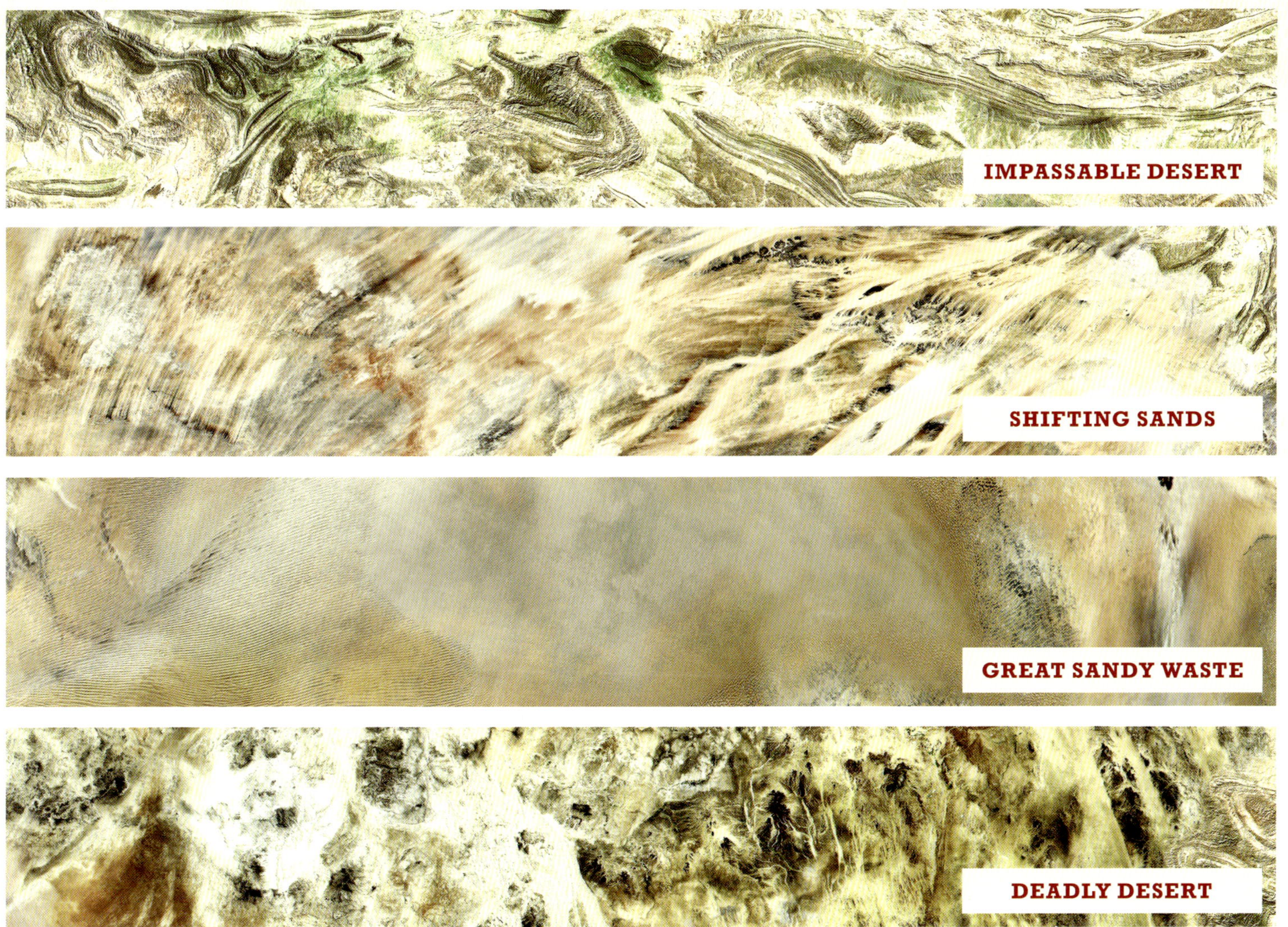

These four panels offer a stunning, exclusive Google Maps overview of each band of the Deadly Desert. The fact that the tetrad—if you will, a personal, "Woggle-Bug approved term" meaning "a set of four"—is permeated with wildly fluctuating surfaces is everywhere apparent in these captures.

As observed earlier in this chapter, the desert was enchanted as a protective device for Oz by the Fairy Queen Lurline, and its shielding effect was later heavily enhanced by Glinda's Barrier of Invisibility. It's true, however, that some magical forces for good have been able to circumvent either or both of their spells, leading to momentous Ozian events. For example, the Wizard made his first trip to and from Oz over the desert, through the air, in his enormous gas balloon. Dorothy came "by air" as well, arriving in a cyclone-propelled farmhouse (of course, the accurate word in this instance is tornado) and whirling away again, "the wind whistling past her ears," thanks to her magic shoes.

In other adventures, people have literally traveled over the Deadly Desert on the rainbow itself; ridden in a specially constructed sandboat; flown across on the back of a small fleet of Orks; actually walked over upon a splendid magic carpet; or been transported by Ozma's Magic Belt. There was also one major historical instance in which the desert's original defenses were overpowered by negative sorcery. This occurred when the Nome King's slaves actually dug below the badlands, opening a vast tunnel so that malevolent legions could march through it to invade Oz.

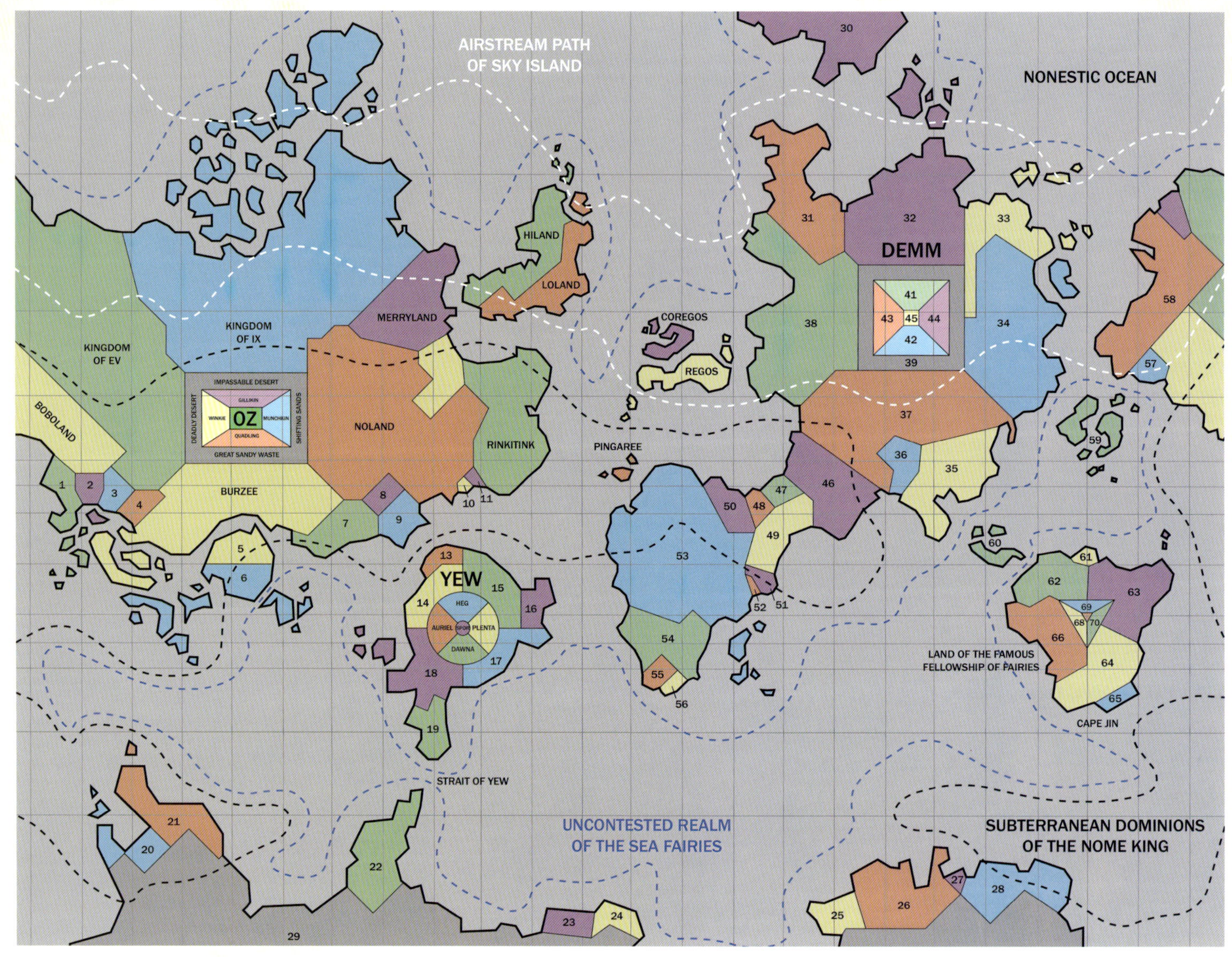

Mr. Gale's global Map of Lurlia shows the five principal continents of that universe, each of which has its own primary shape; this, of course, follows Mr. Baum's discovery of our own rectangular Oz. Three of the continents contain, at their center, an original and favored fairy country: Oz, Yew, or Demm. In my role as the Highly Magnified and Thoroughly Educated Professor of the Royal Athletic College of Oz, I am compelled to share with you my greatest acrobatic stunt in language transliteration: I have told Mr. Gale—as I told Mr. Baum—that I privately and punningly refer to these continents as "Us, You, and Them."

Oh, the cleverness of me!

I will briefly and in general terms describe these global worlds. (As you study Lurlia, however, please note the accompanying numerical list of seventy-one locations not designated by name on the map itself.) Nonestica includes the Land of Oz, surrounded by the four plots of Deadly Desert and additional Baumian fantasy empires. To the south of Nonestica, one finds Mr. Baum's Island of Yew; to the east is the continent controlled by the Land of Demm, which itself is surrounded by four deadly lakes and features its own unique fairy terrain. South of Demm is the land of the Famous Fellowship of Fairies, where Tik-Tok—in his own Baum book, *Tik-Tok of Oz*—had his unexpected and exceptional audience

THE CONTINENT OF NONESTICA

1. Veeva
2. Wheeler Country
3. Ripple Land
4. Happy Valley
5. Burzee's Isle of Dai
6. Burzee's Isle of Nie
7. Whimsie Country
8. Mo
9. Phantastico
10. Ascha
11. If Land
12. Merquee

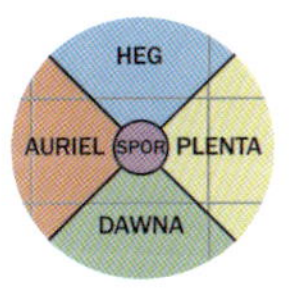

THE ENCHANTED ISLE OF YEW

13. Rohs
14. Meddo
15. Forest of Lurla
16. Slaf
17. Oshan
18. Sado
19. Yew Shore

THE LURLIAN ARCTIC

20. Blueboo Land
21. Wulfhelm
22. Glai Shore
23. Frijid
24. Lulera Landing
25. Fross
26. Wispar
27. Phyord
28. Chadda
29. Lurlian Arctic

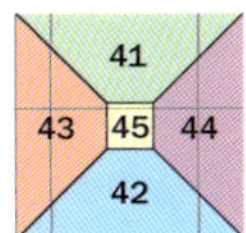

THE LAND OF DEMM

30. Cerenady
31. Ahaland
32. Whiffle Land
33. Whuffle Land
34. Cob
35. Deso Land
36. Slaf
37. Forest of Ervana
38. Shooga
39. Cragglemire Wastes
40. Demm – overall name of Oz-like country
41. Northern Demm – Noomchi
42. Southern Demm – Langen
43. Eastern Demm – Grunkine
44. Western Demm – Pagling
45. Central Demm – Yellow Country, Hunnee City
46. Kurya
47. Auwaik
48. Nune
49. Mown
50. Duskval
51. Lynen
52. Aktoo
53. Mifket Isle
54. Mallo Marsh
55. Fera
56. Zeza Country
57. (Nonestica) Niseland
58. (Nonestica) Rose Kingdom
59. Isle of Phreex
60. Isle of Romance

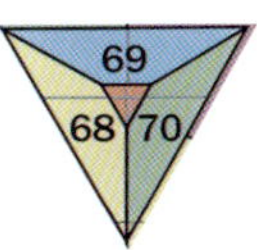

THE LAND OF THE FAMOUS FELLOWSHIP OF FAIRIES

61. Jin's Landing
62. Drangor
63. Phansee
64. The Great Desert of Jin
65. Paeyl
66. Vale of Kaynek
67. Lof-Fof
68. Memree
69. Dreme
70. Ohp
71. Pere

with Tititi-Hoochoo, the Great JinJin. This continent is shaped like a triangle, with Cape Jin at its southernmost point. From the Cape itself, one could board (if one had) the Magic Raft and travel due south to the Lurlian Antarctic.

You will notice that the Gale cartography also incorporates the airstream path of Sky Island, the uncontested (and underwater) monarchy of the Sea Fairies, and the Subterranean Dominions of the Nome King.

For supplementary geographic specifics, you will find above the aforementioned numerical list of sub-countries.

A Few Words about Oz

BY MICHAEL PATRICK HEARN

I'll sing a song of Ozland, where wondrous creatures dwell
And fruits and flowers and shady bowers abound in every dell,
Where magic is a science and where no one shows surprise
If some amazing thing takes place before his very eyes.

—L. FRANK BAUM, *THE PATCHWORK GIRL OF OZ*

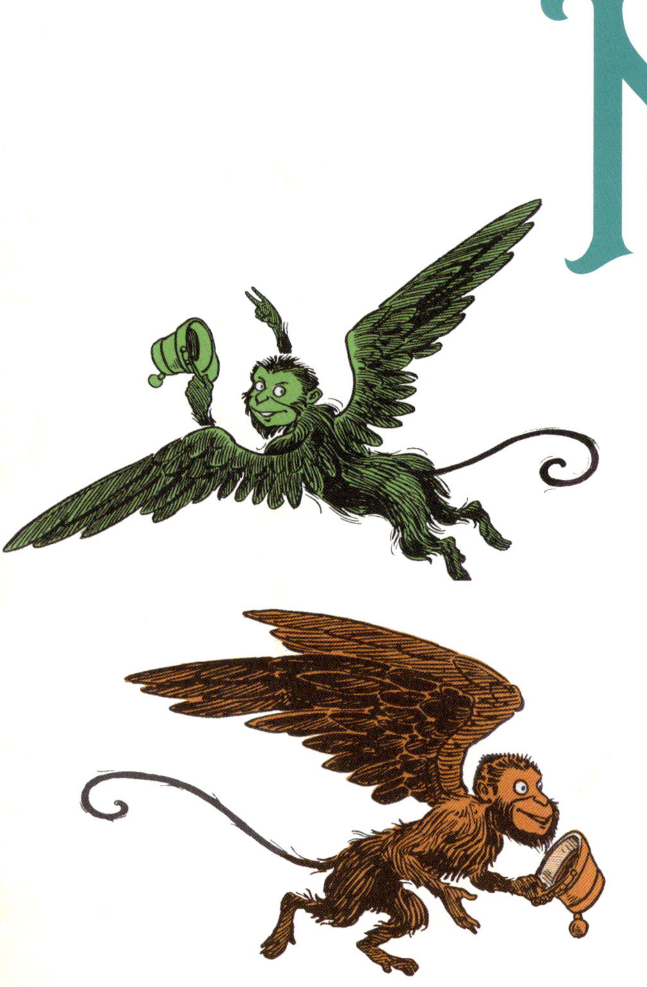

Not so long ago, over lunch, I went through the portfolio of a charming young artist. Leafing through these striking, extraordinarily inventive reinterpretations of the inhabitants of the Marvelous Land of Oz, I thought to myself, Here may well be the future of Oz! Gabriel Gale has brought Dorothy, the Scarecrow, the Tin Woodman, the Cowardly Lion, and Toto, too, up to date. He has almost singlehandedly brought Oz into the twenty-first century in this stunning book for all ages—and for the ages.

One thing is immediately clear from this art: Gabriel Gale is thoroughly immersed in the saga of Oz, not just *The Wonderful Wizard of Oz* but all fourteen original Oz books by Royal Historian L. Frank Baum. He is fully committed to depicting the vast cast in the legacy of Oz, not just the starring roles but even the least important supporting players; not just the classic four but rather the full range of amazing characters known only to the most ardent Oz buffs. He has also considered the Borderlands of

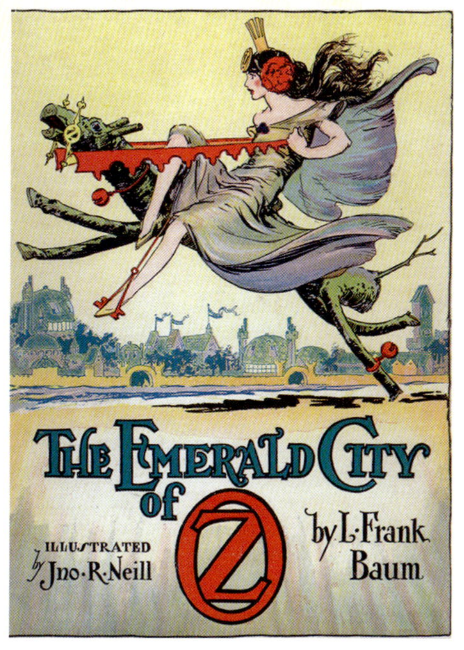

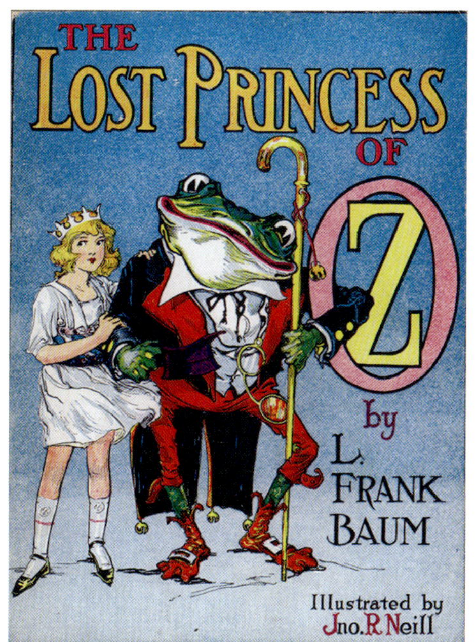

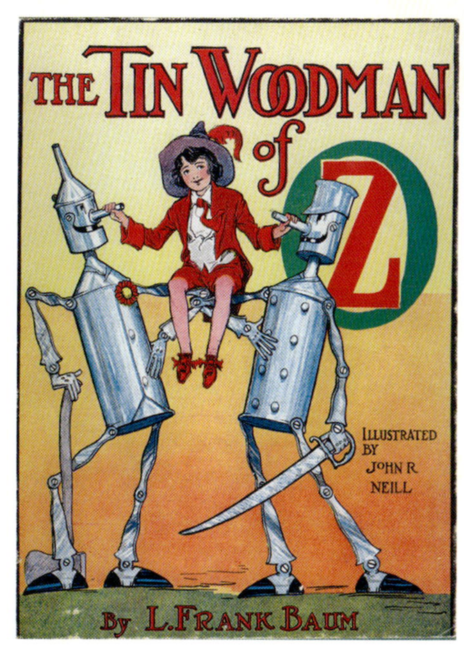

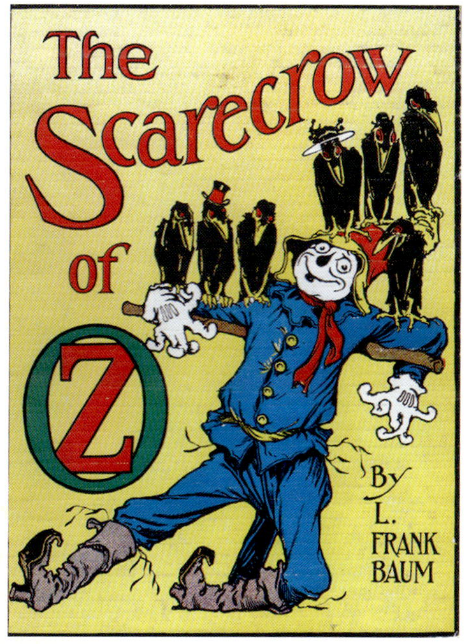

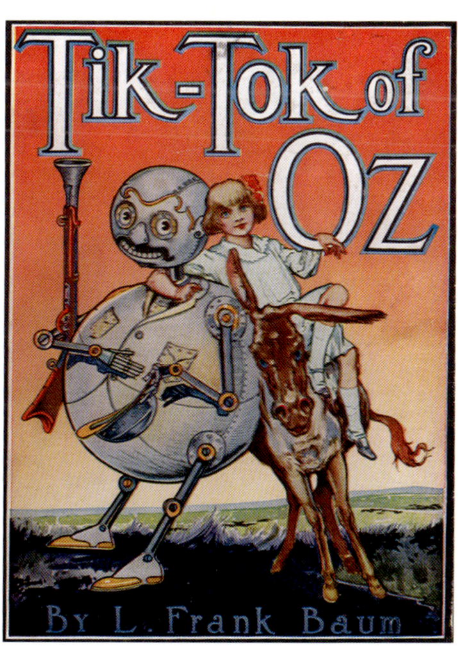

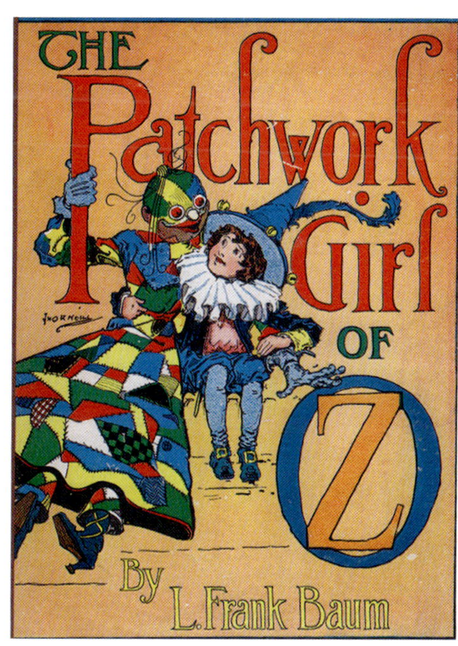

Oz that can be found in the boundless imaginary continent of Nonestica where Oz lies—a world parallel to that of the Great Outside World. He goes even further to call their hidden planet Lurlia after the Fairy Queen Lurline, who enchanted it all. He has expanded on the original Maps of the Marvelous Land of Oz and the Countries near to the Land of Oz, credited to Professor H. M. Woggle-Bug, T. E., and which served as the endpapers of *Tik-Tok of Oz* in 1914. He has made one crucial change. Although Baum described the Blue Country of the Munchkins in the East and the Yellow Country of the Winkies in the West where the sun goes down, Professor Woggle-Bug carelessly reversed them. Gale restores them to where Baum originally placed them in *The Wonderful Wizard of Oz*. As a skilled cartographer and as an illustrator, Gale proudly reports that he has also produced a satellite map of Oz—"the world's only Google Map of a fantasyland, where we can zoom in to see the rivers, mountains, etc."

OPPOSITE: Winged Monkeys by Denslow, *The Wonderful Wizard of Oz*
ABOVE: Six of Mr. Baum's Oz book covers by Neill

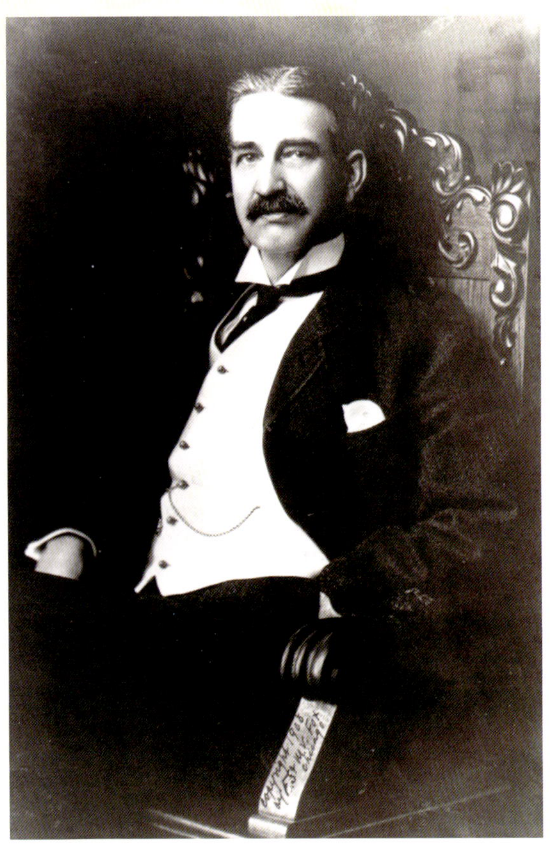

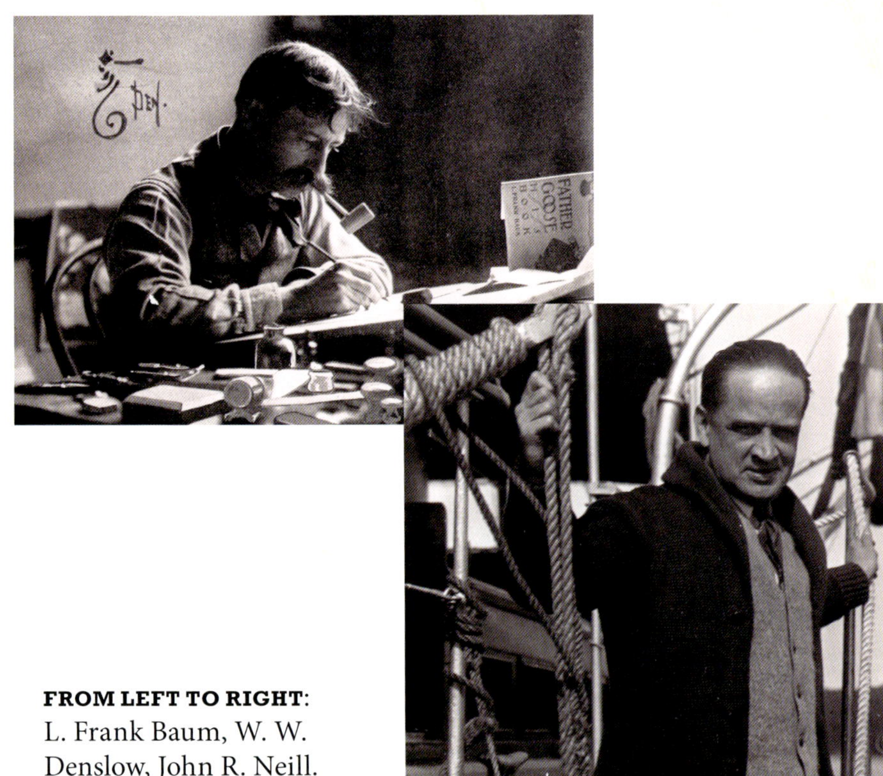

FROM LEFT TO RIGHT: L. Frank Baum, W. W. Denslow, John R. Neill. John Fricke Collection.

Locale is crucial for fairy tales. Gale is a trained architect whose skill as a draftsman is no more evident than in his utopian vision of a modernist Emerald City. "My inspirations for its city planning," he explains, "are the Columbian Exposition of 1893 and the City Beautiful movement, specifically the McMillan Plan for Washington, D.C., of 1901." Gale is sure that the Wizard would have been familiar with them before he landed in Oz and built his magnificent City of Emeralds. The artist says that if you look closely from above at the Emerald City Zoning Plan, you will see the eyes and the smile of the Wizard, who is looking up at the Witches as they fly overhead. The buildings themselves draw on the wild imaginings of visionary architect Antoni Gaudí, with their sleek lines and organic forms that defined the distinctive Spanish Art Nouveau architectural style, exemplified in the famed, and still unfinished, Basílica de la Sagrada Família in Barcelona. And yet Gale still cleverly pays homage to the Beaux Arts amalgamation of towers and walls and minarets that made up W.W. Denslow's original Emerald City. Gale's Scale Comparison chart suggests how his Sapphire and Tourmaline Towers of Oz might literally tower over such renowned landmarks as the Empire State Building, the Willis Tower, and the Eiffel Tower.

Each generation has reinterpreted Oz according to its own tastes. And Gabriel Gale is no exception to this tradition. He combines the Spanish architect's precision of line with a naturalist's demand for anatomical accuracy. Were he recording only the fairyland's fanciful birds, Gale might be called the Audubon of Oz. He shares his fellow American's faithfulness in rendering the creatures of the real world when depicting the full range of men and beasts in Baum's imaginary universe. Gale freely admits that he stands squarely on the shoulders of the original Imperial Illustrators of Oz, Denslow and John R. Neill. Still he adds clever touches of his own from his keen modern observation of his subjects.

In rediscovering Oz, Gale has drawn on a cornucopia of artistic styles. "Yes," he says, "Art

Nouveau was a major aesthetic influence." Princess Ozma, "simply the most important character," looks like she just stepped out of an Alphonse Mucha poster. Although the artist denies any intended similarity, his Frogman looks perhaps more like Beatrix Potter's Jeremy Fisher than he does Neill's drawings in *The Lost Princess of Oz*. Obviously, Gale has long admired the noble sword and sorcery tradition of modern high fantasy that runs from J. R. R. Tolkien through George R. R. Martin; as a consequence, his art is perhaps more suitable for the older child—or the adult with a childlike heart—than are the charmingly old-fashioned illustrations of Denslow and Neill. "The writing of J. R. R. Tolkien was important inasmuch as it inspired me to delve into greater detail with respect to the world-building of Oz," he says. Of course, younger children, too, will find these pictures beguiling.

Baum took from his reading of Theosophy the various classes of enchanted immortals, called Elementals. They exemplified the four ancient Greek elements—Earth, Air, Fire, and Water—as Gnomes, Sylphs, Salamanders, and Undines. Representatives of these branches of fairy creature can be found in Baum's stories. They are Gale's Ethereals, who (like the Witches of Oz) can be either good or wicked depending on their natures. Whether Princess Ozma or Polychrome the Rainbow's Daughter in *The Road to Oz* or assorted Ryls and Sprites who attend Old Saint Nick in the Forest of Burzee in *The Life and Adventures of Santa Claus*, they belong to a fairy fellowship who look after the welfare of mortals. Their sworn enemies are the Nomes, who live underground in *Ozma of Oz*, and the dreaded shape-shifting Phanfasms of *The Emerald City of Oz*. Gale has drawn them with a dreamy romanticism appropriate to Baum's fairy realm.

As the son-in-law of the famous nineteenth-century Feminist Matilda Joslyn Gage, Baum recognized the extraordinary power of women. Gale shares Baum's feminism in the four witches of the four corners of Oz, both the Good and the Wicked. He noticed that "Denslow's drawing of the Wicked Witch of the West depicted reptiles on her outfit. I took that idea as a jumping-off place and imagined each wicked witch with particular 'familiars,' or animal assistants: reptiles, insects, plants, and beasts." One of Gale's favorite characters is Glinda the Good, who to him represents Baum's intellect. She is the one, out of all the many remarkable inhabitants of Oz, with whom Gale most personally identifies. And he does not forget aggressive General Jinjur, who leads her all-female Army of Revolt to seize the Emerald City and overthrow the Scarecrow.

Many of Baum's beasts are as imaginary as any of his fairies. They often incongruously combine characteristics of two or more animals in quite unexpected ways. The most famous are the Winged Monkeys, but Gale does not shy away from the many other extraordinary but obscure monsters of Oz. Although the Winged Monkeys make a relatively brief but significant appearance in *The Wonderful Wizard of Oz*, they so fascinated Gale that he expanded Denslow's comic inventions into a broad army of "all shapes and sizes, ranging from the Orangutan King to the Gorilla Guards, Baboon Infantry, and the Pygmy Marmoset reconnaissance." Gale's deadly Kalidahs, half-tiger and half-bear, are far more menacing than Denslow's typically whimsical creatures, and the Li-Mon-Eags, an odd amalgamation of lions and monkeys and eagles (hence their name), are especially fierce in their new transformation.

All of his passions—artistic, intellectual, spiritual—went into discovering Oz. Gale has dissected the Oz books not just as a scholar or historian but also as a surgeon. According to Baum, Ozland is a place "where magic is a science." Gale builds on this, noting "I have taken a scientific approach with my illustrations of magical characters." The Woggle-Bug is actually an insect unlike Neill's amusing oddity. One would not be surprised to find the Wizard here in a lab coat. Gale

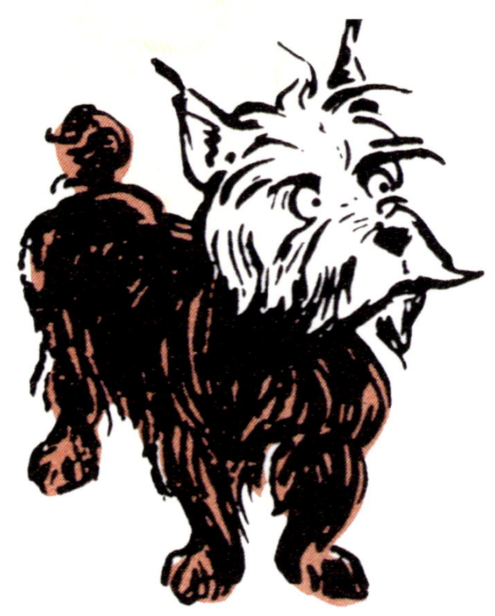

LEFT AND OPPOSITE: Toto casts an approving glance at Gabriel Gale. Art by Denslow, *The Wonderful Wizard of Oz.* Photograph of Gabriel Gale by Brian Keith.

is fascinated with what he calls "the ingenious schematics of their parts and construction." He wanted to see how they actually worked. One can see how his Tin Woodman's head and body move and function. His rendering of Scraps the famous Patchwork Girl is especially clever. He has taken Baum at his word, even including a pair of silver suspender buttons for eyes, two rows of pearls for teeth, and a long scarlet plush tongue. He provides a blueprint of exactly how the boy, Tip, might have manufactured beloved Jack Pumpkinhead in *The Marvelous Land of Oz*. How big does the Gump from the same book have to be to lift six characters? he wondered. He knew that, scientifically, the dimensions of its large palm branch wings had to be far greater than Neill drew them to reasonably carry the Scarecrow, the Tin Woodman, and all the others through the air and over the Emerald City. He then shows the exact wingspan of this peculiar creature.

Gale shares with Baum a deep fascination with mechanical ingenuity and so he is especially dexterous in constructing the Mechanicals, not merely the famous Tin Woodman but all the other lively robots who clink through Baum's books. Tik-Tok, the Clockwork Man of *Ozma of Oz*, is one of his "absolute favorite characters." He also pondered exactly who the gifted men who invented him might have been. "Smith & Tinker have such a minor reference in Baum," the artist explains, "but I am fascinated by them and wanted to investigate their other potential creations in depth, reframing the bickering Smith & Tinker as Thomas Edison and Nikola Tesla, and using the Steampunk aesthetic." That late twentieth-century style of science fiction fuses Victoriana with futuristic machinery. Tik-Tok, like the other Mechanicals, belongs to what Gale calls "Clockpunk." He is a sort of a copper cyborg, a transformer who collapses into a ball that can protect Dorothy when she climbs inside. Smith & Tinker also constructed the mammoth Iron Giant from *Ozma of Oz*; Gale draws it at such a massive scale that the Tin Woodman and Tik-Tok look like tiny trinkets by comparison.

All the other old favorites are here along with many unexpected ones, such as the Wooden Gargoyle from *Dorothy and the Wizard in Oz*; a Fuddle girl—who falls apart like a jigsaw puzzle—from *The Emerald City of Oz*; and the dreadful Yell-Maker and King Anko, the great sea serpent, along with the mermaids and sea devils, all found in Baum's now largely forgotten underwater fantasy *The Sea Fairies*. "The Wheelers, Hoppers, Hammer-Heads, and others have skeletal diagrams to show their magical biology," Gale proudly reports. "The Hammer-Heads and Horners have Darwinesque drawings of the variety of their horns and hammers." He obviously enjoyed

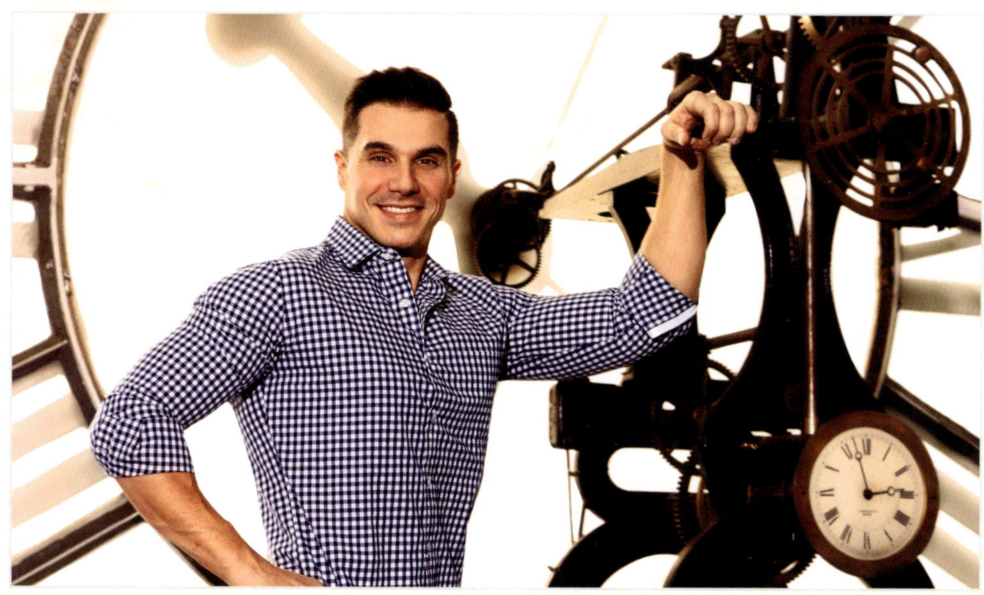

drawing other strange and hostile bands—Mangaboos, Scoodlers, Growleywogs, Flatheads—whom Dorothy must overcome on her adventures in and out of Oz. "I was merely trying to render them as true to Baum's description as I could," Gale says. "As you know, they are very peculiar characters indeed." He readily acknowledges that Baum's obscure characters were more fun to draw than the ones everybody knows. They liberated Gale's abundant imagination. He particularly enjoyed drawing certain characters that Baum mentioned but neither Denslow nor Neill ever depicted in their celebrated illustrations; for example, the fire-breathing Rak of *Tik-Tok of Oz* has become an enormous seahorse-like monstrosity, maybe in part an homage to Denslow who often signed his work with a stylized hippocampus.

One may quibble with Gale's sometimes unconventional depictions of the cherished century-old personages. While Dorothy is shown in period dress, the Cowardly Lion is now a fierce warrior in a cloak of pelts or medieval battle gear. The Scarecrow's head is no longer just an old painted sack with the left eye bigger than the right: Gale has meticulously reconstructed it out of bits of burlap. His Scarecrow is more hunky than husky. He also takes liberties with lesser-known Baum creations: Quox, the benevolent blue dragon of *Tik-Tok of Oz*, and the gigantic monster Choggenmugger, from *Rinkitink in Oz*, have become fantastical dinosaurs. And yet Gale's Ork looks more like Baum's description in *The Scarecrow of Oz* than does Neill's more humorous interpretation.

So here is *The Art of Oz*, an in-depth visual introduction to the remarkable inhabitants of the fascinating Land of Oz, where will be found all the popular old celebrities for modern times, plus many more surprises. "Some of my youthful readers are developing wonderful imaginations," L. Frank Baum noted in his preface to *The Lost Princess of Oz* in 1917. "This pleases me. Imagination has brought mankind through the Dark Ages to its present state of civilization. Imagination led Columbus to discover America. Imagination led Franklin to discover electricity. Imagination has given us the steam engine, the telephone, the talking-machine and the automobile, for these things had to be dreamed of before they became realities. So I believe that dreams—day dreams, you know, with your eyes wide open and your brain-machinery whizzing—are likely to lead to the betterment of the world. The imaginative child will become the imaginative man or woman most apt to create, to invent, and therefore to foster civilization." No doubt Gabriel Gale's splendid illustrations will inspire the imaginations of both young and old for generations to come. Can one really ask any more than that from a work of art?

Acknowledgments

Mr. Gale and Mr. Fricke wish to thank the great-grandchildren of L. Frank Baum—Robert and Clare Baum; Gita Morena; Roger and Charlene Baum—as well as friends on "the Oz circuit": Marc Baum, Colleen Zimmer, Dennis Kulis, the historical foundation and museum staff of All Things Oz and OZ-Stravaganza! (Chittenango, NY); Clint Stueve, Katlyn Stubbeman, Chris Glasgow, and those at the Oz Museum and OZtoberFest! (Wamego, KS); Peter Halikias, Clint Paraday, Ryan Jacobs, Anna Pechtel, Andrew Stege, and Tom "TC" Meller of the Midwest Oz Festival (Tinley Park, IL); Peter Glassman and Books of Wonder, NYC; Peter Hanff and the International Wizard of Oz Club (ozclub.org). Gratitude is also extended to the Justin Schiller Collection for permission to reproduce the Oz maps on pages 176 and 177; to Michael Patrick Hearn for his essay; to Charles Miers, Robb Pearlman, Gloria Nantz, and Jessica Napp at Rizzoli; to Jane Lahr, whose passion and savvy initiated this project, and her associate, Lyn DelliQuadri; and to Lisa Schreiber and Michael Walsh for the dazzling design of these pages.

Mr. Gale expresses appreciation to his greatest supporters: Nicholas, Maria, Dean, Rene, Ralph, Joanna, Karina, and Stephanie; to Arthur Jedrzejczak, who has had the most significant impact on Mr. Gale's illustrations in this book (Arthur thanks his mother, Sylwia, and brothers Sebastian and Michael); to Robert J. Mezquiti of Studio Autoforma, Jean Auguste Alix and Alice Fox; and to John and Johanna Bush and George Makrinos, who have accompanied Mr. Gale since the onset of his Oz adventures. Mr. Fricke offers gratitude to far-flung, faithful family: Patty, Mike and Linda, Erin, Noel, and Haley; to Brent and Frank McCullough-Phillips; to Susie Parry; and especially to Kellen Lindblad, whose advocacy, belief, and love have provided seventeen years of emotional sustenance.

L. Frank Baum's Oz books, some of his "Borderland" stories, and others of the Oz series are today available in a variety of reprints, ranging from text-only to virtual facsimiles of the original printings. The best of these include all the color and black-and-white illustrations by W. W. Denslow and John R. Neill; the fourteen Baum Oz books are published in this superior format by Books of Wonder/HarperCollins.

The magic is theirs; the legacy is ours

Lyman Frank Baum (1856–1919) was a forty-year-old veteran of a dozen careers before he began writing books for children. With *The Wonderful Wizard of Oz* (1900), he created the first American fairy tale and unwittingly launched a fantasy realm that has endured for more than twelve decades. His fourteen Oz novels, Oz short stories, and dozens of other books, stage musicals, and pioneering attempts at multimedia and silent film presentations mark Baum as a unique genius of juvenile entertainment. He came to embody his own philosophy: "To please a child is a sweet and lovely thing that warms one's heart and brings its own reward." **William Wallace Denslow (1856–1915)** warrants recognition as a preeminent children's book illustrator/designer of the early twentieth century. His colorful pictorial approach to three books by L. Frank Baum is proof of such declaration, but Denslow also contributed art to newspapers, magazines, advertising booklets, novel covers, postcards, comic pages, and an outstanding series of storybooks. His concepts of Baum's Oz characters first defined their charm for countless children. **John R. Neill (1877–1943)** illustrated more books in the official Oz series than any other artist: fourteen by Baum, nineteen by Ruth Plumly Thompson, and three for which he also wrote the text. Additionally, he made glorious contributions to newspapers and magazines in the first forty years of the twentieth century and pictured scores of other books. Among these are *The Oz Toy Book* and Baum's *The Sea Fairies*, *Sky Island*, *John Dough and the Cherub*, and *Little Wizard Stories of Oz*. Neill is regarded as the great fan favorite of traditional Oz illustrators; his conceptions remain historically classic.

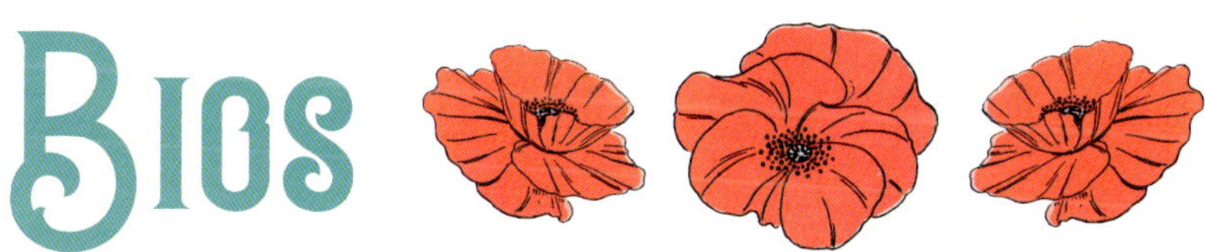

Gabriel Gale's association with Oz is described both in his greeting at the onset of this book and by Princess Ozma in chapter one. He is the creator-conceptualizer of the *Ages of Oz* series, the first two books of which were written by Lisa Fiedler and published by Simon & Schuster: *A Fiery Friendship* and *A Dark Descent*. Born in Brooklyn, New York—where the Bay Ridge branch of the public library provided his initial passage to Oz—he is a graduate of the Cooper Union for the Advancement of Science and Art and the Columbia University Graduate School of Architecture, Planning and Preservation. His illustrated "Oz talks" have delighted students and entertained all ages at bookstores and Oz festivals throughout the country. When not working in Oz, Gale makes his home in New York City. ***John Fricke*** has regularly spent time in Oz since he was five years old and deems it an extraordinary privilege to have interviewed Dorothy and her fellow Ozians for *The Art of Oz* text. This is his ninth book; his earlier titles include two about the entire arc of the Oz phenomenon, two about MGM's *The Wizard of Oz* film, and three about Judy Garland. He received Emmy Awards as coproducer of Garland documentaries for PBS-TV and A&E Network, as well as a Grammy nomination for journalism. Fricke annually emcees the national Oz and Garland festivals and has spoken about Oz and Judy on *The Today Show*, TCM, and NPR; at MoMA, Film at Lincoln Center, and the Paley Center in New York; the Academy of Motion Picture Arts & Sciences in Los Angeles; Deauville Film Festival in France; and National Film Theatre in London. His latest book is *White Christmas: A Pictorial History of the Classic Holiday Film*. ***Michael Patrick Hearn*** is the author of the best-selling *The Annotated Wizard of Oz* (W.W. Norton, 2000) and remains the world's leading L. Frank Baum authority. His other books include *The Annotated Huckleberry Finn*, *The Annotated Christmas Carol*, and *The Porcelain Cat*, illustrated by Leo and Diane Dillon. He has taught at Columbia University, Brooklyn College, Queens College, and Simmons College and has lectured throughout the United States and in Europe and Canada. Hearn has contributed to numerous anthologies and documentaries; he is frequently interviewed on television, radio, online, and in print; and his articles and book reviews have appeared in the *New York Times Book Review*, the *Washington Post*, *the Nation*, and other journals.

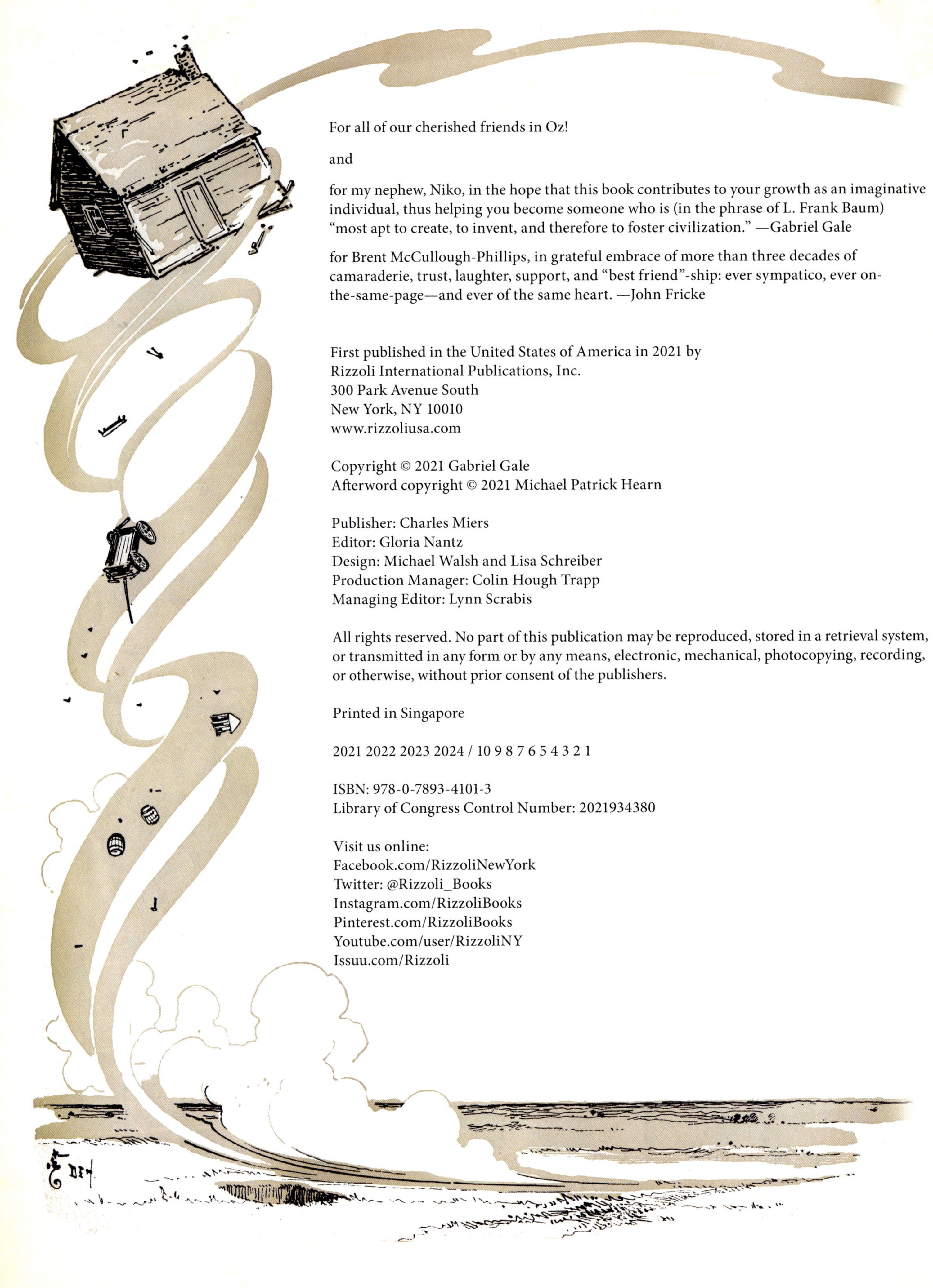

For all of our cherished friends in Oz!

and

for my nephew, Niko, in the hope that this book contributes to your growth as an imaginative individual, thus helping you become someone who is (in the phrase of L. Frank Baum) "most apt to create, to invent, and therefore to foster civilization." —Gabriel Gale

for Brent McCullough-Phillips, in grateful embrace of more than three decades of camaraderie, trust, laughter, support, and "best friend"-ship: ever sympatico, ever on-the-same-page—and ever of the same heart. —John Fricke

First published in the United States of America in 2021 by
Rizzoli International Publications, Inc.
300 Park Avenue South
New York, NY 10010
www.rizzoliusa.com

Publisher: Charles Miers
Editor: Gloria Nantz
Design: Michael Walsh and Lisa Schreiber
Production Manager: Colin Hough Trapp
Managing Editor: Lynn Scrabis

Printed in Singapore

2021 2022 2023 2024 / 10 9 8 7 6 5 4 3 2 1

ISBN: 978-0-7893-4101-3
Library of Congress Control Number: 2021934380

Visit us online:
Facebook.com/RizzoliNewYork
Twitter: @Rizzoli_Books
Instagram.com/RizzoliBooks
Pinterest.com/RizzoliBooks
Youtube.com/user/RizzoliNY
Issuu.com/Rizzoli